Voting for Autocracy

Most autocracies today hold elections. Yet the role of autocratic elections and the behavior of voters and parties in these regimes often appear puzzling. Through the use of simple formal theory, quantitative analysis, and historic narrative, this book develops a broadly comparative theory of the survival and demise of "electoral autocracies" and the strategies they use to resolve intra-party conflict, divide and deter elite opponents, and win political loyalty from the masses. The book illustrates the theory with an analysis of the Mexican Institutional Revolutionary Party (PRI), one of the most resilient autocratic regimes of the twentieth century. An autocratic regime hid behind the façade of elections that were held with clockwork precision. Although their outcome was totally predictable, elections were not hollow rituals. The PRI gave millions of ordinary citizens a vested interest in the survival of the autocratic regime. Voters could not simply "throw the rascals out" of office because their choices were constrained by a series of strategic dilemmas that compelled them to support the autocrats. The book also explores the factors that led to the demise of the PRI and what led to the transformation of autocratic elections into democratic ones.

Beatriz Magaloni is an assistant professor of political science at Stanford University. She is also affiliated with the Center for Democracy, Development, and the Rule of Law and the Latin American Center. She received her M.A. and Ph.D. in political science from Duke University and a law degree from ITAM. Her dissertation won the Gabriel Almond Award for best dissertation in comparative politics granted by the American Political Science Association. Articles she has written have appeared in the *Journal of Theoretical Politics*, *Política y Gobierno*, and edited volumes.

Cambridge Studies in Comparative Politics

General Editor

Margaret Levi *University of Washington, Seattle*

Assistant General Editor

Stephen Hanson *University of Washington, Seattle*

Associate Editors

Robert H. Bates *Harvard University*
Peter Lange *Duke University*
Helen Milner *Columbia University*
Frances Rosenbluth *Yale University*
Susan Stokes *Yale University*
Sidney Tarrow *Cornell University*
Kathleen Thelen *Northwestern University*
Erik M. Wibbels *University of Washington, Seattle*

Other Books in the Series

Lisa Baldez, *Why Women Protest: Women's Movements in Chile*
Stefano Bartolini, *The Political Mobilization of the European Left, 1860–1980: The Class Cleavage*
Mark Beissinger, *Nationalist Mobilization and the Collapse of the Soviet State*
Nancy Bermeo, ed., *Unemployment in the New Europe*
Carles Boix, *Democracy and Redistribution*
Carles Boix, *Political Parties, Growth, and Equality: Conservative and Social Democratic Economic Strategies in the World Economy*
Catherine Boone, *Merchant Capital and the Roots of State Power in Senegal, 1930–1985*
Catherine Boone, *Political Topographies of the African State: Territorial Authority and Institutional Change*
Michael Bratton and Nicolas van de Walle, *Democratic Experiments in Africa: Regime Transitions in Comparative Perspective*
Michael Bratton, Robert Mattes, and E. Gyimah-Boadi, *Public Opinion, Democracy, and Market Reform in Africa*

Continued on pages following the Index

For Alberto

Voting for Autocracy

HEGEMONIC PARTY SURVIVAL AND ITS DEMISE IN MEXICO

BEATRIZ MAGALONI

Stanford University

CAMBRIDGE
UNIVERSITY PRESS

CAMBRIDGE UNIVERSITY PRESS
Cambridge, New York, Melbourne, Madrid, Cape Town, Singapore,
São Paulo, Delhi, Dubai, Tokyo

Cambridge University Press
32 Avenue of the Americas, New York, NY 10013-2473, USA

www.cambridge.org
Information on this title: www.cambridge.org/9780521736596

First published 2006
First paperback edition 2008

A catalog record for this publication is available from the British Library

Library of Congress Cataloging in Publication data

Magaloni, Beatriz.
Voting for autocracy : hegemonic party survival and its demise in Mexico / Beatriz Magaloni.
p. cm. – (Cambridge studies in comparative politics)
Includes bibliographical references and index.
ISBN-13: 978-0-521-86247-9 (hardback)
1. Partido Revolucionario Institucional. 2. Democratization – Mexico.
3. Hegemony – Mexico. 4. Politics, Practical – Mexico. 5. Mexico – Politics and government – 20th century. I. Title. II. Series.
JL1298.R34M34 2006
324.272'083–dc22 2006022357

ISBN 978-0-521-86247-9 Hardback
ISBN 978-0-521-73659-6 Paperback

Transferred to digital printing 2010

Contents

Acknowledgments

This book is the result of almost ten years of research. It started as a dissertation in the Department of Political Science at Duke University. My gratitude goes first to Robert Bates, my mentor, dissertation advisor, and a key influence in my perspective on the politics of development. This book also owes a great deal to two of the leading experts on parties and elections, John Aldrich, who also served as my dissertation advisor, and Herbert Kitschelt, who has closely watched my research as it has evolved over the course of these years. Most of all, I am grateful to Alberto Diaz, my intellectual companion, my most devoted reader, and the coauthor of many papers upon which critical aspects of this book's theory are based. This book also owes a great deal to Federico Estévez. No one understands Mexican politics better than he does. Not only does he know all the "nuts and bolts" of the PRI regime, he is also driven, like me, by a strong passion for empirical research. Throughout my years both as director of the Political Science Program at ITAM and as a faculty member at Stanford, Federico has remained a great friend, critical reader of my work, and coauthor in many projects. Numerous insights in my book are owed to him.

This book was written while Alberto and I ventured in search of two academic positions in a foreign country. Alberto was originally hired as an assistant professor at UCLA, and I was hired at Stanford. We decided from the outset that our first priority was to be together with our children. I am extremely grateful to the Political Science Department at UCLA for hiring me as a visiting professor during Alberto's first year as assistant professor. Dan Posner, Barbara Geddes, and John Zaller were an incredible support that year. Zaller also read all my work, and my theoretical perspective benefited immensely from his comments.

During my years at Stanford, I have had the privilege of working with a distinguished group of scholars. I have learned much from Barry Weingast, my coauthor on several projects about Mexico. In addition, David Laitin has been a decisive influence. Teaching our graduate seminar on comparative politics with him allowed me to place my work within the broader questions that so centrally motivate comparative politics and to understand more fully the comparative relevance of my research. David has also read many chapters of this book and has provided useful feedback. Furthermore, Isabela Mares has been a great friend and colleague. Isabela and I coordinated the comparative speaker series in 2004, and many of our discussions during these seminars or at dinners with the speakers were a tremendous source of inspiration for my work. I am also grateful to Steven Haber, who shares my interest in understanding the politics of autocratic regimes, and who has a keen understanding of Mexico. I thank the Social Science History Institute that Steve directs for critical financial support in helping to pay for research assistance. Jim Fearon has also read and commented on several aspects of my theory. I am grateful for his sharp criticisms that pushed me to refine my arguments, and also for his being a great neighbor. Lastly, Mike McFaul and Terry Karl have also read parts of my research and given me useful comments. Thanks to both!

My research on Mexico has benefited from a large network of friends and colleagues. Special thanks go to several colleagues at ITAM, where I spent several years while doing field research. Denisse Dresser, Federico Estévez, Eric Magar, Alejandro Moreno, Alejandro Poiré, Jeff Weldon, and Margarita Mendoza made those years incredibly fulfilling. I am also thankful to my good friend Jacqueline Martínez, who provided me with invaluable electoral information (now available at the website of CIDAC) and her keen insight in understanding local politics in Mexico. I want to also thank my ITAM students, who served as critical sounding boards for some of the perspectives presented in this book. Also, I am grateful to some of my political science colleagues at CIDE with whom I interacted at different academic events and who helped me to understand Mexican politics better. María Amparo Casar deserves special mention.

Robert Bates, Alberto Diaz, Guillermo Trejo, and two anonymous reviewers deserve special credit for reading the entire manuscript and making detailed comments on each of the chapters. Their input was critical in putting the final manuscript together. I also thank those who commented on articles or individual chapters that were presented at academic conferences. Parts of Chapters 2 and 8 were presented at the conference Advances and Setbacks in the Third Wave of Democratization in Latin America. I am grateful to Frances Hagopian, Scott Mainwaring, and Guillermo O'Donnell for their feedback. Several of the ideas that drive my voting model and Chapter 4 were presented at the conference Citizen–Politician Linkages in Democratic Politics, which took place at Duke University. I am particularly thankful to Herbert Kitschelt, Kanchan Chandra, and Luis Medina. Similar ideas were presented at a conference on vote buying that Alberto Diaz and I organized, Clientelism in Latin America: Theoretical and Comparative Perspectives, and at the conference Frontiers in Latin American Political Economy, both of these at Stanford. I thank Barbara Geddes, Miriam Golden, John Londregan, Jim Robinson, Susan Stokes, Aaron Tornel, and Leonard Wantchekon for their keen insights. I also presented several articles at annual meetings of the American Political Science Association. Particular thanks go to Gary Cox and Olga Shvetsova, who commented on aspects of my work that deal with voter coordination, and to William Keech, who commented on my work on electoral cycles.

I also want to thank the scholars and friends who have participated in various conferences on Mexican voting behavior. Some of these scholars have contributed to the survey data that is employed in several chapters of this book. Jorge Domínguez deserves special mention as a source of intellectual inspiration, and as one of the most critical readers of my work over the course of these years. I also thank the group of scholars involved in the Mexico 2000 Panel Study, particularly Chappell Lawson, for making the group possible, and also Kathleen Bruhn, Miguel Basañez, Roderic Camp, Wayne Cornelius, Joseph Klesner, James McCann, Alejandro Moreno, Pablo Parás, and Alejandro Poiré. I thank Alejandro Moreno, who has helped me to refine my understanding of Mexican voters, and Alejandro Poiré, who is my coauthor on several papers on voting behavior. My gratitude goes to Rafael Giménez, who allowed me to design a survey questionnaire used to test aspects of my theory about the divisiveness of the opposition and who made available the 1997 survey employed in Chapter 7. I thank Alonso Lujambio, Juan Molinar, and Jeffrey and Carolina Weldon, who gave me access to the Council Hall of the Federal Electoral Institute on the night of the 2000 presidential elections, when the PRI finally lost and yielded power peacefully.

I am also grateful to the superb research assistance of Vidal Romero, whose help was critical in writing Chapter 5. He has also assisted me in numerous other projects, and together with Tania has provided incredible friendship. I thank Arianna Sánchez, one of my most driven students from

ITAM (now a law student at Stanford), Sandra Pineda, and Marcela Gómez for helping me put together the dataset in Chapter 4 that allowed me to empirically assess key aspects of my theory of vote buying. My gratitude also goes to Alex Kuo, Jeffrey Lee, and especially to Matt Carnes for their laborious help in editing this book. I am grateful as well to Margaret Levy for her invaluable support and for including this book in the Cambridge Studies in Comparative Politics series. Thanks also to Susan Stokes for her incisive comments and for patiently guiding this book through production. Lew Bateman was also a source of advice and encouragement throughout the process.

Finally, I want to thank my family and close friends. My sisters, Diana, Ana, and Claudia, are my best friends. Simply knowing that they are there together with their daughters provides an immense sense of security and a sense of home. My mother, the strongest person I know, is a central pillar of our family. Her support and love have been decicive in making these years more enjoyable. My father has transmitted to me since early childhood a passion for understanding and also a strong commitment to try my best always. This commitment has brought me far. My Aunt Kiki pushed me to leave Mexico and to seize the opportunities that an academic career in the United States could offer. My cousins, Kristof and Andras, and my brother-in-law, Michael, are also always close to my heart. My three children, Emilia, Nicolas, and now baby Mateo, are the joy of my life. They have taught me about devotion and unconditional love. I also want to thank Reme, Virginia, and Estela, who have provided love and support to our children and have allowed me to keep them close to me while I work at home (although, I must say, always with numerous distractions). However, as a friend once told me, "The whole point of being at home is being available." I also want to thank Lizy, Hernán, Jaana, Andres, Norma, Elvira, Francisco, Pilar, Tony, Mijal, Clara, Samuel, Vera, Alia, Cristian, Belen, Carmelita, Arianna, the Armitanos, Magdalena, and all the Leaping Lizards; the children and parents of Ohlone's room seven; and the loving Bing Nursery School community for being like a family to us and our children while in the United States.

This book is dedicated to my soul mate and partner, Alberto, who is the most loving and generous person I know. Without him, I probably would not have ventured in pursuit of an academic career in the United States. Juggling motherhood, my new status of immigrant, and a professional life would simply not have been possible without his constant support and optimism.

Introduction

In this book I provide a theory of how hegemonic-party autocracies sustain their rule and of the process by which those autocracies can undergo democratization, illustrating this theory with the case of Mexico. Hegemonic-party autocracies are remarkably effective at constructing political order (Huntington, 1968). After the True Whig Party, which ruled Liberia from 1878 until 1980, when it was ousted by a military coup; the Mongolian People's Revolutionary Party (MPRP), which ruled for seventy-five years, from 1921 to 1996; and the Communist Party of the Soviet Union (CPSU), which ruled for seventy-two years, from 1917 to 1989, the Mexican Institutional Revolutionary Party (PRI) was the longest-lived autocratic regime of the twentieth century. The PRI governed for seventy-one years, from 1929, when the precursor to the party was created,[1] until 2000, when the PRI lost the presidency to the long-standing opposition party, the National Action Party (PAN). Unlike the MPRP and CPSU, the PRI held regular elections during all these years for all levels of elective office.[2] Parties other than the PRI were allowed to compete, and Mexico continuously replaced government officeholders electorally, including the president.

Like the Mexican PRI, many other autocracies have perpetuated their rule in spite of regular multiparty elections. Some examples are the Senegalese Socialist Party (PS), which governed for forty years, from the nation's independence in 1960. From the time that Senegal became a multiparty state in 1976, the PS continued to rule until it lost the presidential elections in 2000, when the president, Abdou Diouf, was defeated in a

[1] The PNR (National Revolutionary Party) was created in 1929, was renamed the PRM (Party of the Mexican Revolution) in 1938, and subsequently was renamed the PRI in 1946.

[2] The True Whig Party allowed multiparty competition but differs from the Mexican case in that it was highly exclusionary. See Moore (1970).

second electoral round by an opposition candidate, Abdoulaye Wade. On the other side of Africa, the Chama Cha Mapinduzi Party (CCM) has ruled Tanzania since 1964. In 1992, Tanzania changed its constitution to become a multiparty state. Even with the advent of multiparty elections, however, the CCM continues to rule, and its hegemonic position was reaffirmed in the 2000 elections, when President Mkapa was reelected with 70 percent of the vote. In neighboring Kenya, the KANU (Kenya African National Union) formed as the result of the unification of the two most important pro-independence political movements. A de facto one-party state came into existence when the government banned the Kenya's People's Union (KAPU) and its leaders were put in prison. KANU instituted multiparty elections in 1992. In the 2002 elections, this party was finally defeated by Mwai Kibaki, who won a landslide victory in the run-off presidential election as the candidate of the National Rainbow Alliance Coalition (NARC). In southern Africa, President Robert Mugabe's political party, the Zimbabwe African National Union Patriotic Front (ZANU-PF),[3] has won all of the elections since 1980 by large margins. These elections remain quite controversial, however. Gabon, Côte-d'Ivoire, Cameroon, Djibouti, Egypt, and Gambia also have been governed by hegemonic-party autocracies for prolonged periods of time.

Further examples can be found outside Africa as well. Despite the fact that opposition parties actively contest the elections in Malaysia, they have not been able to supplant the long-entrenched ruling coalition led by the United Malays National Organization (UMNO), which has dominated the country's politics since 1957. For nearly four decades, the Kuomintang (KMT) maintained its rule in Taiwan under a state of martial law and emergency rule. Taiwan began democratizing in the mid-1980s, and the Democratic Progressive Party (DPP) was allowed to field candidates for the first time in the 1986 supplementary legislative elections (previously, non-KMT candidates had been required to run as independents). A constitutional reform in 1994 allowed for direct presidential elections

[3] Still supervised by Britain, the first general elections of 1980 were won by the liberation movements, unified into the Patriotic Front (PF). Just before the elections, the PF divided into its original components, the ZANU-PF (Zimbabwe African National Union) and the PF-ZAPU (African's People's Union), led by Robert Mugabe and Joshua Nkomo, respectively. These factions subsequently split, leaving the ZANU-PF as the sole ruling party. Partly as a result of the inability of the ZANU-PF to penetrate the strongholds of the PF-ZAPU, Mugabe signed a unity agreement in 1987, which merged the two parties into ZANU-PF (Baumhogger, 1999: 965).

to take place in 1996. The reformist Lee Teng-hui was reelected with 54 percent of the vote. The KMT lost enough seats to the DPP, however, to require that members of the two parties negotiate a compromise in order to approve constitutional amendments. The subsequent constitutional reforms led to the abolition of the National Assembly. The KMT was finally defeated in the 2000 presidential elections. Singapore's People's Action Party (PAP) is yet another example of a hegemonic-party autocracy, which has ruled since 1959.

These long-ruling hegemonic-party regimes constitute one of the most common forms of autocracy in the world today. Yet we lack a systematic theory addressing how these autocracies behave: if force is not the key to their political domination, could it be that they retain power because the population supports them? And if so, what accounts for mass support for these autocracies? How can these autocracies survive when they lose the support of the masses? Why do they permit elections instead of simply manufacturing the vote altogether, as occurred in the former USSR and other communist dictatorships? Under what conditions are hegemonic-party regimes expected to commit electoral fraud? What accounts for the establishment of credible commitments to refrain from rigging elections? How do these autocracies democratize? These are some of the central questions I address in this book.

The Point of Departure and the Dependent Variable of the Book

There are several questions about hegemonic-party rule that I do not explore in this book. My theory is not about why hegemonic-party autocracies emerge in the first place. As summarized by Huntington (1970), there are three established theories of why party autocracies emerge. "First, it has been argued, particularly by Africans, that party systems reflect the class structure of societies, and in a society where there are no pronounced differences among social and economic classes, there is no social basis for more than one party" (10). The second view argues just the opposite: the "justification of the single-party is found in the need to counterbalance the fissiparous tendencies of a heterogeneous society" (10). The third view, as advanced by Huntington (1970), is that a "one-party system is, in effect, the product of the efforts of a political elite to organize and legitimate rule by one social force over another in a bifurcated society. The bifurcation may be between socio-economic groups or between racial, religious, or ethnic ones" (11).

The Mexican PRI was established by victorious warlords after a prolonged war in order to construct political order out of chaos. The construction of political order required not only that the warlords give up their arms, but also that a population that had been mobilized for war come to support the new institution.[4] The origins of the PRI can be traced to President Plutarco Elias Calles (1924–28). Calles originated the idea of creating a political party that would draw into a single organization all of Mexico's then-relevant revolutionary leaders, local bosses, and existing political parties, most of which held sway only at the regional level. His National Revolutionary Party (PNR), which was eventually transformed into the PRI, soon became the most important national party organization. In spite of its origin as an essentially elitist organization, by the mid-1930s the ruling party had transformed itself into a party of the masses. President Lázaro Cárdenas (1934–40) created a dense corporatist institutional structure in order to incorporate peasants and workers into the party – organizing workers into the Confederation of Mexican Workers (CTM) and peasants into the National Confederation of Peasants (CNC). He managed to obtain the loyalty of these groups by providing them with direct material rewards, above all, land reform and social legislation. The goal of this form of "statist corporatism" was to control the masses and manage a peaceful transition to mass politics led by the state (Schmitter, 1974; Malloy, 1977).

Thus, part of the reason the Mexican autocracy was highly *inclusionary* is the legacy of its origins. I leave for further research how it is that politicians were able to build this organization, taking as exogenous the emergence of party autocracy. As Huntington (1970: 10) points out, once a party autocracy takes root, it develops "a life of its own." My theory deals with this last aspect – what I call the "mechanics of the survival and demise" of hegemonic-party autocracy.

Survival Through Electoral Fraud?

When analyzing why hegemonic parties are so resilient, journalists and scholars normally focus on electoral fraud. The prevailing argument is that the incumbent party steals the elections in order to allow the regime to

[4] One possible reason why party autocracies such as the Mexican PRI and the Communist Party autocracies in China and the USSR emerged out of civil war instead of democracy, as set forth by Wantchekon (2004), is that in these autocracies one faction was able to establish supremacy after the civil war, while in his story about the emergence of democracy out of civil war there are two factions that face a stalemate and turn to democratic elections to resolve the stalemate.

sustain itself. There is no doubt that the Mexican PRI committed electoral fraud in the 1988 presidential elections, when the party declared that the new computer system had mysteriously collapsed the night of the elections, and it also committed fraud in many local elections.[5] The 1988 elections were the first seriously contested presidential elections. The official results gave the victory to the PRI's presidential candidate, Carlos Salinas, with 50.7 percent of the vote over 32.5 percent given to a former PRI politician, Cuauhtémoc Cárdenas of the National Democratic Front (FDN), which was eventually transformed into the Party of the Democratic Revolution (PRD). As the recently published memoirs of then-president Miguel de la Madrid attest, there is no doubt that the PRI committed fraud against Cárdenas. What is impossible to establish with the available information is whether the PRI needed the fraud in order to retain the presidency, or if the fraud was rather employed to manufacture a 50 percent vote share for the PRI. The 50 percent vote threshold was decisive because with fewer votes, the PRI would not have obtained the cushioned majority it needed in the Electoral College, composed of newly elected congresspersons, to single-handedly ratify the presidential election (Castañeda, 2000: 86, 232).

Yet there are two problems with the view that electoral fraud alone can account for the survival of hegemonic-party regimes. The first is that these parties often rule by either running uncontested or, when the opposition effectively challenges them, winning by impressive margins of victory, manufactured only minimally by fraud. Before the onset of the debt crisis in 1982, which marked the beginning of more than twenty years of economic stagnation, the Mexican PRI was able to win most elections by impressive margins of victory. Electoral fraud played such a minor role during those years[6] that some scholars regarded Mexico as a democracy,

[5] The PRI committed fraud in many local elections, including the infamous case of Chihuahua in 1986, where the ruling party stole the governorship from the PAN. Lujambio (2001) presents an excellent historical overview of how the PAN in Mexico was affected by electoral fraud during its long history of opposing the PRI. Eisenstadt (2004) provides the most comprehensive account of how the opposition parties in Mexico dealt with electoral fraud in the decade of the 1990s.

[6] Molinar (1991) explained this most clearly. He noted that electoral fraud was more prevalent in rural jurisdictions because the opposition normally did not have the reach to monitor the ballots there. In urban political jurisdictions the PRI's leeway to commit electoral fraud was more restricted, as the opposition was normally present to monitor the ballots. In the countryside, however, electoral fraud did not normally make the difference between the PRI winning or losing, because the opposition did not even field candidates in most of the rural jurisdictions. Fraud was mostly employed to boost the party's vote share.

albeit an unusual one – witness the title of one of the best studies of Mexican politics, Frank Brandenburg's (1955) dissertation, "Mexico: An Experiment in One-Party Democracy." In his classic study of democracy, Lipset (1959) also conceived Mexico as belonging to a small group of democracies in the developing world, together with Argentina, Brazil, Chile, Colombia, Costa Rica, and Uruguay, on the grounds that these countries had shared "a history of more or less free elections for most of the post-World War I period" (74). Mexican elections at the time were no more questionable than, for instance, elections in India or Japan. After 1982, elections in Mexico became more competitive, and the practice of electoral fraud more common. Yet even during this more competitive era, the PRI effectively won in the overwhelming majority of political jurisdictions (e.g., single-member districts, municipalities, and gubernatorial races) largely because the opposition had only a meager presence in most of them.

A focus on electoral fraud as the sole reason for the PRI's survival would thus lead to two erroneous conclusions: first, that Mexico was more democratic in the 1950s, 1960s, and 1970s than in the 1980s and 1990s, an odd conclusion given that there was considerably more political competition during the latter period and that the electoral institutions were transformed in the 1990s; and second, that the PRI was not able to win elections cleanly, which for the most part it did. Similar electoral dynamics are observable in most hegemonic-party regimes, where the ruling party either runs uncontested in many races or, even when contested, wins by huge margins. This suggests that electoral fraud is only one of the instruments these autocracies have at their disposal to retain power, and that it is not always the most important one. Moreover, as Diamond (2002) points out, authoritarian rulers turn to their nastiest levels of repression, intimidation, and fraud when they are vulnerable, not when their political domination is secured at the ballot box.

The second fundamental problem with the perception that electoral fraud is the sole cause of authoritarian survival is that this viewpoint simply pushes the problem one step back. The Mexican PRI committed fraud in 1988, and twelve years later this same party stepped down from office, peacefully yielding the presidential seat to the PAN's candidate, Vicente Fox. If fraud was the only means by which the PRI had sustained itself in the past, why did this party not resort to stealing the election again in 2000? What allows hegemonic-party autocrats to get away with stealing elections? What prevents them from doing so? The key to understanding the resiliency of hegemonic parties, and how they democratize, lies in our answers to these questions.

This book provides a theory of the survival and demise of the Mexican PRI, and in doing so it also sheds new light on the politics of what some scholars call "electoral authoritarianism" and its democratization dynamics. Linz writes that "if I were to write a book on comparative democracies, it would have to include a section on ... defective or pseudodemocracies, which I would rather characterize as "electoral authoritarian" regimes ... where a façade covers authoritarian rule" (Linz, 2000: 34). Schedler (2002) calculates that the most common form of autocracy today is hidden behind the façade of elections: "Their dream is to reap the fruits of electoral legitimacy without running the risks of democratic uncertainty" (37). Diamond (2002) and Levitsky and Way (2002) also highlight the prevalence of electoral authoritarianism.

The Role of Elections in Autocratic Regimes

Most autocracies employ at least some repression to disarticulate the opposition – they murder or imprison its leaders (Arendt, 1968; Stepan, 1971; Dahl, 1973; O'Donnell, 1973; Wintrobe, 1998). Evidence suggests that this strategy often backfires: repression can push the opposition into insurgency, which eventually threatens to overthrow the dictator through civil war (see, for example, Wood, 2000). Hegemonic-party autocracies do not ban the opposition, but rather allow elites to organize into independent political parties and to have a place in the legislature.

The conventional argument regarding why autocratic regimes allow elections is that these elections create a democratic façade and thus enhance the regime's legitimacy. For example, according to Crespo (2004), "a hegemonic party like the PRI, insofar as it tried to avoid becoming a one-party system in order to preserve a certain *democratic legitimacy,* had to honor democratic rituals. It was obliged to adopt institutions and procedures typical of a democracy, even though in reality these institutions and procedures lost their original function" (61, emphasis mine).

No doubt autocratic regimes often need to adopt the façade of elections in order to deceive other parties (e.g., international donors). This argument, as Joseph (1999) explains, might to a large extent account for why politicians in some of the poorest single-party autocracies in Africa chose to institute multiparty elections for the first time (although internal political struggles and the discrediting of authoritarian rulers also played a decisive role)

(Bratton and van de Walle, 1997; Bates, 2001). But the PRI did not adopt elections in order to enhance its legitimacy. The PRI was designed with the explicit purpose of preventing personal dictatorship. The Mexican revolution was fought under the banners "*sufragio efectivo, no reelección*"[7] and "*la tierra es de quien la trabaja*"[8] against the dictator Porfirio Diaz, who had ruled Mexico for over thirty years. The political pact that symbolizes the end of the revolution – the 1917 constitution – forbade presidential reelection while establishing multiparty elections. After having modified the constitution to allow for his reelection, President Alvaro Obregón was murdered in 1928. After the murder of Obregón, politicians established the predecessor of the PRI with the explicit intent to transit from a system of "*caudillos*" to one of "institutions." The assassination of Obregón established a powerful focal point that would serve to coordinate a rebellion among ruling party politicians against would-be dictators who aspire to get rid of the elections. The PRI was thus a collusive agreement that allowed ruling-party politicians to divide the rents of power among themselves while preventing any single individual from grabbing it all. To make this pact to share power effective, consecutive elections took place with clockwork precision and presidents stepped down from office every six years.

The decision to allow multiparty elections has momentous implications for the dynamics of autocratic survival. Even if their outcome is totally predictable, elections are not simply mass rituals, devoid of significance. My approach underscores four functional roles of elections in autocratic regimes. First, autocratic elections are designed to establish a regularized method to share power among ruling party politicians. The Mexican autocracy was unique in that elections were employed to replace even the highest office, the presidency. In most other hegemonic-party autocracies, the same president is reelected for prolonged periods, while elections are employed as means to distribute power among lower-level politicians. Autocratic regimes reward with office those politicians who prove most capable in mobilizing citizens to the party's rallies, getting voters to the polls, and preventing social turnmoil in their districts. The autocracy thus forces politicians to work for the benefit of the party and to have a vested interest in the survival of the regime. Second, elections are meant to disseminate public

[7] The English translation is "no reelection and the right to have votes effectively counted."
[8] The English translation is "land for the tiller."

information about the regime's strength that would serve to discourage potential divisions within the ruling party. By holding elections regularly, winning them by huge margins, painting the streets and towns all over the country in the party's colors, and mobilizing voters in great numbers to party rallies and the polls, the PRI sought to generate a public image of *invincibility*. This image would serve to discourage coordination among potential challengers – most fundamentally, those coming from within the party – and to diminish bandwagon effects in favor of the opposition parties among the mass public. High turnout and huge margins of victory signaled to elites that the ruling party's electoral machine was unbeatable because citizens supported the regime. The message to the disaffected party politicians was that the only road to political success was the ruling party, and that outside of it there was nothing but political defeat. To be sure, the PRI also resorted to ballot stuffing and electoral fraud. However, electoral victories obtained simply by stuffing the ballots were insufficient to convince powerful politicians within the ruling party of the regime's might.

The third functional role of elections in hegemonic-party autocracies is to provide information about supporters and opponents of the regime. Wintrobe (1998) proposes that dictators face a dilemma in that that they cannot ever truly know what the population thinks of them. If the dictator is loved, his power is more secure; if the dictator is despised by his people, he is more vulnerable to challenges from potential opponents. Communist dictatorships relied on a combination of strategies to obtain information about their subjects, including the secret police and informants, and they also used competition among subordinates for scarce resources to their advantage (Wintrobe, 1998; Olson, 2000). Hegemonic-party regimes employ elections as a key instrument for obtaining information about the extent of the party's mass support and its geographic distribution. The hegemonic party uses this information to screen voters according to their political loyalties, rewarding supporters with access to government funds and punishing defectors by withdrawing them from the party's spoils system. In doing so, the hegemonic party creates a market for political loyalty and makes citizens vest their interests in the survival of the regime.

The fourth functional role of elections in an autocratic regime is to trap the opposition, so that it invests in the existing autocratic institutions rather than challenging them by violent means. Gandhi and Przeworski (2001) put this idea succinctly: "Under dictatorship, parties do not compete, elections do not elect, and legislatures do not legislate. What, then, is the role of these institutions under dictatorship?" (1) They argue that dictators protect themselves by offering particular groups of the potential opposition a place in the legislature. Autocratic legislatures and elections also serve to divide the opposition. As my model in Chapter 8 makes explicit, the nature of the autocratic electoral game is such that some opposition players are invariably better off playing the "loyal opposition" while leaving others to rebel on their own. By selectively coopting the opposition, the autocracy prevents its opponents from forming a unified front to rebel against the regime.

Alternative Theories of Hegemonic-Party Survival

Hegemonic-party autocracies do not conform to the model of what we normally regard as dictatorships. The communist regimes, for example, aspired to total domination "of each single individual in each and every sphere of life" (Arendt, 1968). In part, this goal was achieved by the atomization of human relationships – the destruction of classes, interest groups, and even the family unit – a process in which terror played a key role. Many military dictators were also very repressive. The military governments in South America, for example, employed the systematic extermination, incarceration, disappearance, and torture of union members and left-wing party leaders and their activists (Stepan, 1971; O'Donnell, 1973). The dictatorships of Central America and South Africa used repression to enforce the labor-repressive institutions upon which racial and class segregation was based, and to disarticulate the political organizations of the oppressed (Wood, 2000). Most theories of autocracy are implicitly or explicitly based on the notion of repression. Wintrobe (1998), who provides one of the most systematic theories of the micro-foundations of autocratic rule, argues that the "existence of a political police force and of extremely severe sanctions for expressing and especially organizing opposition to the government (such as imprisonment, internment in mental hospitals, torture, and execution) is the hallmark of dictatorships of all stripes" (34).[9]

Hegemonic-party autocracies are a more benign form of dictatorship. This is not to say that there is no repression at all. The Mexican PRI was no "tea party," as Castañeda (2000: xiv) puts it. However, "neither was it [repression] similar in brutality, systematicity, scope and cynicism to its counterparts in Mediterranean or Eastern Europe, or in the rest of Latin

[9] Linz (2000) challenges the view that repression is an essential characteristic of autocracies.

America. . . . Repression was truly a last resort" (Castañeda (2000: xiv).[10] From its creation, the PRI permitted the opposition to compete in multiparty elections – although it banned the Communist Party, a decision that pushed radical left-wing movements into insurgency and was largely responsible for the guerilla activity in the 1960s and 1970s. The 1978 electoral reform legalized the Communist Party and managed to co-opt most of the violent opposition to the regime by significantly reducing their entry costs to the legislature.

Reflecting about Mexico, Mario Vargas Llosa argued that the PRI was the "perfect dictatorship": it imposed itself without the people noticing. Vargas Llosa may be taken as suggesting that Mexicans were naïve not to understand that they lived under an autocracy. However, I prefer to interpret this phrase as indicating something about the peculiar nature of these regimes. Hegemonic parties camouflage their autocratic nature with the instruments of democracy, tricking or trapping citizens into supporting them with their votes.

My approach to the resiliency of hegemonic parties differs from some prevailing views of how these autocracies sustain themselves. One popular view argues that hegemonic-party regimes survive because of their forceful imposition against the will of the people – they sustain themselves through autocratic electoral institutions, formal barriers to entry, and electoral fraud, which collectively make it impossible for the opposition to effectively challenge the regime (Sartori, 1976). Molinar (1991) offers the best institutionalist account of the PRI's hegemony. He argues that two sets of institutions were essential for the PRI to maintain its hegemony: first, legal barriers to entry for potential challengers, and second, the centralization of the monitoring and adjudication of elections in the hands of the federal government and the PRI's central bureaucracy.

My approach concurs with the aforementioned arguments in that it recognizes that these autocratic electoral institutions were important for sustaining party hegemony. However, as I further discuss in Chapter 1, barriers to entry and electoral fraud are insufficient to account for the survival of a hegemonic party. Moreover, attributing party hegemony solely to autocratic institutions evades a central question: what allows the ruling party to erect

[10] Repression in Mexico was selective, although in some regions and municipalities in the states of Chiapas, Oaxaca, Guerrero, and Veracruz, political killings on a per capita basis rivaled the levels of per capita repression in military dictatorships. I thank Guillermo Trejo for pointing this out to me.

and sustain these institutions? In order to draft autocratic institutions, the ruling party needs to unilaterally control constitutional change without the need to forge coalitions with the opposition. To do this, the ruling party requires winning with supermajorities rather than a simple majority. My approach to hegemonic-party survival takes institutions as partly *endogenous* to the electoral game. I provide an understanding of the conditions that allow a hegemonic party to sustain its control of the electoral process, and of what might lead this party to give up such control.

A second view concludes that these regimes remain in power through legitimacy derived from their historic origins. Huntington (1968) argues that the "stability of a modernizing political system depends on the strength of its political parties. A party, in turn, is strong to the extent that it has institutionalized mass support" (408). He also notes that one-party regimes tend to emerge out of social revolutions or independence movements, which endow them with a distinctive aura of legitimacy.[11] "The stability of a one-party system derives more from *its origins* than from its character. It is usually the product of a nationalist or revolutionary struggle. . . . The more intense and prolonged the struggle for power and the deeper its *ideological commitment* the greater the political stability" (424, emphasis mine)

My approach to party hegemony builds on Huntington's (1968) in stressing the importance for regime survival of the institutionalization of mass support, with electoral fraud and force playing secondary roles. However, my approach traces the mass support for the hegemonic party to sources other than the regime's historic origin and legitimacy, [12] for three reasons. First, the myth of an historic origin is not enough to ensure political loyalty; if it were, why would the hegemonic party devote so much in fiscal resources, as I demonstrate in this book, to the purpose of party maintenance? Second, explanations of authoritarian durability based on legitimacy are hard to falsify, because citizens under autocracies possess incentives to misrepresent their preferences out of fear (Kuran, 1991; Havel, 1992).[13]

[11] Huntington (1968) also stresses the widespread use of patronage by these regimes. In line with my argument, the use of patronage is an indication that political loyalty stems from sources other than ideological commitment.

[12] I understand legitimacy as "acquiescence motivated by subjective agreement with norms and values" (Lamounier, 1973: 13, quoted in Przeworski, 1991).

[13] The difficulties pollsters face in surveying citizens living under autocracies provide evidence of this point. To overcome the problem of preference falsification (respondents answering that they supported the PRI out of fear), Mexican pollsters had to follow ingenious strategies, such as introducing a form of "secret ballot" and interviewing citizens in the anonymity of the streets (see Domínguez and McCann, 1996: 228).

Third, explanations of regime durability based on legitimacy can easily become tautological. "If by loss of legitimacy we understand the appearance of collectively organized alternatives, [these explanations] are tautological in that the fact that these alternatives are collectively organized means that the regime has broken down" (Przeworski, 1991: 54).

A third approach to the resiliency of hegemonic-party regimes focuses on "performance legitimacy," namely, popular support based on sound economic performance (Hansen, 1974). Many scholars and journalists tend, either implicitly or explicitly, to employ this approach toward understanding why hegemonic parties in the fast-growing Asian economies of Taiwan, Malaysia, and Singapore have been able to sustain themselves for so long.

An approach to authoritarian survival based on "performance legitimacy" is more amenable to empirical testing. Hegemonic-party regimes should be sustained when the economy grows, and should collapse when the economy deteriorates. Yet the evidence suggests that these regimes are quite resilient to economic recession. The UMNO in Malaysia, the PAP in Singapore, the KMT in Taiwan, and the BDP in Botswana have no doubt profited from sound economic performance. Yet many other hegemonic parties have persisted despite deteriorating economic conditions (Geddes, 1999). The Mexican PRI presided over a long period of economic stability and economic growth, which no doubt contributed to its durability. But after the onset of the debt crisis in 1982, this party continued to govern for close to two decades despite a collapse in growth, macroeconomic mismanagement, and widespread poverty.[14] Most of the African hegemonic-party regimes have also sustained their hegemonic positions despite years of deteriorating economic conditions.

The challenge is to understand why citizens support autocracies, even if they often disapprove of them. Kuran (1991) provides a powerful explanation of why, despite despising communism, citizens endured it for so long (see also Havel, 1992) and why political order crumbled so rapidly. Communism in Eastern Europe was brought down in the streets as a result of a "tipping phenomenon." Citizens were afraid of expressing

[14] In her analysis of the electoral effects of the debt crisis in Latin America, Remmer (1993) demonstrates that in countries where elections took place during the 1980s, all the incumbent parties that presided over the debt crisis lost power. Some of the most notable exceptions included the hegemonic-party regimes of Mexico and Paraguay, the one-party communist dictatorship of Cuba, and the military regime of Chile. Her analysis did not include these cases because she focused on democracies.

their opposition to the regime and behaved as though they all supported communism – a form of "preference falsification" resulting from fear. Once citizens realized that there were thousands of other citizens also willing to challenge communism, the dictatorship collapsed. The communist dictatorships were thus highly vulnerable to the *public* expression of political opposition.

Although this theory is extremely useful for understanding why citizens support autocracies, its applicability to the Mexican case is limited. On the one hand, the USSR played a central role in the fall of communism in Eastern Europe. The "tipping phenomenon" Kuran (1991) uncovers would have been impossible had the USSR not given clear signals that this time, unlike the 1950s and 1960s, it would not invade Eastern Europe to repress the population. No such external threat existed in Mexico, which suggests that fear of repression played a more limited role in accounting for the PRI's mass support. Second, unlike communist dictatorships, hegemonic-party autocracies permit the opposition to *publicly* challenge the regime through multiparty elections. Thus, any theory of mass support for these regimes must necessarily uncover the logic of voting behavior under autocracy.

In one of the best existing comparative analyses of autocracies, Geddes (1999) provides a fourth view of the factors that account for the resiliency of hegemonic-party autocracies. In her view, party autocracies (hegemonic-party and single-party) are more resilient than the two other types of autocracies, military regimes and personal dictatorships, because of their relative immunity to elite splitting, an immunity that results from a behavioral equilibrium in which all factions are better off if they remain united than if they split.

> Factions form in single-party regimes around policy differences and competition for leadership positions, as they do in other kinds of regimes, but everyone is better off if all factions remain united and in office. This is why cooptation rather than exclusion is usually the rule in established single-party regimes. Neither faction would be better off ruling alone, and neither would voluntarily withdraw from office unless exogenous events changed the costs and benefits of cooperating with each other. (11)

My approach builds on Geddes's (1999) in stressing the behavioral incentives actors face to remain loyal to the authoritarian regime. However, I move beyond Geddes by focusing on the strategic interaction between elites and masses. In my view, elites possess strong incentives to remain united as long as the population supports the ruling party. If electoral support begins to wither, so do incentives to remain united within the ruling party. A disaffected ruling party politician faces the following choice: remain loyal to the regime and hope to be rewarded with office and spoils in the future, or split and challenge the regime through elections. Only when there is sufficient voter dissatisfaction do party splinters have any real chance of achieving office by challenging the regime on their own. Below, I provide a summary of my theory of hegemonic party survival.

My Theory of Hegemonic-Party Survival

The pillar of a hegemonic-party regime is its monopoly of mass support, which in turn allows the regime to deter elite divisions and to manipulate institutions by unilaterally controlling constitutional change. Unlike democratic parties, hegemonic-party autocracies aspire to supermajorities. Why would a hegemonic party purposely seek to sustain an "oversized coalition?" Would it not be more rational to buy off a minimally winning coalition, as opposed to working to assure a virtually universal coalition? Indeed, as coalition theory predicts, in distributive zero-sum games it generally makes rational sense to form coalitions that include the minimal number of members that guarantees victory (Riker, 1962). Why would a hegemonic party devote so much effort to campaigning and buying votes when, during most of its life, elections are not competitive?

Hegemonic parties are oversized governing coalitions that are largely sustained through the distribution of government spoils and patronage. These autocracies strive to sustain oversized governing coalitions rather than minimally winning ones because, first, as argued earlier, they want to generate an image of invincibility in order to discourage party splits. A second reason why hegemonic-party autocracies aspire to supermajoritiers is to control institutional change to their advantage. In order to manipulate institutional change, these autocracies need supermajorities – most countries require legislative supermajorities, a popular referendum, or a combination of the two to change the constitution. The Mexican constitution exemplifies this phenomenon. It was modified to the ruling party's advantage close to 400 times, and many of these alterations were substantial, including numerous changes in the electoral institutions; the centralization of political power and fiscal resources in the hands of the federal government; the systematic weakening of the judicial power and the Supreme Court; and the restructuring of the system of property rights.

My approach presupposes that for hegemonic parties, co-optation is better than exclusion because the institutional benefits for the ruling clique of having an oversized coalition outweigh the costs of sustaining it. The costs of sustaining an oversized coalition vary through the years. As will become apparent in this book, it is less expensive to buy off a large coalition of the very poor than a coalition of a wealthier middle class. The economic costs of sustaining an oversized coalition also rise as the one-time windfalls of the initial seizure of power are used up and the economy becomes more complex.

The resources used to pay for the hegemonic coalition in Mexico originally belonged to the landowners, who as a class were destroyed or significantly weakened during the revolution.[15] The PRI continued to carry out what became a form of "permanent land reform" until the 1992 constitutional reform, which declared land redistribution to be over. The PRI's agrarian redistributions eventually devastated the agricultural sector – Mexico became a net importer of foodstuffs by the 1960s. In order to sustain the hegemonic coalition, the PRI also resorted to the systematic manipulation of the budget and other policy instruments, as I demonstrate in Chapters 3 and 4. Over time, the PRI ended up undermining the economy and the state's revenue base.

In line with Geddes (1999), this book proposes that party hegemony must be understood as resulting primarily from a behavioral equilibrium where elites *and* masses are better off uniting with the ruling party, and where opponents are trapped in investing in the survival of the autocratic electoral game rather than rebelling against it. I explore the mechanics of authoritarian survival by uncovering the behavioral incentives faced by elites to coalesce with the regime; the calculus of voting under autocracy; and the nature of the opposition's coordination dilemmas in competing against an autocratic ruling party.

Elite Unity

Comparative evidence indicates that elite divisions within a hegemonic party tend to occur when there is a presidential succession. The Kenyan president Daniel arap Moi could not stand for reelection in the 2002 presidential contest. Moi chose a successor, Uhuru Kenyatta. KANU ministers who wanted their party to select its candidate by secret ballot in a

[15] This is in sharp contrast to what happened in Central America, where the landed oligarchies rejected redistribution of land and formed an alliance with the army to repress the masses.

national convention formed a breakaway faction, the Rainbow Coalition, which finally abandoned KANU and joined the Liberal Democratic Party (LDP). A similar sequence of events occurred in Taiwan. The year 2000 marked the end of the term of President Lee Teng-hui. The KMT confronted a major split as a result of the party's presidential nomination. Vice President Lien Chan defeated Taiwan Governor James Soong in the contest to attain the presidency. In response to losing the KMT nomination, Soong ran as an independent. The DPP nominated Chen Shui-bian, a former mayor of Taipei, who won the election with 39 percent of the vote against 37 percent for the independent candidate Soong. However, even when there is no presidential succession, a hegemonic party is vulnerable to elite divisions. For example, just before the 2000 Senegalese presidential elections, Moustapha Niasse split from the PS to stand against the long-time incumbent president, Abdou Diouf. Thus, elections provide a vehicle through which disaffected ruling party politicians can legally challenge the regime. This is the reason why hegemonic-party autocracies, which permit multiparty elections, are far more vulnerable to elite divisions than single-party regimes, where opposition is banned and disaffected elites confront imprisonment if they defy the party.

The Mexican PRI stands out as the only hegemonic-party autocracy where the president was replaced through elections every six years. Disappointed members who failed to be nominated to the presidency were the biggest threat to continued party unity. During its history, the PRI experienced a series of major splits. The most important took place in 1940, 1946, 1952, and 1987, and they all occurred because prominent ruling party politicians objected to the party's presidential nominee. The rule of nonconsecutive reelection for all elective offices, in effect since 1933, gave for ample access to office to a multiplicity of ambitious politicians, ensuring constant circulation of elites (Smith, 1979; Camp, 1995). The benefits of the rule of nonconsecutive-reelection in terms of giving access to office to a large number of party politicians and keeping them hopeful were obvious, but the disadvantage was that every six years the PRI was vulnerable to a major elite division at the top. In most hegemonic-party autocracies, this problem prominently arises only when the president chooses to retire or when he dies, not every six years.[16]

[16] I thank an anonymous reviewer for underscoring the fact that most other hegemonic-party autocracies are less vulnerable to elite divisions because the president is not replaced so often.

Chapter 1 of this book relies on ambition theory to account for elite unity and divisiveness within a hegemonic party. My theory states that hegemonic-party regimes deter party splits through three main mechanisms: first, they strive to create an image of invincibility by overpowering at the polls. Huge margins of victory are costly to obtain because they require "'mobilized' voters – people whose electoral participation (turnout) and/or candidate choice [are] induced by vote buying and coercion" (Cornelius, 2004: 47). Second, hegemonic parties must distribute ample spoils and government jobs to members of the ruling coalition so as to deter elites from splitting. The PRI managed to sustain its coalition by allowing politicians to do business under the umbrella of the state and distributing jobs, privileges, and resources to them. The cement of the hegemonic coalition was ambition and rent seeking, rather than a common ideology. The same is true for hegemonic parties in Africa. As Van de Walle (forthcoming) argues, "African leaders typically used state resources to co-opt different ethnic elites to maintain political stability" (93). Arriola (2004) demonstrates that autocratic regimes in Africa lasted longer when they were able to offer ministerial positions and expand the cabinet in order to co-opt opponents. A third instrument hegemonic parties employ to deter party splits is raising the costs of entry to potential challengers by manipulating the electoral rules and threatening to commit electoral fraud against them and to use the army to enforce such fraud. As argued earlier, institutional manipulation requires that the hegemonic party control legislative supermajorities and often also the capacity to win a national referendum.

A central empirical implication of my approach is that budget cycles around elections will occur even when these are not competitive. With the use of macroeconomic data from the 1930s through 2000, Chapter 3 provides compelling evidence of the occurrence of budget cycles under the Mexican autocracy. I demonstrate that long before the 1980s, when elections first became competitive, the PRI flooded districts at election time with generous amounts of government spending. The distribution of government spoils was central to mobilize voter turnout; to buy off powerful interest groups, such as the party's labor and peasant organizations; and to dissuade party politicians from splitting. I also show that other policy instruments and variables, such as the money supply, wages, inflation, and economic growth, also moved according to the electoral calendar. Chapter 3 also demonstrates that these electoral budget cycles were associated with the PRI's vulnerability to elite splits around presidential elections. My findings suggest that the timing of splits within the ruling party coincided with years when the government spent significantly less, thus failing to distribute sufficient economic resources to hold the coalition together.

Electoral Support

This book endorses the proposition that autocrats, regardless of type, cannot remain in power without some form of mass support. Even the most horrendous autocracies, as Arendt noted, "command and rest upon mass support" (1968: 306). Repression is an alternative instrument autocracies employ to secure their survival. No matter how great the repressive power of an autocracy, however, the fact of the matter is that it can't control too many people simply by threatening to use force. As Wintrobe (1998) puts it, "the people have good reason to fear the ruler. But this very fear (as well as jealousy) will make many among them look for ways to get rid of the dictator" (4). Hegemonic-party regimes instead employ electoral institutions as a means to regularize payments to their supporters and implement punishment to their enemies, among both the elite and the masses, so as to induce them to remain loyal to the regime and to have a vested interest in its survival.

Existing voting theories are unable to explain why voters support autocrats because they make a set of implicit or explicit assumptions that are inconsistent with the electoral settings of autocracies. My theory of voting behavior under autocracy builds on Downs (1957) and Fiorina (1981) in that voters are assumed to be interested in selecting a party that maximizes their expected utility. Yet voters must make their choices in an electoral arena that is different from a democratic setting in three main respects: (1) opposition parties are highly uncertain entities to voters because they have never governed; (2) the ruling party monopolizes the state's resources and employs them to reward voter loyalty and to punish voter defection; and (3) the ruling party can commit electoral fraud or threaten to repress its opponents, in which case violence might erupt. By systematically incorporating each of these traits into the voter's utility function, I am able to provide a model of voter support for autocracies. The "tragic brilliance"[17] of these systems is that the population plays an active role in sustaining them, often despite corruption, inefficient policies, and lack of economic growth. Citizens' choices are free, yet they are constrained by a series of strategic dilemmas that compel them to remain loyal to the regime.

[17] I draw the notion of tragic brilliance from Diaz-Cayeros, Magaloni, and Weingast (2004).

The voting model allows me to derive predictions about the effects of economic performance, modernization, and economic policy reform on authoritarian survival. Following the seminal work by S. M. Lipset (1959), the most recent cross-sectional analyses have established a series of stylized facts about the relationship between development, economic performance, and authoritarian breakdown. Yet the empirical analysis does not constitute an explanation; only theory can provide that. Why are autocracies less sensitive to economic crises than democracies (Przeworski et al., 2000: 111)? Why do short-term economic crises seem to be irrelevant for authoritarian survival whereas longer-term crises do seem to matter (Przeworski et al., 2000: 112)? Why are party autocracies so resilient in the face of economic recession (Geddes, 1999, 2003)? Why is it that development creates the necessary preconditions for democracy to survive but does not account for the establishment of democracy (Przeworski, et al., 2000)? There are a number of possible ways to answer these questions. Here I have chosen to look at the strategic dilemmas voters confront in an authoritarian regime.

My approach contends that economic performance plays an important role in authoritarian survival: autocrats are stronger when the economy booms, and become weaker otherwise. Voters are likely to support the autocrat "sincerely" when it puts in place policies that make the economy prosper, industry develop, and wages and employment increase. Furthermore, if the economy has historically been growing under an autocratic regime voters will be tolerant of short-term economic crisis. Under these conditions, voters will stick with the "known devil" rather than turn the government over to uncertain opponents. Thus, economic crisis is not sufficient to account for the breakdown of hegemonic-party regimes. My theory suggests the following picture about mass support for hegemonic parties and ultimately their survival (Figure 1.1). A hegemonic party's mass support depends on a combination of (a) long-term economic growth; (b) vote buying and the distribution of government transfers through what I call a "punishment regime" or the autocrat's threat to exclude opposition voters and politicians from the party's spoils system;[18] and (c) electoral fraud and force. As this book will make explicit, to effectively opperate a "punishment regime" through which the autocrat delivers payments to its friends and punishments to its enemies, a strong party organization is required that can establish linkages with voters necessary to identify supporters and to

[18] I draw from my previous work with Diaz-Cayeros and Weingast the notion of a punishment regime. See Diaz-Cayeros, Magaloni, and Weigast (2004).

Punishment regime

Long-term economic growth	No	Yes
High	**"Self-destructive authoritarian equilibrium"** Authoritarian survival based on performance and the selective use of fraud and repression • Russia under Vladimir Putin	**"Self-reinforcing authoritarian equilibrium"** Authoritarian survival based on performance and the distribution of spoils. No need for electoral fraud. • Mexico 1940-80 • Malaysia's UMNO • Botswana's BDP • Taiwan's KMT • Singapore's PAP
Low	**"Unstable authoritarian equilibrium"** Authoritarian survival solely based on electoral fraud and represssion • Guinea-Bissau's PAIGC in 2000	**"Self-destructive authoritarian equilibrium"** Authoritarian survival based on the distribution of spoils and the selective use of fraud and repression • Mexico post-1982 • Most of the African hegemonic-party regimes (The PS in Senegal, the KANU in Kenya, the CCM in Tanzania, the ZANU-PF in Zimbabwe, the CPDM in Cameroon, the PDG in Gabon, and the PDCI in Cote-d'Ivoire are some examples.) • Malaysia post-1998

Figure I.1. Authoritarian equilibria, economic performance, and pork.

monitor their behavior. Without effective targeting of government spoils, the autocrat will not be able to create a market for political loyalty and deter defections. Electoral fraud, as Chapter 8 makes explicit, can be employed to boost the electoral returns of the hegemonic party or to overturn a losing outcome. Repression may be used to intimidate, incarcerate, or disappear elite opponents or in the worst cases to crush pro-democracy movements. In Figure I.1, electoral fraud is indicated as a relevant factor for authoritarian survival only inasmuch as it can make a difference between the hegemonic party's losing or winning, although hegemonic parties also may employ fraud to boost their vote margins. As Chapter 8 makes explicit, when autocrats resort to electoral fraud, they are also often ready to use the army against the people. However, if the threat of force is effective in deterring the opposition from confronting the fraud, we might not observe too much repression actually ocurring.

The upper left quadrant is a scenario of high long-term economic growth and no "punishment regime." This constitutes an authoritarian strategy that is "self-destructive" in the long-run. My voting model makes explicit why economic growth has conflicting effects on authoritarian survival: in the short term, economic growth leads voters to support the regime, yet economic growth can eventually turn against the autocrat because as voters become richer, they will become more capable of making "ideological investments," defecting to the opposition parties despite the risk of being excluded from the incumbent party's spoils system and losing government transfers. Wealth works at liberating voters from the autocracy because it reduces their dependence on government transfers. This would be an example of democracy brought about by development, as in endogenous modernization theory (Przeworski et al., 2000; Boix and Stokes, 2003). Examples of this type of autocratic equilibrium are cases where the party organization is too weak to effectively opperate a "punishment regime." Fragile electoral support also translates into elite factionalism. Repression might be used against elite opponents or even against pro-democracy movements. Russia under Vladimir Putin fits this characterization.

The upper right quadrant is a self-reinforcing authoritarian equilibrium. Voters support the regime because the economy improves, and the "punishment regime" works at deterring them from making ideological investments in democratization. The higher the median income of voters, the more transfers and spoils must be distributed in order to successfully deter voter exit and elite divisions. This is an authoritarian equilibrium where electoral fraud is unnecessary for the incumbent party to sustain itself, although hegemonic parties often employ fraud to boost their vote margins. Repression, when employed, tends to be very selective and mostly directed against elite opponents. Mexico between the 1940s and late 1970s fits this characterization. Other examples of hegemonic-party regimes where there is outstanding economic growth and where spoils and government transfers are widely distributed through a "punishment regime" are Malaysia, Singapore, and Botswana. The KMT in Taiwan is yet another example of a strong hegemonic party that was largely sustained because of sound economic performance and patronage. The electoral defeat of the KMT in 2000 must necessarily be understood as a direct consequence of a major elite split within the party.

The lower right quadrant of Figure I.1 is a scenario of deteriorating economic conditions. Since voters are predisposed to switch support to the opposition as a result of poor economic performance, the autocrat increasingly depends on vote buying, electoral fraud, and repression to sustain itself. The poorer the median voter, the more effective the "punishment regime" is in deterring mass and elite defections, and the less need for electoral fraud. Mexico after the 1980s fits this characterization. After the onset of the debt crisis, the PRI became increasingly dependent on vote buying and electoral fraud to sustain itself. Richer voters and those in localities most exposed to international trade were the first to defect to the opposition, mostly to the PAN. The PRI resorted to stealing elections in some of the states and municipalities that defected, although electoral fraud was not universal because the overwhelming majority remained loyal to the PRI, thanks in part to vote buying and the distribution of "pork." The PRI also suffered the most important split of its history, which resulted in the formation of the PRD. Many local elections during those years resulted in violent confrontations between the PRI and the opposition. The PS in Senegal, the CCM in Tanzania, and the ZANU-PF in Zimbabwe, to name a few, are examples of authoritarian equilibria operating despite years of deteriorating economic conditions and sluggish recovery from the economic backsliding of the 1980s (van de Walle, 2001).

Although hegemonic-party autocracies can sustain themselves for many years despite deteriorating economic conditions, this scenario does not constitute a self-reinforcing equilibrium, as my account of the Mexican case illustrates. The imperative of political survival translated into ever-increasing incentives for the PRI to manipulate the economy to stay in office. Opportunistic economic cycles induced by the ruling party devastated the economy and exhausted the resources available for patronage. As a consequence of all of this, the party's popular support was eventually destroyed.

The lower left quadrant is a scenario wherein there is no economic growth and the autocrat lacks resources to sustain a "punishment regime." In this scenario, authoritarian survival depends solely on electoral fraud and coercion, and it is hard to achieve because a very weak autocrat will not be able to enforce an authoritarian imposition against strong opponents, at least in a systematic fashion. These are cases characterized by economic collapse, where the state is bankrupt and lacks access to funds to sustain a patronage network. The PAIGC (African Party for Independence of Guinea and Cape Verde) provides an illustration of this scenario. After twenty-five years of uninterrupted rule and years of economic deterioration, the PAIGC was defeated in the 2000 elections. Although the party was accused of manipulating the elections in 1994, the party was simply too weak and resource-poor to attempt to steal the 2000 elections again from its opponent, Kumba Yalá of the PRS (Party for Social Renewal), because the regime had suffered a defeat in a 1998 regional war (Rudebeck, 2003).

Opposition's Coordination Dilemmas

Opposition coordination dilemmas are the other key factor accounting for the survival of hegemonic-party autocracies.[19] With only 36 and 40 percent of the vote, President Daniel arap Moi won the 1992 and 1997 presidential elections, respectively, because the opposition in Kenya was severely divided, mostly along ethnic lines.[20] The KANU was finally defeated in the 2002 presidential elections by the NARC, which resulted from an alliance between the LDP, led by Raila Odinga, and the National Alliance Party of Kenya (NAK), a super-opposition alliance that included thirteen opposition parties, representing all of Kenya's major tribes.

The opposition in Senegal was also traditionally fractionalized, although the Senegalese Democratic Party (PDS) was the only opposition party with a national presence. None of the opposition parties in Senegal had any ethnic affiliation, and most of the opposition parties were to the left of the PS (Ingham, 1990: 131), making opposition coordination potentially easier than in Kenya. For the first time in Senegal's history, the PS did not obtain an absolute majority of the vote in the first round of the 2000 presidential elections – Diouf got 41 percent, Wade 30 percent, and Niasse 17 percent. In the second round, all seven opposition candidates, including Niasse, swung behind Wade in a coalition, "Alternance 2000," in order to oust Diouf.

In Mexico, the opposition was also divided, mostly along ideological lines. The PAN stood to the right of the PRI and the PRD to the left of the ruling party on a series of economic policy issues. These ideological

[19] The literature on dominant party systems argues that coordination failure plays a key role in sustaining party dominance (Riker, 1976; Sartori, 1976; Pempel, 1990; Laver and Schofield, 1991; Cox, 1997).

[20] The Kenyan population was subdivided into some forty ethnic groups. The largest groups were the Kikuyu (around 21 percent), mainly living in the central part of the country. These are followed by the Luhya (around 14 percent), the Luo (13 percent), the Kalenjin (11 percet), the Kamba (11 percent), the Kissi (6 percet) and the Meru (5 percent) (Foeken and Dietz, 2000: 123).

differences, as I systematically explore in this book, complicated opposition coordination at the mass and elite levels. Opposition leaders from the PAN and the PRD considered forging an all-encompassing opposition alliance for the 2000 presidential race. Although both Cuauhtémoc Cárdenas and Vicente Fox expressed interest in the idea, each wanted to be the candidate to lead the alliance. Eventually, both Fox and Cárdenas entered alliances with minor parties, making it clear that a coalition of left and right was not going to be the means to defeat the PRI. Given that party leaders from the PAN and the PRD did not unite into a single electoral front to dislodge the PRI, opposition voters had a hard time coordinating to support a common opposition candidate capable of defeating the PRI.

The divisiveness of the opposition might be the product of ethnic cleavages (Ordeshook and Shvetsova, 1994; Cox, 1997); it might result from fundamental policy differences among opponents (Riker, 1976; Sartori, 1976; Pempel, 1990; Laver and Schofield 1991; Magaloni, 1996); or it might be the product of personal rivalries among opposition leaders. Electoral rules also play a powerful role in shaping incentives to coordinate (Cox, 1997). Electoral institutions determine the pay-offs that result from forming larger versus smaller electoral coalitions. The simple-majority, single-ballot system, according to Duverger's law, creates incentives for elites to coalesce, leading to the consolidation of a two-party system.[21]

Because autocracies possess ample leeway to manipulate electoral rules, the divisiveness of the opposition is partly *endogenous*, a direct consequence of the ruling party's institutional manipulation (Diaz-Cayeros and Magaloni, 2001; Lust-Okar, 2005). The Mexican PRI drafted electoral rules for the translation of votes into seats in order to accomplish three goals simultaneously: (1) to reward itself disproportionately; (2) to reduce entry cost to the legislature for the smaller opposition parties so as to co-opt them into acquiescing to the existing institutions rather than challenging them through violent means; and (3) to divide its opponents. The PRI accomplished these goals by, among other measures, creating a mixed electoral system for the Chamber of Deputies.[22] The mixed electoral system,

[21] See Riker (1982) for a discussion of Duverger's law and the historical developments surrounding it; for a formulation by Duverger himself, see Duverger (1986). See also Ordeshook and Riker (1968).

[22] There are 500 seats elected under a mixed electoral formula; 300 seats are elected from single-member districts, and 200 come from multimember districts. The electoral formula for distributing the multimember seats is not compensatory and thus is far from proportional.

originally established in 1978, disproportionately rewarded the ruling party, which was the only party that could win a majority of the vote in the single-member districts; at the same time, it allowed opposition parties to win seats from the multimember districts, mitigating Duvergerian incentives to coordinate. Voters could cast only one straight vote, preventing them from strategically dividing their votes in such a way that they would support the stronger opposition contender in the single-member races and vote sincerely for their preferred choice in the multimember races. In the short run, seats from the multimember districts benefited opposition parties by significantly reducing entry costs to the legislature. In the long run, however, these seats helped sustain the PRI's dominance by discouraging coordination among opposition parties and voters.

In my account of authoritarian survival, opposition coordination dilemmas play two fundamental roles. First, defeating a hegemonic party requires mass coordination on the part of voters. Mass coordination is almost automatic when opposition party elites manage to form all-encompassing opposition electoral fronts, as in Senegal in 2000 or in Kenya in 2002. When opposition party elites fail to unite, this form of mass coordination is harder to achieve. Across Africa, ethnic rivalries complicate opposition coordination, although they do not preclude it. Multiparty competition seems to have enhanced ethnic identities (Glickman, 1995) and ethnic voting (Posner, 2005). Citizens tend to vote for individuals of their own ethnic group, particularly in ethnically divided societies, even if this entails wasting their votes on losing candidates (Van de Walle, forthcoming). In Mexico, opposition coordination required that voters put aside their ideological differences and choose to cast a vote for the strongest opposition contender capable of dislodging the PRI.

But even if voters are willing to set their ideological or ethnic differences aside, as long as the hegemonic party cannot be defeated, they are better off voting sincerely for their first choice rather than strategically voting for the strongest contender. This is another reason why perceptions of invincibility help hegemonic parties – these perceptions serve to discourage mass snowballing effects. Strategic voting also requires dissemination of polling results through the mass media so that the parties' relative standings become common knowledge (Cox, 1997). Nonetheless, autocratic regimes exert tight controls over the mass media (Lawson, 2002), allowing them to portray a minuscule opposition and an overpowering ruling party; these messages work to discourage voter coordination.

The second coordination dilemma that I explore is related to electoral fraud and alternation of political power in office. Chapter 8 develops a game-theory model of "electoral transitions" to answer the following questions: under what conditions would a hegemonic party steal the elections and be able to get away with this behavior? What explains why a hegemonic party would credibly choose to tie its hands not to commit fraud, delegating the organization and monitoring of elections to an independent electoral commission? When is a hegemonic party expected to yield power peacefully if defeated? My model suggests that in trying to enforce clean elections, opposition party elites face a complicated coordination problem. Suppose that opposition parties A and B are considering a choice between rebelling against the electoral fraud or acquiescing to it. If both parties rebel against the regime in tandem, the hegemonic party could more easily be dislodged. Yet if party A chooses to rebel against the electoral fraud, party B will face the following strategic dilemma: rebel in tandem and go to war, or acquiesce to the electoral fraud and capture legislative seats and government spoils. Furthermore, electoral incentives are not well aligned to fight authoritarianism. Opposition party elites face the paradoxical result that allegations of electoral fraud might also translate into electoral punishment by what I label *moderate opposition voters*, who are skeptical of allegations of electoral fraud and averse to post-electoral violence. My model of "electoral transitions" thus demonstrates that if party B's electoral base is composed mostly of *moderate* supporters, and if the official results allow this party to acquire enough legislative seats and possibly policy influence, this party will be better off institutionalizing itself as a "loyal opposition;" the result is that the opposition fails to rebel in tandem, which in turn enables the autocrat to engage in various sorts of electoral malpractice with impunity. The model in Chapter 8 thus spells out the reasons why authoritarian equilibria occurring where there is significant electoral corruption can be long-lasting. The tragedy of these autocratic equilibria is that factions of the opposition and voters play a prominent role in sustaining them.

My approach is in line with that of Weingast (1997), who argues that dictators trespass upon citizens' rights by profiting from coordination dilemmas among their opponents. I move beyond Weingast in explicitly bringing voters, political parties, electoral rules, and elections into the story of strategic interaction. Moreover, I provide a theory of endogenous institutional design that helps to explain why an autocrat might sign a "political pact"[23] with the opposition, willingly agreeing not to transgress their electoral rights by delegating the power to control the organization of elections to an independent electoral commission. Such political pacts, which can play a powerful role in enabling society to coordinate against a dictator, are exogenous to Weingast's model and left unexplained. I show that two conditions must hold for a pact creating an independent electoral commission to be signed: the ruling party must believe it can go on winning elections cleanly; and the opposition, under some particular circumstances, must credibly threaten to rebel against the election results, regardless of whether there is fraud or not, unless the ruling party finds a way to guarantee *ex ante* the transparency of the elections. My model of electoral transitions thus spells out how autocratic elections transform into democratic ones and the factors that account for the emergence of the rule of law in the realm of elections.

The Process of Democratization

To understand the dynamics of democratization in hegemonic-party regimes, one must simultaneously look at three arenas. First, the structural and economic factors that enable voters to defect from the hegemonic party must be articulated. My theory of voting behavior under autocracy allows me to derive hypotheses about the structural conditions facilitating voter defection from the hegemonic party and voter coordination. These hypotheses will be assessed using empirical evidence for the case of Mexico in Chapters 2, 5, 6, and 7.

Second, to understand the process of democratization in these regimes, one must spell out the hegemonic party's strategic response to opposition party entry, including how the autocracy manipulates economic policies and its control of state resources in order to halt the deterioration of its core base of supporters, deter voters from defecting, and undermine opposition party building. These issues will be analyzed using empirical evidence for the case of Mexico in Chapters 3 and 4.

Third, to understand the process of democratization in hegemonic-party regimes, one must look at elite bargaining over political institutions. Chapter 8 presents a game-theoretic account of the *process* of transition,

[23] I draw the term from Karl (1990). The meaning of "pact" in my approach is different. A pact entails the redesign of the electoral institutions as opposed to an agreement not to politicize certain issues such as the redistribution of income.

looking at elite bargaining over institutions. The transition game I develop spells out the set of strategic variables that influence the possibility that, once an *apertura* has occurred – with the socioeconomic, international, and structural preconditions fulfilled in such a way that voters are ready to defect to the opposition – the transition might actually happen. In this framework, the peaceful alternation of political power in office is one of the possible equilibrium outcomes, as occurred in Mexico in 2000; but my model also allows for the possibility that the incumbent reverses the outcome of the elections, as occurred in the 1988 presidential elections.

Thus, when it comes to analyzing the dynamics of the transition to democracy in hegemonic-party regimes, approaches that mostly focus on elite bargaining are incomplete. In providing a theory that simultaneously examines elite and mass behavior, this book seeks to bridge the gap between elite-level approaches to the study of democratization that emphasize the *process* of transition and individual agency (e.g., Rustow, 1970; O'Donnell and Schmitter, 1986; Share and Mainwaring, 1986; Di Palma, 1990; Przeworski, 1991) and the structural approaches to democracy that look at the set of "preconditions" that make authoritarian breakdown more likely and democracy possible (e.g., Lipset, 1957, and 1959; Huntington, 1968; Przeworski et al., 2000; Boix and Stokes, 2003; Mainwaring and Perez-Liñán, 2005). In this book, I answer Karl's (1990) call to place elite bargaining within a framework of historical constraints so as to avoid the "danger of descending in excessive voluntarism." My approach to the study of democratization is thus complementary to that of Haggard and Kaufman (1999), in that it "draws on strategic analysis but focuses on the effects of the economic conditions on the preferences, resources and strategies of key political players in the transition game" (76), and to Geddes (1999).

Compared to two of the leading approaches that also employ game theory to account for the politics of regime change (Boix, 2003, and Acemoglu and Robinson, 2006), mine is much less ambitious because I do not claim to provide a theory of transition that applies to all the countries in the world, regardless of the nature of their authoritarian past. There are different "modes" of transition (Karl and Schmitter, 1991), and, like Geddes (1999), I believe that the *dynamics* of transition differ depending on the type of autocratic regime that is being challenged. My approach also differs from these works in another fundamental way. In Boix (2003) and in Acemoglu and Robinson (2004), the distribution of income between rich and poor is *the* central battle of the politics of regime change. Because autocrats are presumed to protect the assets of the rich and democracy is assumed to threaten those assets, the rich must be willing to acquiesce to some redistribution in order for democracy to emerge. Thus, in both of these works, reduced inequality encourages democracy because it makes the rich less fearful of redistribution.

In my approach, rather than rendering the rich less fearful of redistribution, growing equality and economic development encourage democratization because they reduce the value of the strategy of vote buying. The most divisive issue of the transition of these regimes is the pursuit of power and the spoils of office, not income redistribution from rich to poor. This derives from the fact that hegemonic-party regimes are more redistributive than most other dictatorial regimes. Often these autocracies can themselves become a major threat to the assets of the rich if, by redistributing or nationalizing them, they can employ them for the purpose of party maintenance. Witness the Mexican nationalization of the oil industry in 1938 and of the banks in 1982; Tanzania's policy of land collectivization; and the more recent expropriation of white private farms by the ZANU-PF throughout Zimbabwe so as to boost President Robert Mugabe's popularity, to name a few examples. A central trait of hegemonic-party regimes is that they possess extremely strong executives and employ these and other state resources to remove all opposition (see also Bratton and van de Walle, 1997). The major battle of the transition to democracy lies in convincing the autocrat to peacefully yield the enormous power vested in the state.

Why Mexico, and What Is New about This Book?

This book develops a theory about hegemonic-party autocracy and its democratization dynamics. The theory is broadly comparative, although the empirical evidence comes from the analysis of aggregate and individual-level data for the case of Mexico. I chose Mexico for several reasons.

First, the Mexican hegemonic-party autocracy survived under a variety of macroeconomic circumstances, initially presiding over a long period of economic growth until 1982, and then governing during a series of recessions, including the debt crisis of the 1980s and the peso crisis of 1994. Thus, the Mexican case permits an exploration of the behavior of a hegemonic-party regime under favorable economic conditions, when electoral fraud was less necessary, and under unfavorable economic conditions, a time when fraud became more prevalent and necessary. It also allows me to test one conventional view about the survival of hegemonic-party regimes, namely, that economic growth *causes* political stability. Mexico grew until 1982 and stagnated afterward. Yet, although the PRI was significantly weakened, it managed to survive where other regimes would have fallen victim to economic disintegration.

A second reason to study Mexico is that the PRI peacefully stepped down from office in 2000 after an electoral defeat. Yet, in the 1988 election, the PRI committed massive fraud against Cuauhtémoc Cárdenas. A comparison of these two elections is ideal for my theory of transitions to democracy. Seldom does one find in a single case both a "successful" and an "unsuccessful" outcome.

The third reason to focus on the Mexican PRI is that through the years of my study of this regime, I have collected ideal macro- and micro-level data that allow me to test a variety of implications of my theory, both for voting behavior and for the behavior of party elites, including the manipulation of the economy for electoral gain. These types of data are extremely difficult to obtain for most autocratic regimes.

There are excellent research publications on Mexican politics and the PRI's rule;[24] a sizable literature on the voting behavior of Mexicans;[25] and some excellent works that study various aspects of the Mexican democratization process, including electoral reform.[26] Although part of what I study has been treated in these works, this book offers several improvements on the existing literature. First, I offer a theory of how all the different pieces in the puzzle of hegemonic-party regimes (voters, party strategy, the economic structure, the use of patronage and pork, and political institutions) relate to each other to produce authoritarian stability and democratization. Most existing works tend to focus on only one element of the puzzle. Second, this book presents new and better empirical evidence about central aspects of the PRI's rule and its democratization. As will become apparent in the later chapters, much of the empirical evidence I offer is completely new and solves some central scholarly controversies.

[24] Scott (1959), Brandenburg (1964), González Casanova (1965), Ames (1970), Hansen (1974), Cornelius (1975), Smith (1979), Molinar (1991), Dresser (1991), Camp (1995), Collier (1995), Weldon (1997), Loaeza (1999), and Castañeda (2000), among many others.

[25] Klesner (1988), Domínguez and McCann (1995, 1996), Domínguez and Poiré (1999), Gómez Tagle (1997), Moreno (1999b, 2003), and Domínguez and Lawson (2004) constitute some of the most relevant contributions.

[26] See Cornelius, Craig, and Fox (1994), Rodríguez and Ward (1995), Bruhn (1997), Camp (1999), Lujambio (2000), Chand (2001), Lawson (2002), Middlebrook (2004), and Eisenstadt (2004), among others.

Third, I place Mexico in comparative perspective, challenging conventional wisdom about Mexico's "exceptionalism." Although the longevity of the Mexican PRI is remarkable, there are many other cases similar to that of Mexico, in which one party holds power for many years under semiauthoritarian conditions. The literature on Mexican politics tends to ignore the fact that there are many other countries in the developing world where one party rules for years and elections take place under semiauthoritarian conditions, all under conditions of extraordinary political stability.

Castañeda (2000) is careful in highlighting Mexico's distinctiveness *relative to Latin America*. He emphasizes three distinctive traits of the Mexican system relative to Latin America: its political stability, the ambivalent nature of the regime – "neither democratic nor repressive" – and what he calls the system's "uncanny capacity to deliver the goods" (x). Mexico is indeed unique in Latin America. It does not fully correspond to O'Donnell's (1973) category of "bureaucratic authoritarianism," nor does it fulfill the requirements of democracy. Moreover, as Latin America transitioned toward democracy after the debt crisis, the Mexican PRI survived economic stagnation, macroeconomic instability, and a brutal deterioration of real salaries. Only by placing Mexico in broader comparative perspective can we understand that some of these patterns are not so unique. Ultimately, the truly exceptional trait of the Mexican political system is its presidential succession mechanism. Castañeda (2000) has provided a splendid study of the presidential succession and its unique character. In this book I have instead chosen to focus on features that are not unique to Mexico – those elements that the PRI's rule shares with other hegemonic-party autocracies.

Defining Hegemonic-Party Autocracies and the Universe of Cases in the World

Although this book is primarily about Mexico, my theory is applicable to other hegemonic-party regimes. Before I proceed to develop my theory, I will define what I mean by hegemonic-party autocracy and distinguish these regimes from their democratic cousins, predominant-party democracies.

Hegemonic-party autocracy is a system in which one political party remains in office uninterruptedly under semiauthoritarian conditions while holding regular multiparty elections. Unlike single-party systems, hegemonic-party systems allow opposition parties to challenge the incumbent party through multiparty elections. In single-party systems, by contrast, competition, if it takes place, happens under the auspices of a single party, and all the candidates must run on the ticket of that party. I argue that single-party systems transform into hegemonic-party systems if incumbents legalize multiparty elections and remain in power nonetheless. Many of the African single-party autocracies, particularly since the early 1990s, fit this characterization.

Hegemonic-party systems should be distinguished from what Pempel (1990) baptized as "uncommon democracies," namely, regimes that have been governed by one political party for prolonged periods under democratic conditions. Sartori (1976) labeled these democratic regimes "predominant-party systems." Sartori offered the following criterion for distinguishing hegemonic-party systems from predominant-party systems: in hegemonic-party systems, "not only does alternation not occur in fact; it *cannot* occur, since the possibility of a rotation in power is not even envisaged. The implication is that the hegemonic party will remain in power whether it is liked or not" (230). Instead, the "predominant-party system is a type of party pluralism in which – even though no alternation in office actually occurs – *alternation is not ruled out*" (200). The Liberal Democratic Party (LDP) in Japan, the Social Democratic Party (SDP) in Sweden, the Christian Democrats (CD) in Italy, and the Congress Party (CP) in India are some of the best-known examples of predominant-party democracies. Hegemonic-party systems are similar to these regimes in that for years they do not experience an alternation of political power in office. Yet, in studying the PRI in Mexico, the PS in Senegal, or the UMNO in Malaysia, to name some examples, most scholars agree that there are significant authoritarian traits in these party regimes that distinguish them from democracies.

Sartori's emphasis on the possibility of the alternation of parties in political office as a central trait distinguishing democracies from autocracies is on target. The difficulty with this criterion, however, is that there is no clear way of knowing *ex ante* when alternation can or cannot occur (Przeworski et al., 2000). The literature has suggested another possible way of distinguishing between these regimes that focuses on electoral manipulations, as Schedler (2002) proposes: "The idea of democratic self-government is incompatible with electoral farces. In the common phrasing, elections must be "free and fair" in order to pass as democratic. Under electoral democracy, contests comply with minimal democratic norms; under electoral authoritarianism, they do not" (Schedler, 2002: 37). The author presents seven forms of authoritarian manipulation; the presence of any one of these, in his view, should label a country an autocracy. Levitsky and Way (2002) also focus on electoral manipulations and the violation of the existing rules of electoral contestation to distinguish between democracies and electoral autocracies.

It is beyond doubt that these manipulations skew elections in fundamental ways. Yet some of the manipulations that Schedler (2002) underscores can also take place in systems that we normally regard as democratic. Consider, for example, "corrupt political entrepreneurs trying to buy the votes of the poor" (44); "self-serving rules of representation granting them a decisive edge when votes are translated into seats" (45); or the "informal disenfranchisement" of different ethnic groups (44). The Japanese LDP, for example, was able to sustain itself largely through vote buying, patronage, and electoral rules that disproportionately represented rural constituencies (Sheiner, 2006). These practices were also common in Italy under the rule of the Christian Democrats (Golden, 2001), and they were very prevalent in the United States during the long era of machine politics. Malapportionment and gerrymandering are also ways to grant a "decisive edge" to some political contenders, and both are quite prevalent in well-established democracies. The informal disenfranchisement of tens of thousands of voters, mostly African American, was one of the main allegations raised against authorities in the state of Florida in the 2000 elections in the United States. Indeed, democracies are classified as such precisely because they possess fewer undemocratic features, not because these features are not present at all (Tilly, 2004). In distinguishing between autocracies and democracies, the central issue seems to be whether electoral manipulations are *potentially controllable* by existing political institutions, not whether they occur at all (Sartori, 1976: 194).

Przeworski and colleagues (2000) offer a third approach to classifying these regimes, one that focuses exclusively on the alternation of political parties in office. All those systems where alternation of political power has not occurred are classified as authoritarian, unless and until the incumbent actually loses an election and peacefully yields power. The authors employ the so-called alternation rule to minimize what they call type I errors, namely, classifying a system as democratic when it is actually an autocracy. When in doubt, they count a regime as autocratic. An example they offer is Botswana, which has "no constraints on the opposition, little visible repression, no apparent fraud" (23), but whether the ruling party would yield office if it ever lost an election is an open question, until the situation actually presents itself. I am in full agreement with the logic of the alternation rule up to this point. However, a problem arises when the incumbent loses power: the authors classify these systems as democratic *retroactively*, that is, from the moment the incumbent first attained office.

These authors' classification rule presents a serious drawback: it entails the risk of classifying a country as a democracy when it is actually an autocracy, which is precisely the type I error the authors seek to avoid. For instance, since the PS lost the 2000 elections and gave up power, Senegal would be classified as democratic from the time multiparty elections were first introduced through a constitutional amendment in 1976. Throughout most of these years, however, the PS held office under semiauthoritarian conditions. And what about Mexico, where the PRI also yielded power in 2000? Should it be classified as democratic beginning in 1929? Can one classify Kenya as a democracy from the time the KANU instituted multiparty elections, given that this party lost power in 2002? Can Cameroon, Gabon, Egypt, Malaysia, Singapore, Tanzania, or Zimbabwe – to name just a few more examples – be classified as democracies *retroactively* (from the time they first permitted multiparty elections onward) when and if their incumbents are defeated and leave office? I believe the answer is no.

To avoid the problems of the approaches just mentioned, I employ two criteria for distinguishing hegemonic-party autocracies from predominant-party democracies, both of which focus on the nature of the existing political institutions. As Diamond (2002) argues, the distinction between electoral democracy and electoral autocracy "turns crucially on freedom, fairness, inclusiveness and meaningfulness of elections" (p. 27). Rather than relying on difficult judgements about whether elections fit these criteria, my approach focuses on the nature of the existing political institutions. First, hegemonic-party systems are far more overpowering than predominant-party systems, usually controlling more than 65 percent of the legislative seats – so that they can *change the constitution unilaterally*, without the need to forge coalitions with opposition parties. This implies that there is no binding set of constitutional rules, as the incumbent party can change the rules unilaterally. If the ruling party is able to draft the constitution unilaterally, the likelihood of erecting authoritarian institutions increases – the autocrat can stack courts, augment presidential powers, modify electoral rules, limit civil and political rights, and colonize the state security apparatus without constraint. If the ruling party instead needs to forge coalitions in order to create institutions, these institutions are less likely to be autocratic. Democratic predominant parties, instead, win by narrower margins, which means that these parties cannot unilaterally modify the constitution to serve their goals. Also, they often need to seek compromise with the opposition for the enacting of legislation and, in parliamentary regimes, for the formation of governments. Although other scholars have also highlighted either the number of legislative seats or the number of votes as a possible way to distinguish these regimes, to my knowledge no previous work underscores that these seat thresholds are important mainly because of their institutional consequences – the fact that the constitution is endogenous to partisan interests.

Second, in hegemonic-party systems, electoral malpractices are not *potentially controllable* because the hegemonic party has unilateral control of the institutions in charge of organizing, monitoring, and adjudicating elections. As a result, in hegemonic-party regimes, a strong *regime cleavage*[27] over the existing political institutions comes to divide the opposition from the incumbents, for the major opposition contenders do not accept the basic institutions as effective and legitimate means to pursue their goals.

Seat thresholds are important for their institutional consequences and should not be employed in isolation as a way to distinguish hegemonic-party autocracies from predominant-party democracies. A hegemonic party might have enjoyed for years the ability to draft the constitution single-handedly and to erect autocratic institutions. This party might subsequently lose its legislative supermajority necessary to amend the constitution, yet still enjoy veto power for *changing* the existing institutions. Part of the dilemma of the democratization of these regimes is that electoral competition takes place under a set of institutions that are skewed in favor of the ruling party and that these institutions can't be transformed without its cooperation.

To give a sense of how common hegemonic-party autocracies are, I first identify the one-party dominant regimes, both democratic and autocratic. My criteria for including a case as one-party dominant are: (1) there should be regularized multiparty competition, even if limited; (2) the chief executive and the legislature must be elected; (3) the incumbent must have held

[27] This cleavage should be distinguished from Sartori's anti-system, pro-system cleavage. According to Sartori, anti-system parties are those that oppose the regime "in principle" owing to ideological radicalism. Parties such as the fascists and extreme communists, that is, sought to transform the very system of government (Sartori, 1976: 133). The cleavage I am talking about stems not from ideological radicalism, but from the different strategic standings of political parties with regard to the existing rules of the game and the strategies they follow in the transition game. Molinar (1991) was the first author to talk about this cleavage dividing party leaders in Mexico. In Magaloni (1996), I show that this division also exists among the electorate.

office for more than twenty years; and (4) if the incumbent wasn't initially elected in multiparty elections, the ruling party subsequently introduced them, and never lost. The criterion of longevity unfortunately eliminates party regimes in the process of consolidating hegemony, such as contemporary Turkmenistan, Uzbekistan, Belarus, Ethiopia, and Russia, to name some examples. My theory should apply to these cases as well.

To sort these cases into democracies and autocracies, I consider the following scenarios. The first scenario focuses on the alternation of political power in office, as in Przeworski and colleagues' study (2000): where alternation has not occurred, I regard the system as an autocracy, because it is not possible to know *ex ante* if a longtime incumbent would step down from office once defeated. Hegemonic-party autocracies that have not been defeated include the already-mentioned UMNO (1957–) in Malaysia, the PAP (1959–) in Singapore, the CCM (1964–) in Tanzania, the ZANU-PF (1980–) in Zimbabwe, and the BDP (1967–) in Botswana. Other hegemonic-party autocracies that have never lost power include the Gabonese Democratic Party (PDG), in power since 1969; the National Democratic Party (NDP) in Egypt, in power since 1978; Cameroon's People's Democratic Movement (CPDM), in power since 1966; the Front for the Liberation of Mozambique (FRELIMO), in power since 1976; and the Colorado Party in Paraguay, in power since 1947.

Where the party was ousted by a military coup, I regard the system as an autocracy for a similar reason: we can't know if the incumbent would have acquiesced to an electoral defeat had it been confronted with one. Hegemonic-party autocracies that were ousted by military coups include the Democratic Party of Cote d'Ivoire – African Rally (PDCI-RDA), which ruled from 1960 until the military coup in 1999; Gambia's Progressive People's Party (PPP), which governed from 1965 until the 1994 military coup; and Liberia's True Whig Party, which was ousted by a coup in 1980.

When the incumbent has been defeated through elections and alternation of political power in office has occurred, the challenge consists in identifying when precisely the system became democratic. In Przeworski and colleagues' study (2000), once the hegemonic power is defeated, democracy is treated as if it had been born the moment the incumbent party first assumed office. In my approach, democracy can be born at three different moments depending on the nature of the political institutions:

1. The system was a democracy since the hegemonic party first assumed office. In my view, Japan's LDP; India's Congress Party; Sweden's Social Democrats; Italy's Christian Democrats; Trinidad and Tobago's People's

National Movement (PNM), which ruled from 1956 until 1986; and the Bahamas' Progressive Liberal Party (PLP), which ruled from 1967 until 1992, fall into this category. According to most political analysts, the BDP in Botswana stands out for governing under quite democratic rules and practices; if it were to lose the elections, I would classify it as democratic since it first assumed office.

2. The system was an autocracy but it became a democracy *before* the party lost, through some form of political pact (Karl, 1990). Suppose that a hegemonic party credibly commits not to steal the elections by, for example, delegating the organization and monitoring of elections to an independent electoral commission. Or suppose that the hegemonic party reaches an agreement with the opposition parties to erect new political institutions that satisfy the interests of the major political players. After entering into these types of political pacts, the incumbent party might continue to win the elections, despite having established the conditions for elections to take place under democratic conditions. In my view, the PRI in Mexico; the KMT in Taiwan; and the National Party (NP) in South Africa, which ruled from 1948 until 1994, fit this characterization.

I classify the PRI in Mexico as a hegemonic-party autocracy from 1929 until the 1994 electoral reform, negotiated jointly among the major political parties – the PRI, the PAN, and the PRD. Triggered by the Zapatista guerilla uprising in the southern state of Chiapas in January 1994, this electoral reform gave true independence to the Federal Electoral Institute (IFE), the body charged with organizing and monitoring elections. The most significant aspect of the 1994 electoral reform was the establishment of the *Consejeros Ciudadanos* (Citizen Councilmen). Six citizens were to be elected to the IFE's board by a two-thirds vote in the Lower Chamber, and each of the major parties – the PRI, the PAN and the PRD – had the right to propose two of them. With this new arrangement, the government lost control of the IFE's board, and the six citizens came to exercise considerable practical control over the 1994 electoral process. After this reform, the opposition parties largely agreed that the issue of the transparency of the federal electoral process had been resolved and that the remaining reforms pertained to leveling the political playing field. In this respect, the subsequent electoral reform of 1996 was also important because it increased state campaign financing and access to the media for the opposition parties. The 1996 reform also incorporated the Federal Electoral Tribunal into the federal judicial power and allowed the Supreme Court to review the constitutionality of electoral laws (Magaloni, 2003; Eisenstadt, 2004).

3. The system was an autocracy throughout the period of one-party rule up until the time the party lost. Suppose that a hegemonic-party autocrat has ruled for years – rigging the elections, excluding key opponents from the ballot, and coercing groups of voters into supporting the regime. Confronted with an electoral defeat, the hegemonic party will be tempted to reverse the outcome of the elections. What might prevent it from doing so? One possibility, as my model in Chapter 8 makes explicit, is that opposition parties can credibly threaten major social unrest, or even a civil war, if the incumbent were to attempt to reverse the outcome of these elections. Another possibility is that the incumbent autocrat loses the previously unconditional support of the armed forces, so that it is unable to enforce the electoral fraud. In contrast to Przeworski and colleagues' approach (2000), in my view a system where the incumbent party accedes to an electoral defeat under these circumstances should be considered autocratic until the end. Kenya under the KANU (1964–2002); Senegal under the PS (1960–2000); Guinea-Bissau under the PAIGC (1975–1999); and Guyana under the National Congress Party (PNC), in control of government from 1964 until its electoral defeat in 1992, fit this characterization.

Table I.1 presents a summary of some of the basic institutional traits of these regimes, which are sorted into democracies and autocracies. These data reflect that predominant-party democracies and hegemonic-party autocracies are different species, which a view that solely focuses on alternation of political power in office would necessarily overlook. The Polity scores confirm the differences between these regimes: predominant-party democracies show Polity scores of close to 10, the highest value on the scale. The average Polity score in the autocracies is −2.64.

The average number of legislative seats controlled by the incumbent party and the average number of effective veto players reflect the fact that in the autocracies, but not in the democracies, the incumbents possess the leeway to modify the constitution unilaterally and rule unconstrained by veto players. Hegemonic-party autocracies control an average of 76 percent of the legislative seats, and their average number of effective veto players is 1.87, while predominant-party democracies control an average of 55 percent of the legislative seats, and they have an average of 3.79 veto players.

Thus, the autocracies possess ample leeway for institutional manipulation. Consider the following example. With the independence of Zimbabwe, a new constitutional framework was created to accommodate the interests of the different warring factions and those of the white ethnic

Table I.1. *Institutional differences between hegemonic-party autocracies and predominant party democracies*

	Average Polity Scores	Average Number of Legislative Seats	Average Veto Players	Effective Number of Executive Heads	Presidential
Hegemonic-party autocracies	−2.64	76	1.87	2.63	66%
Predominant-party democracies	9.39	53	3.79	4.87	0%

Note: Predominant-party democracies include Japan, India, Italy, Sweden, Trinidad and Tobago, and Bahamas. Hegemonic-party autocracies include Botswana, Cameroon, Cote d'Ivoire, Djibouti, Gabon, Gambia, Guinea-Bissau, Guyana, Kenya, Liberia, Malaysia, Mexico, Mozambique, Paraguay, Senegal, Singapore, South Africa, Taiwan, Tanzania, and Zimbabwe. Polity scores are from Polity IV (Marshall and Jaggers, 2003). Average Polity scores are calculated from the date the party first assumed office until its demise. For those parties that returned to office, all numbers correspond to the first period a party ruled. Average legislative seats are average percentage number of legislative seats in the lower house. Data on legislative seats come from various sources, including Beck et al. (2001); Banks (1976); CIA World Fact Book; the Library of Congress Country Studies; Background Notes (U.S. Dept. of State); www.encyclopedia.com; Auswärtiges Amt: Country Information; Governments on the WWW (www.gksoft.com/govt/). Average number of veto players come from the Database of Political Institutions, Beck et al. (2001). Effective Number of Executive Heads is the inverse of the sum of the squared percentage of years each head of the executive ruled. Data on heads of the executive is calculated from World Political Leaders, Roberto Ortiz Zárate, www.terra.es/personal2/monolith/00index.htm.

minority. Taking advantage of its overwhelming electoral victory in 1980, the then prime minister Robert Mugabe transformed the existing institutional framework. A constitutional amendment in 1987 replaced the Westminster system with an executive presidency, and it abolished the 20 percent reserved parliamentary seats for the "white roll"; this was followed by the abolition of the Senate, where 25 percent of the seats were also reserved (Baumhogger, 1999: 965). The Movement for Democratic Change (MDC) mounted a strong challenge to the ZANU-PF in the 1999 elections, winning 57 of the 120 seats. To revive the party's popularity, President Mugabe engaged in a strategy of racial nationalism, confiscating white-owned farms throughout the country. Hundreds were beaten as a result of the confiscation of property by the government. The Supreme Court ruled this policy of land reform illegal. President Mugabe refused to enforce the Court's decision, and he subsequently decided to employ his constitutional powers to stack the Court with political allies. After the 2002 elections, Mugabe attempted to cement his electoral success, passing a bill intended to ban independent electoral monitors and to concentrate all the electoral functions in his hands (Marshall and Jaggers, 2003, Polity IV Country Reports).

These types of constitutional manipulation are ruled out in the democracies. This is not to say that there is no room for other forms of institutional manipulation – dominant parties in these democracies were all famous for manipulating campaign financing, social legislation, and electoral laws to their advantage. However, in all of these democracies, constitutions were binding because their dominant ruling parties could not modify them without the opposition's consent. Although the Christian Democrats dominated Italian politics for over thirty-seven consecutive years, from 1945 until 1981, after 1953 this party ruled as a member of a parliamentary coalition, which meant that the Christian Democrats not only could not change the constitution but also needed to make compromises with other political players in order to pass legislation. The LDP in Japan never governed as part of a coalition, but on average it controlled less that 60 percent of the parliamentary seats during its thirty-nine consecutive years of rule. By the same token, the Social Democrats in Sweden controlled an average of 48 percent of the legislative seats during its forty-five years of uninterrupted rule. The Congress Party in India was the preeminent force after independence. However, this party never managed fully to colonize all the existing political institutions, including the assemblies of the states and the judicial power, because political power in India was highly fractionalized.

Another distinctive trait of most autocracies is that power is highly concentrated in the hands of one single individual. Table I.1 reports the Effective Number of Executive Heads (ENEH), which is adapted from the Effective Number of Parties (N) used by Laakso and Taagepera (1979). ENEH is the inverse of the sum of the squared percentage of years each head of executive ruled. Thus, for example, in Botswana there have been three presidents from the BDP – Sir Seretse Kama, Quett Masire (now Sir Ketumile Masire), and Festus Mogae. The first ruled for fifteen years, the second for eighteen, and the third had ruled for two years up to 2000. ENEH in Botswana is given by

$$\frac{1}{(.42)^2 + (.51)^2 + (.05)^2} = 2.21.$$

The average ENEH is 2.63 in the autocracies and 4.87 in the democracies. In all of the hegemonic-party autocracies, the head of the executive is an extremely powerful player because he also tends to be the de facto leader of the party. Among the hegemonic-party autocracies, the Mexican PRI stands out. The ENEH under the PRI is 9.72, which is close to Japan's (11.28) and Italy's (9.81). Other hegemonic-party autocracies that dispersed power among various individuals were Liberia (7.08) and South Africa (5.21). The rest of the hegemonic-party autocracies, especially the African ones, are highly *personalistic* and have been ruled for a majority of the time by their founding leader and at the most one other individual. (The average ENEH for the rest of the African autocracies is 1.6, and the average ENEH for the Asian autocracies is 2.71.)

Finally, the table shows that one-party dominant regimes occur almost equally often in parliamentary and presidential systems. Yet 66 percent of the autocracies are presidential, while *all* of the predominant-party democracies are parliamentary. As I discuss in Chapter 8, presidential institutions not only concentrate power in the hands of one single individual, but also maximize the stakes of losing power, augmenting the incentives for incumbent parties to resort to electoral fraud and the use of force in order to retain power.

Plan of the Book

Chapter 1 presents my theoretical framework for understanding elite cooperation within the hegemonic-party system and mass support for the regime. I also discuss voter coordination dilemmas and present a set of hypotheses about party strategy and voters' behavior to be assessed using empirical evidence in subsequent chapters. My theory of the determinants of mass support for the PRI presented in Chapter 1 stresses a series of causal relationships that link the socioeconomic structure with the propensity to support the autocratic regime or to defect to the opposition. Chapter 2 provides empirical evidence, based on aggregate socioeconomic indicators, for several of my theoretical claims. Some of these relationships, and in particular the correlation between underdevelopment and support for the PRI, have long been understood by experts. Other correlations are less clear even to the experts. Chapter 2 also serves to provide some basic "stylized facts" about the dynamics of mass support for the PRI and the decline in that support over the years.

In Chapters 3 and 4 I assess the role of economic resources, pork, and patronage in sustaining the PRI regime. These chapters are highly original contributions even for experts who are versed in the intricacies of PRI patronage. Chapter 3 concentrates on the analysis of budget and business cycles from 1938 until 2000. Chapter 4 analyzes the mechanics of vote buying and its political effectiveness from the PRI's point of view. In addition to vote buying, my voting model states that voters care about economic performance and ideological appeals. Chapter 5 concentrates on the role of economic performance in accounting for mass support of the PRI, focusing on the post-1988 period. In Mexico, as in most other Latin American countries, the 1980s were a lost decade in terms of economic growth. How did Mexican voters react to these dramatic changes in the economic environment? To answer this question, Chapter 5 employs presidential approval ratings from 1988 to 2000 and macroeconomic data.

Chapter 6 explores the role of policy issues and ideological appeals in voting behavior. The chapter reveals that *policy divisions* constituted an important source of the opposition's coordination dilemmas. I demonstrate that those who reported supporting the PAN over the PRD disproportionately favored a set of right-wing economic policies (including liberalization of trade and privatization of the state oil company, PEMEX). They also stood against increases in taxes and wealth redistribution. Conversely, PRD voters preferred a more activist and nationalistic state, including government programs for alleviation of poverty and redistribution of wealth. These voters also opposed the privatization of PEMEX. Thus, on the economic left-right scale, the PAN stood to the right and the PRD to the left of the PRI. However, on the political pro-regime, anti-regime scale, voters of the opposition parties stood together, a fact that implies that the ideological scale in Mexico was multidimensional, and thus that there was room for opposition coordination, as occurred in the 2000 elections.

Chapter 7 answers the following questions: what led Mexican voters to finally decide to "throw the rascals out" of office? What factors hindered or enabled opposition coordination? To answer these questions, the chapter presents an analysis of voting choices in the 1994, 1997, and 2000 elections. Using micro-level evidence, I systematically test my hypotheses of mass support for the PRI and the factors enabling voters to defect to the opposition. Chapter 8 presents my "transition game from hegemonic-party regimes." In this last part of the book, I make use of an "analytic narrative" perspective (Bates et al., 1998) to analyze the *process* of democratization and elite bargaining over the new rules of the game that allowed democracy to emerge in Mexico and led the PRI to yield power peacefully in 2000. Chapter 9 concludes.

1

Equilibrium Party Hegemony

All autocratic regimes face two dilemmas: first, they must deter potential elite rivals, and second, they must induce some form of political loyalty from the masses. How does a hegemonic party manage to solve elite disputes and keep the party united? Why would voters support an autocratic regime? To answer these questions, I present in this chapter my theory of hegemonic-party survival, which will be assessed using systematic empirical evidence in subsequent chapters of this book.

Elite Divisions and the Golden Years of the PRI

During the golden years of the PRI, the most serious threats came from within the party itself (Molinar, 1991). The PRI experienced a series of splits during its history, the most important of which were those of Juan Andreu Almazán in 1940,[1] Ezequiel Padilla in 1946,[2] Miguel Henríquez Guzmán in 1952,[3] and Cuauhtémoc Cárdenas in 1988. All of these splits

[1] Almazán headed the opposition against the PNR's nominee, Manuel Avila Camacho, in 1940. Almazán had support from some sectors in the army and from those who were against the party's shift toward the left during the Lázaro Cárdenas years (Medina, 1978). He officially obtained close to 6 percent of the vote.

[2] Padilla was nominated by the PDM (Partido Democrático Mexicano). He had belonged to the ruling party, holding an important cabinet position during the Avila Camacho presidency. He officially obtained 19 percent of the vote.

[3] Henríquez Guzmán organized a strong opposition against the ruling party. He claimed to represent the "real" principles of the Mexican Revolution, which according to him and his supporters had been betrayed during the Alemán presidency. Henríquez Guzmán was at first supported by Lázaro Cárdenas himself. However, when Alemán named Ruiz Cortínez as the presidential nominee, Lázaro Cárdenas publicly rallied with the PRI. Henríquez Guzmán nonetheless continued his campaign through the Popular Party Front. After the PRI won the presidency, these politicians came back to the party when they where offered

occurred because prominent politicians objected to the party's presidential nominee. The 1988 split was different because it resulted in the formation of a new political party, the PRD.

To understand how a hegemonic party manages to deter party splits and the factors that account for elite divisiveness, consider the following decision-theoretic problem of a politician who is evaluating whether to remain loyal to the hegemonic party or to split. The expected utility of joining the hegemonic party is given by the probability of winning under that party's label, P_I, multiplied by the likelihood of obtaining that party's nomination, N_I, times the utility of office, O, minus the costs incurred in running a campaign under the incumbent's label, C_I. The utility of office can be thought of as access to government spoils, S_I, plus the opportunity to advance some policy goals or ideology, I_I; α and δ refer to the weight the politician attaches to spoils and ideology, respectively. Thus, the expected value of running as a member of incumbent party is defined as:

$$E(U_I) = P_I N_I(\alpha S_I + \delta I_I) - C_I \quad (1.1)$$

The expected value of splitting is given by the probability of winning under an opposition party's label, P_O, multiplied by the probability of obtaining that party's nomination, N_O. When there are no opposition parties, $P_O N_O$ can be thought of as the probability of overcoming legal barriers to entry such that the politician will be able to form and register his own ad hoc, candidate-centered organization to challenge the hegemonic party. The utility of winning office as a member of the opposition is also a function of access to government spoils, S_O, plus the opportunity to advance some policy goals or ideology, I_O, weighted by α and δ. The costs incurred in campaigning under the opposition party's label, C_O, can be understood in various ways, including the lack of access to the government-controlled mass media and harassment by members of the autocratic party. The expected electoral fraud, $E(F)$, should also be subtracted from the politician's expected rewards of splitting. Thus, the expected value of splitting is:[4]

$$E(U_O) = P_O N_O(\alpha S_O + \delta I_O) - C_O - E(F) \quad (1.2)$$

positions in the government. Henríquez Guzmán officially obtained 16 percent of the vote.

[4] To simplify, the framework assumes no repetition of the decision problem. For a formalization of the repetitive decision problem with a very similar framework, see Cox (1997).

A politician who is more ideologically oriented faces a stronger trade-off between the incumbent party and the opposition: if he joins the incumbent party, he will have to compromise his ideology in favor of the ideology of whomever happens to become the next president; if he joins the opposition, he will be able to advance his true policy goals, but only at the expense of access to government spoils.

In this simple choice-theoretic framework, splits are less likely as the politician perceives that the chances of winning elections by joining the ruling party are larger than the probability of gaining office by joining the opposition ($P_I > P_O$). When P_O is close to zero, the incentives to split are minimal. This is why hegemonic-party autocracies strive to create an image of invincibility. By winning with margins of victory of 75 percent or more, a hegemonic party generates a public message that outside of the ruling party there is nothing but limbo. When the autocracy's electoral support begins to wither, potential defectors stand better chances of going on their own and defying the ruling party by mobilizing disaffected citizens to the polls.

During its golden years, the PRI invested in winning huge margins even though the opposition posed no fundamental threat. My approach underscores that one key reason the PRI placed a lot of emphasis on mobilizing voters to the polls even when elections were not competitive was to deter elites from splitting. The PRI developed complex networks of organizations and activities to mobilize voter turnout and distributed particularistic material rewards – everything from land titles to construction materials to public sector jobs – prior to elections. During the golden years of the PRI, reported electoral participation rates were extremely high – they averaged approximately two-thirds of registered voters (Klesner and Lawson, 2004: 68). Why would the PRI care about high voter turnout? When elections were not competitive, the PRI invested in mobilizing voter turnout because low turnout would signal the existence of latent voter dissatisfaction, which might offer factions within the ruling party incentives to split.

In addition, in the ambition-theoretic framework, the threat of electoral fraud reduces the incentives to split. Every ruling party politician who split from the PRI in 1940, 1946, 1952, and 1988 alleged electoral fraud. With the exception of the 1988 presidential elections, electoral fraud in those elections was carried out to boost the ruling party's vote rather than to make the difference between winning and losing. Lower-level politicians stuffed the ballots for various reasons, including a desire to advance their careers within the party. Ballot stuffing also was intended to create a signal to elites that defection would be punished and that there was no hope in defying the party because it would use everything at its disposal, including fraud and force, to prevent opponents from winning. Fidel Velázquez, a longtime leader of the CTM, expressed the threat implicit in the practice of stuffing the ballots with the following words: "With guns in hand we came, and with guns in hand we will leave."

Furthermore, splits are less likely when the value of the government spoils given to elites increases – that is, as the difference between S_I and S_O becomes larger. The PRI offered liberal access to government spoils and opportunities for corruption to the members of the so-called revolutionary family, who were rewarded with plentiful opportunities to do business under the umbrella of the state and with profitable contracts. During the years of heavy state involvement in the economy and industrialization promoted by the state, politics constituted the principal road to economic success. Hank González, a famous PRI politician, summarized this trait of the Mexican political system with the following phrase: "A politician who stays poor is poor at politics."[5] Large government bonuses and direct cash transfers were also distributed to elites prior to elections, as I demonstrate in Chapter 3. These cash transfers given to elites were meant to pay politicians for their continuous loyalty to the ruling party. Since the PRI was in control of the national government and fiscal resources were extremely centralized, a politician who decided to split could expect to be cut off from access to government spoils and profitable state contracts even if he won an election. Thus, in Mexico opposition politicians were by definition "resource-poor" [materially poor] politicians.

As the ambition-theoretic framework also spells out, the likelihood of splits within the ruling party decreases when the probability of obtaining the nomination, N_I, increases. The 1933 constitutional reform established the rule of nonconsecutive reelection for all elective offices – governors, local and federal legislators, and municipal presidents. The constitution also forbade presidential reelection. The rule of nonconsecutive reelection contributed to elite unity by increasing the continuation value of remaining within the PRI. Suppose that a politician does not obtain the party's nomination during this electoral period. The politician will remain loyal to the PRI as long as the continuation value (the payoff from the next period forward) is larger than the expected value of splitting. If the politician remains loyal to the PRI, he gets 0 during this period, but he has a probability, p,

[5] The Spanish phrase is "Un político pobre es un pobre político."

that he will be rewarded with a nomination in the future. Thus, the rule of nonconsecutive reelection allowed the party to offer attractive positions to an ample number of politicians and to circulate elites, continuously, making the Mexican autocracy highly inclusionary (Smith, 1979; Camp, 1995).

On the other hand, the rule of nonconsecutive-reelection implied that the president needed to be replaced every six years. As argued in the Introduction, the relative frequency with which the PRI replaced the president made the party vulnerable to elite divisions prior to the presidential elections. Castañeda's (2000) insightful analysis reveals that presidential succession was accomplished by following certain rules. The PRI endowed the president with the enormous power to nominate his successor through a practice called the *dedazo* (the finger tap). The president also had the strongest say in the nomination of PRI candidates for other important elective offices, including the Chamber of Deputies, the Senate, and the governorships (Smith, 1979; Camp, 1995; Diaz-Cayeros, 2006). The president chose his successor from among the members of the cabinet. "Whoever had harbored dreams of becoming president, but failed to make it to a first-circle cabinet post by the middle of an administration, simply had no chance" (Castañeda, 2000: xix). To encourage these politicians to remain loyal until the end, the president deceived them by making each cabinet member believe that he was to be the chosen one. The president also severely punished candidates who made their desire for the nomination *public.* Fidel Velázquez expressed this trait of the presidential succession in the following phrase: "Whoever moves first will not be included in the picture."[6] The point was that if a politician from the PRI attempted to defy the president by making public his intention to become the party's nominee before the president selected the successor, the politician stood no chance of being chosen. The PRI thus sought to discourage the formation of factions around strong candidates that would divide the party.

Another strategy the PRI employed to deter party splits was to increase the entry costs to the electoral market, making it costly for former ruling party politicians to form opposition parties that would nominate them (this reduced the value of N_O). To enter the electoral market after exiting the PRI, former ruling party politicians needed either to form their own ad hoc partisan organizations and obtain permission from the government to register them, or to obtain a nomination from a preexisting opposition party. The PRI tinkered with the electoral rules in order to raise the cost of

[6] The Spanish phrase is "El que se mueva no sale en la foto."

entry to disaffected ruling party politicians who failed to obtain the ruling party's nomination. After the Almazán split, the 1946 electoral law required parties to register legally in order to compete in elections; to obtain such a registration, the parties had to form *national* organizations with sufficient members distributed across the states. The 1946 law required a party to have 30,000 members nationally, with at least 1,000 members in no less than two-thirds of the states (Medina, 1978). After the split by Henríquez Guzmán, the laws were modified, increasing the requirements for obtaining a legal registry. The new law of 1954 required a minimum of 75,000 members nationally, distributed so that the party had no less than 2,500 members in two-thirds of the Mexican states (Medina, 1978: 28; Molinar, 1991: 36).

As important as these autocratic electoral institutions were in deterring potential challenges, they are insufficient to account for the PRI's hegemony and its success in preventing more splits. During the era of party hegemony, there is scant evidence of the government denying requests for legal party registration. The Frente de los Partidos Populares (Popular Party Front), which nominated Henríquez Guzmán for the presidency, was denied legal status because it had organized an armed attack on a military barrack in northern Mexico. In the 1964 presidential elections, the party nonetheless presented a presidential candidate and other symbolic contenders who had been prisoners in jail since the 1958 railroad workers strike (Bruhn, 1997). Many of its leaders later participated in the 1968 student movement. The Mexican Communist Party was not allowed to compete until it was legalized in the 1978 electoral reform. This reform was also accompanied by an amnesty law that benefited political prisoners and members of rural and urban guerilla groups of the 1960s and 1970s. The 1978 electoral reform also introduced the mixed electoral system for electing the Chamber of Deputies. The new electoral law significantly lowered entry costs for opposition parties that were not able to win single-member races. However, no other party, including those parties that arose from splits within the ruling party, was denied a legal registration. The fact of the matter is that during the years of strong dominance by the PRI, few ambitious politicians sought to form opposition political parties.

It is hardly surprising that the overwhelming majority of Mexican politicians belonged to the PRI, since only through that party could politicians attain office. Some opposition parties opted to survive as "satellite" PRI organizations. These parties fielded candidates in local elections and in some senatorial, congressional, and gubernatorial races, but eventually came always to support the PRI's candidate in the presidential race. Such parties where the PARM (Authentic Party of the Mexican Revolution)[7] and the PPS (Popular Socialist Party), both clearly on the left on ideological grounds. Supporting the PRI presidential candidate became their survival strategy: it not only allowed them to keep their registry, but on two occasions allowed their leadership to reach governorships.[8] These parties, together with the successors of the Communist Party, nominated Cuauhtémoc Cárdenas as their presidential candidate in the 1988 presidential elections. Thus, for many years, the PAN was the only legally recognized opposition party that did not compete as a "satellite" of the PRI.

The ambition-theoretic framework also spells out that splits are more likely among ideologically oriented politicians. The ruling party was ideologically heterogeneous. Analysts traditionally distinguished two major wings in the PRI: the left wing, which in the fashion of President Lázaro Cárdenas (1934–40) stressed income redistribution, land reform, and the party's commitment to social justice; and the right wing, which like President Miguel Alemán (1946–52) stressed the government's commitment to industrialization and state-led capitalist development (Hansen, 1974: 110). Economic polices shifted between presidential terms, emphasizing either private or public property; a stronger or weaker role for the government in economic planning; and more or less social spending. Politicians who succeeded in obtaining the party's nomination for elective office had to compromise their own ideologies in favor of the ideology of whoever happened to become the president.

During the golden years of the PRI, ideology played a critical role in accounting for a politician's disposition to join the PAN, for many years the only truly independent opposition political party. Since the founding of the PAN in 1939, this party had embodied the right-wing alternative to the PRI,

[7] Two generals, Jacinto Trevino and Juan Barragán, formed the PARM. A small group of older revolutionary leaders who opposed Miguel Alemán's polices – including the brother of revolutionary leader Francisco I Madero – decided to gather in a group called Hombres de la Revolución, which later became the PARM.

[8] For instance, General Raúl Madero, a politician from PARM, obtained the PRI's support and became the governor of Coahuila. Francisco Martínez de la Vega, a former PPS politician, switched to the PRI and became governor of San Luis Potosí. Governor Julián Gazcón Mercado was elected on the PPS and PRI ticket in Nayarit. His brother ran on the PPS ticket some years later against a PRI candidate. According to most accounts, he won the elections but the president of the PRI, Muñoz Ledo, offered him instead a seat in the Senate, which he refused, thus ending his political career. The leader of the PPS, Jorge Cruickshank García, accepted the deal, becoming senator for Oaxaca.

emphasizing a smaller role for the state in the economy, a larger role for private property, and fidelity to Roman Catholicism. Originally, the PAN was born as a coalition of conservative politicians who opposed the left-wing economic polices implemented by President Lázaro Cárdenas – including the nationalization of the oil industry and the increasing expansion of the government's role in economic planning – and Catholics who opposed the Cárdenas education policy (i.e., providing a socialist government-led education to all Mexicans) and the anticlericalism of the PRI. The PAN thus emerged as a conservative Catholic party. The party's leaders refused to admit obvious links to Catholic thought and organizations until 1998, when the PAN became a full member of the international Christian Democratic Organization. As Loaeza (2003) explains, "the ambivalence of PAN toward its religious components can be explained by the anticlericalism of the revolutionary regime that explicitly forbade political parties with a religious affiliation" (196). However, this ambivalence should not lead one to underestimate the importance of the ideas and values that Catholicism provided: "this identity enabled PAN to survive the hegemony of the PRI and the indifference of the majority of voters.... The "doctrinal" identity of the PAN was the basis of the image of independence that differentiated it from other opposition parties.... for decades, a specific and original doctrine within the revolutionary regime was all PAN had in the absence of votes, voters and elected representatives" (Loaeza, 2003: 197). One implication of the ambition-theoretic framework is that those politicians who choose to invest their long-term loyalties in an opposition party will predominantly be ideologues motivated by a desire to advance some policy goals or to promote democracy. The more pragmatic and ambitious politicians will not join the opposition parties until elections become more seriously contested, as occured in Mexico in the 1990s.

Finally, splits are less likely as the costs of campaigning as a candidate from the opposition relative to the costs of running as the ruling party's candidate increase ($C_O > C_I$). Lawson (2002) shows how the mass media and compaign finance were skewed in favor of the PRI and how these were linked to autocratic stability.

Opposition parties were presented in an unflattering light, if they were presented at all, and PRI contenders received much greater share of coverage that they did of the popular vote. Although opposition parties had won some access to modest public financing and airtime in the 1970s, and although the resources available to them had been increased in the early 1990s, in practice opposition parties received very little coverage until the 1990s. Consequently, Mexican voters were exposed to a fairly homogenous media message designed to generate support for the ruling party and discredit the political opposition. (Lawson, 2002: 159)

These biases were particularly pronounced on television, where most voters learned about politics. The first time Mexican voters were extensively exposed through the television to the campaign pronouncements of opposition candidates was in 1994, during the first televised presidential debate.

The Mexican PRI also enjoyed indiscriminate access to the government's revenue to run its campaigns. The PRI's proclivity for vast and illegal campaign expenditures is not well documented. Some scandals, which began to be uncovered in the 1990s, suggest the massive amounts of illegal resources to which PRI politicians had access. In June of 1995, leaders of the PRD accused that the PRI governor of the state of Tabasco, Roberto Madrazo, had spent between $40 and $80 million on his campaign for the 1994 gubernatorial election – at least twenty times the legally allowed amount (Lawson, 2002: 144).

To summarize, to keep the hegemonic coalition united and to deter potential splitters, legal barriers to entry and electoral fraud are insufficient instruments. The PRI also needed, first, to offer sufficient material rewards and access to government office to the multiplicity of ambitious politicians within the party. Second, the PRI needed to mobilize voters to come to the polls in sufficient numbers to win by huge margins. Both of these strategies presuppose that maintaining party hegemony is costly and that co-optation is better than exclusion. Third, the PRI employed its control of the mass media and a liberal access to campaign funds to portray an image of invincibility and a minuscle opposition. These messages served to discourage voters from supporting the opposition and elites from defecting from the PRI.

Using this framework, we are now in a position to understand why the Cardenistas split when they did. Ideological considerations played a major role in the Cardenista split of 1987 (the difference between I_O and I_I was large). As is clear from Bruhn's (1997) account of the emergence of the PRD, Cárdenas and his allies strongly disagreed with Miguel de la Madrid's economic polices. They strongly opposed the government's reduction of spending under the IMF stabilization package, the government's decision to continue to pay the foreign debt, and the policies of trade liberalization and the privatization of state-owned enterprises. The Cardenistas instead still believed in the viability of Import Substitution Industrialization

(ISI) and in the need to maintain a strong, active, and nationalistic state.

However, Cuauhtémoc Cárdenas and the group of politicians who left the PRI with him in 1987 did not split from the ruling party only for ideological reasons. Belonging to a radically different political group than the market-oriented technocrats who controlled the presidency, these politicians saw slim prospects for furthering successful political careers within the party (for them, the likelihood of obtaining the party's nomination, N_I, was very slim). As Bruhn's (1997) study documents, the Cardenistas explicitly complained about a strong sense of exclusion during the De la Madrid presidency, arguing that the first circle of power was increasingly controlled by a small group of technocrats who left the politicians, particularly those following a different economic ideology, completely outside. Before splitting, the Cardenistas attempted to "democratize" the PRI. Above all, they opposed the *dedazo,* through which the incumbent president selected his own successor. Once they realized their efforts had failed, they opted to exit from the PRI. The split took place at the party assembly in March 1987, a couple of years after they had formed the Corriente Democrática to attempt to democratize the PRI's nomination procedures.

Cárdenas did not form a new political party prior to the 1988 presidential elections in order to overcome existing barriers to entry. Rather, some preexisting political parties cross-endorsed him (thus he could obtain an opposition party's nomination, N_O). The first party to support his candidacy was the PARM, formerly a "satellite" opposition. Most preexisting left-wing parties also supported Cárdenas. But the nomination procedures within the PRI had always been hierarchical, and there had always been ideological battles within the party. What changed in 1988? One of the most consequential variables in the choice-theoretic framework outlined above is the probability of winning as a member of the hegemonic party, P_I, or as an opposition candidate, P_O. No matter how hierarchical the nomination procedures are or how salient the ideological divisions, if a politician is sufficiently ambitious, his dominant strategy seems to be not to split when there is no real chance of attaining office through other means. What was different in 1988, as we will see in subsequent chapters of this book, was the electoral discontent against the PRI. The anticipation of better electoral prospects outside the PRI is what ultimately provided Cárdenas and his allies the incentive to exit the party.

The 1988 presidential elections thus mark a turning point in Mexican politics. There is no doubt that massive electoral fraud was committed against Cárdenas, who claimed the victory. As will become apparent in Chapter 8, the PRI got away with electoral fraud because the opposition failed to present a unified front to challenge the official election results. The PAN seems to have cut an early deal with the incoming president, Carlos Salinas. The rest of the opposition parties that supported Cárdenas refused to confront the results. As Bruhn (1997) documents, these parties were willing to defend their electoral victories in the Chamber of Deputies, but they were not willing to defend Cárdenas's vote in the presidential race.

This book demonstrates that the PRI's electoral support collapsed after the 1994 peso crisis, when voters began to defect to the opposition in one local election after another. The opposition won fourteen gubernatorial races between 1994 and 2000. The opposition also won majority control of the Chamber of Deputies in 1997. The growth of the PRD was significant during this period. Its biggest prize was Mexico City, which it won in 1997 after elections for mayor of the Federal District were introduced for the first time. But the PRD's growth at the local level during this period must primarily be attributed to PRI splits. Despite having no significant presence in the state of Zacatecas, the PRD won the gubernatorial election of 1998 by endorsing Ricardo Monreal, who split from the PRI when the party denied him the nomination. A similar process took place in Baja California Sur: when Leonel Cota lost the PRI's primary election, he joined the PRD and won the 1999 gubernatorial race. The PRD also won the gubernatorial elections in Tlaxcala and Nayarit in 1999. In those cases, a former PRIísta was backed not only by the PRD but also by a coalition that included most of the state-level opposition parties. The PRI became so vulnerable to party splits in the late 1990s because its popular support had withered.

Prior to the 2000 presidential election, the PRI introduced for the first time in its history a primary election for selecting the party's presidential nominee. Rather than handpicking his successor, President Zedillo allowed the voters to choose the PRI's candidate in an open national primary. Four candidates competed: the interior minister, Francisco Labastida, who was Zedillo's choice; Roberto Madrazo, the governor of Tabasco; Manuel Barlett, the governor of Puebla; and Humberto Roque Villanueva, a former national head of the PRI. Labastida won the primary election with 55 percent of the vote; Roberto Madrazo was second, with 30 percent. In my choice-theoretic ambition theory, a more open nomination process translates into fewer incentives to split. My account suggests that one key reason why the PRI might have chosen to introduce a primary election rather than having the president handpick the candidate was to avoid a bitter struggle over the PRI nomination that would irreversibly divide the party. None of the losing candidates in the primary election, including Roberto Madrazo, decided to split. Consequently, the PRI's ultimate demise in the 2000 elections did not result from divisions within the ruling elite. It came instead as a result of the choices of millions of voters who finally were able "throw the rascals out." Why did it take so long for voters to dislodge the PRI? To answer this question, I develop a theory to explain voting behavior under an autocratic regime.

Modeling Electoral Support in Autocracies

In their seminal analysis of voting choices in Mexico, Domínguez and McCann (1995) propose a "two-stage model" where voters first ask whether to support or oppose the ruling party. The decision at this first stage is mostly explained on the grounds of voters' assessments of what will happen with the national economy if the ruling party loses. It is only at the second stage that issues play a role in accounting for a choice among the opposition parties. My theoretical model builds on this work. It provides insights regarding how voters derive these expectations about the future with or without the ruling party. My model presents three fundamental issues to resolve: first, how voters calculate the expected economic performance under the alternative parties; second, how voters calculate their chances of receiving transfers from each of the parties; and third, what shapes voters' calculations about expected levels of post-electoral violence. I define the voters' utility in the following terms:

$$U_i = \beta_i E[p_j] + \alpha_i E[t_j] - \gamma_i ID_{ij}^k - \lambda_i E[v_j] \tag{1.3}$$

where, dropping the subscript i, $E[p_j]$ is the expected economic performance of party j if elected. $E[t_j]$ represents the transfers a voter expects to receive by voting for party j. ID refers to the issue distance between voter i and party j in the *k* issues – the closer a voter is to party j's positions, the higher the chance of supporting that party. $E[v_j]$ refers to the expected level of post-electoral violence that stems from supporting party j. Constants β, α, and γ are the weights assigned to "sociotropic evaluations," "pocketbook evaluations," and "policy voting." λ is the voter's aversion to violence. Below, I explore how votes derive their expectations about the future.

A Bayesian Logic of Learning and the Economic History of the Regime[9]

When selecting among parties, voters need to assess how those parties will shape future economic performance. Expected party performance, $E[P_j]$, is composed of a set of macroeconomic indicators – growth, inflation, wages, currency stability, interest rates – that party j will deliver if elected. Due to uncertainty about the future and the complexity of the economy, $E[P_j]$ can be represented as a random variable with a normal distribution.

Following Achen (1989, 1992), who builds on Fiorina (1981), I assume that voters calculate expected performance according to Bayesian principles: they hold some prior information, P^J_{iO}, about how party j might perform if elected, which is then updated by considering campaign promises. The available information about the parties differs considerably. The incumbent has effectively been in office permanently, while the challenger has never governed, at least at the national level. The voters priors about the incumbent's performance, P^I_{iO}, can be constructed from a distribution of the observed economic performance experienced by the individual during his political lifetime while the party has been in power. $\overline{P}_{i_0}$ is specifically the mean value of the economic indicators the voter has observed since he became aware of politics at time w, so that:

$$\overline{P^I_{io}} = \frac{\sum_{k=w}^{t-1} P_k}{t - w - 1} \qquad (1.4)$$

The distribution of growth rates is assumed to be normal, $(\overline{P}^I_{i_0}, \sigma^2_{i0})$. Two new pieces of information are then observed: the current state of the economy, Pt, and the incumbent party's campaign announcements or the average growth rate it promises to deliver during the following term, A^I_{t+1}, both of which are random variables resulting from normal distributions, $N(\mu, \sigma^2)$.

Campaign announcements are not taken at face value. Voters can assess the credibility of the ruling party's promises by looking at its record. In particular, voters are presumed to remember what the incumbent party promised to deliver in the previous campaign, A^I_t; and to observe how much the average growth rate it produced, Pt, deviated from that promise.

9 This model is inspired in part by Achen's (1992) model of party identification, which builds on Fiorina (1981) and Downs (1957).

If the incumbent is seen to have lied, voters discount the credibility of $A^{I}{}_{t+1}$ by a factor σ (where $0 < \sigma > 1$), so that

$$\delta = \begin{bmatrix} 1 & \text{if } A_t^I \leq P_t \\ \dfrac{1}{1 + A_t^I - P_t} & \text{otherwise} \end{bmatrix} \qquad (1.5)$$

Hence, voters observe what the incumbent promises to deliver, $A^{I}{}_{t+1}$, qualifying such promises by δ in the manner specified by (1.5). This creates a modified piece of new information, $P^{I}p_{t+1}$, [where $P^{I}p_{t+1} = f(\delta, A^{I}{}_{t+1})$] that voters will use to update their priors.

The expected economic performance of the incumbent during the next term in office, $\overline{P_i}$, is a weighted average of the mean economic performance voter i has observed during his lifetime and the two new pieces of information, namely, the current state of the economy and the incumbent's campaign promises.[10]

$$\overline{P_i}^{I} = \frac{1}{w_0 + w_1 + w_2}\left(w_0 \overline{P_{iO}^{I}} + w_1 P_t + w_2 P_{pt+1}^{I}\right),$$

$$\frac{1}{\overline{\sigma^2}} = w_0 + w_1 + w_2 \qquad (1.6)$$

with

$$w_0 = 1/\sigma_o^2, w_1 = w_2 = 1/\sigma^2.$$

It can be seen that the weights of the prior and current information are proportional to the reciprocal of the standard deviations of the data, represented by w_0, w_1, and w_2. This is an appealing result because it can tell us how much information voters can really extract from each observation: the noisier the information, the less voters can learn. The economic voting model usually assumes that voters focus only on the most recent piece of retrospective information, applying a myopic decision rule that is well captured in the phrase "What have you done for me lately?" (V. O. Key, 1966). Here, voters use all the available retrospective information, not just the current state of the economy, and they also learn from campaign promises.

[10] The posterior density function results from the sequential use of a well-known result of Bayesian analysis when normal distributions are combined (for proof, see Appendix A1.1 in Box and Tiao, 1992: 74).

Voters who find the incumbent party unreliable or its promises too noisy are expected to be more myopic and less sympathetic during an economic recession. History also matters: if the voter has observed the incumbent party performing in a consistently satisfactory manner, he is expected to be more forgiving if there is an economic downturn during the election year. But voters are expected to be rationally forgiving of an economic recession only when the incumbent is reliable and possesses a satisfactory historic record, on the one hand, and when the opposition is not perceived as a superior choice, on the other.

In deriving the opposition's expected performance, two serious complications emerge. First, voters' prior beliefs about the opposition party are formed in a state of almost complete ignorance. The argument is not that prior information about the opposition is completely absent, since voters might still hold *some* beliefs about the opposition party's expected performance. These prior beliefs are, however, generally noninformative. The voter's priors can thus be represented as a diffuse distribution of economic performance of the form $1/\sigma$. The second complication is that voters must update their noninformative priors with current campaign promises, which could very well be interpreted as pure rhetoric, since the credibility of those promises cannot easily be assessed.

The opposition party's expected economic performance during the next term in office results from the combination of a diffuse prior, $1/\sigma$, with a normal distribution, P^0_{Pt+1}, where both μ and σ^2 are unknown:

$$\overline{P_i^{\,0}} = \frac{1}{\sigma} P^0_{Pt+1} \tag{1.7}$$

This equation shows how hard it is for a party that has effectively been out of office permanently to win over voters purely on the grounds of promised economic performance. The total absence of information about opposition party performance means that voters are more likely to discount the opposition's campaign promises as not credible due to uncertainty.

Thus, the hegemonic party has an important advantage over the opposition party due to asymmetries of retrospective information. The role of voter uncertainty in discouraging support for the opposition has been amply recognized by experts (Cinta, 1999; Morgenstern and Zechmeister, 2001). In a sense, σ can be interpreted as the amount of voter uncertainty with respect to opposition parties. This uncertainty is not fixed. An opposition party that has held office at the local level might be regarded with less uncertainty than one that has not had previous local experience. Also, uncertainty is a function of media coverage, with less coverage contributing to increased voter uncertainty. Finally, a party that continuously changes its policy stances might be regarded with more uncertainty than one that is more consistent over time.

To illustrate some of the implications of this model, suppose that countries X and Y have each been governed by hegemonic parties for more than thirty years. To simulate the model, I assume that prior beliefs are a function of the mean growth rates observed by the voter since he first became politically aware. Of course, voters care about a wider set of economic indicators. All voters, that is, desire a healthy macroeconomic system as reflected by many indicators – growth rates, inflation, wages, the value of the currency, employment, and the like. However, since voters might attach different weights to each of these indicators, to simplify the problem the simulations concentrate only on growth rates.

In both countries, the average growth rate has been 6 percent; but in country X growth rates have been very consistent over time, while in country Y they have been erratic, going from boom to bust to boom again for several years. Now suppose that there is an economic downturn during the election year, with the growth rate dropping to 1 percent in both countries. The model tells us that the average citizen of country X will still expect the hegemonic party to deliver, if reelected, average growth rates largely consistent with its past performance record, while the average citizen in country Y will expect mediocre economic performance. Figures 1.1 and 1.2 illustrate these issues by showing the posterior density functions for the hypothesized average citizen in both countries. The curves are the average citizen's prior beliefs (the average of growth rates observed during the individual's life since becoming politically aware), the likelihood density function (the current information, which is composed of the current growth rate), and the posterior density function (the average growth rate that the individual expects the ruling party to deliver during the next term in office). The average citizen's prior density function in country X, with stable growth rates, is given by the normal distribution, $N(6\%, 0.5^2)$; that of country Y, with unstable growth patterns, is given by $N(6\%, 2.5^2)$; for citizens in both countries, the new observation, which is graphed as the likelihood function, is the growth rate in the election year, given by $N(1\%, 1.5^2)$.

We see that after an identical observation – the current economic downturn – the average citizen's beliefs about the expected performance of the parties differ considerably. Although in both countries citizens a priori believe that the hegemonic party will deliver a reasonably high annual

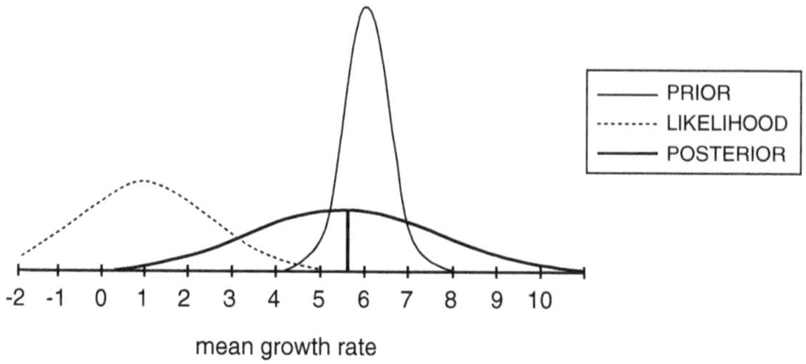

Figure 1.1. Effects of economic recession on voter's expectations: Country X with stable long-term growth.

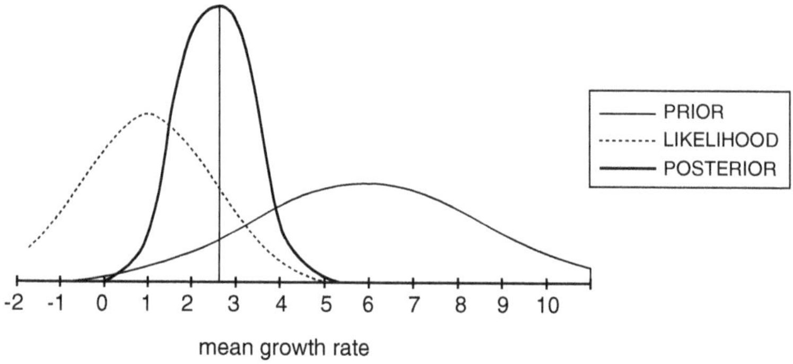

Figure 1.2. Effects of economic recession on voters' expectations: Country Y with unstable long-term growth.

average growth rate of six percent, the current downturn dramatically reduces posterior beliefs in country Y, but not in country X.

Naturally, the economic crisis may hurt party Y's reelection chances much more. In a sense, citizens in country X did not pay much attention to the recent economic downturn in forming their expectations: their posterior opinion of the expected party performance dropped by less than one percent. Citizens in country Y, on the contrary, were much more myopic. This is because the party's performance record is too noisy, forcing voters to focus only on the most current information in making their inferences.

Party autocracies appear to be more resilient to economic recession. The model underscores that voters might be more tolerant of economic

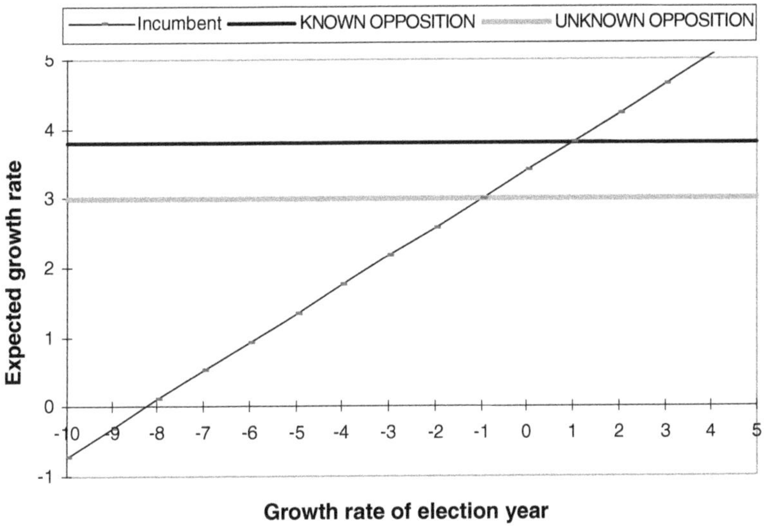

Figure 1.3. Effects of voter uncertainty on voters' expectations.

crises in situations where opponents possess no record in government. This is because of voter uncertainty. To illustrate the role of voter uncertainty with respect to the opposition, Figure 1.3 simulates the model with a set of election-year growth rates for an incumbent party having a good performance record. The prior density function is given by the normal distribution, $N(6, 1.87^2)$, which roughly approximates that of the Mexican PRI from 1940 to 1965, the years of the so-called economic miracle of steady high growth rates. The figure also considers two types of challengers, an "unknown opposition" and a "known opposition," competing in different party systems, a hegemonic-party system and a competitive party system, respectively. Thus, the unknown opposition has never been in office, while the known opposition has. The expected performance of the unknown opposition party is derived from equation (1.7), which uses a diffuse prior and updates it with current campaign announcements. I assume that the challenger mimics the incumbent's campaign promises.[11]

Since the known opposition has previously been in office, its expected performance can be calculated by applying almost the same equation as that used for the incumbent. That is, for this opposition party, the prior information is given by the average growth rate produced when in office, which

[11] Unless otherwise stated, for the purpose of calibrating the model, σ^2 for the challenger is assumed to be equivalent to $1/W_2$.

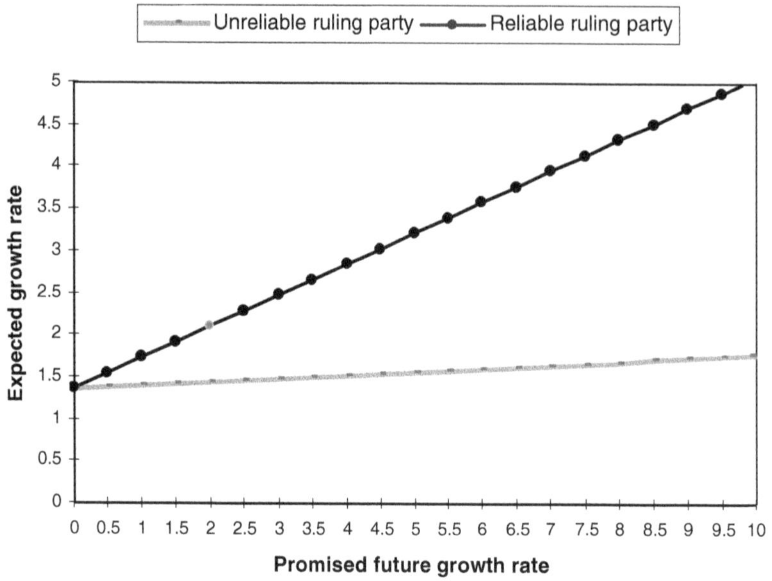

Figure 1.4. Effects of campaign promises on voters' expectations.

voters update with one new piece of information, the current campaign promises. In this simulation, the economic record of the known opposition party is assumed to be slightly less good than that of the incumbent (on average 5 percent, with the same variance). Campaign announcements (the new information) are 6 percent, and voters believe some of the incumbent's promises ($\delta = 0.66$). The lines in the figure correspond to the voter's mean posterior density function (or the mean growth rate he expects each of the parties to deliver during the next term in office). The horizontal axis is the growth rate of the election year – the higher it is, the higher the growth rate the voter expects the incumbent to deliver if reelected. The vertical axis refers to the expected mean growth rate.

The higher the growth rate during the election year, the higher the incumbent's chances of winning, and, conversely the more severe the economic recession, the more likely it is that the incumbent will lose. Figure 1.3 shows that this is true for *both* the competitive and the hegemonic-party systems. However, clearly the threshold needed for the incumbent party to lose the election is smaller when it faces a challenger that holds previous experience in government. The difference between the points at which the unknown and the known opposition parties' expected performance intersect with that of the incumbent party might be called the accountability failure of hegemonic-party systems due to the asymmetric retrospective information and voter uncertainty.

In the model, voters can punish the ruling party for being unreliable and betraying its campaign promises. Because there is no retrospective information on the opposition, voters will not be able to actually "grade" its reliability – how much its words resemble its actions. This is the only *ex ante* asymmetry that can work against the ruling party. To illustrate this point, Figure 1.4 simulates the model assuming two types of ruling parties, one "unreliable" and the other "reliable." The unreliable ruling party has deviated from its promises – the actual growth rate at time t was much smaller than the announced growth rate for that period, such that $\delta = 0.1$. The reliable ruling party has almost always delivered what it promised, such that $\delta = 0.9$. Both ruling parties possess the same record – a prior density function of $(6, 1.87^2)$ – and suffer an economic recession of -1 percent during the election year. It can be seen that no matter how much the unreliable ruling party assures voters that it will produce future economic prosperity, voters no longer believe its promises to turn things around. By contrast, because voters trust the reliable ruling party, they will give it a chance to fix things up.

The model also provides important clues as to who is more likely to start punishing the regime because of an economic crisis. Citizens differ in their prior economic information on the ruling party's performance because they possess different-"length" past political experiences, meaning that they have observed different averages and variances of growth rates depending on their age. In particular, older voters may have observed different periods of party performance – realignment eras, economic booms, recessions, or even wars – not directly experienced by the young. Consequently, if the party's historical record is good, older voters will be less likely to defect from the party in times of economic crisis.

To illustrate this point, consider the Mexican historical economic record. Before the debt crisis, all voters had experienced average annual growth rates of 6 percent or more. The debt crisis generated extremely low prior beliefs among the younger generation, those who became aware of politics after the recession had started. These voters did not experience the so-called economic miracle of stable and high economic growth. When they started to be aware of politics (roughly in the late 1970s and early 1980s), the economy was on the verge of a bust that lasted for almost eight years. During the Salinas presidency, macroeconomic stability was achieved, but the economy barely grew. The 1994 peso crisis represented another serious setback. Thus, voters born roughly after 1960 experienced only deteriorating economic conditions and macroeconomic instability under the rule of the PRI. My model provides a rationale for why Mexico's younger generation was significantly more predisposed to defect from the PRI.

To summarize, with respect to how economic performance shapes support for the hegemonic party, my approach predicts that economic growth should help the regime to survive. However, despite a current economic downturn, voters can rationally believe that the ruling party will be more capable than the opposition of handling the future national economy when (1) the economic history of the regime has been consistently good; (2) the autocracy has kept its promises, so that voters can trust that it will be able to turn things around despite recession; and (3) the opposition is too uncertain. When these conditions hold, voters will be more *forgiving* of economic recession, allowing the autocrat a chance to turn things around in the future. This is how Mexican voters behaved, as I further demonstrate in this book, prior to the 1994 peso crisis.

However, my model does not predict that voters will always be tolerant of economic recession. Since voters learn from experience, they can become *vindictive* when the economic history of the regime has fallen below a "threshold of acceptability" such that they no longer trust the ruling party's competence *or* reliability. The 1994 peso crisis, as I demonstrate in Chapters 5 and 7, caused voters to react in this manner, eventually leading to the PRI's demise.

The Punishment Regime: Side Payments and Deterrence[12]

Back in 1994, a sixty-five-year-old peasant from the state of Morelos told me:

> I have always voted for the PRI because only this party can win. Why would I support the opposition if it can't win? They told me that this time they would also give us checks [he was referring to cash transfers within the then recently instituted Farmers Direct Support Program (PROCAMPO) designed to support small-scale farmers].[13] I must thus vote for the PRI to get my check.

With this impeccable logic, the sixty-five-year-old peasant expressed the reasons why most of Mexico's poor people supported the ruling party.

[12] The deterrence model is from Diaz-Cayeros, Magaloni, and Weingast (2004). This section draws from Magaloni, Diaz-Cayeros, and Estévez, (forthcoming).

[13] PROCAMPO replaced price supports for basic grains with direct cash payments.

Voters are not concerned only about societal outcomes. Like this sixty-five-year-old Mexican peasant, voters also care about government transfers or targeted side payments such as cash transfers, food subsidies, credit, land titles, and the like. The voting literature refers to these as *pocketbook* evaluations, and they are particularly relevant, I argue, for accounting for the voting behavior of the poor. Most scholars agree that government transfers (which are broadly included in the notion of patronage) are a central device that autocracies can use to ensure their survival.[14] Yet there is no systematic attempt to incorporate patronage into a theory of voting behavior (Chandra, 2004, is one of the few exceptions). My approach provides a simple mechanism, based on deterring defection, which explains why patronage is such a powerful device for constructing political order. By incorporating patronage into a model of voting behavior, my approach also permits me to evaluate how support for the hegemonic party should change in response to deteriorating economic conditions, modernization and urbanization, and changes in government polices.

I begin by placing voters in a strategic interaction game with the autocratic hegemonic party, which unilaterally controls fiscal transfers and government programs. Voters must decide between supporting the ruling party or voting for the opposition. The ruling party observes voters' behavior and targets side payments, rewarding supportive voters with patronage funds and punishing defecting voters by withdrawing these funds. The game results in four possible outcomes, which I label A–D. The representation of the sequential game is presented in Figure 1.5.

I assume that the incumbent party prefers to reward its supporters and to punish its opponents (it prefers outcome A over B, and D over C). This assumption about the incumbent's behavior, which is supported by empirical evidence in Chapter 4, rests on the supposition that hegemonic-party regimes seek to maximize the number of votes despite the economic costs of sustaining an oversized coalition so as to deter elite splits and opposition entry. Voters can thus infer that if they support the opposition, they will be punished: they will not receive land from the government, or their subsidies will be cut, or they will be excluded from the government's housing program, or their locality will be punished by

[14] See especially Huntington (1968). The vast literature on clientelism also stresses the role of patronage in the construction of political order. The body of literature on clientelism is considerable. See Lemarchand and Legg (1972), Scott (1972), Lemarchand (1972), as well as the edited volumes by S. W. Schmidt et al. (1977) and Gellner and Waterbury (1977).

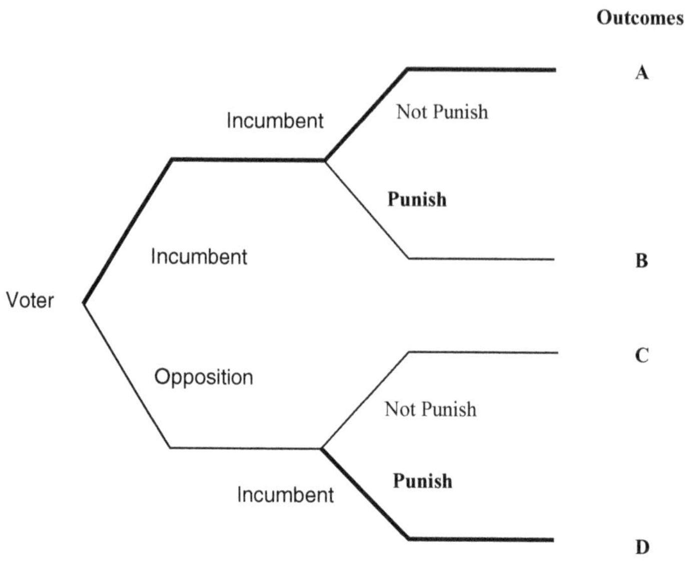

Figure 1.5. Deterrence game and the punishment regime.

cuts in central government funding, or they will not receive a direct cash transfer.

The literature refers to this form of political exchange as "clientelism" (Scott, 1972; Lemarchand, 1972; Kitschelt, 2000). Clientelism is characterized by dyadic personal relationships that are asymmetric but reciprocal: the patron delivers desired material benefits to its clients in exchange for services and loyalty to the patron. In his classic study, Scott (1972) argued that patron-client links are based on inequality, which arises from the fact that "the patron is in a position to supply *unilaterally* goods and services which the potential client and his family *need for their survival* and well being" (125, emphasis added). As a monopolist for critical resources, such as protection, access to arable land, fertilizers, or water and irrigation, the patron is in a position to exploit his market power and demand compliance from those who want a share of those goods. However, if the client did not need these goods so badly, or if she had savings and alternative sources of income to finance her needs, or if she could incur the costs of exiting to another jurisdiction to secure the needed services, the client would not succumb to the patron's domination.

The effectiveness of this "punishment regime" in deterring voter defection largely depends upon the ruling party's ability, first, to *screen* between supporters and opponents and second, to *target* benefits only to those who will vote for the party. The easier it is to target voters with excludable benefits, and the more closely a party can monitor the voters' choices, the more the deterrence logic applies. This is why clientelistic linkages normally entail the provision of excludable material benefits (Kitschelt, 2000).

Stokes (2005) lucidly argues that clientelistic linkages presuppose a commitment problem: once a party gives a transfer to a voter, how can it make sure that she will abide by the implicit bargain and deliver her vote? Magaloni, Diaz-Cayeros, and Estévez (forthcoming) argue that public goods are a riskier political investment because they generate a stronger commitment problem.[15] Once delivered to voters, public goods can be consumed by opposition voters, and they cannot be withdrawn. Private outlays such as jobs and other discretionary transfers are better able to solve the commitment problem: if the voter defects after receiving the transfer, the ruling party can always withdraw the private transfer and cut her off from the party's spoils system.

A political party requires a dense organizational network to mitigate the commitment problem, that is, the possibiliy that the voter may receive the transfer but fail to deliver support. The PAN explicitly prompted voters to behave in this fashion with its creative campaign slogan "*agarra lo que te dan y vota por el PAN*" [take what they give you and vote for the PAN]. To screen loyal voters, the Mexican PRI employed a multiplicity of organizations and agents, ranging from party unions within the CTM and the CNC, to local party bosses, caciques, schoolteachers, and *presidentes ejidales* (the heads of the *ejidos*, a form of communal landholding). During its golden years, the ruling party also resorted to violating the secrecy of the ballot. The PRI could get away with this illegal practice because the opposition did not possess a sufficiently dense organizational network to monitor elections, particularly in rural areas, where the ruling party used to run uncontested (Molinar, 1991). As the opposition grew stronger, the PRI's leeway to violate the secrecy of the ballot gradually disappeared.

Vote buying works better when people's votes can be observed. This is the reason why clientelistic networks are far more effective in small rural communities than in large impersonal cities. In rural settings, local party brokers and caciques possess more *local knowledge* about voters – with whom voters hang out, what their political opinions are, at which political rallies they show up. The story in the large cities is different because in urban

15 On the commitment problem, see also Robinson and Verdier (2002).

areas it is harder for the ruling party to acquire knowledge about voters' types, monitor their behavior, and target private transfers to its loyal supporters.

By 1988, Mexico was predominantly urban, and vote buying through the party's clientelistic machine became exceedingly expensive owing to the transaction costs required for effective targeting and to the number of individual transfers needed to ensure election victories. During the Salinas presidency, the PRI instituted a poverty relief program, the National Solidarity Program (PRONASOL), in an attempt to recover the support of the heterogeneous electorate. PRONASOL distributed private excludable benefits to individuals through the party's clientelistic networks, but the program also provided public works directly to the communities. These *geographically targeted* public goods reduced transaction costs and were more cost-effective per beneficiary, although they involved higher political risks (Magaloni, Diaz-Cayeros, and Estévez, forthcoming). The literature refers to this form of political exchange (the exchange of public works for political support) as pork barrel politics or patronage politics.

Vote-buying and clientelism also take place in well-established democracies. A key difference between clientelistic practices in "competitive" and "noncompetitive" electoral systems, however, is that opposition voters are invariably punished when only one party governs for decades. The introduction to this book makes explicit that noncompetitive systems also exist in democracies. Golden (2003) and Scheiner (2006) study the role of clientelistic practices in sustaining the dominance of the Christian Democratic Party in Italy and the LDP in Japan, respectively. In the introduction, I discussed the differences between these noncompetitive democracies and hegemonic-party autocracies.

The Calculus of Voting and the Trade-off between Ideology and Transfers

Given that the voter's utility function is defined as $U_i = \beta_i E[p_j] + \alpha_i E[t_j] - \gamma_i I D^k_{ij} - \lambda_i E[v_j]$, the utility of voting for the ruling party autocrat increases as the economy grows, as the size of the financial punishment increases, as the ideological distance from the ruling party is smaller, and as the threat of violence increases. Leaving aside the issue of violence for subsequent discussion, a voter will be indifferent between voting for one of the opposition parties, say party O, and the ruling party, I, when

$$\beta_i \mathrm{E}[\mathrm{p_O} - \mathrm{p_I}] - \gamma_i(\mathrm{ID_{iO}} - \mathrm{ID_{iI}}) = \alpha_i \mathrm{T}^*_{\mathrm{iI}} \quad (1.8)$$

where the left-hand side represents the utility differential for voter i between one of the opposition parties and the ruling party that is attributable to economic performance and ideology, while the right-hand side is the voter's "price" – the minimum transfer necessary to make her vote for the ruling party. In order for a voter to choose to defect to the opposition, the utility differential attributable to economic performance and ideological proximity must *outweigh the expected punishment of foregone financial resources.* The voter may support the ruling party "sincerely," either because he expects the ruling party to be better than the opposition at handling future economic performance, or because he prefers the ruling party to the opposition on ideological grounds – although, as demonstrated by Domínguez and McCann (1995), ideology does not seem to play a powerful role in accounting for support for a hegemonic party. The voter might also support the ruling party "strategically," out of fear of economic punishment or fear of violence. Equation 1.8 allows me to derive the following propositions about the calculus of voting under autocracy.

1. The prize necessary to buy off political support, T_i^*, increases as the ideological distance between the voter and the ruling party increases. Voters may care about a series of economic policy issues such as taxation, social policy, tariffs, and the exchange rate. I call this the *socioeconomic* dimension of party competition. If the parties are primarily ethnic-based, I assume that ethnicity maps onto some meaningful economic policy divisions. For example, as Bates (1989) argues, ethnic groups tend to be geographically concentrated, and their interests are largely shaped by what they produce. Export crop producers possess dramatically different preferences with respect to exchange-rate polices than those producing food for the internal market. In authoritarian settings, voters may also care about a series of political issues ranging from democratization to protection of human rights, freedom of expression, political participation, and electoral reform. I call this the *regime dimension* of party competition. Voters' preferences on the socioeconomic and regime dimensions are independent of each other – that is, voters may intrinsically value democracy and civil liberties, or they may value democracy because of its ability to reduce corruption and increase government accountability. The ruling party will need to devote more transfers to buy off voters who are most committed to democracy and political reform. It will also need to

devote more resources to buy off those who are most opposed to the government's economic policies.

2. The prize necessary to buy off political support increases as the voter is less concerned about financial punishment. The weight attached to transfers, α, can vary inversely with voters' income. This is a standard assumption in the literature on distributive politics. As Dixit and Londregan (1996) note, higher marginal utility among the poor makes them "more willing to compromise their political preferences for additional private consumption" (1144). This means that middle- and high-income voters will be more likely to make "ideological investments" in democratization despite the risk of financial punishment. By contrast, poorer voters who mostly care about transfers are most likely to support the autocratic ruling party. The implication of this result is that hegemonic-party autocracies will have the poor and those most dependent upon the party's spoils system for their survival as its most loyal followers – a point that has been extensively established by experts on Mexico (Ames, 1970; Cornelius, 1975; Klesner, 1988; Molinar, 1991) and has also been highlighted in the context of Africa (Cowen and Laakso, 2002). The middle class and the rich will be more predisposed to support the opposition. Wealth allows voters to make "ideological investments," so to speak, choosing to support the opposition despite the risk of economic punishment.
3. T_i^* increases as the economic situation deteriorates. Deteriorating economic conditions compel hegemonic-party autocracies to increasingly rely on vote buying, pork, and patronage to survive in office. Conversely, as the economy improves, T_i^*decreases because voters become predisposed to "sincerely" support the ruling party. This conclusion applies also to rich and middle-class voters, who will rationally support autocracies that can make them prosper. Note, however, that economic growth has conflicting effects on authoritarian survival. Because voters support governments that can make the economy prosper, in the short term economic growth can strengthen the autocratic regime. But since economic growth also increases the income of voters, in the long term economic growth can eventually work against the autocrat, because wealth liberates voters from their dependence on the state and permits them to make ideological investments in democratization.
4. The more fiscal resources, subsidies, and economic regulations are under the government's control, the more leeway the autocrat will

have to buy off electoral support and deter voter exit. This is consistent with the finding in the comparative literature that oil wealth can inhibit democratization (Karl, 1997; Ross, 2001). By the same token, market-oriented reforms and trade liberalization are expected to weaken the autocracy, as these polices imply that the ruling party loses its monopoly over economic sanctions and selective payoffs in the form of government regulations, subsidies, tariffs, and the like. Indeed, as Dresser (1994) explains for the case of Mexico, "the system of resource allocation that evolved in Mexico during the era of Import Substitution Industrialization (ISI) created a broad-based 'populist distributive coalition' of organized interests.... The coalition flourished on state business such as public credit, production subsidies, tariff protection, tax incentives and purchasing contacts" (145). There is consensus in the literature on Mexico that the efficacy of this "social pact" began to erode in the 1980s and 1990s, with the economic recession and the market-oriented reforms that followed. These polices implied a fundamental restructuring of the traditional alliance of interests.

5. Vote buying should primarily be directed toward the poor and ideologically akin voters. In the Mexican context of a divided opposition, this means that it should be less expensive for the PRI to sway voters who are likely to defect to the left-wing opposition party, the PRD, than those who might defect to the more ideologically distant PAN. At the mass level, there is no doubt that PRD supporters and PRI supporters look more alike in terms of social composition, both parties drawing support from poorer and left-leaning voters, as I demonstrate in Chapters 6 and 7. At the elite level, however, PAN and PRI politicians have appeared more alike since the government began to follow neoliberal policies in the mid-1980s.[16]
6. Because the effectiveness of this "punishment regime" in deterring voter defection largely depends upon the ruling party's ability to distinguish between supporters and opponents, it follows that hegemonic-party autocracies will receive more support in smaller rural localities, where it is easier to acquire *local knowledge* about

[16] However, PRI politicians have been ideologically heterogeneous. The national leadership and their closer allies, including most of the successful candidates, have been more right-wing since at least 1982. The rest have been very leftist, which explains why most of the former ruling party politicians who split have defected to the PRD, not to the PAN.

voters and where the party's clientelistic networks are likely to be more effective. It is in these settings that party autocrats also tend to get away with violating the secrecy of the ballot more easily. As urbanization and voter heterogeneity increase, support for the autocrat should diminish.

The Autocrats' Optimal Strategy: Economic Growth and Poverty Traps

The theoretical finding that autocratic ruling parties are helped by economic growth but hurt by economic development raises the following fundamental question: what is the autocrat's optimal strategy? If economic growth helps the autocrat but will turn against it in the long run, what types of economic policies should the autocrat put in place? The Mexican PRI resolved this paradox by simultaneously promoting state-led industrialization and creating a poverty trap to guarantee for itself an electoral base. During its golden years, the PRI enacted a series of economic policies to promote rapid industrialization and urbanization. These policies, as I will demonstrate in subsequent chapters, threatened the party's survival as wealthier voters and those living in more affluent cities began to defect from the PRI beginning in the early 1950s. To secure for itself a loyal base of support, the PRI simultaneously put in place a series of policies and institutions that prevented peasants from rising out of poverty and made them systematically dependent on state patronage for their survival.[17] Policies that were designed with this purpose in mind included the "permanent land reform" (in effect until 1992) and the establishment of the *ejido*, through which the state distributed land without granting property rights to peasants. Through the years, Mexican peasants received land, but it was of increasingly poor quality and of unprofitable size. Further, peasants could not legally sell, rent, or give land as collateral for credit. They thus were unable to obtain access to various markets, including the credit market, and became fully dependent on the state's support, credit, and subsidies for their survival. The PRI thereby achieved high rates of economic growth and rapid industrialization and at the same time prevented peasants from becoming independent farmers. In doing so, the party guaranteed for itself an electoral base of loyal voters, the so-called Green Vote. A broad implication of these arguments is that autocratic regimes will possess

[17] These ideas come from joint work with Alberto Diaz and Barry Weingast on a project studying land reform in Mexico.

strong incentives to follow economic policies that simultaneously promote economic growth, allow them to distribute pork and patronage, and keep a solid base of support dependent and trapped by the party's clientelistic practices.

Mass Coordination Dilemmas

Democratization requires massive coordination on the part of voters. There are two types of mass coordination dilemmas voters need to overcome in order to dislodge a hegemonic-party autocracy. The first is confronted by ruling party voters who support the ruling party out of fear of economic punishment. The elderly peasant from the state of Morelos cited earlier fits this characterization. Without the assurance that many other voters will support the opposition, these ruling party voters are likely to play it safe and support the incumbent. Democratization requires, first, that ruling party supporters defect en masse. I call this type of voting behavior "strategic defection," which is motivated by the perception that the hegemonic party can lose. Chapter 7 explores strategic defection by ruling party voters in the 2000 presidential elections.

The second mass coordination game entails deciding which opposition party to support. When opposition party elites do not form electoral fronts, mass opposition coordination is extremely hard to achieve. To represent both of these coordination dilemmas, the deterrence model presented earlier in this chapter can be extended in a natural way. First, let the game be about N voters or N electoral districts, simultaneously making decisions whether to support the hegemonic party or the opposition. Nothing assures that they will coordinate on their decision.

Second, the aggregate decisions of these voters or districts determine whether the hegemonic party or the opposition controls the national government. The preferences of the hegemonic party over the outcomes are the same as in the previous model: it seeks to punish defectors with reduced funding, and to reward its supporters with transfers. I assume that the opposition's preferences mirror those of the ruling party.

Finally, there are two or more opposition parties, $O_1, O_2, O_3, \ldots\ldots O_n$. I assume that these parties hold common political stands on a regime/anti-regime dimension in that they all seek to renegotiate the rules of the game, defeat the autocrat, and establish a democratic system; the parties differ, however, in their economic policy stances, some standing to the left and others to the right of the autocrat on a second, socioeconomic dimension.

If the parties are primarily ethnic-based, I assume that ethnicity maps onto some meaningful economic policy divisions. The policy space is thus multidimensional. If the number of voters supporting the ruling party exceeds a certain threshold d, $V_I > d$, the ruling party wins control of the national government. But the threshold d can be very low if coordination dilemmas are not overcome. It can be shown that coordination is more likely when the following conditions hold:

1. Coordination requires that voters perceive that the hegemonic-party autocrat can effectively be defeated. If voters cannot infer that other voters are also willing to defect, coordination is likely to fail due to the threat of punishment. This assumes that the ruling party can somehow monitor people's votes. Monitoring is reasonable for a subset of voters who live in smaller rural localities, where local party bosses possess more local knowledge and can identify supporters, and where they often violate the secrecy of the ballot.
2. In systems with a divided opposition, there is no rational reason to cast a strategic vote in favor of the strongest opposition party when opposition voters perceive that only the autocrat can win. "Strategic voting" (or abandoning one of the trailing opposition parties in order to support one of the front-runners) requires that the ruling party can effectively lose, for otherwise the voter will be wasting his vote by supporting a challenger that has no real chance (on the logic of strategic voting, see Riker and Ordeshook, 1968; Riker, 1982; and Cox, 1997). Perceptions of invulnerability are thus essential to prevent opposition coordination and mass wagon effects against the regime.
3. Coordination is more likely the less the opposition vote, Vo, is divided among opposition parties, where opposition fractionalization, $Vo = Vo_1 + Vo_2 + Vo_3 + \ldots Vo_n$, can be expressed as the effective number of opposition parties, namely $No = 1/\sum V_{Oi}^2$. As No increases, the threshold needed for the hegemonic-party autocrat to win, $VI > d$, becomes smaller. Thus, hegemonic parties thrive where the opposition is divided.
4. Coordination against the hegemonic party is more likely when the difference between the number of votes for the strongest and the second-strongest opposition party increases, so that voters can strategically rally behind the strongest opposition party. When two, three, or more opposition parties are equally strong, voters will have a hard time coordinating to support the strongest challenger. Thus, for coordination

to take place, the ratio between the second-strongest and the strongest opposition party should be closer to zero than to one (Cox, 1997).[18]

5. Opposition coordination requires that voters set aside their ideological (or ethnic) differences in order to dislodge the autocrat. Naturally, if the strongest opposition parties both lie either to the right or to the left of the autocrat, or if the opposition is not divided along ethnic lines, voters will have an easier time coordinating to dislodge the autocrat. Yet, contrary to what Riker (1976) implied when analyzing party dominance in India, an "ends-against-the center" coalition is possible even when the ruling party lies between both opposition parties on the socioeconomic dimension. I have argued that party competition in hegemonic-party autocracies is generally multidimensional. This means that voters might still be able to coordinate, provided that they more heavily value the regime/anti-regime dimension as opposed to the socioeconomic or ethnic dimension. The soliency of these dimensions might vary from one election to another.

One way to assess how voters value these dimensions is by constructing complete voter preference profiles (Magaloni, 1996). If a voter first prefers a left-wing opposition party, O_L, to a right-wing opposition party, O_R, and prefers both of these to the hegemonic party autocrat, I, such that his complete preference ranking is $O_L > O_R > I$, it is clear that he will be willing to set ideology aside, casting a strategic vote in favor of the right-wing opposition party if it is the strongest challenger. I call this type of voter a nonideological or tactical opposition voter, whose priority is to dislodge the autocrat.

If, on the contrary, the voter's complete preference ranking is $O_L > I > O_R$, ideology will prevent him from casting a strategic vote to dislodge the autocrat. I call this type of voter an ideological opposition voter, whose priority is to support whichever opposition party is closest to his policy preferences even if that party has no chance of defeating the autocrat. Opposition coordination requires that there be more tactical than ideological voters among the supporters of the trailing opposition party.

The same logic can be applied to cases where the opposition is divided along ethnic lines. In these cases, opposition coordination will be harder

[18] Cox (1997) proposes the second-to-first loser vote ratio (SF ratio) to assess coordination failures. Duvergerian equilibria, where voters successfully coordinate behind the strongest contenders, occur when the SF ratio is closer to zero. Non-Duvergerian equilibria (coordination failures) occur when the SF ratio is close to one.

to achieve when there are serious ethnic rivalries among opponents such that voters would rather waste their votes or support the ruling party than support an opposition party of a different ethnic identify.

6. As in all tipping games, information dissemination about the preferences of the other players, and the relative standing of the alternatives at the polls, is essential for coordination to take place (Lohmann, 1994; Cox, 1997). Yet in hegemonic-party autocracies, there are normally no independent sources of information because the government controls the mass media (Lawson, 2002). Control of the media is an important tool autocrats employ to prevent voter coordination and diminish snowballing effects.

The Game of Fraud and Expectations of Post-electoral Violence

In hegemonic-party autocracies, voters must make their choices without being certain of whether the players will respect the election results or if a violent confrontation might occur. An additional difficulty voters confront is that the "game of fraud" takes place in a state of imperfect information: it is not possible to know for certain whether the ruling party actually won or lost.

The strategic calculation of voters can be more fully appreciated in the following simplified version of the transition game to be presented in Chapter 8. The simplified version of the game, which includes only the strategy sets with two opposition parties that coordinate their actions, is given in Figure 1.6.

The voter must choose without knowing whether the ruling party will win or lose. The box at the second node represents the aggregate decisions of N voters. If the number of voters supporting the ruling party exceeds d, $V_I > d$, the ruling party wins control of the national government; if $V_o > d$, then the opposition wins control. Once the aggregate decisions of the voters have determined which party holds national office, the parties decide on their strategies: the ruling party can choose either to refrain from stealing the elections (not fraud) or to steal the election from the opposition (fraud). The opposition must then decide how to respond: it must either accept the official results, or contest them through mass demonstrations and rallies.

The ruling party must decide whether to commit fraud or not. If the ruling party commits fraud, the unified opposition challenges the official results. If the ruling party holds clean elections, the opposition accepts the

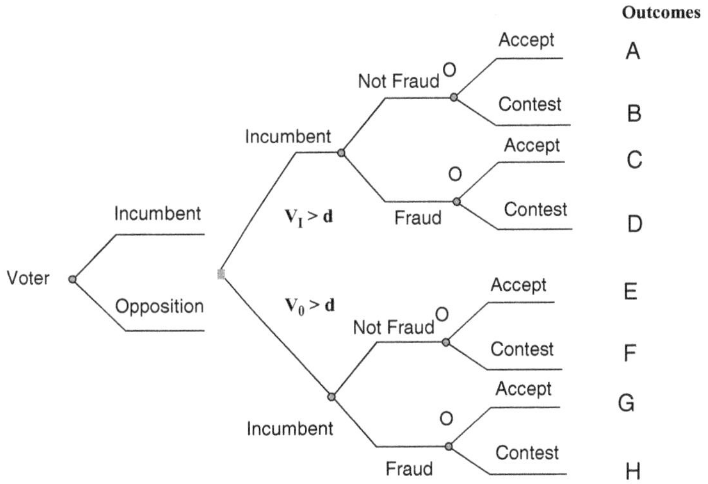

Figure 1.6. Simplified version of the transition game with a unified opposition.

results. Looking down the game tree, the ruling party refrains from committing fraud if it wins and the opposition accepts its defeat. This outcome is denoted by the letter A. In the fully specified game with a divided opposition, the ruling party can commit fraud even if it wins so as to boost its vote margins when it anticipates that the opposition parties will not coordinate in contesting the results.

The real risks emerge when the ruling party loses: will it accept defeat and yield power peacefully, or will it chose to steal the election from the opposition, even if this entails serious post-electoral conflict? A peaceful alternation of political power in office is denoted as outcome E: the ruling party loses, refrains from committing fraud, and the opposition has no incentive to contest the results. But the other possibility is that the ruling party chooses not to allow the opposition to take office, by stealing the election through electoral fraud and threatening to use the army. In the simplified version of the game with a unified opposition, the opposition contests the official results, and post-electoral conflict results (outcome H). The conflictual outcome can range from political instability, resulting from the temporary lack of a legal government, to violence or, in the most extreme cases, civil war. To simplify, I will denote such an outcome as Violence. In the fully specified game with a divided opposition, the ruling party can get away with stealing the election when the opposition fails to coordinate to contest the electoral fraud.

In the simplified version of the transition model, the voter must consider two possible outcomes: retaining the existing political regime with no post-electoral violence (outcome A), or a lottery between violence (outcome H) and alternation of political power with the opposition winning (outcome E). The expected value of the voter's decision can be represented as:

$$\begin{aligned} Ei[I] &= pR \\ E_i[O] &= (1-p)[(1-q)A - qV], \end{aligned} \tag{1.9}$$

where *p* stands for the probability that the ruling party will win a majority of the vote. R is the value of keeping the existing political regime with no post-electoral conflict. The term inside the parentheses is a lottery between the alternation of political power in office (A) and violence (V), where $V \geq 0$ – ranging from simple post-electoral conflict to outright civil war. The probability of violence occurring is *q*.

The implication of this expression is surprisingly stark: the expected costs of post-electoral conflict (where V > 0) are discounted from the opposition. This derives from the fact that the voter knows that, by supporting the opposition, she can trigger an authoritarian response from the ruling party that may generate violence. In this game, the risks of violence are insignificant when the opposition cannot win (e.g., when *p* is close to one). But as the opposition strengthens, the risk of violence becomes more salient. The costs to the voter of the regime's authoritarian response can range from simply not having her vote counted, to having to follow opposition leaders into the streets to defend the vote, to, in the worst case, being physically threatened in the parties' feuds. My account thus parallels that of Wantchekon (1999), who argues that "violence-prone candidates . . . are more likely to win elections when voters fear a collapse of the political process" (p. 246). My approach departs from his, however, in linking the risk of violence directly to the autocrat's electoral manipulations and threat of repression and to the opposition's responses to the electoral fraud.

In my model, there are two types of opposition voters, categorized by their preconceptions regarding the existing political regime and their tolerance for violence, represented as λ in equation 1.3. More tolerant of violence and highly distrustful of the democratic credentials of the regime, *radical opposition voters* will support opposition parties that challenge the electoral fraud. By contrast, *moderate opposition voters*, who are more concerned about political stability, will be suspicious of allegations of electoral fraud, and they will side against parties that engage in post-electoral battles. Note that this presupposes that voters possess no way of knowing the actual election results. Thus, one key quandary in the transition game is that allegations of electoral fraud and post-electoral mobilization can paradoxically work to discourage support for the opposition.[19]

To dissuade the ruling party from rigging the election, the opposition must be endowed with a large enough number of *radical voters* who develop an unwavering commitment to democratization for its own sake and who place that commitment over the disagreements they might have on other issues. If the opposition's electoral base is mostly *moderate*, the ruling party will find it easier to co-opt one of its opponents into acquiescing to the electoral fraud.

Conclusion

Hegemonic parties are collusive pacts among ruling party politicians to divide the spoils of office among themselves. The party's central dilemma consists in deterring potential elite challengers, particularly those coming from within. As long as they are given access to government spoils and are rewarded with office, elites will remain united. However, elections pose a fundamental dilemma for the hegemonic party – politicians who are denied the party's nomination will be inclined to split and challenge the regime as opposition.

My theory of autocracy underscores that hegemonic parties require mass support to survive. These autocracies rely on the mobilization of the masses as a means to deter intra-elite divisions. When the party keeps its monopoly of electoral support, elites possess strong incentives to remain loyal to the hegemonic party because it is the "only game in town." Thus, even when elections are not competitive and the opposition can't even dream of winning, autocracies need to mobilize electoral support. When electoral support begins to wither, party autocracies become more vulnerable to elite splits and opposition rivals.

Hegemonic parties mobilize mass support by establishing a complex system of incentives that compel citizens to support the regime, even if reluctantly. My theory conceives support for an autocratic regime as a function

[19] In their study of mass politics in Mexico, Domínguez and McCann (1996) were the first to highlight this paradox. One of the key electoral implications of the perceptions of electoral fraud they found was voter abstention, which had effects that were not neutral, but tended to harm the opposition. "A significant number of voters believe the opposition's claims about the pervasiveness of electoral fraud and stay home on election day, making it easier for the PRI to win" (Domínguez and McCann, 1996: 164).

of a combination of factors: the state of the national economy; government transfers; ideological commitments; and voters' fears of what may happen to the political order if the autocracy is defeated. Richer voters will pay more attention to the state of the national economy, and they may continue to support the autocrat because of a general distrust of opposition parties' capacities to handle future economic performance owing to uncertainty about these parties. Poorer voters will mostly focus on government transfers and may continue to support the autocratic regime because of fear of being excluded from the party's spoils system if they defect to the opposition.

Economic growth promotes voter support for an autocracy. Voters are likely to support the autocrat when the economy prospers, industry expands, and wages and employment increase. Furthermore, when the long-term economic record of the regime is satisfactory, voters will be tolerant of short-term economic recession. Under these conditions, risk-adverse voters may prefer to stick with the "known devil" rather than turn the government over to the uncertain opposition. However, if the economy deteriorates in a more systematic way, voters will embrace political change regardless of the risks.

Economic growth has conflicting effects on autocratic survival, however. As voters' incomes increase, they are more capable of making "ideological investments" in democratization despite the risks of economic punishment that come with defecting from the ruling party. The autocrat thus possesses strong incentives to promote economic growth and at the same time put in place policies that will keep a loyal base of support dependent on state transfers for survival. The Mexican PRI attained this goal by promoting growth and industrialization and simultaneously establishing polices that created a poverty trap for peasants, who remained the most loyal base of support for the autocratic regime up until it was defeated in 2000.

As the economy deteriorates, the autocrat becomes more dependent upon the distribution of pork and electoral fraud to survive in office. Autocratic survival is thus a function of economic growth, modernization, and the availability of the state resources that the party employs to glue the hegemonic coalition together. The more resources the party has at its disposal, the better able it will be to regularize payments to its supporters, at both the elite and the mass levels, and survive in office. Trade liberalization, privatization, and market reforms weaken autocratic parties because they destroy their monopoly of economic rewards and sanctions and imply a necessary reduction in the state resources available for patronage.

Equilibrium Party Hegemony

The effectiveness of what I have called the "punishment regime" in securing voter support is directly related to voters' incomes, on the one hand, and to the party's ability to monitor people's votes and target benefits, on the other. The poorer the median voter, the more effective the "punishment regime" will be in ensuring the autocrat's survival. To monitor people's votes, autocrats often resort to violating the secrecy of the ballot. They also employ dense organizational networks in order to acquire knowledge about voters' loyalties and to target benefits. As localities become more urban and voter heterogeneity increases, party autocracies become less able to deliver payments to their supporters and implement punishment to their enemies. Thus, as in modernization theory, my approach underscores that economic development and urbanization debilitate autocracies. Development works to mitigate voters' need to submit to the party's clientelistic practices, and urbanization makes it more difficult for the party to monitor and target voters.

A weak hegemonic party will resort to electoral fraud and the use of force to survive in office. Opposition parties are in a strategic dilemma when confronted with electoral malpractice. Electoral incentives are not well aligned to fight authoritarianism, as opponents can be punished for engaging in post-electoral battles and violence. This conclusion derives from two assumptions about voters' behavior: first, most voters dislike violence, and second, since there is no way for voters to know the actual election results, many will distrust allegations of electoral fraud.

One of the implications of these findings, as we will see in Chapter 8, is that the autocrat will find it easier to co-opt a fraction of the opposition elites whose electoral base is composed mostly of *moderate* voters into acquiescing in the electoral fraud and playing the "loyal opposition." To fight electoral fraud, the opposition must count on a sufficiently large base of *radical* voters who develop an unwavering commitment to democracy and are willing to risk violence to make their votes count.

My approach thus underscores the reasons why citizens support autocrats often despite corruption, the violation of fundamental rights, restrictive economic regulation, and even failure to foster economic growth. The equilibrium is tragic in that citizens are often compelled to accept these features, and brilliant in that the autocrat induces citizens to play an active role in maintaining the system.

2

Structural Determinants of Mass Support for the PRI

My theory of the determinants of mass support for the PRI presented in the previous chapter stresses a series of causal relationships that link the socioeconomic structure with the propensity to support the autocratic regime or to defect to the opposition. This chapter provides empirical evidence, based on aggregate socioeconomic indicators, for several of my theoretical claims. Some of these relationships, and in particular the correlation between underdevelopment and support for the PRI, have long been noted in classic studies of Mexican politics. Other correlations are less well understood. This chapter also serves to provide some basic "stylized facts" about the dynamics of mass support for the PRI and the decline of that support over the years.

Economic Performance and Support for the PRI

From 1929 until 1982, the PRI was successful in generating political stability and economic growth. The PRI's predecessor, the PNR, emerged in 1929 as a compromise among warlords and revolutionary leaders to put an end to a long period of political violence. The compromise was successful, and for more than seventy years political elites in Mexico settled their disagreements through the regime's institutional channels, seldom resorting to violence.

The PRI also produced economic growth. Before the founding of the PNR, the economy was in dismal shape, at least in part due to internal political instability. Indeed, the average growth rate in the twenties was −0.93 percent.[1] The economy began to grow after 1933, soon after Mexican

[1] Author's calculations using data from INEGI.

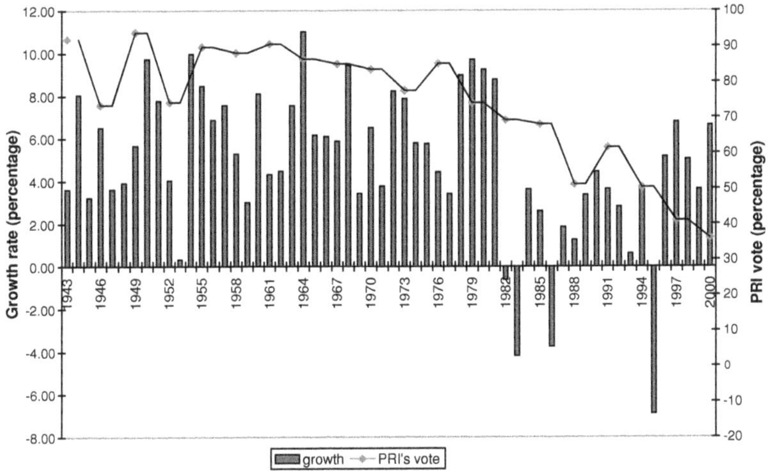

Figure 2.1. The PRI's support and economic growth, 1943–2000. *Source:* Growth rates are from the Estadísticas Históricas de México, Instituto Nacional de Estadística, Geografía e Informática. Electoral data is from Molinar, 1991; Presidencia de la República, V Informe de Gobierno, 1993; and the Federal Electoral Institute (www.ife.org.mx).

politicians organized the PRI to put an end to political violence. From 1933 until 1981, the Mexican economy had positive growth rates (an average of 6 percent a year), and during most of these years there was also impressive macroeconomic stability.

As will be further discussed in the following chapter, the populist interlude of the 1970s destroyed macroeconomic stability. Furthermore, during the eighties and nineties, long-term growth collapsed: from 1982 until 1989, the economy grew on average by only 0.51 percent, and the average growth rate during the following decade was only 2.9 percent.[2] Since 1982, Mexico has experienced two serious economic recessions, the first between 1982 and 1988, as a result of the debt crisis, and the second during 1995–96, as a result of the devaluation of the peso. Both crises produced high inflation rates, devaluations, and a brutal deterioration of real wages.

What impact did economic performance have on support for the PRI? Figure 2.1 graphs the vote for the PRI in federal elections from 1943 until 2000. Three general trends reflected in this figure should be underscored. First, there is a secular decline in support for the PRI: its vote share falls

[2] Author's calculations using data from INEGI.

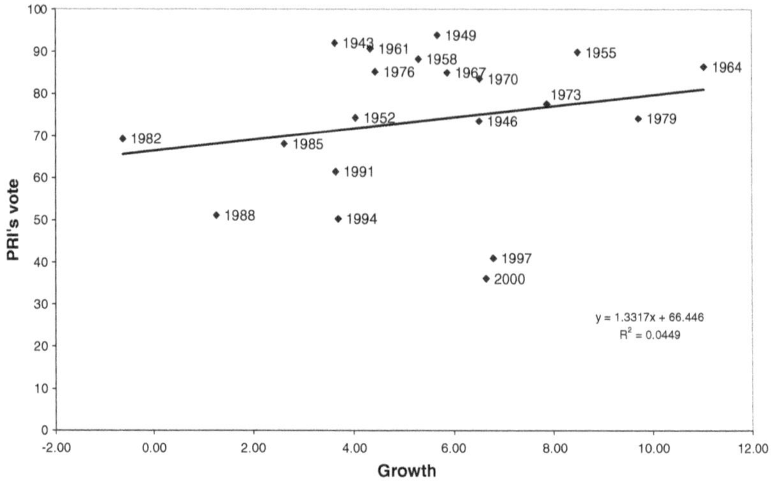

Figure 2.2. Annual growth rates and the PRI's vote. *Source:* Growth rates are from the Estadísticas Históricas de México, Instituto Nacional de Estadística, Geografía e Informática. Electoral data is from Molinar, 1991; Presidencia de la República, V Informe de Gobierno, 1993; and Instituto Federal Electoral (www.ife.org.mx).

with the passing of time, with the exception of two elections – the election of 1976, when the opposition did not even field a presidential candidate, and the midterm election of 1991, when Carlos Salinas managed to recover most of the lost vote that had gone to Cuauhtémoc Cárdenas in the 1988 presidential elections (an issue to which I return later in this book). Second, elite splits within the PRI (in 1940, 1946, 1952, and 1988) translated into sharp electoral losses for the party. Third, the secular decline in PRI support accelerates after the debt crisis of 1982, and this pattern is even clearer in the local elections.

Thus, in general, electoral support for the PRI was stronger when the economy grew, and weaker when the economy deteriorated. However, the relationship between economic growth and support for the PRI is not so straightforward. Although support for the PRI significantly weakened during the post-1982 era of economic stagnation, the party managed to survive, while many other autocratic regimes collapsed, victims of similar economic disintegration (Remmer, 1993; Haggard and Kaufman, 1995). Voting trends are not strongly correlated with economic growth. Figure 2.2 plots the PRI's vote share against the election-year growth rate; the figure also shows a regression line and its formula. There is a positive correlation between growth rates and the PRI's vote, but this correlation is not strong.

The PRI received surprisingly strong support in the worst years of the economic recession of the eighties, namely 1982 and 1985, which seems to indicate that voters were not reacting in accordance with the simple economic voting model that tells them to punish incumbents when the economy deteriorates and to reward them when the economy improves (Downs, 1957; V.O Key, 1966). The limitations of this model are also reflected in the 1997 and 2000 elections, when the PRI was punished at the polls despite the relatively high growth rates of those two years.

A theory of retrospective voting does not adequately account either for support of an incumbent during recession or mediocre economic performance, as shown by Mexican voters between 1985 and 1994, or for voters turning against the incumbent despite an objective improvement of economic conditions, as Mexicans did in 1997 and 2000. Electoral fraud cannot be the sole explanation for why voters appeared to remain loyal to the PRI despite recession. Studies employing individual-level data on the federal elections since 1988 similarly demonstrate that voters supported the PRI in 1988, 1991, and 1994 despite holding very negative retrospective economic evaluations, and that they turned against the PRI in 1997 and 2000 despite the fact that the economy was improving (Domínguez and McCann, 1996; Magaloni, 1999; Magaloni and Poiré, 2004a; and Chapter 7 of this book). My model of Bayesian learning can account for both of these paradoxes, as I will demonstrate later in this book.

Modernization and the Decline in the PRI's Support

Because voters do not like to support incompetent governments, economic recession debilitated support for the PRI and economic growth strengthened it. In the short and medium term, growth helped the PRI to survive. Yet, in the long term, growth threatened the PRI because the richer voters became, the more willing they were to make "ideological investments" by defecting to the opposition despite the risk of economic punishment, as the theoretical model presented in the previous chapter made explicit.

Figure 2.3 shows a scatter plot of vote shares and income per capita. The figure also reports a regression line and its formula. Economic development and national vote trends are highly intertwined, and the correlation is significantly stronger than that between economic growth and support for the PRI.

To assess the conflicting effects of economic growth and modernization on the PRI's survival, I use an OLS pooled time-series analysis of the PRI's

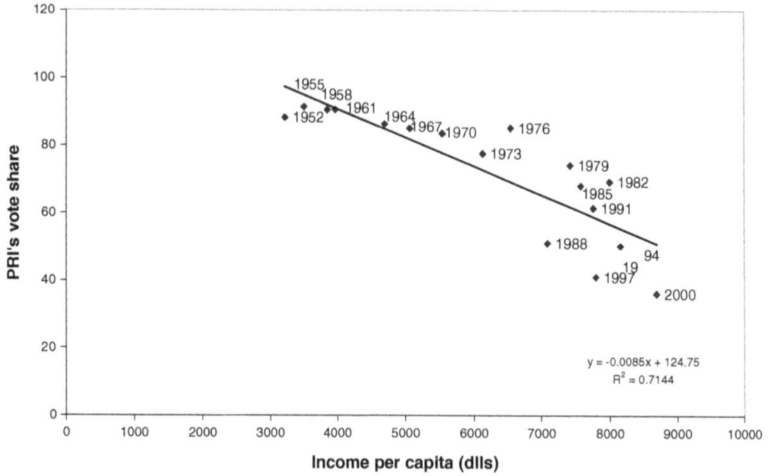

Figure 2.3. Effects of modernization on the PRI's support. *Source:* Income per capita is measured in real dollars and comes from the Penn World Tables, Version 6.1. Electoral data is from Molinar, 1991; Presidencia de la República, V Informe de Gobierno, 1993; and Instituto Federal Electoral (www.ife.org.mx).

vote in presidential elections for each of the thirty-one states of Mexico from 1958 until 1994. The dependent variable is the change in the PRI's vote share from one presidential election to the next. Since the PRI's vote share falls with the passing of time, most observations are negative. The main independent variables are the logarithm of the level of development per state (as indicated by the gross state product, GSP) and the average state-level growth rate during the presidential term. The OLS regression employs fixed effects. My theory expects economic growth to have a positive impact and level of development (as measured by the state's gross product) to have a negative impact on change in support for the PRI. The results of the regression, which are shown in Table 2.1, confirm my expectations: economic growth increases support for the PRI, and level of development hurts the party.

Figure 2.4 simulates the results of this model by varying from their minimum to their maximum values either level of development (as measured by the state's gross product) or the average growth rate, holding the other independent variables at their mean values. It can be seen that development sharply accelerated the rate at which the PRI lost votes. In the short term, the PRI could halt its rate of decline by promoting economic growth: if

Table 2.1. *Change in PRI support per state in federal elections, 1958–94 (fixed effects)*

Independent Variables	Coefficient	Std. Err.
PRI vote lagged	0.02	0.11
Log GSP	−12.72***	2.41
Growth	187.27***	52.42
Constant	38.24***	14.18

N = 160
No. groups: 32
F(3,125) 17.85
Prob F > 0
R-sq.: 0.30

Note: The dependent variable is the change in PRI support per state in federal elections. Log GSP is the logarithm of states' gross product, and growth is its percentage change from one presidential term to the next. *** significant at the 95% confidence level.

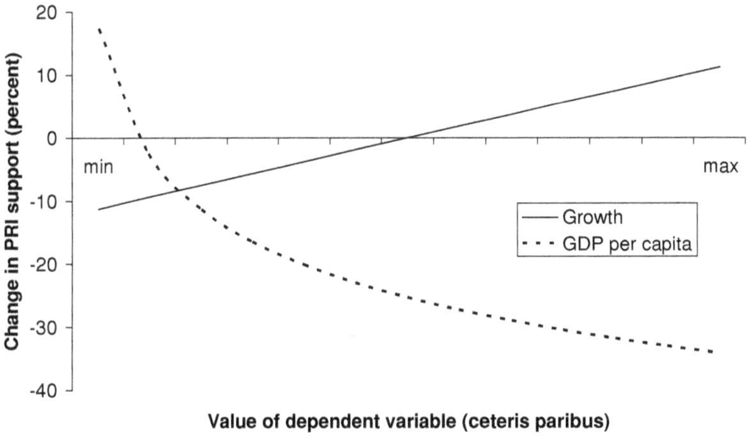

Figure 2.4. Effect of growth and development on changes in the PRI's Support. *Note:* Simulation of model in Table 2.1. Data corresponds to state-level PRI returns in federal elections, 1958–94.

a state grew at an average rate of 11 percent, the best observation in the sample, the model predicts that the PRI would gain 11 percentage points. By contrast, if the local economy stagnated and the average growth rate was −.02 percent, the worst observation in the sample, the model predicts a loss for the PRI of 11 percentage points.

Table 2.2. *Municipalities won by the three mayor parties and the CONAPO deprivation index, 1990–99 (percent)*

	Richest 1	2	3	4	Poorest 5	Total
PRI						
1990	0.92	0.92	0.92	0.94	0.96	0.93
1993	0.81	0.90	0.92	0.96	0.96	0.93
1996	0.72	0.71	0.81	0.85	0.80	0.79
1999	0.46	0.63	0.68	0.79	0.79	0.69
PAN						
1990	0.05	0.02	0.01	0.01	0.00	0.01
1993	0.16	0.06	0.03	0.02	0.00	0.04
1996	0.24	0.19	0.07	0.04	0.04	0.11
1999	0.43	0.20	0.12	0.09	0.04	0.15
PRD						
1990	0.01	0.05	0.05	0.03	0.01	0.04
1993	0.00	0.02	0.04	0.02	0.03	0.03
1996	0.02	0.08	0.09	0.09	0.14	0.09
1999	0.11	0.15	0.16	0.11	0.15	0.14

Source: Electoral data is from CIDAC. The CONAPO index is from the Consejo Nacional de Población.

Poverty and the Partisan Distribution of Municipalities

The PRI's long-lasting hegemony was solidly based on poverty and underdevelopment. Between 1940 and 1980, the Mexican economy did grow, but development was highly unequal and unbalanced. The PRI kept the support of the poorest localities, while the prosperous and wealthiest regions began to defect to the opposition, most notably to the PAN (Ames, 1970; Klesner, 1988, Molinar, 1991).

Table 2.2 reports the percentage of municipalities governed by the PRI, the PAN, and the PRD between 1990 and 1999, classified by level of development. Development is measured using the Conapo deprivation index.[3] The index is grouped into five categories, from the wealthiest localities to

[3] The Conapo index is a measure produced by the Mexican government that reflects the level of deprivation per municipality. It is calculated using a set of indicators that include the percentage of the employed population earning below the minimum wage; illiteracy; housing with access to sewage, electricity, and drinking water; and the population living in rural localities.

the poorest. The wealthiest localities include, for example, Mexico City and many of the state capitals of the richer states in the North. The poorest localities are small, highly isolated and marginalized rural municipalities scattered around the country, many of them in the South.

In 1990, the PRI controlled 93 percent of the municipalities, which were distributed across all levels of development. By 1999, the PRI controlled 69 percent of the country's municipalities, and most of these were heavily concentrated among the poorest and second-to-poorest groups. The PAN tended to win in the exact opposite type of locality than did the PRI. In 1990, the PAN governed only 1 percent of the country's municipalities, and the overwhelming majority of those were among the richest municipalities, according to the Conapo index. By 1999, the PAN controlled 15 percent of the country's municipalities; 43 percent of those came from the richest and 20 percent from the second-richest municipalities, while only 4 percent were among the poorest. The PRD, for its part, possesses a more even representation across the whole spectrum of development. In 1990 and 1993, most of the municipalities governed by the PRD were concentrated in the middle level of development. In 1996, the PRD performed surprisingly well among the poorest municipalities but had only a meager presence in the richest. By 1999, however, the PRD possessed a very even distribution across all levels of development. Thus, among the opposition parties, the PRD was the most successful at competing for the core base of supporters of the PRI, found in the poorest municipalities. However, the PRD was not able to truly penetrate those municipalities and mount a more serious challenge to the PRI until 1996. As noted earlier, the PRD largely relied on ruling-party splits during this period to acquire a more significant and broadly distributed presence across the states.

Opposition Entry in Local Elections

Mexico's democratization, as Lujambio (2001) has lucidly noted, must necessarily be understood in the context of the country's federal structure, and thus within a process that gradually enabled the opposition to enter local electoral markets to challenge the PRI. There are 31 states in Mexico and more than 2,400 municipalities. Governors are elected every six years, and state assemblies and municipal presidents are elected every three years. The staggered electoral calendar means that there are gubernatorial elections every year except the second year of the presidential term, and that there are municipal elections every year.

The PAN had a long history of opposing the PRI. Its presence in the localities can be traced back at least to the 1950s (Lujambio, 2001; Loaeza, 1999, 2003; Magaloni and Moreno, 2003). Until the 1980s, however, the PAN's electoral strength at the local level was marginal. The debt crisis and the nationalization of the banks in 1982 both contributed to the PAN's growth in the localities, particularly in the northern states (Chand, 2001). At first, the PRI was highly reluctant to let the PAN advance at the local level. Witness, for example, the infamous electoral fraud in the gubernatorial elections in Chihuahua of 1986, where there is credible evidence that the PRI stole the election from the PAN (Molinar, 1987; Lujambio, 2001).

The PAN's first gubernatorial victories must be understood in the context of larger bargains struck between the PAN's national leadership and the federal government during the Salinas presidency. During this period, the PAN came closer to the government than ever before. In the 1988 elections, the PRI had lost the supermajority necessary to modify the constitution single-handedly. This meant that Carlos Salinas needed the support of the PAN to pass his economic agenda, much of which required constitutional changes. (The privatization of the banks, for instance, required constitutional reform, and so did the restructuring of land tenure arrangements in the countryside.) The PAN traded its support for the president's economic agenda – which was fairly similar to the PAN's economic platform – for the PRI's approval of two electoral reforms, one in 1990 and the other in 1993, which established a more independent federal Electoral Tribunal and a Federal Electoral Institute. (I will turn to the issue of institutional reform in Chapter 8.) The PAN further used its power in government to entice Carlos Salinas to deliver on his promise to back the PAN vis-à-vis local PRI bosses. As I discuss in Chapter 8, the deal with the president, which came as a side payment for the PAN's agreement not to challenge electoral fraud in the 1988 presidential elections, enabled the PAN to obtain official recognition for many of its electoral victories at the local level and even to benefit from the so-called *concertacesiones*: post-electoral bargains through which the president transferred the election from the PRI to the PAN, regardless of the actual vote count, when local elections had unclear or contested outcomes.

The first PANista victory in a gubernatorial election occurred in Baja California in 1989 (see Table 2.3). Next, after a post-electoral bargain between the PAN and Carlos Salinas, the state of Guanajuato was given to this opposition party, which claimed that the PRI's official victory in the 1989 election had been the result of electoral fraud. The PAN also

Table 2.3. *Gubernatorial elections in Mexico, 1993–99*

State	Year	PRI	PAN	PRD	NP	Coalition	Victory	Previous	SF Ratio
		Percentage of Vote							
Coahuila	1993	65.50	27.00	0.00	1.97		PRI	PRI	0.0370
Chiapas	1994	50.40	9.20	34.90	2.58		PRI	PRI	0.2636
Morelos	1994	75.80	7.90	0.00	1.65		PRI	PRI	0.1265
Tabasco	1994	57.50	2.60	38.70	2.08		PRI	PRI	0.0672
Baja Calif.	1995	42.30	50.90	3.30	2.27		PAN	PAN	0.0309
Guanajuato	1995	32.90	58.10	7.00	2.22		PAN	PAN	0.2134
Jalisco	1995	36.60	51.90	3.90	2.45		PAN	PRI	0.1568
Yucatán	1995	48.70	44.40	3.00	2.29		PRI	PRI	0.0868
Michoacán	1995	38.90	25.50	32.40	3.11		PRI	PRI	0.7869
Campeche	1997	48.00	3.10	41.20	2.46		PRI	PRI	0.1679
Colima	1997	42.60	38.20	16.30	2.82		PRI	PRI	0.4263
DF	1997	25.60	15.60	48.10	3.06		PRD	PRI	0.6085
Nuevo León	1997	41.90	48.50	3.20	2.41	PRD + PVEM	PAN	PRI	0.0751
Querétaro	1997	39.50	45.40	7.40	2.71		PAN	PRI	0.1834
S. L. Potosí	1997	49.50	41.40	9.10	2.36		PRI	PRI	0.3236
Sonora	1997	41.80	31.60	23.50	3.03		PRI	PRI	0.7181
Chihuahua	1998	50.30	42.20	5.50	2.3	PT + CDP	PRI	PAN	0.1298
Zacatecas	1998	39.80	13.50	46.70	2.53		PRD	PRI	0.3377
Durango	1998	39.90	30.30	8.40	3.29		PRI	PRI	0.7027
Veracruz	1998	49.00	27.20	17.90	2.88		PRI	PRI	0.6589
Aguascalie.	1998	38.00	53.10	6.90	2.31		PAN	PRI	0.1800
Oaxaca	1998	48.90	10.20	37.60	2.56		PRI	PRI	0.2720
Tamaulipas	1998	54.90	26.60	16.10	2.51		PRI	PRI	0.6033
Puebla	1998	55.50	29.70	11.20	2.44		PRI	PRI	0.3760
Sinaloa	1998	47.50	32.70	18.10	2.73		PRI	PRI	0.5392
Tlaxcala	1998	44.30	8.60	34.00	2.38	PRD + PT + PVEM	Coalition	PRI	0.2764
B. Calif. Sur	1999	37.40	6.30	55.90	2.19		PRD	PRI	0.1672
Hidalgo	1999	53.50	32.10	14.40	2.44		PRI	PRI	0.4491
Q. Roo	1999	44.40	17.40	36.10	2.79		PRI	PRI	0.4807
Guerrero	1999	49.80	1.70	47.70	2.1	PRI + PRS and PRD + PT +PRT	PRI	PRI	0.0334
Nayarit	1999	44.80	52.90	0.00	2.08	PRD + PT + PVEM	Coalition	PRI	0.0189
Estado de México	1999	42.50	35.50	22.00	2.82	PAN + PVEM and PRD + PT	PRI	PRI	0.6208

Source: Diaz-Cayeros and Magaloni (2001). The SF ratio in the last column is the second-to-first loser vote ratio used to assess how much the opposition coordinated. The closer to one the ratio is, the more the opposition failed to coordinate (Cox, 1997).

won Chihuahua in 1992. Thus, during the Salinas presidency, the right-wing opposition party was finally able to gain access to political office at the gubernatorial level in three states. During the Salinas presidency, the PAN also won control of 331 municipalities, while during the Miguel de la Madrid presidency (1982–88) it had won only 140.

For its part, the PRD did not win any gubernatorial races during the Salinas presidency – although it won in 366 municipalities, many of them rural and sparsely populated. Thus, contrary to assessments by many political commentators, the PRD's growth at the local level was impressive, especially considering that most of its victories came in the face of violent confrontations between PRI local elites and PRD contenders. By the PRD's count, during the Salinas presidency close to 500 of their activists were murdered in these electoral confrontations. Virtually every competitive election involving the PRD against the PRI ended up in post-electoral battles, many involving violence (Eisenstadt, 2004). These violent events, together with an explicit media campaign to portray the PRD as violence-prone, discouraged voters from supporting the party (Bruhn, 1997). As I will further demonstrate in Chapter 4, another reason why the PRD's growth at the local level during the Salinas presidency was slower than the PAN's must be attributed to PRONASOL, the poverty relief program that was purposely designed to prevent the PRI's core poorer supporters from defecting to the opposition, particularly to the PRD (Molinar and Weldon, 1994).

The opposition's victories at the local level significantly accelerated after 1994. After the second recession, the opposition won fourteen gubernatorial races (see Table 2.3): the PAN was reelected in Guanajuato and Baja California in 1995, but it lost Chihuahua to the PRI in 1998. The PAN also won Jalisco in 1995, Querétaro and Nuevo León in 1997, Aguascalientes in 1998, and the state of Mexico in 1999. The PRD won Mexico City in 1997. But the PRD's growth at the local level during this period must primarily be attributed to PRI splits. The PRD won the gubernatorial election of Zacatecas in 1998 by endorsing Ricardo Monreal, who had split from the PRI. A similar process took place in 1999 in three other states, Baja California Sur, Tlaxcala, and Nayarit.

The opposition's growth at the municipal level during the eighties and nineties is depicted in Figure 2.5, which reports the municipalities won by the PAN and the PRD between 1980 and 2000 and the percentage of the population governed by these parties each year. In 1980, the PAN controlled only 7 out of Mexico's more than 2,400 municipalities. The economic

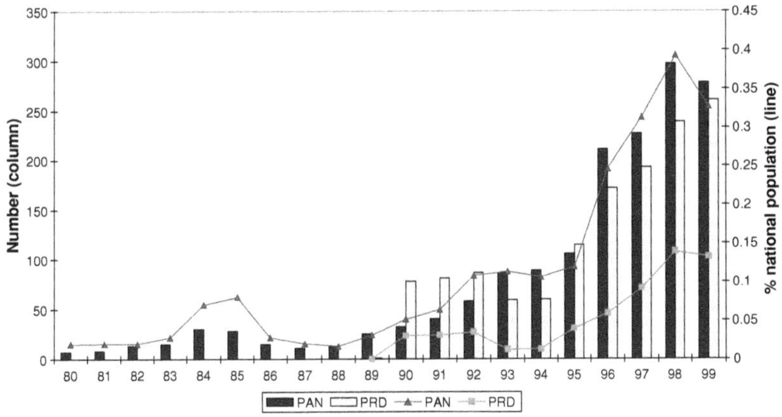

Figure 2.5. Opposition municipalities, 1980–99. *Source:* Electoral data from CIDAC and BANAMEX-ACCIVAL, Estadísticas Federales y Locales 1970–2000.

recession of the 1980s translated into more municipal victories for the PAN – in 1984 and 1985, the PAN controlled close to thirty municipalities, mostly urban ones. Between 1986 and 1988, the PAN's growth at the municipal level reversed, but then it gradually began to increase after 1990. The expansion of the opposition in the municipalities, and in particular the PAN, accelerated after the 1994 peso crisis. The jump is particularly strong in 1996, although the overwhelming majority of those gains resulted from victories in the elections taking place in 1995. Between 1995 and 1997, the PRI lost the majority of the vote in the deputy and/or municipal elections of Aguascalientes, Durango, Puebla, Sinaloa, Yucatán, Estado de México, Coahuila, and Morelos. The PAN won most of the important cities in dispute during those elections, including the capital cities of Jalisco, Baja California, Yucatán, Michoacán, Oaxaca, Chiapas, Puebla, Aguascalientes, Coahuila, Sinaloa, and Morelos.

The PRD starts to grow quite rapidly after its creation in 1989 – note that the PRD controls a larger number of municipalities than the PAN in 1990, 1991, and 1992, although the number of people governed by the PRD is much smaller because, contrary to the PAN, the left-wing opposition party tended to win in more rural localities. The PRD's expansion at the local level reverses in 1992 and 1993, however. It is only after the economic recession of 1994 that the PRD begins to grow again.

The opposition's dramatic growth at the local level after 1994 may be attributed to three factors. First and foremost, the 1994 peso crisis generated massive defections from the PRI. With the exception of some states located in the North, the overwhelming majority of localities reacted in a *forgiving* way to the economic recession of the 1980s. After the 1994 peso crisis, by contrast, most voters, including those situated in the poorer states of the South, became *vindictive*, defecting en masse to the opposition. Second, the opposition's victories in the gubernatorial and municipal elections of 1995, 1996, and 1997 produced a powerful demonstration effect, creating a growing belief among Mexican voters that the long-ruling hegemonic party could effectively be defeated and that the opposition could gain political office peacefully. Third, national party elites had reached a new understanding that elections would be respected. This understanding began with the 1994 electoral reform, which established the independence of the IFE, and culminated with the 1996 electoral reform, which contributed to leveling the playing field by significantly increasing the campaign financing and media access of the opposition parties. Although these elite pacts affected only federal elections (the IFE does not possesses jurisdiction over local elections), they had a diffusion effect in some states, which transformed their electoral institutions to fall in line with the new federal arrangements. Others states, however, adamantly maintained their old institutional structures, which continued to give ample leeway to local PRI bosses to manipulate the elections in their states. The analysis of these state-level electoral institutions is beyond the scope of this book.

To assess the difference in voters' reaction to the economic recession of the 1980s and the 1994 peso crisis, a simple comparison between the PRI's vote shares in the gubernatorial elections preceding and following each of these recessions can be employed.[4] For example, there were gubernatorial elections in the state of Jalisco in 1982, 1988, and 1995. The effect of the debt crisis can be assessed by subtracting the PRI's vote share in 1988 (61 percent) from that party's vote share in 1982 (56 percent), which gives a 6 percent vote loss for the PRI. The effect of the 1994 peso crisis can be assessed by subtracting the PRI's vote in Jalisco in 1995 (37 percent) from its 1988 vote, which gives a 23 percent vote loss for the PRI. Performing

[4] Thus, to obtain the average loss for the PRI in the 1980s, the PRI's vote share in a state's gubernatorial election preceding the debt crisis (1979, 1980, 1981, or 1982) was subtracted from that party's vote share in the next gubernatorial election (1985, 1986, 1987, or 1988). Data for gubernatorial races in the 1980s and 1990s comes from CIDAC.

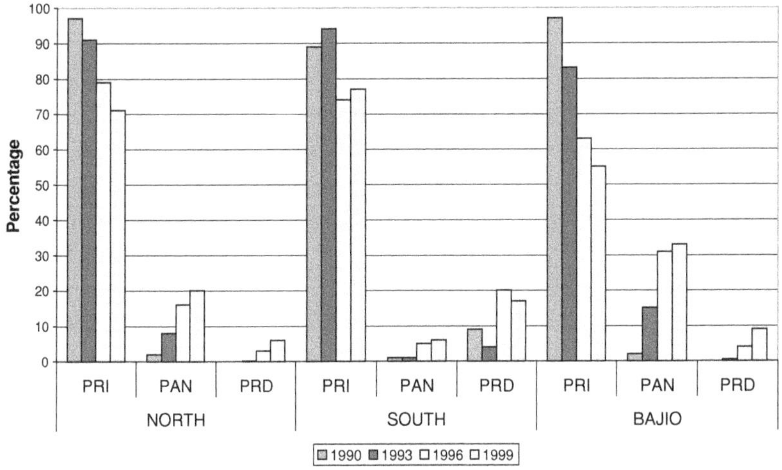

Figure 2.6. Regional distribution of municipalities governed by the three major parties, 1990–99. *Source:* Electoral data from CIDAC.

the same comparison for all states gives an average loss for the PRI in the gubernatorial elections preceding and following the 1982 debt crisis of 8 percent. The average loss for the PRI in the gubernatorial elections preceding and following the 1994 Peso Crisis was 23 percent, more than twice as large as the average PRI loss of the 1980s.

The North-South Division, Trade Liberalization, and Remitances

There is a geographic pattern in the distribution of the parties' support and the PRI's losses. Support for the PAN disproportionately came from the more internationalized localities situated in the North and the El Bajío region. The largest losses for the PRI during the eighties were heavily concentrated in those regions and primarily benefited the PAN. Support for the PRD, by contrast, disproportionately came from poorer localities located in the South (see Figure 2.6). The largest losses for the PRI after the 1994 peso crisis were primarily concentrated in that region and in the states where the ruling party had split.

The internationalization of the Mexican economy played an important role in the expansion of the PAN. Beginning in 1985, the Mexican economy became increasingly integrated with that of the United States. This tendency was significantly accelerated with the signing of NAFTA in 1993. Many states and municipalities in northern Mexico and the El Bajío region possess vibrant economies with deep connections to the United States. The liberalization of trade beginning in 1985 implied a dramatic transformation of state-society relations and federalism in Mexico. With ISI policies, local economies were geared toward the center, where markets for their goods and inputs were concentrated. Before 1985, close to 80 percent of Mexico's exports came from the state-owned oil company; the manufacturing sector was geared toward the internal market and was tightly regulated by the central government. Policies such as multiple exchange rates, tariffs, permits, subsidized credit, and strict regulations on foreign direct investment and the transfer of technology all meant that producers had no chance unless they courted the central government. The dismantling of these policies meant that the remote central government, and hence the PRI, increasingly lost control of the local economies, many of which began to seek new opportunities in international markets. Golden (2004) provides a very similar argument about the role of internationalization in the demise of the Christian Democrats in Italy.

Support for the PRD came disproportionately from the states and municipalities of the South, poorer localities that were not highly internationalized in terms of trade in goods and services. However, they did experience a significant form of internationalization through labor migration to the United States. For these poorer localities, the economic crisis of the 1980s and the subsequent implementation of orthodox stabilization intensified the pressure for labor migration to the United States. By moving abroad in search of jobs, those most dissatisfied with the economy exercised an option for "exit" instead of seeking greater "voice" within the nation, and ultimately provided an escape valve for social tensions (Hirschman, 1981). As a consequence, it could be argued that labor migration contributed to delaying democratization in these poorer regions.[5] Over time, however, labor migration worked against the PRI because the remittances sent home by migrant workers enabled poorer local economies to liberate themselves from their economic dependence on the government. Systematic empirical evidence of the connection between remittances and support for the PRD is provided in my work with Diaz-Cayeros and Weignast (Diaz-Cayeros et al., 2004).

[5] I thank Terry Karl for this observation.

Conclusion

This chapter has provided some of the basic "stylized facts" about the structural factors that account for mass support for the PRI and its decline over the years. The chapter has taken the economic structure as given. Chapters 3 and 4 will take a different approach. They will emphasize the PRI's strategic manipulation of economic policies and the economic cycle.

3

Budget Cycles under PRI Hegemony

A central empirical implication of my theory presented in Chapter 1 is that there would be budget cycles or an increase in government spending around elections, when the hegemonic coalition is most vulnerable to potential challengers, including those resulting from splits within the ruling party. Budget cycles would occur even when elections were not competitive, and would become more pronounced when the opposition strengthened. My approach also predicts that splits within the ruling party would tend to occur in part due to failures to distribute enough material rewards to the members of the ruling coalition. This chapter tests these hypotheses against the empirical evidence. I answer the following questions: first, is there systematic empirical evidence that the PRI flooded districts at election time with generous amounts of government spending? Second, is there evidence that electoral business cycles took place even when elections were not competitive? Third, do other policy instruments and variables, such as the money supply, inflation, and economic growth, also move according to the electoral calendar?

The chapter unfolds as follows. The first section summarizes the literature on electoral business cycles, which was developed for competitive democracies. The second section presents a discussion of budget cycles in light of some conventional views about the Mexican political system. The third section analyzes government spending patterns between 1938 and 2000. The fourth and fifth sections present evidence of the movement of inflation, the money supply, nominal wages, and the exchange rate according to the electoral calendar. The sixth section focuses on the temporal variability of economic growth according the electoral calendar. I present my conclusions in the final section.

Existing Literature on Electoral Business Cycles

The literature on electoral business cycles was initially developed for advanced industrial democracies. The seminal article was authored by Nordhaus (1975), who formalized the idea of an opportunistic political business cycle, where current employment is boosted through expansionary aggregate demand policies, at the cost of higher inflation later on. In the late eighties, "rational political business cycles models" questioned both the idea that voters are myopic and the existence of an exploitable trade-off between inflation and unemployment (Cukierman and Meltzer, 1986; Roggoff and Sibert, 1988; Persson and Tabellini, 1990). These models suggest that although observable output and unemployment cycles are not likely to occur, "pre-electoral manipulations of policy instruments for 'signaling' purposes are likely to be the norm, rather than the exception" (Alesina et al., 1993: 3). The new generation of models thus stresses political budget cycles wherein policy instruments, such as taxes and expenditures, are manipulated.

A parallel line of models on the interaction between elections and politics focuses on partisanship. These models assume that elections matter and that groups of politicians and voters contest economic policies through elections (Keech, 1995). The classic work is that of Hibbs (1987), who argues that Democrats conventionally target lower-income, blue-collar wage earners and are hence more averse to unemployment than Republicans. He systematically shows that under Democrats, unemployment tends to decrease and output to increase, and vice versa for Republicans. Alesina (1987, 1988) also provides a partisan model but assumes rational expectations. The model generates milder Phillips-like cycles if wage contracts are signed at discrete intervals and if electoral outcomes are uncertain.

Much less research exists on the relationship between electoral politics and the economy for less developed countries. The most important contribution is that of Ames (1987), a broadly cross-sectional analysis of spending decisions in Latin American nations between 1947 and 1982. He concludes that even Latin American military dictators in danger of being overthrown were opportunistic, using public expenditures to please key constituencies, particularly the military. "Military governments may opt for austerity once they are safe, but in their first year of power they cover their political bases" (Ames, 1987: 33). Ames finds no evidence that the competitiveness of elections matters for increasing the magnitude of budget spurs prior to elections. This result leads him to conclude that "even in polities like Mexico, where the opposition only dreams of winning, elections play a powerful role for lower-level politicians trying to demonstrate their political skill" (1987: 12). Although Ames is correct in underscoring the importance of elections in Mexico, his explanation for why spending might spike before elections is insufficient. Given the enormous fiscal centralization prevailing in Mexico, lower-level politicians have little control over the dispensation of economic resources. Thus, the reasons why the national PRI leadership, in control of its vast resources and in control of nominations, would choose to reward vote mobilization efforts as opposed to other political skills remain unclear.

A different line of research that employs assumptions similar to those of the "partisan models" for developed countries is that of "populist cycles." The argument is that left-wing "populist" governments destroy the economy and eventually democracy (Dornbush and Edwards, 1991). Populist cycles are defined as sets of unsustainable expansionist macreconomic polices – monetary and fiscal – aimed at redistributing wealth. Populist governments are often followed by authoritarian right-wing regimes that seek to reverse these redistributions.

Remmer (1993) systematically explores the connection between elections and macreconomic performance in Latin America during the post-1980s period and finds no evidence of populism, not even of "classic" business or budget cycles. She concludes that elections in Latin America "should perhaps be seen less as threats to economic stability than as catalysts for policy reform and responsible economic management" (Remmer, 1993: 403). Remmer explicitly chose to exclude Mexico from her analysis, based on the argument that non-competitive elections pose a different incentive structure from that presupposed by the business cycles literature.

There are few systematic attempts to assess the occurrence of electoral cycles in Mexico.[1] Heath (1999) presents evidence of what he aptly calls the "*sexenio curse*" – currency devaluations and serious economic volatility occurring around presidential successions. Since Heath's analysis is about only four presidential successions, it is not possible to assess from it the extent to which his findings reflect a systematic trait of the PRI regime – in fact, currency devaluations around presidential successions had not taken place in Mexico prior to 1976. González (2002) provides a more

[1] Since Ames (1987) relied on a pooled time series, it is hard to assess from his results the extent to which electoral cycles occurred in Mexico or to gauge their magnitude.

systematic assessment of the incidence of budget cycles occurring as a result of purposeful manipulation of policy instruments prior to elections. Drawing on "rational political business cycles models," she claims that the PRI manipulated policy instruments in order to "signal competence." She also shows that the magnitude of the election cycle was exacerbated during the "country's most democratic episodes" (p. 204). The reasons why the PRI might have needed to "signal competence," even when the opposition could not dream of winning, are not spelled out.

Increased Spending by a Lame Duck and Presidencialismo *in Mexico*

With only a few exceptions, the literature on Mexican politics has tended to take party hegemony for granted. Haggard and Webb (1994), for example, argued that "the PRI's dominance of the political system meant that elections did not pose *any fundamental uncertainties*" (13, emphasis mine). Scholars of Mexico have also tended to neglect the central importance of elections for the PRI regime. Schedler (2000), for example, proposes that "[s]ince 1934, presidential elections have been held with clocklike precision, punctuating a dense calendar of regular legislative, gubernatorial and municipal elections. Yet these democratic forms were *hollow* rituals, given the systematic absence of minimal democratic guarantees" (6, emphasis mine).

My approach challenges these views. The PRI was vulnerable even when elections were not competitive because it was subject to division from within. By winning the elections with huge margins of victory, the PRI attempted to disseminate an image of invincibility that would discourage splits within the ruling party and snowballing effects among the mass public. Thus, the "ritual" of elections, even though their outcome was virtually certain, was by no means devoid of significance, but played a powerful role in the maintenance of the system.

Although the literature on Mexico has paid much attention to the presidency, my approach stresses the ruling party. Formally, the Mexican president was not a very powerful player. The president dominated the other branches of government only because he *was* the leader of the PRI, and that party was extremely disciplined (Weldon, 1997; Casar, 2002). The PRI delegated great informal powers to the president, including that of handpicking his successor and determining the direction of public policy without much constraint. However, one must necessarily look at other political players to account for budget cycles. On the one hand, it does not seem reasonable to assume that the sitting president's main motivation is the reelection of th PRI – a desire to maximize his legacy or to grab as much as possible from the public pie might also motivate the president, and such goals might conflict with the PRI's reelection (Romero, 2005). On the other hand, the president lost almost all his powers during his last year in office, and the PRI's machine took control. Thus, to account for election cycles, one needs to focus on the PRI, its legislators, and also the ministers of finance and budget, who stood the best chance of being nominated as presidential candidates. My findings about political budget cycles challenge a common view about the Mexican political economy that attributes a great deal of "insulation" to the so-called technocrats (see, for example, Haggard and Kaufman, 1992, 1995). The structural adjustment literature has misunderstood the Mexican political system. The technocrats could not possibly have been insulated from electoral markets. Because the president chose his successor from the members of his cabinet, the technocrats' ambitions were too closely tied to the electoral fortunes of the PRI. As likely presidential nominees, the technocrats shared an interest in maximizing the party's reelection chances and keeping the hegemonic coalition united by distributing government spoils prior to the elections.

Budget Cycles, 1938–2000

To assess whether the PRI increased expenditures before elections, I employ a monthly time series for the central government budget that comes from two sources. For January 1938 to December 1976, the data comes from the Finance Ministry.[2] For January 1977 to December 2000, the information comes from the Central Bank.[3] My test of the temporal variability of expenditures in response to the electoral cycle merges the two datasets, using only those accounting concepts where there is a close match in both series.[4] There are three years of overlap (1977–79) in the two series, which

[2] Secretaría de Hacienda y Crédito Público (SHCP) in its *Estadísticas de Finanzas Públicas*. I am extremely grateful to María de los Angeles González for generously sharing the electronic compilation of this data with me.

[3] The *Indicadores Económicos y Financieros* published by the Banco de México are available at <http://www.banxico.gob.mx/eInfoFinanciera/FSinfoFinanciera.html>.

[4] These two series use different methodologies to account for and classify federal public expenditure. Some of the differences are related to the way expenditure is accounted through time (accrual basis).

Table 3.1. *Summary statistics for various components of the budget, 1938–2000, real 1994 pesos (billions)*

	N (I)	Mean (II)	Std. Dev (III)	Mean Electoral Year (IV)	Mean Non-Electoral Year (V)	Difference (IV–V)
Total expenditure	756	9.08	9.35	9.66	8.79	0.87*
Budgetable expenditure	756	5.35	4.93	5.74	5.15	0.59**
Current expenditure	756	1.80	1.56	1.93	1.73	0.20**
Capital expenditure	756	2.17	2.15	2.35	2.08	0.27**
Current transfers	756	2.05	2.57	2.24	1.96	0.28*
Revenue sharing	755	1.12	1.41	1.20	1.07	0.13

t-test (one-tailed): * 90% significant; ** 95% significant.
Note: Budgetable expenditure refers to total expenditure minus interest payments, debt expenditure, and revenue shares to the states. Current expenditure is the current expenditure of the federal government minus total (current) transfers. Capital expenditure includes capital expenditure and capital transfers. Current transfers are total (current) transfers. Revenue sharing refers to revenue transfers that the federal government gives to the states under the Revenue Sharing Agreement.

allowed me to verify the consistency of the merging for each accounting concept.[5] To transform the data into real pesos, a long time series for inflation was needed; I draw on several different sources in order to create such a price index.[6] The budget figures employed in this analysis are expressed in real pesos of 1994.

Table 3.1 provides summary statistics for the various components of the budget. The last columns of the table present the mean expenditures during election and nonelection years, and the difference between these two (including a test for significance). There were eleven presidential elections and ten midterm elections between 1938 and 2000. The table provides

[5] The average discrepancy in the monthly figures between the two series in the three years of overlap varies depending on the variables (available from the author). The largest differences are in capital expenditures and interest payments, which are precisely the type of variables that are most likely to be affected by employing different accounting rules. Unfortunately, current expenditure, investment, and transfers could not be disaggregated in the estimations merging the two datasets because the discrepancies between the series are too large to justify assuming that they are measuring similar forms of expenditure. All of the figures were originally in current pesos.

[6] I employed various sources to obtain a price index. The General Wholesale Price Index for Mexico City: Banco de México from January 1938 to December 1956; *Anuario Estadístico-Secretaría de la Economía Nacional* from January 1957 to December 1966; and from January 1967 to July 2003, the Consumer Price Index (INPC).

tentative evidence of the occurrence of electoral budget cycles, since expenditures are consistently higher in election years than in nonelection years.

To systematically test for the occurrence of budget cycles, I employ OLS time-series regressions of monthly real expenditures. Lagged variables are included for the monthly expenditure of the same month of the *previous year*. The autoregressive specification for the dependent variable is chosen as the best, using standard techniques.[7] The independent variables are dummies for the two quarters prior to elections, the election quarter, and two quarters after the elections. My expectation is that expenditures should increase prior to elections and should decrease afterward. Since expenditures consistently increase in December, due to legally mandated wage premiums of at least one extra month (*aguinaldo*) given to employees during the Christmas month, I add a dummy for that month.

I also employ a dummy variable for the last quarter of the presidential term. I expect to find strong increases in *current government expenditures* at the end of the presidential term. Since the regressions control for the month of December, which should capture increases in government spending resulting from legally mandated wage premiums, whatever additional increase in current government spending taking place during the last quarter of the presidential term should thus be attributable to an increase in *discretionary bonuses and monetary transfers* received by government employees and politicians prior to the termination of their current positions. In Mexican political parlance, these corrupt expenditures at the end of the presidential term were referred to in the phrase "it's the year of Hidalgo [the founding father of independence], you're a sucker if you leave anything."[8] I expect to find a positive impact of the variable for the last quarter of the presidential term for current expenditures.

I also employ dummies for the presidencies during different periods of economic policy in Mexico commonly highlighted by the literature: the stabilizing development period (1952–70), a period known for high growth rates with impressive price and currency stability; the populist period (1970–82) of high growth accompanied by systematic increases in government expenditures and public indebtedness, which culminated in

[7] I follow Alesina and Roubini (1997) in not reporting the lag coefficients for the purpose of making the presentation of the results more concise.

[8] In Spanish the phrase is "el año the Hidalgo, ch . . . su madre el que deje algo."

the debt moratorium of 1982 and the oil boom; and the neoliberal period (1982–2000), an era of economic recession, macroeconomic volatility, and structural adjustment.

Expenditures should be lowest in the era of stabilizing development. During that period, the state played a moderate role in the economy, leaving more room for the private sector. Economic growth was impressive during the period, and the PRI enjoyed extremely high levels of electoral support. However, the benefits of economic development were not broadly distributed, and there were some signs of popular discontent with economic polices: first, the strike of the railroad workers, which president López Mateos (1958–64) repressed; and second, the student movement, to which president Díaz Ordaz (1964–70) responded with a brutal slaughter of hundreds of students during the demonstration of October 1968.

Budgetable and current spending should be highest during the populist period. The Echeverría administration (1970–76) attempted to restore the loss of the government's credibility by dramatically increasing expenditures, food and housing subsidies, land distribution, and state control over a wide range of economic activities. President López Portillo (1976–82) continued with these expansionist economic polices, assisted by the oil boom and massive increases in foreign borrowing. The spectacular rise in international interest rates led Mexico to declare a moratorium on its debt payments in August 1982, and money suddenly dried up, leaving the country in bankruptcy.

President Miguel de la Madrid (1982–88) had to cope with the fiscal collapse of the Mexican state, macroeconomic instability, and the debt crisis. His administration adopted various IMF-sponsored orthodox stabilization packages, which meant a dramatic decrease in government spending. Because of interest payments and debt expenditure, total expenditures should be very high during this administration. However, budgetable, current, and capital expenditures should be lower than they were during the populist era.

The PRI's electoral base began to wither as a result of the economic recession of the 1980s. Since my argument is that the PRI becomes more dependent upon government spending for its survival *as mass support deteriorates*, my expectation is that the following two presidencies, especially that of Carlos Salinas (1988–94), should significantly increase budgetable, current, and capital spending. Carlos Salinas, as I will demonstrate in the following chapter, was particularly successful at recovering mass support for the PRI, and he managed to do so in part by increasing government transfers to voters.

Finally, the models add a dummy variable for the years in which PRI splits occurred: 1940, 1946, 1952, and 1988. My argument is that the PRI needs to distribute funds in order to keep the hegemonic coalition united. I expect to find a systematic drop in expenditures in the election years during which the party suffered a major elite split. The drop in expenditures could be attributed to an economic recession or to failure on the part of the government to amass enough fiscal resources from taxes and other sources, such as oil. Unfortunately, information on quarterly growth rates exists only since 1982, so I cannot include growth as an independent variable in the regressions. The dummy for the year of a PRI split should thus have a negative sign and be statistically significant. For each budgetary item, I run the following regressions

$$\begin{aligned} \mathrm{B_t} = {} & \beta_0 + \beta_1 \mathrm{B_{t-1}} + \beta_2 \mathrm{B_{t-2}} + \cdots + \beta_n \mathrm{B_{t-n}} + \beta_{\mathrm{n+1}} E_{\mathrm{q-n}} + \beta_{\mathrm{n+2}} E_q \\ & + \beta_{\mathrm{n+3}} \mathrm{E_{q+n}} + \beta_{\mathrm{n+4}} \mathrm{Dec} + \beta_{\mathrm{n+5}} \mathrm{E_q endterm} + \beta_{\mathrm{n+6}} ARC \\ & + \beta_{\mathrm{n+7}} ALM + \beta_{\mathrm{n+8}} GDO + \beta_{\mathrm{n+9}} LEA + \beta_{\mathrm{n+10}} JLP \\ & + \beta_{\mathrm{n+11}} MMH + \beta_{\mathrm{n+12}} CSG + \beta_{\mathrm{n+13}} EZP + \beta_{\mathrm{n+14}} Split + \varepsilon_{\mathrm{t}}, \quad (3.1) \end{aligned}$$

where $\mathrm{B_t}$ is the monthly real expenditure. The Es are dummies for the q − n and q + n election quarters, where q stands as the election quarter. The dummies take a value of 1 for the three months comprising a given quarter and 0 otherwise. *Dec* is a dummy for the month of December, and $E_q endterm$ is a dummy for the last quarter of the presidential term. The rest are dummies for the presidencies. Each presidency is labeled by the initials of the president's name (for example, Luis Echeverría Alvarez is LEA). Presidents during the era of stabilizing development were Adolfo Ruiz Cortines (1952–58), Adolfo López Mateos (1958–64), and Gustavo Díaz Ordaz (1964–70). The populist presidents were Luis Echeverría Alvarez (1970–76) and José López Portillo (1976–82), and the neoliberal presidents were Miguel de la Madrid Hurtado (1982–88), Carlos Salinas de Gortari (1988–94), and Ernesto Zedillo Ponce de León (1994–2000). *Split* refers to a dummy for the years in which the PRI split. Results are shown in Table 3.2.

My results show an impressive movement of the budget according to the electoral calendar. Total, budgetable, current, and capital expenditures systematically increased one quarter prior to the elections (*Election Q-1*) and during the election quarter (*Election Q*). The effects are substantial.

Table 3.2. *Budget cycles, 1938–2000*

	Total Expenditure	Budgetable Expenditure	Current Expenditure	Capital Expenditure
Election Q-2	0.56	0.28	0.22***	0.16*
	(0.38)	(0.20)	(0.07)	(0.09)
Election Q-1	0.70**	0.65***	0.33***	0.44***
	(0.38)	(0.20)	(0.07)	(0.09)
Election Q	0.76***	0.43**	0.20***	0.42***
	(0.38)	(0.20)	(0.07)	(0.09)
Election Q+1	0.34	0.58**	0.054	0.33**
	(.51)	(0.28)	(0.10)	(0.12)
Election Q+2	−0.71*	−0.27	−0.10	−0.14
	(0.38)	(0.20)	(0.07)	(0.09)
End term	0.91	−0.33	0.35***	−0.13
	(0.70)	(0.38)	(0.13)	(0.17)
PRI SPLIT	−1.65***	−0.65***	−0.29***	−0.35***
	(0.48)	(0.26)	(0.09)	(0.12)
ARC	−0.08	0.022	−.0008	.0008
	(.40)	(0.21)	(0.08)	(0.01)
ALM	0.16	0.13	0.15**	−.0004
	(0.4)	(0.22)	(0.08)	(0.01)
GDO	0.77**	0.46**	0.29***	0.11**
	(0.41)	(0.22)	(0.08)	(0.01)
LEA	2.61***	1.41***	0.72***	0.82***
	(0.45)	(0.25)	(0.01)	0.10
JLP	5.88***	1.80***	0.94***	1.52***
	(0.60)	(0.33)	(0.12)	0.16
MMH	6.50***	−0.384	0.29**	0.31**
	(0.89)	(0.37)	(0.13)	0.16
CSG	3.56***	1.58***	0.59***	0.96***
	(0.78)	0.29	(0.12)	0.14
EZP	5.94***	1.54***	0.30***	0.34**
	(0.76)	(0.38)	(0.11)	(0.14)
Dec	1.32	0.64***	0.40***	0.56***
	(0.41)	(0.22)	(0.08)	(0.10)
Constant	0.32	0.09	0.03	0.02
	(0.25)	(0.14)	(0.05)	(0.06)
	N = 732	N = 732	N = 732	N = 732
	Adj R2 = 0.92	Adj R2 = 0.91	Adj R2 = 0.89	Adj R2 = 0.90

*** significant at the 99% confidence level; ** significant at the 95% confidence level; * significant at the 90% confidence level.

Note: The autoregressive specification of the dependent variable is chosen as the best using the Aikake and Swartz tests. Coefficients of the lagged dependent variables are not shown. The acronyms stand for presidents. *PRI split* is a dummy for years in which the ruling party split. *Dec* is a dummy for the month of December. *End term* is the last quarter of the presidential term. *Election Q* is the election quarter.

Relative to the average monthly expenditure, total expenditures in an election month will be 8 percent larger. Current expenditures will be 12 percent, 20 percent, and 11 percent larger in the two quarters prior to elections and in the election quarter, respectively. Capital spending is 20 percent larger both in the quarter prior to elections and in the election quarter, and it continues to increase in the quarter after the elections (*Election Q+1*). As expected, the end of a presidential term (*End term*) is associated with a systematic increase in current expenditures – relative to average monthly expenditures, current expenditures are 20 percent larger in the last quarter of the presidential term. Since the regressions control for the month of December, when *aguinaldos* to state employees are paid, the increase in current expenditure during the last quarter of the presidential term must be attributable to an increase in *discretionary bonuses and monetary transfers* received by government employees and politicians prior to the termination of their current positions – in other words, to an increase in government corruption.

The years in which the PRI experienced a major elite split are systematically associated with a dramatic drop in government spending. The drop in government spending is substantial: relative to the average total expenditure, total expenditure was 20 percent less in the years in which the PRI split. The drop in government spending during these years could result from an economic crisis or from the failure to generate enough fiscal resources to finance government spending. Fewer resources to distribute to the members of the ruling coalition translated into higher incentives to split.

As expected, during the populist era there was a spectacular increase in government spending. Capital expenditures witnessed a particular boost during the López Portillo administration. During the era of economic recession and adjustment, total expenditures continued to be extremely high – although, as mentioned earlier, much of this spending comes from interest and debt payment. More informative are the fluctuations in budgetable, current, and capital expenditures. As expected, relative to the populist era, there was a dramatic decrease in budgetable, current, and capital spending during the Miguel de la Madrid presidency. Carlos Salinas significantly increased budgetable, current, and capital spending, which are the items in the budget more subject to political manipulation, and decreased total spending or interest and debt payments. During the Ernesto Zedillo (1994–2000) administration, current and capital expenditures were cut almost by half relative to the Carlos Salinas presidency.

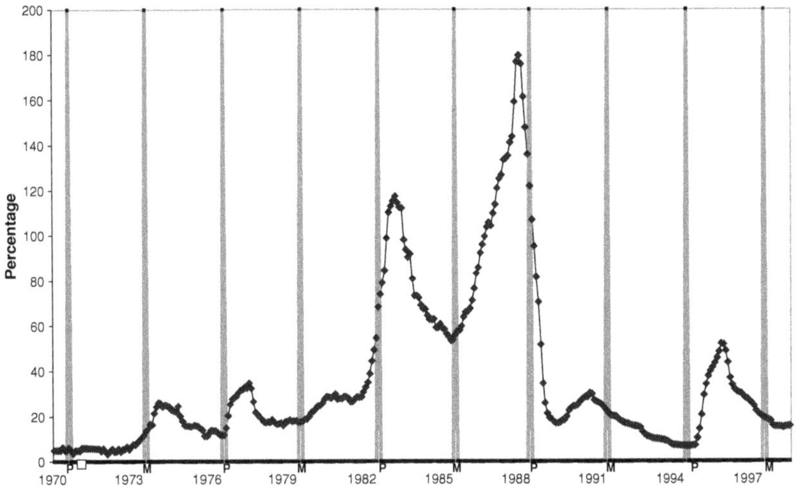

Figure 3.1. Annual rate of inflation and the electoral cycle. *Source:* Banco de Mexico. Election dates highlighted with lines. P indicates presidential election; M stands for midterm.

1970–2000: Macroeconomic Instability and the Shift toward Neoliberalism

Is there evidence that other policy instruments and output variables, such as the money supply, inflation, and wages, also moved according to the electoral calendar? To answer this question, I focus on the post-1970 period. Between 1934 and 1970, there was impressive macroeconomic stability. Mexicans were accustomed to having a stable currency and virtually no inflation. Prior to 1970, there is no evidence that inflation moved according to the electoral calendar (econometric results available from the author). Presidents during the seventies accelerated public investment programs and expanded social services. Without an increase in tax revenues, the expansionist polices were financed by large budget deficits, an explosion of foreign borrowing and oil revenues, and consequentially led to an increase in inflation.

Figure 3.1 presents the annual rate of inflation from 1970 to 2000. The figure also indicates when presidential and midterm elections took place. During the populist era of the 1970s, inflation appears to increase precisely after the elections – the post-electoral peaks are highest in 1973, 1976, and particularly in 1982. Although inflation became problematic after the 1973 midterm elections, it is not until the 1980s that it became an acute fiscal problem, in some years reaching annual rates of above 100 percent. Inflation in the eighties was largely inherited, a result of the expansionist macroeconomic polices of the seventies and highly unfavorable international conditions. During the neoliberal era, inflation appears to follow the opposite pattern from that of the populist period with respect to the electoral calendar, with politicians attempting to reduce inflation prior to elections. It can be seen in Figure 3.1 that the pre-electoral stabilization, although particularly noticeable in 1988, also is evident in the 1991 midterm election and in the 1994 presidential race.

The de la Madrid government initiated a dramatic shift in economic policy, implementing an orthodox IMF-sponsored stabilization package that included the restructuring of public finances, abrupt devaluation of the currency, and raising public sector prices. Despite this fiscal adjustment, the government could not control inflation until the National Solidarity Pact was signed in December of 1988. The Solidarity Pact was an agreement between labor, capital, and the government, in which the government agreed to an orthodox monetary regime, and labor and capital agreed to restrain wage and price increases and to renegotiate contracts according to a previously specified calendar. One of the crucial aspects of the Solidarity Pact, as I discuss in the following section, was the fixing of the exchange rate, which then served as a key coordinating device. The Solidarity Pact thus included orthodox and heterodox measures and was particularly successful. During the Salinas government, the yearly inflation rate was under control – although generally above 10 percent. The lowest yearly inflation rate was reached in 1994, around the time of the presidential election. With the peso crisis of December 1994, macroeconomic stability was again destroyed.

The conventional interpretation of the shift in macroeconomic polices during the 1980s is a change in government ideology. Indeed, Luis Echeverría and López Portillo subscribed to structuralism and state-led growth. Miguel de la Madrid, Carlos Salinas and Ernesto Zedillo were believers in monetarism and free markets. The relative influence of the labor movement within the PRI also changed between the 1970s and the 1980s (Middlebrook, 1986). Labor was more influential during the populist period. Workers in the formal sector of the economy were the main beneficiaries of the expansionist economic polices of Presidents Echeverría and López Portillo. With the oil boom of the late 1970s and early 1980s, real wages reached their peak, as can be seen in Figure 3.2.

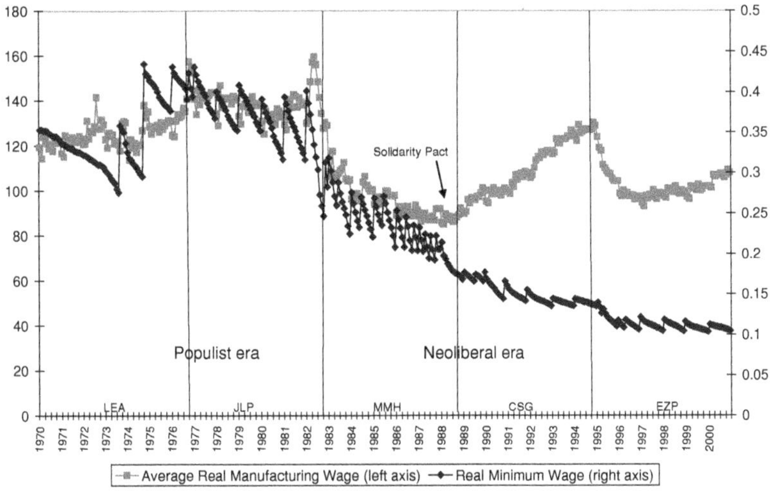

Figure 3.2. Evolution of real wages, 1970–2000. *Source:* INEGI. Lines separate presidential terms. LEA is Luis Echeverría Alvarez; JLP is José López Portillo; MMH is Miguel de la Madrid Hurtado; CSG is Carlos Salinas de Gortari; EZP is Ernesto Zedillo Ponce. The "populist era" is 1970–82; the "neoliberal era" is 1982–2000.

Workers' bargaining strength dramatically declined during the neoliberal era (Collier, 1992; Middlebrook, 1995; Bensusán, 2004). After 1982, nominal wage increases always lagged behind price increases, an indication that workers' bargaining power vis-à-vis capital had diminished. Between 1982 and 1988, real wages lost 60 percent of their value, consistently deteriorating until the Solidarity Pact was signed and inflation was controlled. During the Salinas presidency, real wages in the manufacturing sector recovered to about their pre-crisis level, with minimum wages lagging behind. In the post-1980 era, wage negotiations were increasingly carried out in a decentralized fashion, causing the official CTM to lose its monopoly representation over labor and its political clout. There was also a significant increase in wage drift, with workers in the most productive and internationalized sectors of the economy earning the highest wages and the others lagging far behind. The 1994 peso crisis represented yet another dramatic setback in the evolution of real salaries, as can be seen in Figure 3.2.

During the neoliberal era, the PRI thus neglected the interests of workers and began to pay more attention to the national and international financial communities and also to the middle class. To consume by credit, the middle class had a strong preference for low inflation and an overvalued currency, both of which the Salinas government delivered. During those years, middle-class Mexicans heavily borrowed to purchase cars, houses, trips, and all sorts of consumer products, most of which were imported.

Thus, there were systematic differences between the populist and the neoliberal administrations. Populist administrations believed in structuralism, were more pro-labor and statist, and followed expansionist economic policies. Neoliberal administrations believed in monetarism, were more pro-capital and pro-consumer, and emphasized state retrenchment, low inflation, and trade liberalization. I thus expect to find systematic differences in the way these two types of administrations manipulate economic policies for electoral gain. Populist administrations should, first, increase the money supply before the elections, which should translate into systematic increases in inflation after elections; and second, they should employ their control of centralized wage negotiations to ensure nominal wage increases before elections. Neoliberal administrations should not increase the money supply before elections. Quite the contrary, in order to please consumers, neoliberal administrations should attempt to stabilize the macroeconomy prior to elections. Moreover, I do not expect to find a systematic relationship between elections and nominal wage increases during the neoliberal era.

To test these hypotheses, I employ OLS time-series regressions of the monthly rate of inflation, the yearly change in the money supply, and nominal wage increases from 1970 until 2000. The regressions for nominal wages employ the wage index as the dependent variable, controlling for the consumer price index (INPC). Obviously, nominal wages increase as prices increase. The independent variables are dummies for different pre-electoral and post-electoral quarters plus the election quarter and lagged variables of the dependent variables. The regression for nominal wage increases also controls for the month of December because, as already noted, wages systematically increase during that month. Results are shown in Table 3.3.

For inflation, M1, and nominal wages, the table reports results for three models. The first uses data from the period 1970–2000; the second employs data from the populist era (1970–82); and the third model reports data from the neoliberal period (1982–2000). Results in Table 3.3 largely confirm my expectations about inflation and the money supply. Populist governments stimulated the economy through an expansion of the monetary base,

Table 3.3. *Monthly inflation rate, M1, real wages, and the electoral cycle*

	Monthly Inflation			M1			Nominal Wages		
		Populist	Neoliberal		Populist	Neoliberal		Populist	Neoliberal
	1970–2000	1970–1982	1982–2000	1970–2000	1970–1982	1982–2000	1970–2000	1970–1982	1982–2000
Election Q-2	−0.16	0.62	−0.55*	0.76	0.44	1.25	−82.51	−0.32	−147.02*
	(0.23)	(0.34)	(0.30)	(1.28)	(1.02)	(2.12)	(59.57)	(0.25)	(86.76)
Election Q-1	−0.38*	0.04	−0.68**	−1.18	−0.95	−1.28	3.38	0.68***	9.01
	(0.22)	(0.30)	(0.30)	(1.29)	(1.02)	(2.13)	(56.58)	(0.23)	(83.38)
Election Q	0.11	0.64***	−0.21	1.88	3.41***	0.96	15.70	0.10	25.40
	(0.22)	(0.31)	(0.30)	(1.28)	(1.03)	(2.12)	(55.34)	(0.23)	(82.05)
Election Q+1	0.38	0.63***	0.14	−2.07	0.17	−2.70	57.41	−0.19	127.35
	(0.22)	(0.31)	(0.30)	(1.30)	(1.18)	(2.12)	(56.84)	(0.24)	(84.17)
Election Q+2	−0.12*	−0.37	−0.04	−1.66	−0.51	−2.37	−50.09	−0.01	−79.89
	(0.24)	(0.38)	(0.30)	(1.47)	(1.40)	(2.18)	(61.61)	(0.28)	(84.62)
INPC							8.51***	27.48***	7.19***
							(1.83)	(3.41)	(2.04)
December							645.16***	2.94***	1106.07***
							(58.31)	(0.24)	(83.83)
Constant	0.26**	0.10	0.38***	1.67***	2.36**	2.18**	−40.62	−0.58***	−57.71
	(0.10)	(0.15)	(0.14)	(0.64)	(1.18)	(1.04)	(23.03)	(0.12)	(37.02)
	Adj. $R^2 = .75$	Adj. $R^2 = .65$	Adj. $R^2 = .79$	Adj. $R^2 = .96$	Adj. $R^2 = .88$	Adj. $R^2 = .95$	Adj. $R^2 = .98$	Adj. $R^2 = .95$	Adj. $R^2 = .95$
	N = 369	N = 153	N = 216	N = 369	N = 153	N = 216	N = 368	N = 152	N = 216

Note: The autoregressive specification for the dependent variable is chosen as the best using the Aikake and Swartz tests. Coefficients for lagged dependent variables are not shown. *INPC* is the monthly price index. December is a dummy for the month of December, when workers receive legally mandated wage premiums. *** significant at the 99% confidence level; ** significant at the 95% confidence level; * significant at the 90% confidence level.

creating an inflationary spurt around elections and in the quarter following elections, while neoliberal governments reduced inflation in the two quarters prior to elections. The drop in inflation during the neoliberal era cannot be solely attributed to the Solidarity Pact. When a dummy is added to control for the first six months of 1988, the drop in inflation in the quarters prior to elections survives. There is no evidence of monetary expansion or contraction taking place prior to elections during the neoliberal era.

Table 3.3 provides evidence that populist governments systematically increased nominal wages in the quarter prior to elections. Neoliberal governments, for their part, did not increase nominal wages prior to elections; nominal wages actually decreased during the first quarter of the election year, when inflation was also dropping, as has been shown. During both of these periods, nominal wages increased as inflation increased, although the magnitude of the coefficient is twice as large during the populist era, which indicates that during that period centralized wage negotiations adequately compensated for price increases, while in the neoliberal era they did not.

Achilles' Heel of the Mexican Political Economy: Exchange Rate Cycles and the Presidential Succession, 1970–2000

The era of macroeconomic instability was also accompanied by chronic currency devaluations, most of them taking place around presidential elections. Figure 3.3 reports the real exchange rate index from 1970 to 2000. The index is constructed by dividing the nominal exchange rate expressed in pesos per dollar by the consumer price index. If the currency is appreciating in real terms, it means that the value of the Mexican peso, relative to the dollar, is "improving" because the rate of inflation is greater than the rate at which the peso moves.

Devaluations are seen as the sharp declines in the exchange rate index. The figure also reports the monthly rate of change of the exchange rate. Devaluations are seen as increases in the monthly rate of exchange (right axis). A crucial question is whether Mexican politicians could strategically time devaluations to occur after the elections. The pattern is by no means systematic. There are post-electoral devaluations in 1976, 1982, 1985, and 1994. In 1982, López Portillo devalued the peso both prior to the elections and after the elections. The presidential succession of 1988 took place in an environment of serious macroeconomic instability, but the government devalued the peso six months prior to the elections, not after the elections.

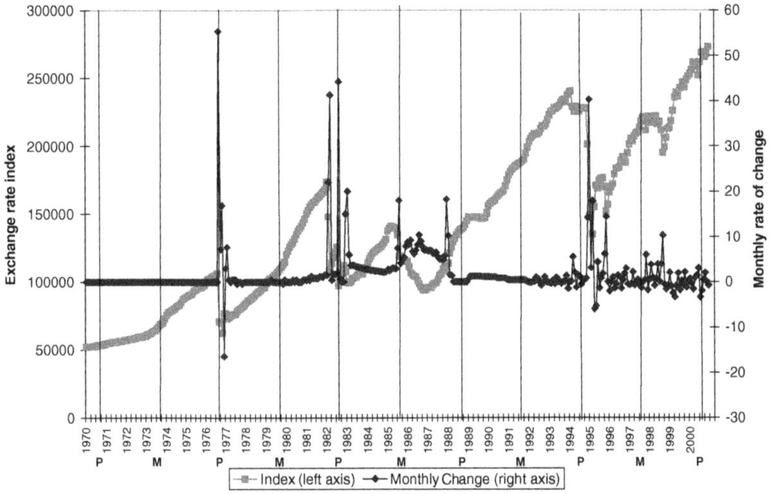

Figure 3.3. Exchange rate and the electoral cycle. *Source:* Banco de Mexico. Election dates highlighted with lines. P indicates presidential election; M stands for midterm

The currency remained stable during the presidential successions of 1970 and 2000 and in the midterm elections of 1991.

Despite the fact that it was not always possible for Mexican politicians to postpone devaluations of the peso until after the elections, there is evidence that the currency followed the presidential cycle, as shown in Figure 3.3, with appreciations systematically occurring throughout the presidential terms and depreciations tending to come at the end of these terms, often after the elections. Neoliberal governments were more prone to engage in this type of behavior. Table 3.4 presents the results of three OLS models on the temporal variability of the exchange rate between 1970 and 2000. As before, I present a model using the entire time series alongside one for the populist period and another for the neoliberal era. The dependent variable is the exchange rate, and the independent variables are dummies for different pre-electoral and post-electoral quarters plus the election quarter and lagged variables of the dependent variables. The regressions also control for the consumer price index.

The models provide some evidence that the exchange rate is tied to the election calendar. For the entire sample, most of the variance in the dummies for the quarters around presidential elections is captured by the post-electoral adjustment of the exchange rate. However, once the sample

Table 3.4. *Exchange rate and the electoral cycle*

Independent Variables	Model 1 (1970–2000)		Model 2 **Populist** (1970–1982)		Model 3 **Neoliberal** (1982–2000)	
	Coeff.	S.E	Coeff.	S.E	Coeff.	S.E
INPC	−0.0004	0.0005	0.0057***	0.0024	−0.0002	0.0007
Election Q-2	−0.0014	0.0276	0.0014**	0.0006	−0.0046	0.0467
Election Q-1	0.0024	0.0269	0.0004	0.0006	0.0033	0.0468
Election Q	−0.0271	0.0266	0.0017**	0.0006	−0.0527	0.0469
Election Q+1	0.0147	0.0267	0.0008	0.0006	0.0255	0.0475
Election Q+2	0.0949***	0.0293	0.0008	0.0007	0.1417***	0.0477
Constant	0.0045	0.0116	−0.0016**	0.0005	0.0191	0.0249
	Adj. R^2 = .97		Adj. R^2 = .96		Adj R^2 =.98	
	N = 358		N = 152		N = 216	

Note: The autoregressive specification for the dependent variable is chosen as the best using the Aikake and Swartz tests. Coefficients for lagged dependent variables are not shown. *** significant at the 99% confidence level;. ** significant at the 95% confidence level;. * significant at the 90% confidence level

is split in two, the results reveal a lack of consistent pattern in the dynamics of currency devaluations: although all the devaluations come during election years, not all occur precisely *after* the election. During the populist era, exchange rate adjustments take place prior to elections and during the election quarter, and in the month immediately following the election. For the neoliberal era, the most common pattern is for a devaluation to take place in the second quarter after the presidential election.

As shown in Figure 3.3, the appreciation of the exchange rate occurred during all the presidential terms but was most pronounced during the neoliberal era, especially during the Salinas administration, but also during the Zedillo presidency. In an environment open to international trade, such as that of Mexico since the liberalization of trade in 1985, an appreciation of the currency brings about an increase in imports, because foreign goods become artificially cheaper. Prior to the 1994 peso crisis, the dramatic increase in internal demand was driven by an extravagant expansion of consumer credit. During the Salinas years, middle-class Mexicans borrowed to purchase imported goods. Imports were financed by the massive amounts of portfolio investment entering the country throughout the Salinas presidency. The balance-of-payments disequilibrium became problematic, however, when capital flows stopped and even reversed, as occurred during the election year of 1994.

The results in this and the preceding section thus uncover partisan-like cycles in Mexico between 1970 and 2000; we see that populist and neoliberal governments engaged in different forms of political manipulation depending on their ideological predispositions, the relative bargaining power of labor, and the different economic settings each government faced. The populist cycles consisted of (1) an increase in government spending during the entire period, with spending spurts systematically occurring before elections; (2) an increase in the money supply before the elections; (3) the occurrence of an inflationary spike around election time and in the quarter after the elections; and (4) a systematic increase in wages, with nominal wage increases disproportionately occurring in the quarter prior to elections. The neoliberal cycles consisted of (1) a reduction of inflation in the two quarters prior to elections; (2) an increase in government spending prior to elections; and (3) the appreciation of the currency throughout the presidential term, with devaluations tending to occur after the elections. Given that during the neoliberal period the economy was highly internationalized, the appreciation of the exchange rate coupled with spending spurts and the expansion of credit prior to elections translated in consumption bubbles around the time of elections.

A Boom-and-Bust Economy and the Electoral Cycle

Between 1934 and 2000, there was systematically lower economic growth during the first year after each new president assumed power. Table 3.5 shows the average annual growth rate from 1934 to 2000 according to the year of the presidential term. Growth was consistently lower during the first year of the presidential term, precisely after the transfer of presidential power. When an OLS time-series regression is run, the drop in growth rates after the presidential election is statistically significant (results available from the author).

Interestingly, with the exception of the 1988 and 2000 elections, there was no real uncertainty as to which party would win the presidency in Mexico. What, then, accounts for the systematic decline in growth after presidential elections? The most likely explanation is that the post-electoral output drop was driven by the importance of government contracts for the Mexican economy. Most of these contracts did not survive from one presidency to the next, and thus investment decisions in Mexico were highly influenced by the presidential cycle. The decline in growth rates after the presidential election can also be accounted for by the fact that there was

Table 3.5. *Average annual growth rate according the presidential term*

Year of Presidential Term	Annual Growth Rate	President	Average Annual Growth Rate Per Presidency	Growth during First Year	Variance in Annual Growth Rates per Presidency
First year (post-election)	**2.70**	Cárdenas (1935–40)	4.54	**7.56**	3.02
Second year	6.49	Avila Camacho (1941–46)	6.15	**9.68**	2.50
Third year	5.64	Miguel Alemán (1947–52)	5.79	**3.61**	2.48
Fourth year	5.40	Ruiz Cortinez (1953–58)	6.41	**0.32**	3.37
Fifth year	5.20	López Mateos (1959–64)	6.41	**3.01**	3.0
Sixth year	4.55	Diaz Ordaz (1965–70)	6.24	**6.15**	1.92
Average	4.99	Echeverría (1971–76)	5.97	**3.76**	1.79
		López Portillo (1977–82)	6.57	**3.39**	4.23
		De la Madrid (1983–88)	0.23	**–4.20**	3.35
		Salinas (1988–94)	3.08	**3.35**	1.33
		Zedillo (1995–97)	1.40	**–6.90**	7.35

a significant drop in government spending after the elections. Given the importance of the state sector for the Mexican economy, a systematic decline in government spending after elections inevitably translated into a decline in growth rates.

A central question that emerges from these results is why Mexicans' "rational expectations" failed to inoculate them from these cycles. Probably the Mexican business community tolerated these cycles as long as they expected to benefit personally from political corruption, which for the most part they did. It was only when the economy became more internationalized that the costs of these political business cycles became acute for the middle class and the business community, which began to resort to capital flight. Another factor to take into account is that until just before the 1980s, the state sector played a disproportionate role in Mexico's economy, and there is no reason to expect this sector to disinvest in anticipation of business cycles.

The last columns of Table 3.5 provide more detailed information on the distribution of growth rates between and within each of the different presidential terms. While growth drops during the first year of the presidential term in almost all of the presidencies, it is after 1982 that the start of a new presidency is associated with economic recession. Two out of the three presidencies since 1982 begin with negative growth rates. It should be noted, moreover, that the average growth rate during each of the last three PRI presidencies is low compared to previous ones. In addition, with the exception of the Salinas presidency, the variance in growth performance has been particularly large in the last presidential terms.

These data reveal why the generation born in the last thirty-five years is usually referred to as the "crisis generation" and why, as I demonstrate in further chapters, the PRI tended to receive significantly less support from the young (see also Magaloni, 1999). Voters who became politically aware during the 1980s never experienced a period of continuous growth and low inflation during the PRI's rule. All they saw were recurrent economic crises.

The debt crisis and the peso crisis had very different causes. The former resulted mainly from fiscal deficits and expansionist economic policies in the context of an overinsulated economy during the presidential terms of Luis Echeverría and López Portillo. Miguel de la Madrid, Carlos Salinas, and Ernesto Zedillo adopted a series of economic policies that emphasized the opposite principles, namely, fiscal restraint, macroeconomic stabilization, trade liberalization, and a full integration into the flows of international capital. The 1994 peso crisis thus represented a serious setback to the new market-oriented strategy. It resulted from quite different problems, mainly having to do with imbalances in the external account produced by the government's exchange-rate policy, excessive growth in credit and consumption, and a poorly regulated financial system. Although the economy recovered from this latter crisis very rapidly, in part thanks to the structural transformation itself, Mexican voters reacted in a bitter and unforgiving manner, as I further demonstrate in Chapters 5 and 7.

Conclusion

The results discussed in this chapter demonstrated an impressive movement of the Mexican economy – the budget, economic growth, inflation, the money supply, nominal wages, and the currency – according to the election calendar. I have demonstrated that budget cycles took place even when elections were not competitive. My results compellingly show that elite splits within the PRI tended to occur systematically when expenditures dropped. I also uncover *partisan-like* cycles where the "populist" administrations of the 1970 manipulated economic policies around elections in ways that differed from those of the neoliberal administrations of the 1980s and 1990s.

Although the PRI's opportunistic manipulation of the budget and other policy instruments seems to have worked for the most part, the economic consequences of these manipulations became severe, and eventually contributed to the party's demise. The macroeconomic stability inherited from the so-called stabilizing development period was destroyed in the 1970s. The populist period (1979–82) was characterized by high growth rates accompanied by systematic increases in government spending financed by public indebtedness and the oil boom. These policies culminated in the debt moratorium of 1982 and the economic recession of the 1980s. Beyond the manipulation of the budget, the results in this chapter demonstrate that populist presidents engaged in a systematic increase in the money supply and nominal wages prior to elections, which translated into higher inflation around election time. These cycles are similar to those formalized by Nordhaus (1975).

The neoliberal period (1982–2000) was an era of economic recession, macroeconomic volatility, and structural adjustment, which was also accompanied by a deterioration of the PRI's vote share and the party's most severe internal split. Due to the economic recession and the fiscal adjustments undertaken, neoliberal governments faced stronger budget constraints. Despite limited space for maneuvering, these administrations employed the budget in strategic ways, as I will further demonstrate in the next chapter. The results also demonstrate that neoliberal administrations tended to reduce inflation in the two quarters prior to elections and raise the value of the currency throughout the presidential term, with devaluations tending to occur after the elections. Given that during this period the economy had become highly internationalized, the appreciation of the exchange rate coupled with spending spikes and the expansion of credit prior to elections translated into consumption bubbles around the time of elections.

The results suggest that with the passing of time, the economic costs of the PRI's opportunism became more pronounced, with economic busts tending to come after elections. Economic growth systematically dropped during the first year of the presidential term in almost all the presidencies. Yet it is only since 1982 that the start of a new presidency has been associated with serious economic recession. Two out of the three presidencies after 1982 began their terms with negative growth rates and serious macroeconomic instability.

There is no doubt that these economic difficulties also resulted from unfavorable international conditions, as most Latin American countries were also experiencing similar challenges. Existing analyses have found little evidence, however, that in the rest of Latin America inflation, currency depreciation, and the budget were associated with elections during this period (Remmer, 1993). What is striking about Mexico is their strong correlation with elections and with the presidential succession.

4

The Politics of Vote Buying

There is wide consensus among experts on Mexico about the key role played by patronage politics in maintaining the PRI regime (Ames, 1970; Cornelius, 1975, 2004; Collier, 1992; Cornelius et al., 1994; Dresser, 1994; Fox, 1994, among others). As Cornelius (2004) explains,

> [F]rom the party's creation in 1929 until the early 1990s, authoritarian mobilization of voters was a key ingredient of the PRI's electoral success. A steadily shrinking but still crucial bloc of voters, concentrated in the country's most economically underdeveloped electoral districts, routinely voted for the ruling party's candidates in response to pressures from local caciques and PRI-affiliated peasant and labor leaders. Particularistic material rewards – everything from minor kitchen appliances to land titles to public-sector jobs – were routinely and systematically used to purchase electoral support. (48)

Despite the fact that most scholars agree that patronage played a key role in the system, there are significant disagreements about the *actual mechanics* of vote buying, on the one hand, and its political *effectiveness* for the PRI's survival, on the other. This chapter deals with these issues. The empirical evidence will come from a systematic analysis of municipal-level allocations from the PRONASOL, a poverty relief program implemented by the Mexican government from 1989 to 1994. The database employed is the first to include municipal-level allocations from PRONASOL distributed to the country's more than 2,400 municipalities during the entire life of the program.

Around 30 percent of PRONASOL's funds were private, excludable benefits, and the rest were public works targeted to towns, municipalities, or regions (Magaloni et al., forthcoming). As argued in Chapter 1, the PRI was able to target transfers to individuals by using its dense corporatist apparatus. This apparatus began to fail as the country became more urban and modern and the PRI was less able to, on the one hand, acquire local knowledge about voters – something that could be feasibly done mainly in smaller communities – and, on the other, monitor voting behavior. Here I focus on the *geographic allocation* of total PRONASOL resources rather than on the allocation of transfers to individual voters. Thus, my analysis examines the political logic of pork barrel politics, patronage or public work provision, rather than individual vote buying through excludable benefits, which the literature equates with clientelism (Kitschelt, 2000).[1]

Most scholars agree that PRONASOL was employed for the purpose of "perpetuating the official party or state-party status of the PRI" (Collier, 1992). However, when it comes to providing systematic empirical evidence about the specific political logic of the program, scholars have been able to offer only very tentative conclusions derived from regressions carried out at an inappropriate level of analysis – state-level allocations (Molinar and Weldon, 1994) – when in fact PRONASOL funds were targeted at municipalities. When analysts have focused on municipal-level allocations, they have studied only a few states (Hiskey, 1999).

Drawing on my work with Diaz-Cayeros and Estévez,[2] this chapter overcomes the existing limitations in the literature by employing a municipal-level PRONASOL database for the entire country. The government did not report total municipal-level expenditures in an easy, machine-readable format. Our database took almost three years to collect, and it comes from *Hechos de Solidaridad*, a government report on project-by-project PRONASOL expenditures per municipality during the five-year life of the program. Our database is thus the closest approximation to actual or exercised municipal-level expenditures.[3]

There are basically two alternative theories about the political logic of PRONASOL. The seminal work, by Molinar and Weldon (1994), concludes that PRONASOL was mostly employed to "buy back opposition voters" – specifically, those who defected to the PRD – a strategy that is

[1] For analysis of the provision of private benefits within the PRONASOL program, see Magaloni et al. (forthcoming).

[2] Together with Diaz-Cayeros and Estévez, I am currently involved in writing a series of articles about PRONASOL. The data I employ in this chapter, and many of the theoretical insights, come from this project. Our papers written thus far are cited in the bibliography.

[3] The total overall figure obtained from our dataset is smaller than what the government presented as total PRONASOL expenditures, normally disaggregated by state. These government-reported figures tend to be overestimations of actual expenditures, possibly because government intermediaries illegally appropriated some of the program's funds.

consistent with swing-voter models of distributive politics (Lindbeck and Weibull, 1987; Dixit and Londregan, 1996). Alternatively, in his dissertation work on municipal-level allocations from PRONASOL to 237 municipalities in Jalisco and Michoacán, Hiskey (1999) claims that PRONASOL's funds were disproportionately targeted to places were the PRI received more votes. He concludes that the program was motivated by a "reward the loyal municipalities" strategy, which is consistent with core-voter models of distributive politics (Cox and McCubbins, 1986).

The central theoretical claim of this chapter is that the logic of the geographic allocation of discretionary expenditures by a hegemonic party under threat cannot be fully accounted for using existing models of distributive politics, which were developed for democratic systems. Core-voter models envision a rather naive incumbent party that wastes resources rewarding its most loyal followers, those who are likely to support the hegemonic party no matter what. Swing-voter models rightly argue that the incumbent party should invest resources where the electoral payoff, in terms of making a difference between voters supporting the incumbent or the opposition, is largest. However, since there is no "punishment regime" in these models, they generate the paradoxical result that voters who elect the opposition by small margins end up being rewarded, which in a hegemonic party regime would generate the wrong type of incentive, that is, reward defection. In swing-voter models, there is no punishment because "swing voters" are treated equally, regardless of whether they elect the incumbent or the opposition.

My approach stresses that an electoral monopoly under threat will follow an "entry-deterrence strategy." First, the party will react in an unforgiving fashion toward defectors by withdrawing funds from those municipalities that elect opposition representatives. Second, the ruling party will disproportionately invest in its supporters who can more credibly threaten to exit, rather than its most loyal followers, who are likely to support the party regardless. In the context of Mexico's municipal elections, this means that the PRI should invariably punish municipalities governed by the opposition and simultaneously divert more funds to those loyal municipalities that are more vulnerable to opposition entry. The entry-deterrence logic is consistent with case studies that underscore the difficulties opposition municipalities and states faced in attempting to govern with fewer fiscal transfers (Rodríguez, 1995; Rodríguez and Ward, 1995).

Before I proceed to explore the political logic of PRONASOL, something must be said about the institutional context. The political logic of discretionary expenditure that I propose presupposes the existence of multiple layers of government, as occurs in federalism. The central government controls the lion's share of the money, however. By financing local PRI governments and punishing opposition ones, therefore, the PRI could seriously disrupt a local opposition government's ability to govern and perform well and undermine their opposition party-building. PRONASOL was one of the most important federal programs providing additional federal funds to the municipalities. To be eligible, the municipality and the state had to match federal funds, although the federal government retained ultimate control of their distribution.

The chapter is organized as follows. The first section presents the context in which PRONASOL was introduced. The second section presents the main theoretical and empirical debates about PRONASOL's political logic. The third section presents my empirical analysis of the program. The fourth section analyses the political effectiveness of PRONASOL. The final section presents my conclusions.

Failing Corporatism and the Introduction of PRONASOL

Patronage politics played a key role in sustaining the PRI regime. The literature stresses that, in order to sustain its broad coalition of interests, the PRI relied on its corporatists wings, the CNC and the CTM, which had monopoly representation of two key socioeconomic sectors. The PRI could control and mobilize the support of peasants through a complex system of "land tenure arrangements (including the promise/threat of land expropriation and distribution under the terms of postrevolutionary agrarian reform legislation), government management of extensive credit and marketing facilities, and the hierarchical organization of rural producers (especially agrarian reforms beneficiaries) through 'official' party-affiliated organizations that reached up from the local ejido leadership to the national party structures" (Middlebrook, 2004: 32). Labor was brought into the alliance by providing economic growth and employment opportunities, raising real wages, and expanding social welfare benefits. The CTM also controlled significant material benefits (e.g., access to government housing and health care), and it exercised strong administrative controls on labor participation through selective repression (Middlebrook, 2004: 32).

There is also consensus in the literature that the efficacy of this "social pact" and the party's corporatist wing began to erode in the 1980s and 1990s with the economic recession and the market-oriented reforms that followed. These polices implied a fundamental restructuring of the traditional alliance of interests. The shift to market-led development significantly weakened the CTM's bargaining power, as well as that of the labor movement overall, and its mobilizational capacity (Bensusán, 2004). Workers, as I showed in the previous chapter, were the biggest losers during the era of structural adjustment. One of the consequences was that the CTM, as Middlebrook (1995: 293–4) notes, failed to deliver votes for the PRI in the 1988 presidential elections. The reform of the land-tenure arrangements introduced by Carlos Salinas in 1992, which declared land reform to be over and allowed for the privatization of the communally owned *ejido*, as well as for the penetration of agribusiness into the countryside, weakened the state's ability to buy off the "green vote." "By greatly reducing the regulatory intervention of state officials in ejido's and agrarian communities' internal affairs, the economic reform process eroded the political controls over peasants" (Middlebrook, 2004: 33).

The consequences for the PRI's survival of the shift in Mexico's development strategy became evident in the 1988 elections, when there was massive electoral fraud and the ruling party came close to losing.[4] To respond to this challenge, Mexico's political elite designed an ingenious program, the National Solidarity Program, which permitted the elite to reconstruct a patronage network for the PRI across the country, particularly with low-income individuals and localities. PRONASOL sought to establish new relationships outside the failing corporatist mechanisms and state bureaucracies. As Dresser (1994) explains, the economic crisis "affected most systems of representation and the economic functions associated with them; as a result, their traditional members were recast by the state elite essentially as consumers of PRONASOL's benefits – electricity, scholarships, paved streets – instead of beneficiaries of traditional state protection in the form of wage increases, subsides, and agrarian reform" (147).

PRONASOL was at least in part a demand-driven program for poverty relief. It targeted funds directly to municipalities based on proposals from community organizations and municipal governments. In order for a project to receive PRONASOL funds, matching grants were always required from state and municipal governments, along with resources provided in-kind by the recipient community. PRONASOL deliberately bypassed the traditional corporatist arrangements and the preexisting entrenched bureaucracies. The Carlos Salinas government centralized allocation decisions

[4] The 1988 electoral fraud will be explored in more detail in Chapter 8.

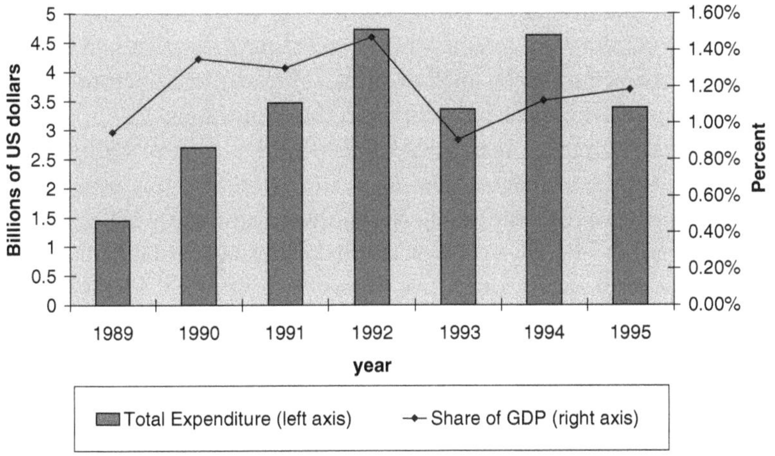

Figure 4.1. Size of PRONASOL.

under the control of the executive and sought to establish a more direct link between the center and the localities, making use of local program administrators and state officials.

PRONASOL soon became the cornerstone of the government's social policy. Its resources represented, on average, 1.18 percent of GDP each year (Magaloni et al., forthcoming). Figure 4.1 graphs total PRONASOL expenditures per year both absolutely and as a percentage of each year's GDP. There is ample agreement in the literature that PRONASOL's objective was more to serve the political survival imperatives of the PRI than to alleviate poverty (Collier, 1992; Molinar and Weldon, 1994; Dresser, 1994; Bruhn, 1996 and 1997, among others). Many analysts even claim that the PRI's landslide victory in the 1991 midterm elections should be largely attributed to PRONASOL (Dresser, 1991). However, there is considerable debate in the literature regarding how PRONASOL actually worked. The literature also reflects disagreement about the political effectiveness of PRONASOL. The terms of this debate are explored below.

The Mechanics of PRONASOL: Theoretical and Empirical Controversies in the Literature

Who benefited from PRONASOL's funds? Were these funds employed to reward loyal followers or to buy back voters who had defected to the opposition? Is there evidence that the PRI employed these funds to punish municipalities that defected to the opposition? Or were these funds instead employed to target swing municipalities, including those that had elected opposition representatives by small margins? The existing literature has not been able to provide conclusive answers to these questions.

The seminal empirical analysis of PRONASOL is that of Molinar and Weldon (1994). They analyze state-level allocations for this program in 1990. The main goal of their article was to show that PRONASOL allocations were *political*. Their most critical empirical findings can be summarized as follows: poverty shows a negative impact on state-level PRONASOL allocations; the PRI spent *less* in states where Cárdenas got more votes in 1988. When the Cárdenas vote is multiplied by a dummy for states holding gubernatorial elections in 1991, the result is that the PRI spent *more* where the Cardenistas got more votes in 1988. The PAN vote share in 1988 shows no statistically significant effect, but the interactive term PAN vote multiplied by gubernatorial election is negative, which means that among the states holding gubernatorial elections in 1991, the PRI spent less in PANista strongholds.

Despite the fact that these authors deserve ample credit for being the first to attempt to test the mechanics of PRONASOL statistically, their work exhibits several shortcomings. As noted earlier, the regressions are carried out at the inappropriate level of analysis, because PRONASOL allocations were at the municipal level, not the state level. From state-level data, they conclude that poverty is decisively not driving PRONASOL allocations. However, when municipal-level data is employed, it turns out that more was spent in poorer localities (see Hiskey, 1999, for evidence on Michoacán and Jalisco; for evidence from the entire country, see Diaz-Cayeros et al., 2000, and the following discussion).

Judging from these results, it is all but impossible to provide an answer to the key question that motivates this chapter: who benefited from the PRONASOL funds? The authors offer two provocative speculations about the implications of their results. On the one hand, they suggest that "it appears that there was an effort on the part of PRONASOL planners to spend more money in areas that had supported the FDN [the National Democratic Front, led by Cárdenas, which eventually became the PRD] in 1988. This strategy may be one of buying back defectors" (131). On the other hand, they speculate that "PRONASOL planners allocated more funds in states where the opposition has gained strength, but that those funds are locally distributed more to PRI supporters than to opposition sympathizers" (131). Without disaggregated data and careful econometric analysis, it is impossible to adjudicate between these alternative political rationales for PRONASOL allocations.

The second major attempt to assess the political determinants of PRONASOL empirically is that of Bruhn (1996). She also employs state-level data. Her dependent variables are per capita PRONASOL allocations for 1989 and 1990 and an ingenious measure of the "reorientation" of social spending, which compares spending under the regional development line of the previous administration's federal budget (Ramo XXVI) with spending through PRONASOL in 1989 and 1990. Her empirical results can be summarized as follows. For the model on per capita state-level allocations, only the PRI vote share in 1988 is positive and statistically significant at the 95 percent confidence level. None of the socioeconomic controls are significant in this first model. For the model examining the reorientation of social spending, the left vote share in 1988 is positive, although it is statistically significant at the 90 percent confidence level only. As the author carefully points out, the overall explanatory power of these models is extremely low (R2 of only .07 and .09, respectively), which means that it is not possible to draw any decisive conclusions from them.

Hiskey (1999, 2003) represents the third major attempt to assess the political logic of PRONASOL. Unlike the previous authors, he employs data for the appropriate level of analysis, namely, the municipality. However, one limitation of his work is that it studies PRONASOL's allocations only in two states, Michoacán and Jalisco. Hiskey's main hypothesis is that PRONASOL was informed by a "reward the loyal" strategy where "more support for the PRI in a municipality translates in a positive linear fashion into more PRONASOL money" (64). He also claims that the "reward the loyal" strategy is backward-oriented, with the incumbent choosing to reward *after the elections* those voters who remained loyal, but doing nothing beforehand to influence voters who might be tempted to defect in the coming elections. This backward-looking strategy is clearly stated in the following terms: "knowing that PRONASOL funds were used as rewards to loyal municipalities, the political variable [PRI vote] should emerge as most significant in the period immediately following an election (Hiskey, 1999: 77).

Hiskey's main empirical results can be summarized as follows: he finds both for Jalisco and Michoacán that the higher the PRI vote share in the municipal elections taking place during the period, the greater the funds allocated through PRONASOL.[5] The author offers systematic evidence that the PRI withdrew funds from municipalities that elected opposition municipal presidents only for the single case of Michoacán in 1993. He concludes that "unlike Jalisco, where a general pattern of rewarding the loyal emerged in PRONASOL spending patterns, PRD municipalities in Michoacán were singled out and consistently denied access to PRONASOL funding" (107).[6]

Hiskey's (1999) results should be taken with caution because they suffer form a "simultaneity" problem. As Schady (2000) discusses, the simultaneity problem emerges from using the parties' vote shares to account for allocation decisions. This problem arises because electoral outcomes are in part the product of expenditures during the previous period(s). Schady discuses the simultaneity bias in the following terms: per capita expenditures in province p at time t, Exp_{pt}, are the product of the outcome of an election in province p at time t−1, $Elec_{pt-1}$; a vector of other variables, $Z1_{pt}$; and an error term, ε_{pt}. If the error term is autocorrelated over time, it can be expressed as $\varepsilon_{pt} = p\varepsilon_{pt} - 1 + Vpt$, where here p stands for the autocorrelation coefficient.

Expenditures can then be expressed as:

$$Exp_{pt} = \alpha + \beta Elec_{pt-1} + \delta Z1_{pt} + p\varepsilon_{pt-1} + Vpt \tag{4.1}$$

Politicians attempt to manipulate expenditures because they expect to influence the outcome of elections, such that:

$$Elec_{pt} = \chi + \gamma Exp_{pt} + \eta 1 + \eta Z2_{pt} + Wpt, \tag{4.2}$$

where $\eta Z2_{pt}$ is a vector of variables that affect election outcomes, and Wpt is the error term. Schady (2000) explains that if both equations hold, estimating the parameter β by OLS will produce results that are biased and inconsistent. "Since there may well be serial correlation and an effect of expenditures on elections, studies that disregard the possibility of simultaneity must be treated with caution" (298)

[5] Hiskey reports that the correlation between the PRI vote share and PRONASOL is linear. When a quadratic term for PRI vote is introduced, "none of the variables were significant" (75, n. 33). This means that, according to his results, more PRONASOL funds were sent to municipalities in which the PRI won by a landslide.

[6] Hiskey does not explain why he did not include dummies for municipalities controlled by the opposition in any of the Jalisco regressions, or in the regressions for Michoacán for other years or for total expenditures.

The standard solution to the simultaneity problem is the use of instrumental variables. The solution is not simple, because one must find a variable that affects elections and does not shape expenditure decisions. The Mexican case offers an ideal solution because it is possible to treat the local election results prior to the 1988 presidential elections as exogenous to the model. Indeed, the 1988 presidential elections represented a tremendous shock to the political system; voting patterns were dramatically transformed after those elections, because the PRI split and a new opposition party, the PRD, was formed. Politicians instituted PRONASOL as a response to the 1988 debacle, and, as I discuss below, capital expenditures per municipality were powerfully influenced by the results of the 1988 presidential elections. Since the municipal elections taking place after 1988 were all influenced by PRONASOL's expenditures, electoral returns for the period 1988–94 cannot be legitimately conceived as exogenous. However, the municipal elections of 1985, 1986, and 1987 were not affected by PRONASOL, and this program was not decided on the basis of what transpired prior to 1988. Below I employ the results of the municipal elections prior to 1988 as instruments in order to solve the simultaneity problem.

The Political Logic of PRONASOL

Model Specification, Independent Variables, and Hypotheses

To assess the political logic of PRONASOL's allocations, I use GLS maximum likelihood estimations of the per capita allocations in the more than 2,400 municipalities from 1989 to 1994. One lag of the dependent variable (Lag) is used to control for serial correlation. The dependent variable is the natural log of total per capita expenditures. Since PRONASOL was a poverty relief program, any model assessing the determinants of expenditures needs to include appropriate independent variables for municipal-level socioeconomic characteristics – most importantly, the level of development. Since these variables do not vary each year, a fixed-effects GLS estimate is *not* appropriate, because it would drop them. To control for local idiosyncrasies, however, I add dummies for each of the states rather than for each of the municipalities.[7]

The reason for using state-level dummies is that allocations in the PRONASOL program were partly driven by state-level idiosyncrasies – in

[7] I employ STATA's *xtreg* procedure.

particular, the political connections between the state governor and the central government, on the one hand, and the political clout of the state-level delegate of PRONASOL, sent by the federal government, and his particular political network of civic associations and politicians in the state, on the other (Kaufman and Trejo, 1997). By adding dummies for each of the states, I control for these and other state-level idiosyncrasies for which I lack appropriate measures.

I employ three sets of independent variables, testing PRONASOL allocations as a function of poverty, budget constraints, and electoral politics. The variables are the following:

To control for the level of development (*develop*), I employ the deprivation index from the Consejo Nacional de Población (CONAPO). This index is constructed using a factor analysis of the 1990 census variables commonly associated with deprivation (illiteracy; lack of elementary school; dwellings lacking access to drinking water, sanitation, and electricity; density of inhabitants; quality of construction; population living in rural localities; and workers earning less than two minimum wages). The index was rescaled to take values on a positive scale from 0 to 5. The rescaling was carried out in order to introduce a quadratic term that tests whether development has a curvilinear relationship with the dependent variable. Since PRONASOL was a poverty relief program, the expectation is that, ceteris paribus, more funds should have been allocated to poorer municipalities. The effect of the deprivation index should thus be positive. If there is a curvilinear effect of development and the quadratic term for the deprivation index (*developsq*) is negative, this would mean that municipalities at middle levels of development received more per capita funds and that there was an urban bias in PRONASOL.

To control for the size of the municipality (*size*), I employ the natural log of population. Data comes from an interpolation of the 1990 census and the 1995 vote count as provided by INEGI. Since there is a high fixed cost to introducing public works, these should be more expensive in per capita terms in smaller localities. The expectation is thus that smaller localities should receive more funds per capita.

Financial restrictions must play a key role, and these are highly political in Mexico. I employ revenue sharing transfers *(sharing funds)* and local tax collection *(taxes)* as controls for other funds that may be complements to or substitutes for PRONASOL funds. Both variables are measured in logged per capita terms. Revenue sharing distributions from the federal government to the states are governed by formulas, and in this sense they are not discretionary. However, after the funds arrive in the states, governors possess a great deal of discretion to distribute them to the municipalities. My expectation is that revenue-sharing funds will complement PRONASOL projects.

If this is correct, and if the effects of the political variables are as expected, this would mean that municipalities controlled by the opposition are net losers in the overall system of federal transfers, receiving less in PRONASOL funds and smaller amounts of revenue-sharing funds, but collecting more in taxes. Indeed, Diaz-Cayeros (2004) has demonstrated that, controlling for levels of development, PRI governments collected less in taxes than opposition governments because the latter were compelled to collect more of their own resources, since they tended to receive less in federal transfers. I thus expect local taxes to have a negative impact on the dependent variable, meaning that the more taxes a municipality can collect, the fewer PRONASOL funds it will receive.

I identify each municipality by the partisan affiliation of the municipal government. The variables are dummies identifying the municipalities governed by the PRD, the PAN, and the PRI *(PANgov, PRDgov,* and *PRIgov)* in a given year. These are the most consequential variables for testing the "punishment regime," namely, that the PRI punished opposition municipalities by withdrawing funds from them. Municipal presidents typically take office the year following an election, although this varies according to the specific electoral calendar. Our database codes for the precise year in which the new municipal administrations took office.

Since governors played an important role as intermediaries between the federal government and the municipalities, I add a dummy for the municipal governments controlled by the PAN within states controlled by a PANista governor (*yuxtapan*). During this period, as discussed in Chapter 2, three governorships were controlled by the PAN – Baja California beginning in 1989, Guanajuato beginning in 1989, and Chihuahua beginning in 1992. Since governors had a say in allocation decisions, exercised through the matching funds they would draw from the state and municipal coffers, I expect that opposition governors will seek to reward opposition municipalities in their states. This variable should thus have a positive coefficient.

I also employ the margin of victory in the election, namely, the vote share of the largest winning party minus the vote share of the first losing party. To solve the simultaneity problem discussed earlier, an instrumental approach is necessary. I thus employ the *predicted margin of victory* (*marginhat*) coming from a first-stage estimation, where the margin of victory in the coming municipal election is the dependent variable. The estimation employs as an instrumental variable the margin of victory in the municipal elections preceding the 1988 debacle and the initiation of PRONASOL (namely, those of 1985, 1986, and 1987). The other independent variables in the model are the same as those employed in the model for total expenditures. My expectation is that, contrary to Hiskey (1999), the PRI should spend *less* in municipalities that it expects to win by landslides after controlling for the identity of the municipal presidents. The effect of this variable should thus be negative.

I test the hypothesis that the PRI sent *more* resources to municipalities where it won with higher vote shares against my hypothesis that, once corrected for the simultaneity problem, the PRI should spend *less* in the municipalities that it expects to win by a landslide. To do so, I employ the predicted PRI vote share *(Prihat)* in the corresponding municipal elections. As with *marghat*, the estimation employs the PRI's vote share from pre-1988 municipal elections (namely, those of 1985, 1986 and 1987) as an instrumental variable.

I also use dummies for the electoral cycles (*Elec fed* and *Elec mun)* to test whether the timing of federal and municipal elections shapes allocation decisions. The electoral calendar in Mexico implies that there are municipal elections every year. Federal elections took place in 1991 and 1994. I expect to find a positive effect for these variables, meaning that the PRI increases PRONASOL expenditures as elections approach.

Finally, I employ the vote shares for the 1988 presidential elections *(Card88*, *PAN88*, and *PRI88)*, which are the percentage of votes obtained by the Cardenistas, the PAN, and the PRI in the 1988 presidential elections, disaggregated to the municipal level. This variable was extremely hard to obtain, since information about the actual results of the controversial 1988 elections is elusive.[8] My hypothesis is that the party's municipal-level vote shares in the 1988 presidential elections should be a key electoral consideration in making PRONASOL allocation decisions. In particular, this variable allows me to test whether PRONASOL planners allocated more funds to municipalities where the Cardenistas were strong in 1988 and hence more vulnerable to an opposition victory in future municipal elections.

[8] Federico Estévez obtained the information for our joint project from a prominent public official who had access to the PRI's data and who has asked to remain anonymous.

I interact the parties' vote shares in 1988 with the dummy for federal elections *(fed*Card88, fed*PAN88,* and *fed*PRI88)* and with the dummy for municipal elections *(mun*Card88, mun*PAN88,* and *mun*PRI88).* If these variables are significant, it would mean that PRONASOL planners employed the parties' vote shares in the 1988 elections in making allocation decisions, both in municipal and in federal elections.

Explaining PRONASOL: Alternative Hypotheses

To test my hypotheses against the existing alternative hypotheses, I proceed in several steps. First, I begin with a model that includes only the parties' vote shares in 1988 and their interactive terms with federal and municipal elections. My goal is to assess whether the PRI devoted more resources to places where it saw its hegemonic position threatened by the Cardenistas. If the evidence shows that the Cardenista support is positive and significant, this would contradict Hiskey's (1999) claim that PRONASOL was simply a "reward the loyal supporters" strategy.

Second, to further adjudicate between the "reward the loyal supporters" strategy and my approach stressing that the PRI rewarded those voters who were most likely to defect, I present two models, one employing the PRI municipal vote share and the other the predicted PRI vote share, drawn from the instrumental variable model. My goal is to demonstrate that without the instrumental approach, one would reach the same incorrect conclusion as Hiskey (1999), namely, that the PRI spent most where it received the most votes. But once the simultaneity problem is addressed with the instrumental variable approach, the conclusion is that the PRI sent fewer resources to places where it won with higher vote shares.

Third, I present a final model to test my hypotheses about the entry-deterrence logic of PRONASOL allocations, according to which the PRI reacted in an unforgiving fashion by withdrawing funds from municipalities controlled by opposition municipal presidents and diverting funds to the loyal municipalities that were more vulnerable. This model adds the dummies identifying the opposition-held municipal governments, the predicted margin of victory in the coming municipal election, and the parties' vote shares in the presidential elections of 1988. All of the abovementioned models include the same socioeconomic and financial independent variables plus dummies for each of the states. To simplify the exposition, I do not present the coefficients for the state dummies and do not discuss the results for the socioeconomic and financial variables until I present the fully specified model.

Effects of the 1988 Presidential Elections on PRONASOL Funds Table 4.1 presents the results of the first models assessing the effects of the 1988 presidential elections, controlling for levels of development, population, and the financial variables. The coefficients for *mun*card88* is positive and statistically significant, which indicates that the PRI spent more in municipal elections where the Cardenistas had been a stronger threat to the ruling party in the 1988 presidential elections. The coefficient *fed*card88* is also positive, although significant only at the 90 percent confidence level. This suggests that the PRI also assigned more funds in the federal elections of 1991 and 1994 to the municipalities where Cárdenas was stronger in 1988. These results give a solid indication that PRONASOL planners employed vote returns from the federal elections of 1988 to map areas of discontent against the PRI, and that they used this information to increase their vote-buying efforts in the subsequent local and federal elections as a way to halt the deterioration of the party's base of support. The results also show that the PRI spent less in the municipal and federal elections in municipalities where the PAN received more votes in the 1988 presidential elections (the coefficients *mun*pan88* and *fed*pan88* are negative and statistically significant).

Thus, Molinar and Weldon's (1994) hypothesis that PRONASOL was disproportionately targeted to areas where the Cardenistas were strong has a great deal of empirical merit. PRONASOL was initiated as a direct response to the PRI's debacle in the 1988 presidential election, which the Cardenistas claim to have won. However, as I will show, once election results for states are disaggregated into those from their constituent municipalities, it turns out that the PRI was extremely careful not to disburse funds to municipalities that were already in the hands of the opposition, *including the PRD*. Thus, the results of the 1988 federal elections were employed to map areas of voter discontent and to target vulnerable municipalities that could defect in the coming municipal electoral cycle.

PRONASOL was, to a large extent, designed to convince voters in vulnerable municipalities not to invest their partisan loyalties in the PRD. However, if after the 1988 presidential elections voters remained, so to speak, "stubborn enough" to elect an opposition municipal president, including one from the PRD, the PRI would punish them in order to create a demonstration effect.

Table 4.1. *Effect of votes shares in the 1988 presidential elections on PRONASOL's municipal-level per capita funds, 1989–94*

Model 1			Model 2		
Independent Variables	Coefficient	Std. Err.		Coefficient	Std. Err.
lag exp	0.25***	0.01	*lag exp*	0.26***	0.01
sharing funds	0.11***	0.01	*sharing funds*	0.11***	0.01
taxes	0.00	0.01	*taxes*	0.00	0.01
develop	0.20***	0.05	*develop*	0.23***	0.05
developsq	−0.02***	0.01	*developsq*	−0.02***	0.01
size	−0.16***	0.01	*size*	−0.15***	0.01
PAN88	0.05	0.13	*PRI88*	0.05	0.07
Card88	−0.15*	0.08	*elec mun*	0.07	0.06
Elec mun	−0.13***	0.03	*elec fed*	0.13***	0.05
Elec fed	0.12***	0.03	*mun**pri88*	−0.23***	0.08
*mun**pan88*	−0.36**	0.16	*fed**pri88*	−0.02	0.07
*mun**card88*	0.45***	0.10			
*fed**pan88*	−0.44***	0.15			
*fed**card88*	0.15*	0.09			
constant	4.68	0.19	*constant*	4.52	0.19
N = 9,549			N = 9,879		
No. groups = 2,237			No. groups = 2,340		
Log likelihood = 10590.36			Log likelihood = 10964.69		
LR chi2(42) = 5086.79			LR chi2(42) = 5165.79		
Prob > chi2 = .0000			Prob > chi2 = .0000		

* significant at the 90% confidence level; ** significant at the 95% confidence level; *** significant at the 99% confidence level. The dependent variable is expressed in logarithmic terms. Coefficients come from a random effects ml regression. Dummies for states were employed but are not displayed. *Lag exp* is the lagged dependent variable. *Sharing funds* is the logarithm of per capita revenue sharing transfers of the corresponding municipality. *Taxes* is the logarithm of per capita municipal taxes. *Develop* is a development municipal-level index, and *developsq* is the index squared. *Size* is the natural log of population of the corresponding municipality. *PRI88*, *PAN88*, and *Card88* are vote shares in the 1988 presidential elections, disaggregated at the municipal level. *Elec mun* and *Elec fed* are dummies indicating whether a municipal election or a federal election took place that year, respectively. *Mun**pri88*, *mun**pan88*, and *mun**card88* are the interactive terms of *Elec mun* and *PRI88*, *PAN88*, and *Card88*, respectively; *fed**pri88*, *fed**pan88*, and *fed**card88* are the interactive terms of *Elec fed* and *PAN88* and *Card88*.

These findings contradict Hiskey's (1999) conclusion that more resources were targeted to places that received higher PRI vote shares. As shown in Model 2 of Table 4.1, the PRI actually withdrew funds from municipalities where the PRI was strongest, according to the 1988 presidential vote shares (the coefficient for *mun**pri88* is negative and statistically significant).

Table 4.2. *The simultaneity problem: PRI municipal vote shares and PRONASOL municipal-level per capita funds, 1989–94*

Model 3			Model 4		
Independent Variables	Coefficient	Std. Err.	Independent variables	Coefficient	Std. Err.
lag exp	0.23***	0.01	*lag exp*	0.23***	0.01
sharing funds	0.10***	0.01	*sharing funds*	0.10***	0.02
taxes	0.00	0.01	*taxes*	0.00	0.01
develop	0.21***	0.05	*develop*	0.21***	0.05
developsq	−0.02***	0.01	*developsq*	−0.02**	0.01
size	−0.16***	0.01	*size*	−0.17***	0.01
yuxtapan	0.24***	0.11	*yuxtapan*	0.24**	0.11
Elec mun	−0.07***	0.02	*Elec mun*	0.23***	0.07
Elec fed	0.09***	0.02	*Elec fed*	0.09***	0.02
PRIvote	0.09**	0.04	*PRIvotehat*	−0.46***	0.10
time	0.06***	0.01	*time*	0.05***	0.01
constant	4.63***	0.20	*constant*	4.82***	0.20
N = 9,491			N = 9,059		
No. groups = 2,328			No. groups = 2,282		
Log likelihood = 10476.844			Log likelihood = 1004.386		
LR chi2(42) = 5134.06			Prob > chi2 = .0000		
LR chi2(42) = 4905.08			Prob > chi2 = .0000		

* significant at the 90% confidence level; ** significant at the 95% confidence level; *** significant at the 99% confidence level. Coefficients come from a random effects ml regression. Dummies for states were employed but are not displayed. *Lag exp* is the lagged dependent variable. *Sharing funds* is the logarithm of per capita revenue sharing transfers of the corresponding municipality. *Taxes* is municipal per capita taxes. *Develop* is the rescaled CONAPO deprivation municipal-level index. *Developsq* is the index squared. *Size* is the natural log of population of the corresponding municipality. *Yuxtapan* is a dummy for municipalities controlled by the PAN in a state controlled by a PANista governor. *Elec mun* and *Elec fed* are dummies indicating whether a municipal election or a federal election took place that year, respectively. *PRIvote* is the PRI's vote share in the corresponding municipal election. *PRIvotehat* is the instrumented PRI's vote share. *Time* is a time trend.

Vote Shares and the Simultaneity Problem Table 4.2 presents the results of two additional models. Model 3 employs municipal-level vote returns to account for PRONASOL funds. As explained earlier, this strategy implies a serious simultaneity problem. Model 4 corrects for this simultaneity problem with an instrumental-variable approach, employing the predicted PRI vote shares using a model where the "instrument" is given by electoral returns from the municipal elections of 1985, 1986, and 1987 plus the rest of the independent variables. The models also include the dummies for federal and municipal elections, to test for my hypothesis that the PRI was forward-looking (increasing spending prior to elections) as opposed to backward-looking (simply rewarding loyal voters after elections, as in Hiskey, 1999). The models also add a dummy for municipalities controlled by the PAN in PANista states *(yuxtapan)* and a time trend (*time*) to control for the fact that PRONASOL spending increased through the years, while the PRI vote in municipal elections tended to erode in a secular mode through time.

There is a direct connection between PRI vote shares and the municipal election dummies (*Elec mun*). When the PRI vote share is zero, it indicates that there was no election that year. Thus, the results of these variables should be read jointly, where a positive vote share means that it should be multiplied by one plus whatever the value of the coefficient for vote share is.

The model that does not solve for the simultaneity problem, Model 3, indicates that there was more PRONASOL spending is municipalities that had higher PRI vote shares, which is what Hiskey (1999) finds. However, after correcting for the simultaneity problem, Model 4 shows that, as expected, the PRI tended to spend less where it expected to get more votes. The coefficient for *PRIvotehat* is negative and statistically significant, which indicates that the PRI spent more in highly contested elections, not where it expected to win by a landslide. The dummy for municipal election (*Elec mun*) also becomes positive, meaning that the PRI spent more in municipalities that conducted elections. The reason why the dummy variable for municipal races is negative in Model 3 and positive in Model 4 is that the variable for PRI vote shares in Model 3 captures the effect of increased spending in municipalities that have elections as part of the endogeneity problem.

The results of the instrumental variable approach are consistent with those presented in Models 1 and 2. These results provide solid evidence that a simple "reward the loyal supporters" strategy was not what PRONASOL was about. What remains to be shown is that the PRI employed an entry-deterrence strategy, reacting in an unforgiving fashion by withdrawing funds from municipalities controlled by opposition municipal presidents and diverting funds to those loyal municipalities that were more vulnerable.

An Entry-Deterrence Logic of PRONASOL Expenditures Table 4.3 presents the results of a final model that tests the entry-deterrence logic. All the political independent variables of interest behave as expected. The results can be summarized as follows. First, unlike most of the conventional

Table 4.3. *The PRONASOL entry-deterrence strategy*

	Model 5	
Independent Variables	*Coefficient*	*Std. Err.*
Lag exp	0.22***	0.01
Sharing funds	0.09***	0.02
Taxes	0.00	0.01
Develop	0.16***	0.05
Developsq	−0.01	0.01
Size	−0.17***	0.01
PRDgov	−0.11**	0.05
PANgov	−0.13**	0.06
yuxtapan	0.33***	0.12
marghat	−0.33***	0.09
Card88	−0.15*	0.09
PAN88	0.01	0.14
Elec fed	0.10***	0.03
Elec mun	0.02	0.06
*Fed*Card88*	0.16*	0.09
*Fed*PAN88*	−0.41***	0.16
*Mun*Card88*	0.40***	0.11
*Mun*PAN88*	−0.46***	0.18
timetrend	0.06***	0.01
constant	4.97***	0.21
N = 8,574		
No. groups = 2,169		
Log likelihood = 9485.93		
LR chi2(42) = 4763.67		
Prob > chi2 = .0000		

* significant at the 90% confidence level; ** significant at the 95% confidence level; *** significant at the 99% confidence level. Coefficients come from a random effects ml regression. Dummies for states were employed but are not displayed. See notes to Tables 4.2 and 4.3 for meaning of variables.

wisdom that argues that PRONASOL was not allocated to the poor, my results demonstrate that, ceteris paribus, the poorest municipalities got the most resources. Unlike the previous models, where the quadratic of the development index was negative and significant, in this last fully specified model this variable is not significant, which means that after controlling for the political variables, there is no evidence that more PRONASOL funding went to municipalities at middle levels of development.

Second, as expected, PRONASOL funds were disproportionately targeted to municipalities that received more federal transfers in the form of revenue shares. This suggests that PRONASOL projects were more likely to be sent to places already benefiting from higher federal transfers within the revenue-sharing system, most notably those controlled by PRI municipal presidents, as Diaz-Cayeros et al. (2004) demonstrate. However, there is no evidence that fewer resources were sent to municipalities that collected more taxes.

Third, with respect to the political logic of PRONASOL, the results provide ample evidence for my hypotheses. As expected, the PRI spent more in vulnerable municipalities where the Cardenistas had been stronger in the 1988 presidential elections. The variables *fed*Card88* and *mun*Card88* are both positive and significant, yet the magnitude of the effect (and the statistical significance) of the *mun*Card88* variable is much larger. The variables *mun*PAN88* and *fed*PAN88* are both negative and highly significant. These results thus confirm the hypothesis that the PRI focused on preventing its supporters from further defecting to the PRD rather than to the PAN. The PRI, in fact, seems to have considered PANista strongholds as sure losses, and thus chose to abandon them altogether by withdrawing funds from them. Instead, the PRI probably considered those municipalities where the Cardenistas had been strongest in 1988 as volatile places where, for the coming cycle of municipal and federal elections, resources could actually make a difference between the municipalities' choosing to remain loyal to the incumbent or electing an opposition municipal president.

To defend its electoral hegemony, the PRI targeted more funds to municipalities where the Cardenistas were strong in the 1988 presidential election. But if voters were daring enough to elect an opposition municipal president, *including one from the PRD*, the PRI punished them by withdrawing funds from their municipality. The coefficients for *PRDgov* and *PANgov* are both negative and significant, which provides solid evidence for the "punishment regime," through which the PRI withdrew funds from opposition municipalities in order to undermine opposition party building. My results are the first to provide systematic econometric evidence about the "punishment regime," using expenditure data from PRONASOL for the entire country.[9]

[9] Existing empirical analyses of the "punishment regime" are at best fragmentary. In her analysis of Michoacán, Bruhn (1997) finds that PRONASOL funds did reach the opposition, but in ways that ensured that these parties could not profit from them. However, Gershberg

The variable *yuxtapan* is significant and of the expected sign: if a municipality controlled by the PAN is in a state where the governor is also a PANista, the results show that, ceteris paribus, that municipality received more funds. These results indicate that despite ample and often well-grounded criticism of PRONASOL's extreme centralization (e.g., Bailey, 1994), the program must necessarily be understood in the context of Mexico's federalism. Although key decisions were made at the federal level and by the president, governors played a decisive role in how these funds eventually were distributed.

The predicted margin of victory in the municipal election *(marghat)* also performs as expected. After controlling for the identity of the municipal presidents, the PRI assigned *less funding* to the municipalities that it expected to win by landslides and more to those that were more contested. If the predicted PRI vote is used instead of the margins of victory, the same results hold: fewer resources are sent to municipalities that are expected to be won with higher vote shares.

With respect to the timing of expenditures, there is evidence that the PRI significantly increased PRONASOL expenditures prior to federal elections (*Elecfed*). For the average municipality, there was not a significant increase in expenditures prior to municipal elections. However, if these elections were expected to be highly competitive, expenditures systematically increased, as can be seen by the effect of *marghat*. All of these results confirm the hypothesis that PRONASOL planners were forward-looking rather than backward-looking.

Finally, it should be noted that although the effect of the lagged dependent variable is positive and significant, its magnitude is relatively small. What this means is that PRONASOL allocations were highly volatile from year to year, varying mostly according to the political imperatives of the PRI and the yearly challenges posed by the municipal and federal elections.

Obtaining an intuitive interpretation of the magnitude of the effects of the variables is not simple, because the dependent variable is expressed in logarithmic terms. To interpret the results, I evaluate expenditures at their mean value. Figure 4.2 presents the simulated effects of margin of victory by the partisan affiliation of the municipality. The figure compellingly

(1994) finds tentative evidence that opposition municipalities received fewer resources. His focus is PRONASOL educational investment. Hiskey (1999) finds that the PRI punished PRD municipalities in Michoacán but reports no similar evidence of punishment of PAN municipalities in Jalisco.

illustrates both the "punishment regime" and the strategic allocation of expenditures to loyal municipalities that are more vulnerable. On average, PAN-affiliated and PRD-affiliated municipalities received 17 and 14.5 pesos per capita less, respectively, than PRI-affiliated ones. As the margin of victory increases, so do per capita funds – every ten-percentage-point increase in the margin of victory decreases expenditures by 4.4 pesos per capita. This means that PRI-affiliated municipalities that were expected to be won by huge margins received thirty-five pesos per capita less than PRI-controlled municipalities that were expected to be won by very small margins.

Opposition bastions – namely, those opposition-affiliated municipalities that were expected to be lost by huge margins – received fewer funds than opposition-affiliated municipalities that could be recovered. Thus, the PRI devoted more resources to places where their expected return was highest, in the sense that they could make a difference between voters' remaining loyal or defecting to the opposition. One key difference between the swing-voter model and my results, however, is their differing accounts of how the PRI dealt with opposition municipalities. It can be seen in Figure 4.2 that an opposition-affiliated municipality that could be recovered easily (an expected margin of victory of zero) received around 120 pesos per capita, which is roughly the same as the expenditures allocated to a PRI-affiliated municipality that was expected to be won by 40 percentage points. The swing-voter model would predict, instead, that these "marginal" opposition municipalities should receive the most funds.

The average PAN-affiliated municipality was significantly punished. However, if the municipality was situated in one of the three PANista states, it received thirty-six pesos per capita more than a PAN-affiliated municipality situated in a PRIísta state. The results highlight the strategic value for the opposition of controlling a governorship. Although opposition governors needed cooperation from the federal government to get funds, once these were channeled to their states they could disproportionately divert them to their own municipalities. If, instead, opposition municipalities were found in PRIísta states, they would inevitably receive less funding, and be punished. The evidence about opposition states receiving less PRONASOL funding is mixed. The coefficients for the dummies of the three states governed by the PAN were 0.62 for Baja California, −0.25 for Chihuahua, and −0.34 for Guanajuato, all three significant at the 99 percent confidence level (the omitted category was Zacatecas). Thus, although Chihuahua and Guanajuato received less funding, Baja California was among the states

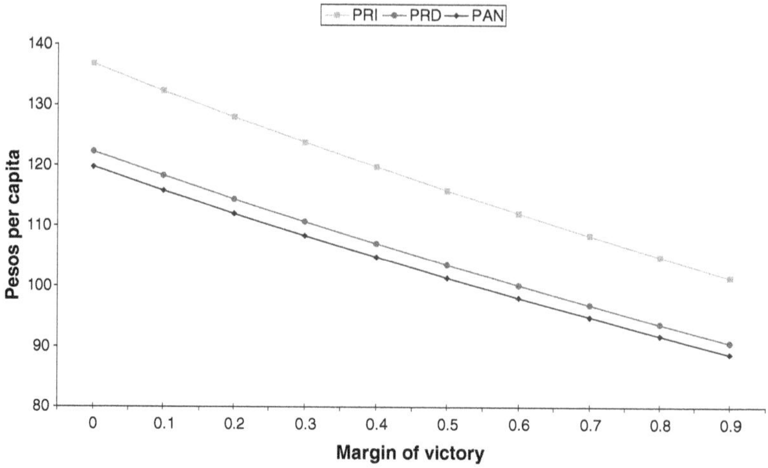

Figure 4.2. Simulation of effect of margin of victory by partisan affiliation of municipality.

which received the most (coefficients for states' dummies are not displayed). If a dummy for opposition states is added to the econometric models, there is no evidence that states governed by the PAN were systematically punished.

The Political Effectiveness of PRONASOL

Was PRONASOL politically effective from the PRI's point of view? Looking at aggregate vote returns, PRONASOL does seem to have been effective: in the 1991 midterm elections, support for the PRI jumped from 50 to 61 percent, while support for the Cardenistas fell from 31 to 8 percent. Fraud inflated the PRI vote returns in 1988, but the 1991 elections appear to have been relatively clean. Hence, the PRI's recovery in 1991 was even more impressive than these figures suggest. The PRI also won the 1994 presidential elections in a fraud-free election with 52 percent of the vote. Although much less impressive than its 1991 performance, the 1994 results were outstanding compared to the 1988 electoral debacle. A central question is whether PRONASOL had something to do with this or not.

The existing literature displays significant disagreement about the political effectiveness of PRONASOL. In their regression analyses of state-level vote swings from 1988 to 1991, Molinar and Weldon (1994) find that "in states where elections for governor were not scheduled in 1991, the PRI did somewhat *worse* in the federal elections for every extra peso spent on PRONASOL.... However, in states where gubernatorial elections were held, the sign of the slope becomes strongly positive and the PRI receive more votes with greater expenditures by Solidarity" (137). With respect to patterns of voting for the Cardenistas, the authors find that "there appears to be no effect of PRONASOL spending on the FDN vote" (139), whereas support for the PAN declines slightly in those states where gubernatorial elections took place in 1991 and more PRONASOL money was spent. Although they conclude that the program was effective, their results are counterintuitive, because in states where no gubernatorial elections were held in 1991, PRONASOL seems to have *hurt* the PRI.

Bruhn (1996) sharply disagrees with these authors' conclusions about PRONASOL's political effectiveness. Using a more straightforward model specification and defining the dependent variable in a similar way – the change in PRI vote share between 1988 and 1991 – she finds no evidence that PRONASOL expenditure helped the PRI and undermined the left: "a more systematic analysis does not support the hypothesis that Solidarity spending accounts for left losses and PRI gains" (162). Hiskey (1999) concludes that "given all the attention devoted to political business cycles, pork-barrel politics and the political use of social funds as a necessary ingredient in the consolidation of neoliberal economic reforms, the political impact of PRONASOL funds is noteworthy for its insignificance" (128).

This section of the chapter seeks to assess PRONASOL's efficacy by looking at federal elections – the PRI's vote swing from 1988 to 1991 and from 1991 to 1994 – with an appropriately disaggregated municipal-level database.

I test models that measure the impact of PRONASOL municipal-level expenditures from 1989 to 1991 on the change in the party's vote share between 1988 to 1991, and the impact of expenditures from 1992 to 1994 on the change in the PRI vote share between 1991 and 1994, controlling for socioeconomic and regional variables.[10] Expenditures are expressed in

[10] Northern states are Baja California, Baja California Sur, Nayarit, Sinaloa, Durango, Sonora, Coahuila, Chihuahua, Nuevo León, San Luis Potosí, and Tamaulipas. Southern states are Morelos, Oaxaca, Guerrero, Chiapas, Veracruz, Yucatán, Tabasco, Quintana Roo, and Campeche. Bajío states are Aguascalientes, Colima, Michoacán, Jalisco, Guanajuato, and Zacatecas. The omitted category is Center, including Hidalgo, Estado de México, Puebla, Querétaro, and Tlaxcala.

logarithmic terms. We know from previous works that the PRI performs better in poorer areas of the country and that the party's vote is affected by regional variables. I also add dummies for state capitals. The expectation is that the PRI should perform worse in richer municipalities and in state capitals. Moreover, the party's recovery in 1991 may also be attributed to higher voter participation and efforts to get out the PRI vote (Bruhn, 1996: 163). I thus include a variable for voter turnout in the concurrent municipal elections and expect to find a positive impact of turnout on the PRI's vote swing. Because of the notion of "regression toward the mean," I also control for how much a party's municipal vote share in the presidential elections deviated from the party's mean vote in those elections. The expectation is that the coefficient of this variable should be negative, meaning that where a party performed unusually well in the preceding presidential election, its positive swing in the coming election is expected to be much lower. The regressions also add dummies for states that held gubernatorial and/or municipal elections in 1991 and 1994. Results for the vote swings of the three major parties between 1988 and 1991 are presented in Table 4.4. The table also reports results for vote swings between 1991 and 1994 as a function of total municipal-level per capita PRONASOL expenditures, expressed in logarithmic terms, from 1992 to 1994 and the same other independent variables used above.

My results reveal that PRONASOL was an effective vote-buying program that simultaneously served to increase support for the PRI and to undermine both of the opposition parties. The results for the party's vote swings from 1988 to 1991 reveal that the remarkable recovery of the PRI in the midterm elections can be accounted for in part by PRONASOL's expenditures from 1989 to 1991 and the higher voter turnout in 1991. The PRI also recovered more votes among the poorest municipalities, as measured by the CONAPO marginality index, and in the North. Its vote swings were larger where concurrent municipal elections took place and smaller in capital cities and in the South and el Bajío regions.

The PRI recovered fewer votes in states where concurrent gubernatorial elections took place, which casts doubt on Molinar and Weldon's (1994) claim that the effectiveness of PRONASOL as a vote-buying effort directed toward defectors should be evaluated primarily by looking at these gubernatorial elections. It turns out that the PRI's recovery was disproportionately small in these states.

The Cardenista vote loss in 1991 looks almost like a mirror image of the PRI's vote gain: the PRD lost more votes in municipalities that received

Table 4.4. *The electoral efficacy of PRONASOL*

Change in PRI Vote, 1988–91	Coeff.	Std.Err.	Change in PRI Vote, 1991–94	Coeff.	Std.Err.
LogPRONASOLpc	0.006***	0.001	*LogPRONASOLpc*	0.006***	0.001
Reg mean	−0.747***	0.017	*Reg mean*	−0.535***	0.019
Develop	0.033***	0.004	*Develop*	0.018***	0.003
Elec mun91	0.052***	0.008	*Elec mun94*	0.037***	0.006
Elec gov91	−0.043***	0.012	*Elec gov94*	−0.036***	0.009
Turnout91	0.049***	0.011	*Turnout94*	−0.039***	0.010
capital	−0.048**	0.024	*capital*	−0.021	0.024
north	0.020**	0.010	*north*	0.033***	0.009
south	−0.042***	0.008	*south*	−0.066***	0.008
bajio	−0.039***	0.010	*bajio*	−0.017*	0.010
constant	0.448***	0.018	*constant*	−0.196***	0.020
N = 1,976; Adj R2 = .52			N = 1,867; Adj R2 = .38		
Change in FDN/PRD Vote, 1988–91			Change in PRD Vote, 1991–94		
LogPRONASOLpc	−0.003***	0.001	*LogPRONASOLpc*	−0.004***	0.001
Reg mean	−0.830***	0.014	*Reg mean*	−0.178***	0.024
Develop	−0.009***	0.003	*Develop*	0.012***	0.003
Elec mun91	−0.075***	0.007	*Elec mun94*	−0.050***	0.006
Elec gov91	0.041***	0.009	*Elec gov94*	0.037***	0.008
Turnout91	−0.034***	0.009	*Turnout94*	0.030***	0.010
capital	−0.026	0.018	*capital*	0.005	0.023
north	−0.016**	0.007	*north*	−0.007	0.008
south	0.042***	0.006	*south*	0.101***	0.007
bajio	0.077***	0.007	*bajio*	−0.002	0.010
constant	−0.091***	0.012	*constant*	0.116***	0.019
N = 1,874; Adj R2 = .66			N = 1,867; Adj R2 = .27		
Change in PAN Vote, 1988–91			Change in PAN Vote, 1991–94		
LogPRONASOLpc	−0.001	0.001	*LogPRONASOLpc*	−0.003***	0.001
Reg mean	−0.484***	0.017	*Reg mean*	−0.350***	0.019
Develop	−0.018***	0.002	*Develop*	−0.042***	0.002
Elec mun91	−0.003	0.004	*Elec mun94*	0.022***	0.003
Elec gov91	0.036***	0.006	*Elec gov94*	0.019***	0.005
Turnout91	0.004	0.006	*Turnout94*	0.016***	0.006
capital	0.041***	0.013	*capital*	−0.018	0.014
north	0.005	0.005	*north*	−0.031***	0.005
south	−0.017***	0.004	*south*	−0.038***	0.004
bajio	−0.018***	0.005	*bajio*	−0.019***	0.006
constant	0.011	0.008	*constant*	0.121***	0.011
N = 1,976; Adj R2=.30			N = 1,867; Adj R2 = .34		

* significant at the 90% confidence level; ** significant at the 95% confidence level; *** significant at the 99% confidence level. *LogPRONASOLpc* is per capita municipal-level expenditures expressed in logarithmic terms. *Reg mean* is how much a party's municipal vote share in the presidential elections deviated from the party's mean vote in those elections. *Develop* is the CONAPO marginality index. *Elec mun* and *Elec gov* are dummies for municipalities and states that have elections concurrent with the federal elections. *Turnout* is turnout in those municipal elections. *Capital* is dummies for state capitals. The rest are regional dummies.

higher PRONASOL expenditures and where voter turnout in 1991 was higher. Vote loses for the PRD were much smaller in the South and in the el Bajío region, where the party's stronghold, Michoacán, is located. Thus, PRONASOL does account for left losses, contrary to Bruhn's (1996) conclusion. Indeed, there was a great deal of stability in the left vote in Michoacán, as she rightly points out, suggesting that partisan loyalties to the PRD had begun to develop. However, most other municipalities where Cárdenas was strong in 1988 chose to support the PRI in 1991, partly as a result of PRONASOL spending. The correlation between municipal-level vote swings for the PRI and the Cardenistas in 1991 was −0.71 and statistically significant, suggesting that the PRI gains did come at the expense of Cardenista losses.[11]

The PAN's vote swing in 1991, for its part, cannot be accounted for by PRONASOL spending, which suggests that this party's base of supporters was more loyal and immune to conversion through intimidation and economic punishment. These results for the opposition vote swings in 1991 sharply contradict Molinar and Weldon's (1994) claim that PRONASOL harmed the PAN and not the PRD.

The results for the 1991–94 vote swings are similar in many respects. The PRI's gains continue to be larger where PRONASOL spending was higher between 1992 and 1994 and where the municipalities were more underdeveloped. The PRI also gains more when there are concurrent municipal elections and in the North, and loses more in the South and el Bajío regions. A significant difference from the earlier results is that higher voter turnout does not account for the greater ruling party gains in the later period. Quite the contrary, higher turnout in 1994 is systematically related to vote swings in favor of both of the opposition parties. A second difference in the results for the 1994 vote swings is that this time PRONASOL spending between 1992 and 1994 is systematically related to losses for both of the opposition parties, not just for the PRD. These last results suggest that those who supported the PAN in 1991 were no longer immune to conversion through spending. This result can probably be accounted for by the fact that in 1991 the PAN received support from many left-leaning voters, according to Domínguez and McCann (1996), and these voters were not equally loyal to the PAN.

[11] At the district level, Bruhn (1996) finds that there is no statistically significant correlation between PRI gains and Cardenista losses (163). However, once the election returns are disaggregated to the municipal level, a strong negative correlation appears.

Conclusion

The goal of this chapter was to provide empirical evidence for two of the theoretical claims of this book: first, that vote buying constituted an essential glue for the maintenance of the PRI regime, and second, that the PRI's vote-buying strategies were consistent with the theoretical claims presented in Chapter 1. The PRI responded to opposition entry by using an entry-deterrence strategy, reacting in an unforgiving fashion by withdrawing funds from localities controlled by the opposition and simultaneously diverting funds to those loyal localities that were more vulnerable to opposition entry.

In this chapter, I have demonstrated that, first, the PRI targeted more PRONASOL resources to vulnerable municipalities where the Cardenistas had been strongest in the 1988 federal elections and *less funding* to loyal bastions where the PRI had won with larger vote shares in those elections. Second, I have shown that the PRI actually diverted funds from municipalities that it expected to win by large margins and concentrated resources where they could make a difference between voters' remaining loyal to the regime or defecting. Third, I have provided compelling evidence of the "punishment regime," or the fact that the PRI withdrew funds from municipalities governed by the opposition. Fourth, I have demonstrated the value for an opposition party of controlling a governorship: in states where the PAN controlled the governorship, its municipalities received more resources. Fifth, I have demonstrated that PRONASOL's expenditures systematically increased before federal elections.

My findings are thus consistent, in part, with Molinar and Weldon's (1994) state-level findings that the PRI targeted more funds to vulnerable places where the Cardenistas were strong in 1988, and inconsistent with Hiskey's (1999) claim that PRONASOL's funds were disproportionately targeted to places were the PRI received more votes. However, unlike Molinar and Weldon's (1994) simple "buy-back the opposition" logic, which generates the paradoxical result that opposition voters end up being rewarded, my results demonstrate that the PRI *systematically withdrew funds from municipalities controlled by the opposition*, including those governed by the PRD. By doing so, the PRI was able to halt the deterioration of its core base of supporters, discourage voters from defecting, and undermine opposition party building.

With respect to the political effectiveness of PRONASOL, this chapter has offered some definitive conclusions. The literature has given a great deal of attention to this program as a key instrument in the PRI's electoral recovery and the PRD's debacle. Nonetheless, most empirical analyses have concluded that PRONASOL's political effectiveness, for the PRI's point of view, was disappointing. Thus, the PRI's recovery in 1991 has remained a big mystery. Looking at municipal vote swings in the federal elections of 1988–91 and 1991–94, I have demonstrated that PRONASOL and poverty predict gains for the PRI and losses for the PRD in 1991, and vote swings in favor of the PRI and against both opposition parties in 1994. Thus, I have been able to provide systematic empirical evidence for two of the central theoretical claims of this book, namely, that support for the PRI can be accounted for in part by vote buying, and that the poor are particularly predisposed to respond to it. The following chapter will assess how economic performance also shaped the fortunes of the PRI in those critical years.

5

Judging Economic Performance in Hard Times

In the voting model presented in Chapter 1, voters are motivated by patronage and vote buying, by government performance, by ideological appeals, and by expectations of political violence. The previous chapter assessed the logic of vote buying and its effectiveness in maintaining the PRI regime. This chapter assesses the role of economic performance in maintaining support for the autocratic regime.

As shown in Chapter 2, from its creation in 1929 until the late 1970s the PRI presided over a long period of economic growth. In Mexico as in most Latin American countries, the 1980s was a lost decade in terms of economic growth. High inflation rates, sharp deterioration of real wages, and underemployment in the cities characterized the decade. The Mexican economy had two-digit average annual inflation rates (or more), and real wages declined by more than 60 percent. In the 1990s, President Carlos Salinas achieved macroeconomic stabilization. Yet, despite macroeconomic stabilization, the Mexican economy remained stagnant during his administration, barely growing at an average annual rate of 3 percent.

The 1994 peso crisis represented another serious setback. The first two years of the Zedillo administration saw a sharp economic decline: in 1995, GNP dropped by almost 7 percent – for Mexico, a recession comparable to the crash of 1929. Industrial wages declined in real terms by more than 30 percent in just two years, and the currency was devalued, by around 250 percent overall, between December 1994 and December 1996. However, although serious, this second recession was short-lived. By 1997, the Mexican economy had recovered – just in time for the upcoming federal elections.

How did Mexican voters react to these dramatic changes in the economic environment? This chapter employs presidential approval ratings and macroeconomic data from 1988 to 2000 to answer this question. I focus on this period because data on presidential approval before 1988 is not available. The chapter unfolds as follows. The first section places my approach to economic voting within the comparative literature. The second section discusses the economic background. The third section places my approach within the Mexican literature on presidential approval. The subsequent sections present my analysis of presidential approval.

Comparative Economic Voting

The question of how voters react to economic performance has been the subject of an important debate within the comparative literature. The economic voting model posits that voters act as "gods of vengeance and reward," rewarding the incumbent party for prosperity and punishing it for recession (Key, 1966). If this model were correct, voters in the developing world should universally turn against economic reforms, which produce at least temporary deterioration in economic conditions. Analyzing the prospects for market-oriented reforms, Przeworski (1991: Chapter 4) predicted that incumbents would either be tempted to abandon economic reforms before the next elections or would end up abandoning democracy. This pessimistic account of the prospects for structural reforms is implicitly based on the notion that voters react according to the economic voting model.

However, Stokes (1996, 2001) compellingly demonstrates a large variance in voter reactions to economic deterioration. She classifies forms of voter reaction to economic recession into four categories, according to whether voters are pessimistic or optimistic about the future, and whether they support or oppose the incumbent. (1) The *intertemporal* model of voting behavior implies that despite current deterioration in the economy, voters are optimistic about the future and support the incumbent because they believe that reforms, to be successful, require a temporary decline in economic conditions. Voters may also come to support risky reforms over less risky alternatives after suffering losses, as in hyperinflationary environments (Weyland, 2002). (2) The *exonerating* model implies that voters are pessimistic about the future but support the incumbent because they believe that some other party, not the incumbent, is responsible for their present economic misery. (3) The *distributional* model posits that voters punish the incumbent despite their optimism about the future because they seek to manifest solidarity with other voters who have been hurt by economic reforms. (4) The *economic voting* model argues that voters are pessimistic about the future and punish the incumbent for recession.

Stokes's (1996 and 2001) approach is extremely useful because it highlights the limits of the economic voting model and identifies other modes of voter reaction to economic recession. Yet it lacks a unified voting model that can describe why voters react the way they do. Implicit in Stokes's framework is a model of voter learning akin to my Bayesian model of learning presented in Chapter 1.

Recall that my voting model posits that voters are future-oriented and base their choices on a *comparative prospective assessment* – they compare the expected economic performance of the ruling party and that of the opposition, and elect the party that is expected to deliver the best prospects for the future of the national economy. Voters are also motivated by patronage and vote buying and by ideological appeals.

My model provides for deviations from the economic voting model based on what voters *learn* from experience about the incumbent and the opposition, on the one hand, and based on the incumbent's ability to deliver side payments to voters, on the other. Despite a current economic downturn, voters might support the government when the incumbent party delivers "selective incentives" to buy them off. This mode of behavior, I have demonstrated, applies most notably to poor voters, who are more willing to compromise their ideology for immediate private consumption.

Voters might also support the government despite deteriorating economic conditions, behaving as future-oriented *bankers*, when they decide that the ruling party is more capable than the opposition of handling future economic performance. This form of voting behavior applies most notably to higher-income individuals, who focus more on government performance and ideological appeals and less on government transfers. As my model makes explicit, given a current economic downturn, voters can continue to be optimistic about the ruling party's expected economic performance relative to the opposition when (1) the long-term economic record of the ruling party has been consistently good, so that voters can rationally believe in its competence *and* reliability, as in the intertemporal vote model; and (2) voters do not find the opposition's promises credible, either because of uncertainty or because its past performance record while in office is dismal, as in the exonerating model.

My argument is that during the Salinas presidency, rich and middle-class voters behaved like future-oriented *bankers*,[1] approving of the president because they trusted his capacity to lead the country out of the recession and because they remained suspicious of the uncertain opposition, and not because voters saw an improvement in the country's objective economic conditions. Their behavior was consistent with the intertemporal voting model. By contrast, poor voters behaved more like *peasants*, rewarding Salinas for vote buying. The poor tolerated the economic situation because they responded to "selective incentives."

Voters' mode of behavior changed during the Zedillo presidency. The 1994 peso crisis paved the way for the PRI's ultimate demise because it completely destroyed the party's reliability. By the 2000 presidential elections, economic performance was outstanding. Voters gave extremely high approval ratings to Ernesto Zedillo but were no longer willing to vote in favor of the PRI because they predicted another post-electoral bust, as I further demonstrate in Chapter 7. I now turn to a discussion of these background economic conditions.

The Economic Background

Macroeconomic instability and a brutal deterioration of real salaries characterized the decade of the 1980s in Mexico. During the entire decade, the Mexican economy had average annual inflation rates of two digits or more, peaking at an unprecedented annual rate of 180 percent in December of 1988.

The de la Madrid government attempted to lower inflation by implementing an IMF-sponsored stabilization package that included restructuring public finances, abruptly devaluing the currency, and raising public sector prices. During his presidential term, de la Madrid reduced the government's budget deficit from 15.63 percent to 9.32 percent of GDP. This adjustment was more radical than the figures suggest. The government was facing extremely large interest payments on both the internal and external debt, and the interest payments of the internal debt, in particular, were affected by the high inflation rates of those years.

Despite the fiscal adjustment, the government could not control inflation until the National Solidarity Pact was signed in December 1987, six months before the presidential election. The National Solidarity Pact was aimed

[1] I take the notion of *bankers* and *peasants* from MacKuen et al. (1992).

at curbing inertial inflation and restoring investment credibility. Business agreed to keep prices fixed. Workers received a compensatory increase of 15 percent in contractual wages in December 1987 and a 20 percent rise in the minimum wage in January 1988. The government increased revenues, cut subsidies, tightened monetary policy, lowered maximum tariffs from 45 percent to 20 percent, and eliminated almost all import permits. The exchange rate was depreciated by about 20 percent and then left fixed as a nominal anchor. Through the National Solidarity Pact, the government managed to lower the rate of monthly inflation from 15 percent in January 1988, to 3 percent in April 1988, to 0.6 percent in September of 1988. The fixed exchange rate served, throughout the Salinas term, as a focal point to coordinate expectations in the economy: as long as the currency remained stable, prices and wages followed suit.

High inflation levels shrink the incomes of voters, especially those of the poorest voters. Between 1982 and 1988, the minimum and industrial wages of Mexicans lost almost 60 percent of their real value. Only when inflation appeared to be under control did average real industrial wages start to increase, with minimal wages still lagging behind. The draconian era of de la Madrid was not accompanied by a significant increase in open unemployment. Unemployment rates were almost constant between 1978 and 1985, with the largest increase, to 6.6 percent, occurring in 1984.[2] Low levels of unemployment can be explained, as Lustig (1992) argues, by the sharp decline in real wages. Such a decline allowed firms and the government to reduce labor costs without having to resort to layoffs.

When Carlos Salinas took office, the annual inflation rate had dropped to around 20 percent. The Salinas government further moved toward macroeconomic stabilization, renegotiating the external debt, balancing the budget (using, among other strategies, the privatization of state-owned enterprises), and deepening trade liberalization by negotiating NAFTA with

[2] These measures, however, are not very informative for developing countries, for they say nothing about what economists call "disguised unemployment." More informative, as Lustig (1992) has argued, is the comparison between the growth of the labor force and the growth rate of formal employment, because it shows the ability of the economy to "absorb" labor. The formal employment growth rate had been 4 percent in the 1960s. However, during the 1982–86 period the growth of employment was only 0.2 percent, while the growth of the labor force was 3.6 percent. Thus, since open unemployment was low, it seems that the informal sector and migration to the United States were absorbing most of the labor supply. Consequently, the economic crisis led workers to engage more than before in low-productivity and sparsely remunerated activities, or to leave the country.

the United States and Canada. However, the Mexican economy did not grow at particularly high rates during the Salinas years. During the six years of his presidential term, the average annual rate of GDP growth was only 3 percent. Nonetheless, all the macroeconomic indicators started to improve.

Inflation was dramatically reduced, and real industrial wages consistently increased, recovering to about where they were in the early 1980s, at least until the end of 1994, when another crisis hit the country. Before the Solidarity Pact was signed, central minimum wage negotiations had constrained real wage increases in the industrial sector. With the Solidarity Pact, a new practice was established: centralized minimum wage negotiations stopped constraining real wages in the manufacturing sector. Wages of workers in the formal sector of the economy were improving relative to what they had been in the 1980s. In addition, over the entire Salinas presidential term the exchange rate appreciated, which, as argued in Chapter 3, translated into an extravagant expansion of imports and a consumer bubble. The balance-of-payments disequilibrium became problematic, however, when capital flows stopped and even reversed during the election year of 1994.

The 1994 Peso Crisis and Its Aftermath

Because both Luis Echeverría and Jose López Portillo finished their presidential terms by abruptly devaluing the currency, the end of a *sexenio* came to be associated with above-average exchange rate risk. Heath (1999) has aptly labeled the end-of-term risks as the "*sexenio* curse." Given the appropriate warning, wealthier Mexicans took their assets out of the country, which explains why the transmission of presidential power in 1994 was difficult to manage.

Because of his high levels of public approval, Salinas was confident in his ability to pass power to a candidate from the PRI who would easily win the August 1994 elections and continue the party's program of economic change (Domínguez and McCann, 1996). Nevertheless, the end of the Carlos Salinas *sexenio* turned out to be more difficult than expected. Three unprecedented political events took place during the election year. First, the Chiapas uprising of January 1994 saw Mayan peasants organize the Zapatista National Liberation Army (EZLN), named after Emiliano Zapata, the famous revolutionary peasant leader in the state of Morelos. The rebelling Zapatistas opposed the government on a wide range of issues:

the North American Free Trade Agreement, Salinas's "illegitimate" presidency and his economic reforms, and the recent constitutional reform of Article 27 that had ended land reform.

Second, on March 23, 1994, the PRI's presidential candidate, Luis Donaldo Colosio, was assassinated. Though the gunman was arrested, the issue of whether he was part of a broader conspiracy was never resolved. The Colosio assassination signaled the existence of deeply rooted divisions within the ruling party. The PRI was forced to improvise, in the middle of the campaign year, the selection of a new presidential candidate. The choice was Ernesto Zedillo, a technocrat trained in economics.

Third, in September 1994, just after the presidential elections, Francisco Ruiz Massieu, the secretary general of the PRI, who was to become the majority leader in the lower house of Congress, was also assassinated. Within two weeks, Manuel Munoz Rocha, a PRI congressman, was linked to the assassination; then it emerged that Rocha had been assassinated. Two weeks later, the assistant attorney general investigating the case, Mario Ruiz Massieu (the brother of the assassinated politician) resigned, arguing that high officials within the ruling party were blocking the investigation.[3]

However, investors did not perceive all of these events as equally risky. Only the Colosio assassination triggered significant amounts of capital flight. Contrary to the official rhetoric, the Chiapas uprising did not lead investors to take their assets out of the country. After the Chiapas uprising became common knowledge, the Central Bank's international reserves even increased from January to February, by $5 billion. It was only the murder of Colosio that triggered a significant amount of capital flight. After that political assassination, international reserves dropped from $25 billion in March to $15 billion in April. Capital flight, nonetheless, soon stopped, and international reserves remained stable from April until October of 1994. Unlike the murder of Colosio, the assassination of Ruiz Massieu did not trigger capital flight. The largest amounts of capital flight took place only when Ernesto Zedillo, the new PRI president, took office in early November. Thus, in the average investor's view, the exchange rate risk increased most with the *transmission of presidential power.*

From the Colosio assassination until the presidential transfer of power, international reserves remained constant, which suggests that the Salinas

[3] In February 1995, Mario Ruiz Massieu was arrested in Newark, New Jersey, carrying $46,000 in cash. The U.S. government found seventeen million-dollar accounts linked to Mario Ruiz Massieu. A link with drug traffic seems quite plausible.

government had recovered investors' confidence. Nonetheless, his government paid a very high price for this confidence. To stop investors from rushing out of the country, the government chose to assume the exchange rate risk by shifting government borrowing from peso-denominated instruments, CETES, to short-term dollar-denominated ones, TESOBONOS. Investors perceived a high currency risk, for they rapidly switched from the peso-denominated instruments to the dollar-denominated ones. Just after the assassination of Colosio, the number of CETES decreased dramatically, by more than 10 billion pesos. This implies that Colosio's assassination was a perceived source of significant exchange-rate risk, and thus that investors opted to rush out of the peso-denominated instruments in order to protect their assets. From March until August, there was a systematic and constant increase in the issue of TESOBONOS, which increased from less than ten billion pesos to more than sixty billion, and a systematic decrease in CETES, dropping by half (from around forty billion pesos to twenty billion).

Given the amount of dollar-denominated government indebtedness, when Ernesto Zedillo took office there was a new perceived risk, namely, government default. The perceived risk of government default was realistic, for if the peso were devalued, the cost to the government of dollar-denominated short-term debt instruments would become monstrous.[4] Indeed, after the devaluation of the peso implemented in December of 1994, the government's debt almost doubled, jumping from 60 billion pesos to close to 120 billion. The Zedillo government quickly stopped issuing TESOBONOS, and had it not been for a U.S.-led credit line of $50 billion, the probability of default would have been extremely high.

The 1994 peso crisis destroyed what today would be regarded as false optimism. Instead of being seen as a new pathway to growth, the Salinas term came to be perceived as a bubble in the midst of recurrent economic crises and a period of long-term stagnation. The crisis also contributed to destroying the PRI's credibility. Soon after Ernesto Zedillo assumed office, a serious economic recession comparable to the decline of 1929 occurred. The so-called *cartera vencida* (the portfolio of nonperforming bank loans) reached unparalleled levels, forcing the Zedillo government to rescue the banks from bankruptcy by socializing most of the short-term costs of bailing them out through the so-called FOBAPROA program.

[4] This was an intended feature of the structure of the Tesobonos: the government was effectively held hostage to keeping the exchange rate stable.

Judging Economic Performance in Hard Times

During the final three years of the Zedillo administration, the economy began to recover at impressive rates. This quick recovery can possibly be attributed to the fact that the Mexican economy had been transformed in fundamental ways and was now highly integrated into the U.S. market. The economy began to recover just in time for the 1997 elections, and was growing at an outstanding rate by the time of the 2000 presidential election. Nonetheless, as will become apparent in this chapter, Mexican voters did not reward the PRI for this economic recovery.

Existing Research on Presidential Approval in Mexico

The relationship between presidential approval and the performance of the macroeconomy has been understood alternatively according to a "retrospective" and a "prospective" voter logic. According to MacKuen and colleagues (1992), there are basically two ways that economic conditions might translate into approval ratings, each of which has different implications for how citizens manage to keep rulers accountable. On the one hand, voters may judge the government on the basis of present personal experiences, based on the answer to the question "What have you done for me lately?" On the other hand, voters may ignore current conditions and instead focus on the question "What are the prospects for the national economy?" MacKuen and colleagues (1992) claim that the first mode of reaction corresponds to the view of a "peasant," the latter to that of a "banker," and argue that "bankers" are less likely to fall prey to political opportunism and short-term budgetary strategies that seek to make the economy appear artificially strong before elections (Nordhaus, 1975; Lindbeck, 1976; Tufte, 1978). According to the authors, a sophisticated electorate, which reacts anticipating future economic conditions, is not at the mercy of opportunistic politicians (Rogoff and Sibert, 1988; Rogoff, 1990; Alesina and Roubini, 1997).

The Mexican literature on presidential approval presents evidence of voters acting both as *peasants* (Buendía, 1996, 2001) and as *bankers* (Villareal, 1999). However, it is unclear from this literature which kinds of mechanisms trigger each kind of behavior – what makes voters judge the incumbent on the basis of retrospective versus prospective evaluations? Furthermore, the existing literature presents contradictory conclusions, particularly with respect to Salinas's approval ratings: Buendía (1996, 2001) concludes that Salinas's approval ratings strongly corresponded to objective economic conditions, while Villareal (1999) claims that his approval ratings did not correspond to actual economic performance (the "Salinas paradox"). He attributes this "distortion" in voters' reactions to positive expectations generated by the economic reforms and media effects. However, although it is quite plausible, Villareal (1999) does not present conclusive evidence that the media was responsible for voters' optimism.

Reflecting on the economic policy reforms, Kaufman and Zuckermann (1998) argue that voters' retrospective evaluations of the national economy and the state of their personal finances impacted their support for Salinas's policies, as measured at two points in time, 1992 and 1994. However, they do not explore the extent to which these subjective economic evaluations might correspond to objective economic conditions, or on the other hand might result at least in part from voter rationalization, with those more supportive of Salinas evaluating the economy more favorably. Furthermore, the authors fail to disentangle the *endogeneity* problem, namely, the extent to which support for the economic reforms was shaped by Salinas's approval and presidential approval in turn shaped by support for the economic reforms.

There are a series of methodological drawbacks in this existing work that I overcome in this chapter. Villareal (1999) draws his conclusions from GEO surveys, which included only Mexico City, and he employs individual-level dependent variables and aggregate-level independent variables, a method that is likely to produce inflated t-scores when compared to the models that only employ aggregate-level data. I follow MacKuen and colleagues (1992) in employing aggregate approval ratings and objective economic conditions to assess the manner in which the electorate judges the incumbent president. As they argue, an aggregate time-series analysis offers an important degree of inferential leverage that individual analysis cannot deliver. "A compelling advantage of macro analysis is that idiosyncratic sources in economic judgments cancel out. Judgments whether the economy will improve or falter, for example, may be too noisy for worthwhile analysis at the individual level. But their noise cancels out in the aggregate, to provide the powerful measure of collective judgments" (86). An additional advantage of employing aggregate approval ratings is that economic data measuring inflation, unemployment, and real wages are themselves averages of economic performance.

Buendía (1996, 2001) employs the surveys conducted by the president's office during the Salinas term because they are far more representative of the country than the ones employed by Villareal (1999). This data presents a problem, however, in that it was not gathered on a regular calendar.

To deal with this problem, Buendía (1996) ran a model with the available observations and then "estimated the predicted probabilities of presidential approval for the missing months" (575). This is an inappropriate method for imputing the missing observations, and it is likely to bias the results.

To overcome the limitations of Buendia's analysis, I impute the missing values for presidential approval with Amelia 2.0 (King et al., 2001). Amelia uses a multiple imputation model for missing data. Given that we do not actually know the real value of a missing observation, it seems wrong to use a particular number in the database, as Buendía (1996, 2001) does. Instead, Amelia generates a vector of possible values for each missing observation, based on parameters from the variables in a proposed model. As a result, the missing observation is transformed into a distribution of potential values.

After correcting for both of these shortcomings in the existing literature, my results demonstrate that, first, aggregate approval ratings during the Salinas presidency did not respond to objective economic conditions. The average Mexican voter acted more like a *banker*, approving of the president despite the fact that the economy was barely growing. Second, poorer voters tended to be more sensitive to objective economic conditions, punishing Carlos Salinas for inflation and rewarding him for macroeconomic stabilization. Third, during the Zedillo administration, voters behaved as *peasants*. As unemployment, inflation, and real wages worsened, voters turned against the president, and when their economic conditions began to improve, they rewarded the president. Fourth, improvements in voters' economic conditions after the post-1997 recovery led voters to approve of the president, but not to trust the PRI. Instead, even as economic growth began to improve as the 2000 elections neared, voters became *more pessimistic about the future of the national economy* and less willing to continue to support the PRI. Presidential approval was no longer fungible for the PRI. This suggests that after the 1994 peso crisis, Mexicans had become quite distrustful of the party in power. With their memories of past economic crises around election times, voters had learned to discount good pre-electoral performance because they anticipated a post-electoral crisis, a point that is further demonstrated in Chapter 7.

Thus, even though Mexican voters behaved more like *peasants* in their approval of Zedillo, this by no means made them more vulnerable to electoral opportunism. Although voters increased their approval of the president due to the economic recovery, that approval was no longer transferable to the PRI because they no longer trusted that party.

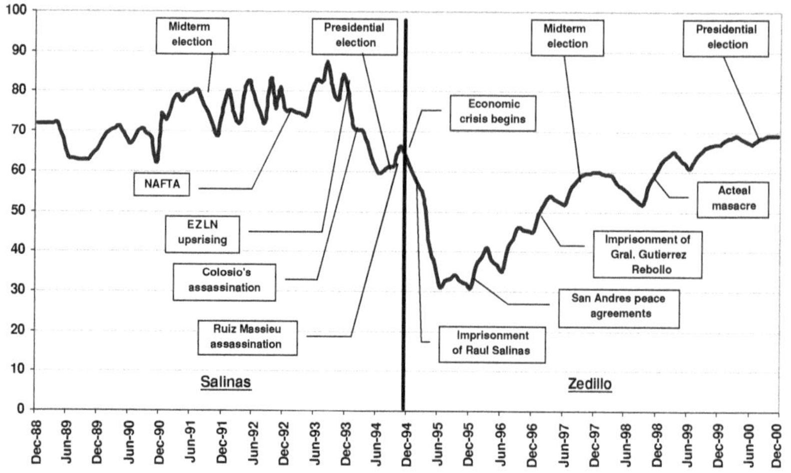

Figure 5.1. Presidential approval in Mexico, 1988–2000.

The Approval Time Series, 1988–2000[5]

I rely on two sources for constructing the presidential approval series: the surveys conducted by the president's office during Salinas term and the approval surveys conducted by *Reforma* newspaper during the Zedillo administration. Surveys by *Reforma* newspaper were regularly conducted on a quarterly basis. However, the president's office did not conduct its surveys on such a regular schedule – there are monthly surveys, but out of the seventy-two months of the *sexenio*, twenty-four months lack observations. As noted earlier, I imputed the missing values for presidential approval during the Salinas presidency using Amelia 2.0 (King et al., 2001).

Figure 5.1 presents the presidential approval series for the period from 1988 to 2000. The figure also indicates the Salinas and the Zedillo presidential terms and a series of events transpiring during those twelve years. The first thing to note is that Salinas's approval ratings are much higher than Zedillo's – the average approval of the former was 73 percent and of the

[5] I thank Vidal Romero for his assistance in the collection of the Carlos Salinas series. I also thank him for assistance in the econometric analyses of the Salinas data, and for help in the multiple imputation procedure that I employ. The analysis of Zedillo's presidential approval draws from my paper "Judging the Economy in Hard Times," presented at the Latin American Studies Association in 2000. Romero also assisted in replicating some of the results of that paper.

latter was 53 percent. The political campaigns for the 1991 midterm elections appear to have given a strong boost to Salinas's popularity, which reached its peak at more than 80 percent in 1993, the year after the signing of NAFTA and the year before the Zapatista uprising in January 1994. During 1994, the year of the presidential election, Salinas's popularity plunged, first as a result of the guerilla rebellion and later as a consequence of the murder of Luis Donaldo Colosio.

Ernesto Zedillo began with high public approval, but this support immediately plunged due to the 1994 peso crisis. As a result, his approval ratings were extremely low during the first two years of his term; thereafter, his popularity gradually increased until the end of his presidential term. The midterm elections of both 1991 and 1997 took place when presidential approval was improving. Before the midterm elections, however, Zedillo's approval was twenty points lower than that of Salinas. Not surprisingly, the PRI lost the majority of the Chamber of Deputies in the 1997 elections. Zedillo's approval rating reached its peak at close to 70 percent just before the presidential elections of 2000 (which the PRI lost, nonetheless), a point to which I shall return.

Presidential Approval and the Economy

To what extent does economic performance shape presidential approval? To measure the status of the national economy, I employ three economic indicators: inflation, real wages, and unemployment.[6] I also use a "misery factor" that combines inflation and unemployment. Given the period's high inflation rates, it would be misleading to employ the widely used "misery index," which is simply the sum of inflation and unemployment, because it would weight inflation disproportionately. Instead, I employ factor scores of both variables. I employ as dependent variables monthly approval ratings during the Salinas term and quarterly approval ratings during the Zedillo presidency as a function of one lagged approval variable plus current values of the economic variables. This is the standard approach in the literature – a distributed lag model, using a Koyck transformation (see MacKuen et al., 1992). Regressions for quarterly approval ratings are run using monthly

[6] Inflation is calculated as the rate of change in the price index of month j with respect to the same month of the previous year. Unemployment is the monthly rate of open unemployment. Real wages are measured as the percentage change in real wages of month j with respect to the same month of the previous year. Data comes from Banxico and INEGI.

values for the economic variables, taking the last month of the quarter as the relevant data point.

Since I am interested in assessing the difference in voters' reactions during the two presidential terms, I ran separate models for Salinas and Zedillo. A reason to run separate regressions for each presidential term is that, as noted earlier, approval data for Salinas required multiple imputation generated by Amelia using Clarify (Tomz et al., 2003). Clarify appropriately combines the results from the imputed datasets from Amelia, and the coefficients take into account the noise of the imputed data (see King et al., 2001, for further details). The models for Zedillo did not require using data from several imputed datasets, and hence it would be inappropriate to run a single model for both presidencies. Results are reported in Table 5.1. None of the economic variables shows a statistically significant impact on Salinas's approval. Further, the results do not vary if I introduce a dummy variable for the 1994 election year, when Salinas's approval rates dropped owing to the Zapatista uprising and the murder of Colosio. However, all of the economic variables contribute to Zedillo's approval ratings in the expected manner.

As inflation and unemployment increased, voters turned against the Zedillo government, and as real salaries increased, voters favored the president. The last columns of the table present the models using the "misery factor." This shows no effect on Salinas's approval, but powerfully shapes Zedillo's approval in the expected way – as "misery" increases, Zedillo's approval decreases, and the effects are substantial and statistically significant. The 1994 peso crisis thus transformed voters' modes of behavior. Ernesto Zedillo had campaigned under the slogans "welfare for your family" and "continuity to consolidate the changes," referring to the economic reforms implemented during the previous administration. The currency crisis destroyed the PRI's perceived reliability. Instead of being seen as a new pathway to economic prosperity, the economic reforms appeared to voters as false promises; voters became quite "vindictive," severely punishing the president for the objective economic deterioration.

By contrast, during the Salinas period the average voter did not behave according to the economic voting model. My results are at odds with those of Buendía (2001), who finds that during the Salinas presidency unemployment and price increases resulted in decreased presidential approval. He concludes that during the Salinas term "the Mexican public behaved in a way consistent with normal economic voting" (143). With respect to Zedillo's presidency, my results are consistent with Buendía's – we both find

Table 5.1. *Economic performance and presidential approval, 1988–2000*

	Salinas Model 1	Zedillo Model 2	Salinas Model 3	Zedillo Model 4	Salinas Model 5	Zedillo Model 6	Salinas Model 7	Zedillo Model 8
Approval lag	0.71***	.13	.70***	0.12	.7000***	.40*	.71***	−0.16
	(.11)	(.25)	(.11)	(0.17)	(.1065)	(.23)	(.11)	(0.17)
Inflation	.00	−.84***						
	(.09)	(.26)						
Unemployment			−.7576	−6.60***				
			(1.3737)	(1.30)				
Wages					.2703	0.85**		
					(.2425)	(0.36)		
Misery factor							.3757	−14.43***
							(.9612)	(2.15)
Constant	21.02**	66.46***	23.690***	73.28***	20.04**	34.55**	21.167**	63.27***
	(8.67)	(19.02)	(8.3048)	(13.77)	(7.65)	(13.07)	(7.9063)	(9.12)
	N = 71	N = 21	N = 71	N = 23	N = 71	N = 23	N = 71	N = 23
R-sqr.		0.82		0.86		0.78		0.91

* significant at the 90% confidence level; ** significant at the 95% confidence level; *** significant at the 99% confidence level.

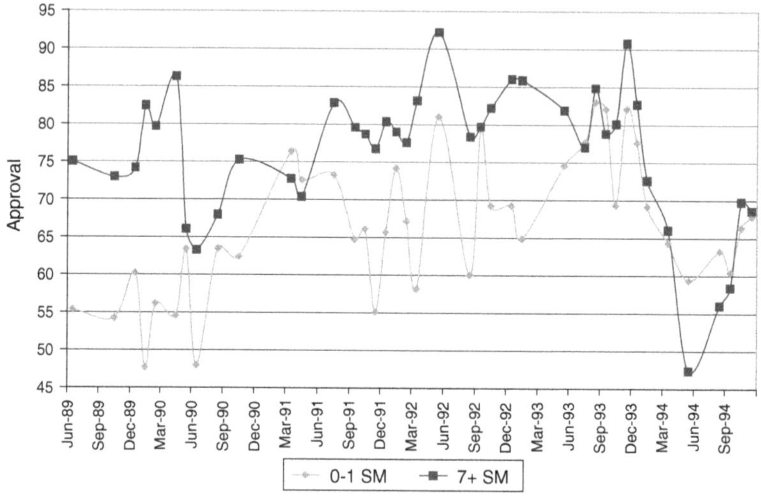

Figure 5.2. Salinas approval by income, poor versus rich.

that he was judged on the basis of objective economic conditions. "Even if the political context – a new administration inheriting an economic crisis – was conducive to acceptance of the government's self-exonerating arguments, the Mexican public did not buy them: they punished Zedillo when the economy deteriorated and rewarded him when the economy began to improve" (Buendía, 2001: 156).

Presidential Approval and Income

The Salinas presidency brought a dramatic shift in economic policy. The structural adjustment and market-oriented reforms that Miguel de la Madrid had initiated were significantly deepened during Salinas's term. It is conventionally assumed that lower-income groups should oppose these neoliberal reforms. Indeed, as Figure 5.2 shows, poor voters (those earning between zero and one minimum wage) tended to regard Carlos Salinas less highly than did rich voters (those earning above seven minimum wages), which is an indication that the poor originally had stronger opposition to his economic agenda. However, Salinas managed to recover support among the poor in a dramatic way. When his term began, only 55 percent of the poor approved of him. By December of 1993, more than 80 percent did, an increase of twenty-five percentage points. To a large extent, Salinas popularity among the poor was linked, of course, to the success

Table 5.2. *Effect of objective economic conditions on Salinas's approval by two income groups*

	Poor	Rich	Poor	Rich	Poor	Rich	Poor	Rich
Approval lag	0.36***	.70***	.41***	.67***	.46***	0.68***	.37**	.67***
	(.13)	(.13)	(.14)	(.14)	(.13)	(.1300)	(.13)	(0.14)
Inflation	−0.30**	0.09						
	(.15)	(.12)						
Unemployment			4.19	−3.29*				
			(3.20)	(1.88)				
Wages					−.06	0.40		
					(.39)	(.33)		
Misery factor							−3.51**	1.9017
							(1.58)	(1.28)
Constant	47.29***	21.41**	26.04***	35.13**	35.82***	21.44**	41.53***	24.70**
	(9.93)	(9.93)	(9.12)	(13.96)	(9.25)	(9.49)	(9.02)	(10.47)
	N = 71	N = 71	N = 71	N = 71	N = 71	N = 71	N = 71	N = 71

* significant at the 90% confidence level; ** significant at the 95% confidence level; *** significant at the 99% confidence level.

of PRONASOL, discussed in the previous chapter. The approval of both voter groups plunged during the 1994 election year, when political violence erupted in the country. The rich reacted more strongly to these violent events, however, as Salinas's approval among them dropped by more than forty percentage points in that year.

To further investigate how income levels shape approval ratings, I ran a series of models for the aggregate approval ratings for poor and rich voters. I focus only on the Salinas presidency for two reasons. First, unfortunately, the Zedillo approval series did not include income. Second, approval ratings during the Zedillo administration are very straightforward – strongly shaped by economic performance – while the Salinas approval ratings remain puzzling. The results of the time-series regression analyses for the aggregate approval series of the poor and the rich are shown in Table 5.2.

Inflation strongly contributes to Salinas's approval ratings among the poor but does not impact the behavior of the rich. This runs counter to Buendía (1996), who claims that inflation "has a more pronounced impact on approval of the president [Carlos Salinas] among the wealthy than among the poor" (580), but is consistent with the findings of Villareal (1999), who argues that the "higher-income respondents exhibit no sensitivity to inflation" (141). A somewhat counterintuitive result is that unemployment shows the inverse effect – as it increases, there is less support for Carlos Salinas among the rich – although it is barely significant at conventional statistical levels.

These results suggest that Carlos Salinas managed to reconstruct support among the poor through a combination of macroeconomic stabilization policies and poverty relief spending through the PRONASOL program, as explored in the preceding chapter. The average voter during the Salinas term, however, did not respond to objective economic conditions.

The Zedillo Paradox: Intertemporal Weakness of Will and Electoral Opportunism

Why did Zedillo's approval ratings not translate into support for the PRI? To answer this question, one needs to understand how objective economic conditions and presidential approval translate into expectations about the future. The topic of this section is thus the relationship between economic conditions, perceptions about the future of the national economy, and presidential approval. I focus exclusively on the Zedillo presidency because the data on Salinas does not include a time series on economic perceptions, namely, how voters evaluated the past and the future of the national economy and their personal finances. The economic perception questions that I employ are the following:

- Sociotropic evaluations about the current state of the economy ("Would you say that the present state of the economy is better, the same, or worse than a year ago?").
- Pocketbook evaluations or assessments of the state of the voter's personal finances (owing to the lack of the usual pocketbook question for the whole time series,[7] I use as a proxy: "How successful do you believe Ernesto Zedillo has been in handling real wages?").
- Future prospects for the national economy ("Now, looking ahead, do you think that a year from now the country as a whole will be better off, or worse off, or just about the same as now?").

[7] The typical pocketbook question is "Would you say that the present state of your personal finances is better, the same, or worse than a year ago?" Unfortunately, responses to this question are available only since September 1997. The correlation of this shorter time series with the question I use is .80, significant at the 99 percent level.

I seek to explore the *causal framework* that governs the relationship between economic conditions, economic perceptions, and presidential approval. This *casual framework* can work in a variety of ways. Objective economic conditions should shape collective perceptions about the past and the future. Presumably, growth should mostly shape sociotropic retrospective perceptions, which are evaluations of the current state of the *national* economy. Variables such as wages, inflation, and unemployment should mostly shape pocketbook evaluations or evaluations of the current state of the voter's personal finances. Sociotropic and pocketbook perceptions should in turn shape voters' assessments of the future of the national economy in the expected ways – as voters perceive that things have improved, they should become more optimistic about the future. Voters' assessments about the future of the national economy should also be influenced by how the mass media filter economic information to the public (MacKuen et al., 1992). Voters' perceptions should in turn shape presidential approval. If voters behave more like *peasants*, presidential approval should mostly be driven by voters' retrospective evaluations – specifically, their pocketbook evaluations. If voters behave more like *bankers*, approval rates should be driven mostly by voters' evaluations of the prospects for the future of the national economy.

Following MacKuen and colleagues (1992), I begin by performing a standard Granger causality test for assessing the causal framework that governs the relationship between objective economic conditions, collective perceptions, and presidential approval. The questions are, first, the extent to which objective economic conditions shape perceptions about the economy, and second, whether these perceptions shape presidential approval.

To see if economic conditions shape collective beliefs about the present state of the national economy, I regressed sociotropic evaluations on their own lagged values and on the lagged values of different economic conditions (on the one hand, GDP growth; and on the other, unemployment, inflation, and real wages). Using a standard F-test, I evaluate whether the coefficients of the economic variables are statistically different from zero.

Table 5.3 presents the results, which are organized following MacKuen and colleagues (1992, Table 1). The columns represent the potential causal effects of economic conditions, economic perceptions, and presidential approval on the different variables in the rows. Each cell contains the p-values associated with different F-tests. The first column indicates that GDP growth shapes economic perceptions – equations under (1)

Table 5.3. *Granger causality tests (probabilities of no causal effect)*

	Causal Variables			
	Economic Conditions			
Dependent Variable	GDP Growth	Inflation Wages Unemployment	Economic Perceptions	Presidential Approval
(1)				
Sociotropic retrospective evaluations	.01	.13	–	–
Pocketbook retrospective evaluations	.00	.07		
Sociotropic expectations	.03	.46	–	–
(2)				
Presidential approval	.13	.00	–	–
Presidential approval	–		.00	–
(3)				
Presidential approval (Shape approval independent of economic perceptions?)	.00	.00	.00	–
(4)				
Sociotropic retrospective evaluations	.00	.07		.15
Pocketbook retrospective evaluations	.00	.00		.42
Sociotropic expectations (Shape perceptions controlling for approval?)	.02	.26		.68

produce p-values below .05. Note from column two, however, that inflation, unemployment, and real wages *do not* shape sociotropic retrospective and prospective evaluations. This is an important finding. It tells us that sociotropic evaluations, both retrospective and prospective, actually reflect judgments about the state of the *national economy*, as measured, for example, by GDP. On the other hand, collective judgments about the voters' current well-being (pocketbook evaluations) seem to be driven by the evolution of wages, inflation, and unemployment (though with a p-value of .07).

Similarly, under (2), I show the p-values associated with different F-tests that examine whether economic conditions and economic perceptions shape presidential approval. While GDP does not shape approval, unemployment, real wages, and inflation do. Moreover, as can be seen from column four, economic perceptions also shape presidential approval. In section (3), I test the causal effects of the real economy and economic perceptions while controlling for each of these variables in turn (MacKuen et al., 1992: 600). The idea is to see whether the effect of the real economy on approval is channeled completely through mass perceptions, or if the economy shapes approval without the electorate noticing it. If the economy shapes approval in this way, the economic variables should pass the multivariate Granger tests. With p-values below .01 for GDP growth and unemployment, inflation, and real wages, they pass the Granger test, a result that markedly differs from that of MacKuen and colleagues (1992). Presidential approval seems to respond to economic conditions not only to the extent that the economy alters public perceptions: the economy also shapes approval ratings without the electorate recognizing the process. Also under (3) in column four, I establish that economic perceptions shape approval even when they are not directly caused by economic conditions. Perceptions seem to matter only inasmuch as economic data, and particularly unemployment, do not completely dominate.

The last part of the table serves to eliminate a potential *endogeneity* problem – namely, presidential approval shaping economic perceptions. With p-values of .15, .42, and .68, we can state quite confidently that individuals do not make their current or future economic judgments on the basis of their evaluation of the president during the previous quarter. Thus, I have greater confidence that the data for Zedillo are not plagued by rationalization, as Kaufman and Zuckermann (1998) could not rule out for their analysis of Salinas's approval ratings. Also, I can concentrate on modeling how the economy shapes perceptions and approval ratings without having to worry about *endogeneity*.

Effects of Perceptions on Presidential Approval

From this discussion of the Granger tests, it is clear that perceptions matter. Now I assess, first, whether sociotropic or pocketbook evaluations matter most for presidential approval, and second, whether Mexican voters are backward-looking *peasants* or forward-looking *bankers*. Table 5.4 presents the results of various regression analyses of presidential approval where I test which of these economic perceptions matters most. Independent of

Table 5.4. *Effect of collective perceptions on presidential approval, 1994–2000*

	I		II		III	
	Coeff.	S.E.	Coeff.	S.E.	Coeff.	S.E.
Constant	32.41**	8.40	71.55***	21.42	78.25***	20.14
Approval t−1	0.53**	0.14	0.32*	0.167	0.207	0.16
Sociotropic evaluations	0.24**	0.06	8.95E-02	0.096	9.46E-02	0.11
Pocketbook evaluations			0.52**	0.265	0.58**	0.27
Prospective evaluations					−0.32**	0.13
Dummy midterm election					5.58	4.04
	Adj.R^2 = .80 N = 18		Adj. R^2 = .84 N = 18		Adj. R^2 = .89 N = 18	

* significant at the 90% confidence level; ** significant at the 95% confidence level; *** significant at the 99% confidence level.

economic conditions, perceptions shape approval, though not in the expected ways. The results can be summarized in the following ways:

1. Sociotropic retrospective evaluations seem to perform quite well as predictors of presidential approval, but only when they do not have to compete against pocketbook retrospective evaluations or future expectations (column one).
2. Once pocketbook retrospective evaluations are introduced, the significance of sociotropic assessments disappears (column two). This finding is uncommon in the comparative literature, which finds that sociotropic evaluations dominate pocketbook evaluations (Kiewiet, 1983; MacKuen et al., 1992). Instead, voters in Mexico during this period were more narrowly self-interested in their behavior, assessing the president primarily by focusing on their own pocketbooks.
3. The last model introduces voters' evaluations of the prospects for the future of the national economy, controlling for the 1997 election. Expectations about the future of the national economy shape presidential approval in a very unusual manner: as voters become more optimistic about the future, approval decreases. This means that voter optimism about the future *hurts* the president.

Table 5.5. *Voters' evaluations of the prospects for the future of the national economy, 1994–2000*

	I	II	III	IV	V
Constant	−8.56***	−11.50**	−16.41	−4.40*	24.17***
	(3.14)	(5.91)	(6.92)	2.25	5.31
Prospective −1ag	0.24	0.25	0.18	0.50***	0.49***
	(0.20)	(0.20)	(0.20)	0.18	0.12
1997 elections	15.62***	15.56***	16.41***	11.58**	
	(5.71)	(5.75)	(5.48)	4.65	
Real wages	−0.24				
	(0.27)				
Inflation		0.15			
		(0.19)			
Unemployment			1.98		
			(1.37)		
GDP				−1.054***	−1.05***
				(0.37)	(0.26)
GDP-1				0.319	
				(0.41)	
Sociotropic retrospections					0.35***
					(0.06)
Time					−1.19***
					(0.32)
	Adj.R^2 = .41	Adj.R^2 = .40	Adj.R^2 = .45	Adj.R^2 = .64	Adj.R^2 = .64
	N = 18	N = 18	N = 18	N = 18	N = 18

* significant at the 90% confidence level; ** significant at the 95% confidence level; *** significant at the 99% confidence level.

Effects of Economic Conditions on Expectations about the Future

Why would voters decide to reward the president when they see that their personal economic situation has improved in the recent past, but to punish him when they see good times ahead? To answer this question, we must understand how economic conditions shape expectations about the future, a task to which I now turn. In Table 5.5, I present results of several OLS regressions that use collective expectations about the future state of the economy as the dependent variable. I obtain the following results:

1. Inflation rates, unemployment, and real wages do not shape collective expectations about the future of the national economy.
2. Growth rates have a negative, statistically significant impact, which means that the higher the current growth rate, the less optimistic voters are about the future. I interpret this result to mean that, in

light of Mexico's history of economic booms and busts during the last twenty years, a high growth rate is perceived by voters as a signal that difficulties lie ahead, because "good things can't last."

3. Retrospective evaluations of the present state of the national economy are employed to make inferences about the future. More positive views about the current state of the economy increase optimism about the future.
4. Time has a negative, statistically significant impact on collective beliefs about the future of the national economy. Voters have learned that the future prospects of the national economy always worsen as the next presidential election approaches. The impact of time is significant even after controlling for growth rates.

My results indicate that Mexican voters during the Zedillo administration rewarded the president for an increase in their real wages and severely punished him for unemployment and inflation. Presidential approval responded more to retrospective pocketbook assessments than to sociotropic ones. In addition, my results show that inflation, unemployment, and real wages powerfully shaped pocketbook evaluations of current well-being. Mexican voters thus acted as *peasants* in their evaluations of Zedillo. Nevertheless, the electorate was capable of making predictions about the future, even though these expectations shaped behavior in unusual ways. Unlike conventional forward-looking voting models, which predict that voters will support a party that is expected to improve their economic situation in the future, I showed *that optimism about the future hurts the incumbent*. As the country grew and the end of the term approached, voters became more pessimistic about the future because they feared an electoral bust after the impending presidential elections.

Even while anticipating an end-of-term crisis, Mexican voters absolved president Zedillo: they approved of him because their pocketbooks were recovering. Yet they did not absolve the PRI: as the national economy improved, they became more pessimistic about the future, and this collective pessimism hurt the party in the 2000 elections. These results, together with what I find in Chapter 7, explain why the PRI could not profit from the outstanding growth rates of the two years before the 2000 elections: voters had learned to distrust the party's electoral opportunism and to interpret economic improvements prior to elections as a sign that the economy would collapse after the election.

6

Ideological Divisions in the Opposition Camp

Opposition coordination failure played a significant role in sustaining the dominance of the PRI. Patterns in local elections during the last twenty years demonstrate that the PRI tended to win more often where the opposition stood divided. By contrast, the PRI tended to lose more often in states or municipalities where a bipartisan mode of party competition prevailed, with the PRI competing against one major opposition party, or where all-encompassing opposition coalitions were forged (Diaz-Cayeros and Magaloni, 2001).

Do policy divisions play a role in inhibiting opposition voter coordination? To answer this question, I designed, with Rafael Giménez, a survey that was conducted by *Reforma* newspaper in July of 1995. A total of 509 respondents were surveyed in three cities: Mexico City, Guadalajara, and Monterrey.[1] Seventeen issues were included in the survey, following the standard National Elections Study format of seven-point policy scales. Respondents were asked to locate their own position on the scale and then to locate their perceived positions of the PRI, the PAN, and the PRD on the same scale. The survey is not representative of the rural poor, and I do not claim that any of the findings in this chapter extend to the Mexican countryside.

[1] Unfortunately, a nationwide survey could not be conducted. Nonetheless, these cities are the largest in the country. I should point out that few surveys in Mexico have been designed with the specific intention of measuring policy positions. To a large extent, pollsters have assumed that issue voting is irrelevant and hence have failed to ask the questions necessary to assess their assumptions. I also intervened in designing the 1997 survey that will be analyzed in the following chapter, which also includes a variety of issue questions similar to those included in the 1995 survey I employ here. Many other surveys do include a couple of issue questions, but the question wording is not appropriate.

The chapter unfolds as follows. I first discuss the research on coordination failure. The following section seeks to provide evidence of chronic voter uncertainty about the parties' issue positions. Finally, the chapter estimates the impact of the issues on voting intentions.

Coordination Dilemmas and Party Dominance

As summarized by Cox (1997), the literature on dominant-party systems argues that coordination failure plays a key role in sustaining party dominance. Analyzing party dominance in India, Riker (1976) argued that coordination failure was essentially the product of the central ideological location of the Congress Party. Opponents "scattered to the right and left of Congress would have had to create an ends-against-the-center coalition in most districts in order to unseat Congress, followed by an ends-against-the center coalition in the Lok Sabha to unseat Congress ministers. The difficulty of pulling off this kind of coordination kept Congress in power" (Cox, 1997: 239). Sartori (1976), Laver and Schofield (1991), and Pempel (1990) all provide a similar argument, which is based on the dominant party's central location, to explain dominance in Japan, Italy, Israel, and Sweden.

Cox (1997) moves beyond these authors in highlighting a variety of causal mechanisms that may inhibit or enhance coordination among political parties and voters. According to Cox, failure to coordinate might stem from three sources: electoral institutions, social cleavages, and election-specific dynamics. First, electoral institutions determine the payoffs of forming larger versus smaller electoral coalitions. The simple-majority, single-ballot system, according to Duverger's law, creates incentives for the consolidation of a two-party system. Duverger's law applies for two reasons (Duverger, 1963). First, the plurality-vote system has a "psychological" effect. Some voters who prefer a candidate or party who they think cannot win will cast a vote for their first choice among the parties that have a better chance of winning. This type of electoral behavior is called strategic voting. Second, the plurality-vote-win system has a "mechanical" effect that influences strategic behavior by political parties. Plurality-vote-win systems give large parties a more-than-proportional share of seats and small parties a less-than-proportional share. Smaller parties may win many votes nationwide but fail to gain a plurality of the vote and thus obtain no electoral payoff. Small parties interested in winning thus face an incentive to form alliances that can plausibly win a plurality of votes.

The most recent interpretations of Duverger's law all tend to agree that the effective number of parties is predicted primarily by district magnitude rather than by electoral formula (Taagepera and Shugart, 1989; Reed, 1990; Cox, 1991; Cox, 1997). Strategic voting, in equilibrium, will tend to reduce the number of parties to M + 1, where M is the district magnitude.[2] Cox (1997) attributes the failure of opposition parties to coordinate against the long-lasting LDP in Japan largely to the single-nontransferable-vote electoral system (SNTV) that prevailed during the era of dominance of the LDP. In Diaz-Cayeros and Magaloni (2001), we argue that electoral rules inhibited coordination among opposition parties in Mexico. Our argument is that electoral rules facilitated the dominance of the PRI through two mechanisms: electoral rules for the Chamber of Deputies disproportionately rewarded existing majorities; at the same time, the rules discouraged potential majorities from forming. More specifically, given the mixed electoral system,[3] the rules disproportionately rewarded parties that could win a majority of the vote in single-member districts; but at the same time, they rewarded minority parties with seats from multimember districts, thereby mitigating Duvergerian incentives to coordinate behind a single challenger. In the short run, seats from the multimember districts benefited opposition parties by significantly reducing entry costs to the legislature; in the long run, however, these seats helped to sustain the PRI's dominance by discouraging coordination among opposition parties and voters in the single-member districts.[4]

Furthermore, the existing rule for the cross-endorsement of presidential candidates, established in the electoral reform of 1993, significantly increased the cost of coordination for the opposition parties in presidential elections. After the 1988 experience, the PRI changed the rule that allowed parties to nominate common presidential candidates while keeping a separate identity for concurrent congressional and senatorial races. The 1993 rule implies that if two parties want to nominate a common presidential

[2] This refers to the generalization of Duverger's law to single-nontransferable-vote (SNTV) systems, of which simple-majority single-ballot systems are a special case, where district magnitude (M) is one, which yields M + 1 or two parties. See Cox (1997).

[3] As discussed in Diaz-Cayeros and Magaloni (2001), there are 500 seats elected using a mixed electoral formula; 300 seats are elected from single-member districts, and 200 come from multimember districts. The electoral formula for distributing the multimember seats is not compensatory and is thus far from proportional.

[4] Voters could cast only one straight vote for both the single-member districts and the multimember districts.

candidate, they must also share candidates in all the congressional and senatorial races – all of the 628 other races at stake. If parties intend to coordinate, they must do so long before the start of the campaign. The rule thus implied that if opposition parties wanted to cross-endorse a presidential candidate, they first had to craft alliances for each of the races taking place simultaneously and consequently sacrifice their internal dynamics for the distribution of seats within the party. This course of action clearly involved great transaction costs.[5]

Second, social cleavages can also inhibit coordination. Social cleavages can be reflected in policy divergences among parties and voters, as in the aforementioned approaches, and these policy divergences might prevent voters from coordinating. For instance, a left-wing voter is not likely to cast a strategic vote in favor of a right-wing party. Riker (1976) employs this approach to explain why the opposition could not coordinate in India against the Congress Party. However, ethnic differences among parties are another powerful social cleavage that can inhibit social coordination (Ordeshook and Shvetsova, 1994; Cox, 1997). Regional differences are yet another potential source of coordination failure. As I demonstrated in Chapter 2, the PAN was stronger in the more affluent urban states of the North and El Bajío, and the PRD was stronger in the poorer and more rural states of the South. For a long time, failure of these opposition parties to have national reach seriously complicated opposition coordination at the national level.

One way to assess the dimensionality of the policy space, and the potential for voter coordination, is by looking at voters' preference profiles, as suggested in Chapter 1 (see also Magaloni, 1996). In the Mexican case, opposition coordination required that opposition voters rank the PRI third. I call these voters who ranked the PRI third "nonideological or tactical opposition voters."[6] Preference profiles such as (PAN P PRD P PRI) or (PRD P PAN P PRI), where P is the preference relationship, fit this

[5] Another restriction on the cross-endorsement of presidential candidates, as Diaz-Cayeros and Magaloni (2001) note, is that the electoral code awards each alliance the amount of public funding that its largest constituent party would have received, rather than the sum of the financing that each party in the alliance would have received had it fielded a separate candidate.

[6] In Magaloni (1994, 1996) and in Magaloni and Poiré (2004b), I called these voters "radical opposition voters." In this book I prefer the term "nonideological opposition voters" because I employ the term "radical opposition voters" for a different purpose (see Chapter 8).

characterization. Nonideological or tactical opposition voters saw more commonalities among the opposition parties and were more concerned about defeating the PRI regardless of party or economic platform. Voters can also see sharp ideological differences between the opposition parties and possess preference profiles such as (PAN P PRI P PRD) or (PRD P PRI P PAN). I call these voters, who perceived larger incompatibilities between opposition parties than between either the PAN or the PRD and the PRI, "ideological opposition voters." If the distribution of preference profiles among the Mexican electorate was such that both ideological and nonideological opposition voters existed, it would mean that the issue space was multidimensional, or that voters and parties were divided along a socioeconomic left-right dimension where the PRI was between the opposition parties, and a pro-regime, anti-regime dimension where opposition parties stood next to each other. In Magaloni (1996), I demonstrated that the distribution of preference profiles among the mass electorate was such that the issue space in Mexico was indeed multidimensional (see also Magaloni and Poiré, 2004b).[7]

Thus, since party competition was multidimensional in Mexico, opposition coordination failure cannot be accounted for solely by arguments akin to those of Riker (1976) or the other authors cited earlier, who focus on the dominant party's central location. These arguments assume, on the one hand, that party competition is one-dimensional, and on the other, that the dominant party is positioned in the middle, so that the overwhelming majority of opposition voters rank that party second. Opposition coordination in Mexico was possible as long as the majority of the opposition electorate attached a higher saliency to the political than to the ideological dimension. This is how voters behaved in the 2000 presidential elections, as I demonstrate in the following chapter. Conversely, if the majority of opposition voters attach a higher saliency to the ideological dimension, as my results in the following chapter indicate occurred in the 1994 presidential elections, opposition coordination would fail. To successfully dislodge the ruling party, voters must hence develop a strong commitment to democracy and political change, and this commitment must be more important than

[7] Using different approaches to assess the dimensionality of the policy space at the mass level, other authors have also highlighted it (see Domínguez and McCann, 1995, 1996; Moreno 1998, 1999b). Molinar (1991) was the first to note the multidimensionality of the issue space in Mexico. His focus was on party elites.

the disagreements they might have on other economic issues or than their ethnic rivalries.

Coordination failure may also arise from election-specific dynamics, or voters' probabilistic assessments of each party's expected chance of winning. According to Cox (1997), failure to coordinate might result when (1) a voter believes that only one party has a real chance of winning, so that there are no incentives to cast a strategic vote; (2) when the second and first loser are so close for second place that voters do not know which party to discount; or (3) when voters do not possess strict preference orders among the three major contenders. In hegemonic party regimes, there are thus few incentives to cast strategic votes because only one party possesses any real chance of winning. This is why strategic voting, as Domínguez and McCann (1996) rightly observe, became thinkable in Mexico only after 1988. Further, if there is no reliable public information about the relative standing of the parties at the polls, coordination will fail (Cox, 1997). This is why control of the media by an autocratic government, as in Mexico well into the mid-1990s (Lawson, 2002), can play a powerful role in inhibiting voter coordination or mass bandwagon effects in favor of the opposition parties.[8]

Opposition coordination during the 1994 and 2000 elections will be assessed in Chapter 7. In this chapter, I concentrate on the issue divisions inhibiting opposition coordination. What were some of the main policy issues that divided opposition voters in Mexico? What were the central policy issues that these voters had in common?

Policy Issue Positions of the Three Major Parties

The survey questionnaire included a series of questions on economic issues that broadly correspond to the four major areas of economic policy making that, according to Lijphart (1984), are invariably present in any political system. The four areas are (1) public versus private property in the means of production; (2) a strong versus a weak role for the government in economic planning; (3) support for versus opposition to the redistribution of wealth through taxes; and (4) support for versus opposition to the expansion of government social programs. International trade, not included by

[8] On the role of the media in Mexican political life, see Lawson (1999, 2002, 2004a). On the role of the media in voting behavior, see especially the articles by Lawson and Moreno in Domínguez and Poiré (1999) and in Domínguez and Lawson (2004).

Lijphart on the list, constitutes a fifth major area of economic policy, one that has become a central point of political division. The division is generally manifested in terms of support for versus opposition to trade liberalization and/or industrial policy.

In addition to economic policy issues, the survey questionnaire included a series of questions on political issues that are meant to capture divisions along the *regime cleavage* dimension, where parties and voters divide with respect to their evaluations of existing political institutions and the scope and pace of political reform. Moreno (1999b) demonstrates in his comparative analysis of political cleavages in democratizing countries that the regime cleavage is the most salient. Finally, the survey questionnaire also included a set of questions on value-related issues, such as opinions on abortion, state-church relations, marriage through the church or free union, the autonomy of indigenous communities, and equality between men and women.[9]

I develop a spatial representation of the parties and voters along the political spectrum by presenting median placements of the parties and median self-placement on each of the issues. Employing median party perceptions instead of mean perceptions is useful because they tend to reflect more accurately the differences among the parties, particularly when the distributions of responses about perceived party placements are not normal. In a sense, median perceptions weight more heavily the opinions of the majority.

Economic Issues

Figure 6.1 provides the median perception of the parties' stands, the median-self-placement, and the percentage of respondents who placed themselves at each point on the scale on all of the economic issues. The first thing to note is that the two opposition parties offer clearly distinct economic platforms; their median placements on most of these issues are two or more full points apart. The PRD was consistently placed to the left of the midpoint on most issues. It was perceived as opposing the privatization of the state oil company, PEMEX; standing against NAFTA and foreign trade; favoring government guarantees of jobs and a good living standard; supporting redistribution of wealth through taxes; standing for an increase in government spending and subsidies to alleviate poverty; and supporting a strong role for the state in economic planning. All of these polices are conventionally favored by left-wing alternatives. The average

[9] The full survey questionnaire is provided on my website <www.stanford.edu/~magaloni>.

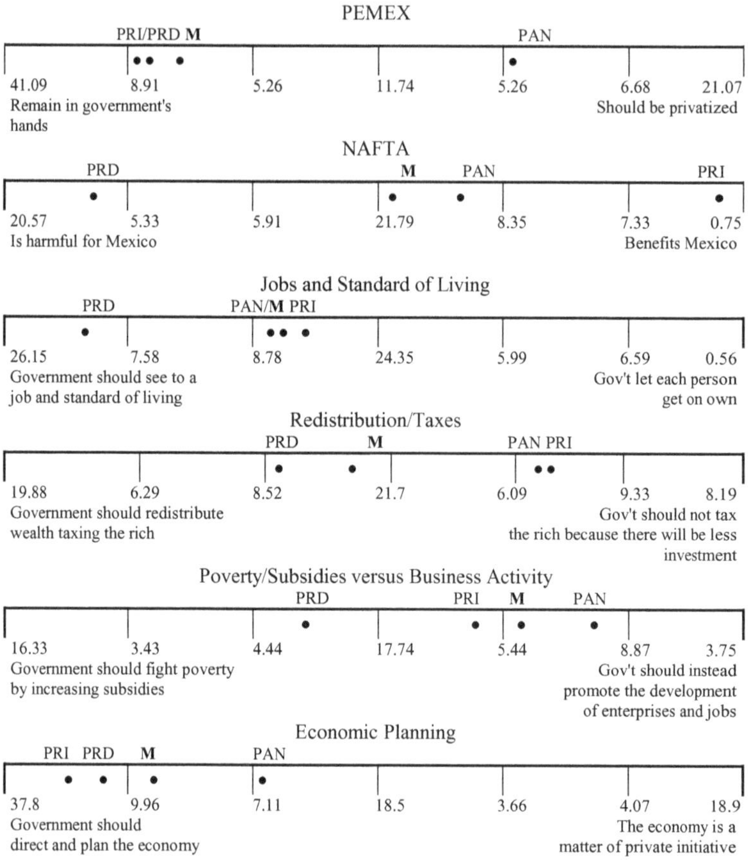

Figure 6.1. Median placement of the parties and median self-placement (M) on economic issues (numbers are percentage that self-placed at each point on the scale).

median placement of the PRD on the economic issues was 2.41, clearly to the left of the mid-point of 4.

The PAN was placed to the right of the midpoint on most economic issues. The median perception was that the PAN favored the privatization of PEMEX, stood against redistribution through taxes, and supported the development of business activity to generate jobs. The PAN's position was regarded as more centrist on NAFTA, economic planning, and government guarantees for jobs and living standards. The PAN received an overall median placement on the six economic issues of 4.56, slightly to the right of the midpoint. Thus, this party was perceived as right-wing but not as supporting a purely free-market approach. As noted earlier, on all of the economic issues, the median placements of the PAN and the PRD were almost two points apart, meaning that according to the median response in the survey, the two opposition parties offered clearly different economic platforms.

On all issues except NAFTA and poverty alleviation, the PRI was perceived as standing together with either opposition party. The PRI was not perceived as a nationalistic party; its median placement was strongly in favor of the free-trade agreement, at point 7 on the scale. However, the ruling party was perceived as a statist alternative, favoring a strong role for the government in the economy and opposing the privatization of PEMEX. In issues that deal with the redistribution of wealth and government guarantees for jobs and living standards, the PRI was seen as standing to the right of the midpoint, meaning that it was regarded as experiencing a "rightist swing" – a perception that was quite accurate. The average median placement of the PRI was centrist at 4.02, between the two other parties.

Figure 6.1 also shows the percentage of respondents who placed themselves at each point on the scale and the median self-placement. The median respondent stood to the left of the midpoint on most economic issues. The median self-placement was clearly to the left on the following issues: privatization of PEMEX (3), government guarantees of jobs and a good standard of living (3.3), and economic planning by the state (2.31). The median respondent was more centrist in his evaluations of NAFTA and foreign trade and on the issue of redistribution through taxes. Only on one issue, increasing government spending to alleviate poverty versus promotion of business activity to generate jobs, was the median respondent clearly to the right on the scale, at 5.29. Overall, the average median response on all economic issues was 3.62, slightly to the left of the midpoint and closer to the PRD on most issues.

Political Issues

Figure 6.2 provides the spatial distribution of the parties on the political issues. The two opposition parties were perceived as having similar positions on the political issues. On the issues of democracy, corruption, and respect for human rights, the median placements of both opposition parties were practically identical. The issue of corruption shows a similar pattern. Both opposition parties were seen as favoring "ruthless punishment, even with jail, of all the corrupt politicians and public authorities." The PRI was

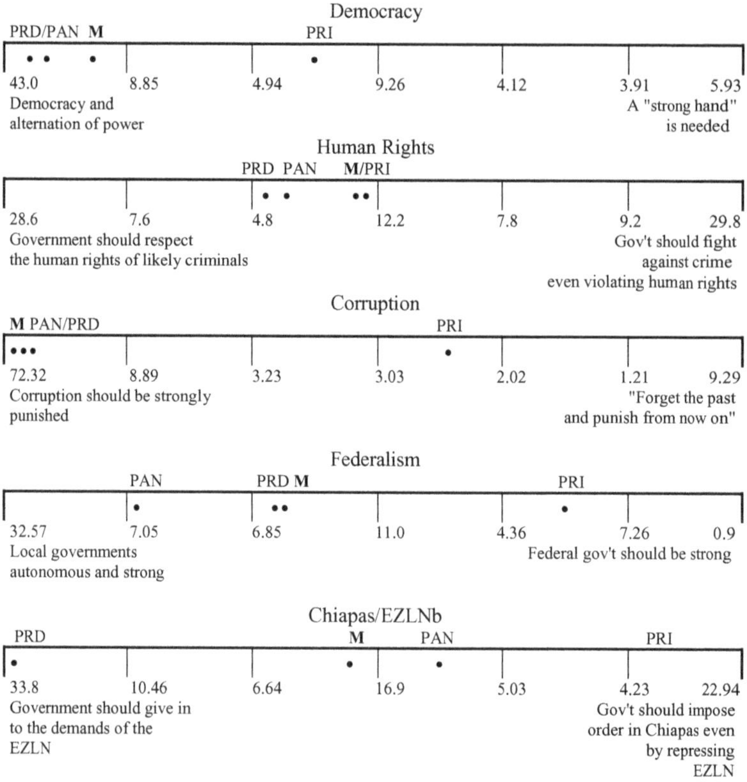

Figure 6.2. Median placement of the parties and median self-placement (*M*) on political issues (numbers are percentage that self-placed at each point on the scale).

placed to the right of the midpoint as favoring a different solution, which was that "the government should forgive what is already in the past, punishing corruption from now on, in order to avoid political revenge among politicians."

On the issue of human rights – whether the government, when fighting crime, should strictly respect the human rights of criminals or instead should be tough on crime even though this might imply violating human rights – the PRI was perceived close to the midpoint, but not too far from both opposition parties. On the issue of federalism, although the median placement of the PAN was slightly to the left of the PRD, meaning that the PAN was perceived as more in favor of decentralization, the difference between the two parties is not very significant (the parties' median placements are less than one point apart). The PRI was perceived as a highly centralist alternative, close to the right-hand side of the scale. On the issue of Chiapas, the positions of the two opposition parties were clearly different. The PRD was perceived as highly sympathetic to the Zapatistas; the PAN was perceived as standing between the other two parties; and the PRI was located to the right, favoring the alternative of sending the army to Chiapas to "put order in the state" (which makes sense, since the army was already in Chiapas and the government had repeatedly refused to withdraw).

As with the economic issues, there was strong disagreement among respondents on these political issues. On the issue of democracy, 43 percent placed themselves at the origin of the scale, favoring democratic elections and alternation of power. Although this percentage is very high, close to 26 percent still favored a "strong hand" – naturally, these respondents were closer to the median perception of the PRI than to that of the opposition parties. On only one issue, corruption, is there almost absolute agreement among respondents, 72.32 percent placing themselves at the origin of the scale.

Value-Related Issues

Figure 6.3 provides the spatial distribution of the parties and of respondents on the value-related issues and the percentage of respondents who placed themselves at each point on the scale. On all of the issues but abortion, respondents leaned toward the liberal side of the scale, and the PRD's median placement was closer to the median respondent on almost all of them. However, on the abortion issue, the median respondent leaned toward the conservative side of the scale – although the distribution of self-placements was slightly bimodal, with 27 percent supporting a pro-choice option and 37 percent a pro-life alternative. Although the three parties were perceived as standing to the right of the midpoint, clearly supporting the notion that "abortion should always be forbidden by law," the PAN was perceived as the party holding the most pro-life position located farthest from the median respondent.

On the issue of state-church relations, the PRD and the PRI were both perceived as anticlerical parties, supporting the notion that the church should not "intervene in politics and that the government should not allow priests to make their political opinions public, to get involved in political organizations or to vote." Voters continued to perceive the PRI

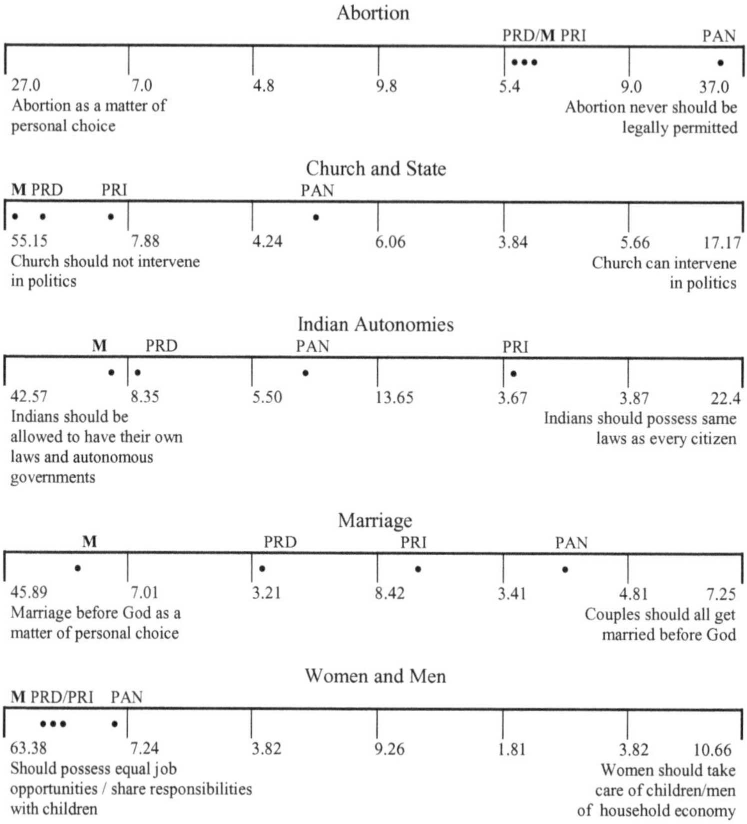

Figure 6.3. Median placement of the parties and median self-placement (*M*) on moral issues (numbers are percentage that self-placed at each point on the scale).

as anticlerical, notwithstanding the constitutional changes that were promoted by Carlos Salinas, through which official anticlericalism came to an end. These constitutional changes were supported by the PAN. Although the PAN was not perceived as favoring strong political involvement of the church in public matters (or as a confessional party), its position was seen as far more friendly toward the church. The median self-placement on this issue was clearly anticlerical.

The issue of autonomy for indigenous communities was an important debate that emerged after the Zapatista uprising. The debate centered on whether indigenous groups should be allowed to possess politically autonomous territories. The median respondent stood in favor of the autonomy of indigenous groups and closer to the average perception of the PRD. The PRI was perceived, on average, as standing against the autonomy of indigenous groups, and the PAN was perceived as standing between the other two parties. On the issue of whether a couple, in order to live together and have sex, must get married before the church or the state, versus the notion that it is "perfectly all right" to live with someone without getting married, the PAN was perceived, again, as holding a more conservative position, more than one and a half points to the right of the midpoint, while the PRD was perceived as holding the most liberal position, slightly to the left of the midpoint. The PRI was perceived as standing between the other two parties. The median respondent was clearly on the liberal side of the scale at 1.58, standing closer to the PRD. On the issue of equality between men and women, all parties were perceived as favoring it; however, the PRD was again perceived as more liberal than the other two parties.

The picture that emerges from these results is that the average voter was quite capable of placing the parties in correct positions. The PAN and the PRD were perceived as offering clearly different economic and values-related packages, the first consonant with right-wing conservative polices and the second with left-wing liberal ones. On all of the economic issues, the mean placements of the PAN were statistically different from the mean placements of the PRD, the PAN always standing to the right of the PRD (results not shown). Further, on almost all of the value-related issues, the mean placements of the three parties were statistically different from each other (results not shown), with the PAN perceived as holding more conservative positions, the PRD more libertarian ones, and the PRI as standing between the other two parties. The opposition parties, however, were perceived as having very similar positions on the political issues – although the average respondent thought that the PRD was more opposed to the political status quo than the PAN because of its sympathies with the Zapatistas.

These results are consistent with the findings of Estévez and Magaloni (2000), where we observed rightist stances for both PAN *voters* and PAN *legislators* on a series of economic policy issues related to taxation, size of government, and redistribution, and leftist stances for both PRD *voters* and PRD *legislators* on these policy issues. Moreno (1998, 1999b, 2003, 2004) found that PAN supporters tended to be positioned in the "center" on the left-right *ideological* scale. The difference between his findings and mine stem from the fact that the left-right ideological scale that Moreno employs to position voters comes from the question: "In politics, people talk about 'left' and 'right.' On a scale of 0 to 10, where 0 is 'left' and 10 is 'right,' where would you place yourself?" My results instead look at disagreements among the parties and voters on a series of economic *policy issues*.[10]

Voting Choices

The final task of this chapter is to assess whether issues shape stated voting intentions. The goal is not to estimate the effect of issues on *actual* voting intentions, but to see how issues translate into the party system. This is a relevant distinction, particularly considering that a high percentage (24 percent) of respondents in the survey did not report a party preference. Among those who reported a party choice, I expect to find a systematic relationship with the issues, meaning that voters should support the party which is "closest" to them.[11]

I follow Alvarez and Nagler (2000) in employing a multinomial probit (MNP) for estimating the impact of issues on stated voting intentions.[12] The prediction of the Downsian spatial model is that voters should vote for the party whose issue positions are closest to their own views. To assess this hypothesis, I employ the square root of the sum of the squared distances between the voter's position and each party's actual position on the issues, where actual position is defined as the median position of the party in the survey data such that:

$$ID_{ijn} = \sqrt{\sum_{k=1}^{K}(P_{jk} - V_{ik})^2}, \qquad (6.1)$$

where ID_{ij} stands for the issue distance between voter i and party j, P_{jk} are party j's actual position on the k issues, and V_{ik} are voter i's issue positions. The sign of the issue coefficients should be negative, meaning that the

10 In the Mexican case, voters' self-placement on the left-right scale seems to reflect their standing on the so-called regime cleavage more than their position on the economy (Zechmeister, 2002).

11 Unfortunately, I cannot evaluate the impact of voter uncertainty on stated voting intentions. Since there are reasons to think that voter uncertainty is in part endogenous (i.e., the product of party choice), a two-stage procedure would be needed to estimate the impact of uncertainty on stated voting intentions. However, the survey does not permit me to perform such a procedure, because, as noted earlier, other relevant variables for estimating voter uncertainty were not included in the survey.

12 On details of the model, see Alvarez and Nagler (2000).

closer a voter is to party j's positions, the higher his chance of supporting that party.

I am particularly interested in highlighting which issues matter for voters in deciding *between the two opposition parties*. Thus, I estimate an MNP model employing the PRD as the base category. Therefore, the coefficients of the model should be interpreted as the effects of a particular variable on PRI or PAN support, *relative* to support for the PRD. My expectation is that political issues will *not* be relevant determinants of voting choices when the comparison is between the PAN and the PRD. However, given that these two parties differ on economic and values-related issues, voters must take these issues into account when choosing between the parties. Regarding the behavior of PRI voters, I expect political issues to be relevant when comparing the ruling party to the PRD. I do not have any a priori expectations about the impact of economic and value-related issues on a vote for the PRI over the PRD. Since the prediction of the Downsian spatial model is that voters should vote for the party whose issue positions are closest to their own views, I expect the issue distance coefficients to be negative.

Table 6.1 presents the results of the MNP analysis.[13] It can be seen that all of the issue coefficients are correctly signed and that quite a few reach statistical significance. The first thing to note is that, as expected, economic-issue distances are statistically significant and have a strong effect on the choice of the PAN over the PRD. This implies that the closer a voter is to the PAN on the economic issues, the higher his chance of supporting that party relative to the PRD.

Since we know that the PAN is located on the right-hand side of the scale on all the economic issues, we can conclude that voters who hold right-wing preferences, and who are thus closer to the PAN's economic-issue positions, tend disproportionately to vote for the right-wing opposition party over the PRD. It should be noted that the political issues are not significant in the case of the PAN, which implies that what makes a voter choose the PAN over the PRD is economics, not politics. Economic issues are also significant for a choice of the PRD over the PRI, meaning that the closer a voter is to the PRD on all of the economic issues, the lower his chance of supporting

[13] Following Alvarez and Nagler (2000), I attempted to control for the correlation of at least one pair of error terms – preferably, those between the PAN and the PRI. However, the matrix of coefficients could not be inverted. This is probably due to the lack of sufficient observations, since the MNP model is quite data-intensive and, unfortunately, the sample size is limited. Results should be read as independent multinomial probit estimates.

Table 6.1. *Multinomial probit analysis (PRD base category)*

Independent Variables	PAN	PRI
Constant	2.630	3.642***
	(.4530)	(.7394)
Education	.0066	−.3098***
	(.0883)	(.1155)
Gender	.2484	−.0324
(1 = Male)	(.2315)	(.2443)
PAN economic distance	−.1477**	
	(.0599)	
PAN political distance	−.0647	
	(.0541)	
PAN moral distance	−.0783	
	(.0571)	
PRI economic distance		−.1510**
		(.0657)
PRI political distance		−.2496***
		(.0841)
PRI moral distance		.0318
		(.0774)
*p < .10	Predicted correctly = 70%	
**p < .05	N = 292	
***p < .01	ll −0.8768	

Note: Issue distances are constructed applying equation 6.2.

the PRI over the PRD. As expected, political issues are also significant and quite strong in the case of a vote for the PRD over the PRI. In neither case were the value-related issues significant.

Thus, these results compellingly demonstrate that before the PRI lost in 2000, there were two highly relevant policy-issue dimensions of party competition in Mexico – a political one and an economic one. On the political dimension, voters and parties divided along an anti- and pro-political-status-quo continuum. Voters tended to take these issues into account when making their choices, with PAN and PRD supporters holding similar views that turned them into "opposition voters." On the economic dimension, voters and parties were divided along a left-right continuum. There were powerful disagreements that divided the opposition parties among themselves on several major areas of economic policy making, such as public versus private property in the means of production; a strong versus a weak role for the government in economic planning; support for versus opposition to the redistribution of wealth through taxes; support for versus opposition to the expansion of government social programs; and support for versus opposition to trade liberalization. Values-related issues were not highly salient to voters. Although the average respondent perceived the PAN as conservative and the PRD as libertarian, voters did not appear to employ these issues in their voting decisions. The low salience of moral issues might stem from the fact that, when the survey was collected, opposition parties had seldom stressed these value-related issues in political campaigns. However, since both voters and parties hold rather divergent views on these issues, values-related issues are *potentially salient*, meaning that if parties start to stress them during the campaigns, voters might act accordingly.

Conclusion

This chapter has analyzed several factors contributing to the policy divisions among the three major parties in Mexico. I first showed that the average respondent could place the three parties' relative policy positions accurately. On most of the economic issues, the PRD was placed to the left, the PAN to the right, and the PRI between the opposition parties, though it sometimes shared left stances with the PRD and sometimes shared right positions with the PAN. On the political issues, both opposition parties were seen as sharing anti-political-status quo positions, and the PRI was placed as the pro-political-status quo party. On the values-related issues, the PRD was perceived as libertarian, the PAN as conservative, and the PRI was placed between the other two parties.

Finally, I demonstrated that before the PRI's defeat in 2000, there were two highly significant dimensions dividing Mexican society. Parties and voters were divided along a political dimension, with opposition voters, relative to PRI voters, disproportionately coming from those who sought to transform the political status quo – to install democracy, decentralize resources, fight corruption in government, and so forth. Political forces were also divided along a left-right economic dimension. I demonstrated that those who reported support for the PAN over the PRD disproportionately favored a set of right-wing economic policies, including liberalization of trade, privatization of PEMEX, and promotion of business activity versus poverty alleviation. They also stood against increases in taxes and wealth redistribution. Conversely, PRD voters preferred a more activist and nationalistic state, government programs for poverty alleviation, and redistribution of wealth. They also stood against the privatization of PEMEX.

This highlights one of the crucial coordination dilemmas faced by opposition forces in Mexico. While opposition parties and voters held similar views on the political dimension, showing the potential to form a united political front against the PRI, on the economic dimension they truly differed. The following chapters will further explore the coordination dilemmas of opposition forces in Mexico.

7

How Voters Choose and Mass Coordination Dilemmas

EVIDENCE FROM THE 1994, 1997, AND 2000 NATIONAL ELECTIONS

What finally allowed Mexican voters to "throw the rascals out" of office? What factors hindered or encouraged opposition coordination in presidential elections? To answer these questions, this chapter presents an analysis of voting choices in the 1994, 1997, and 2000 elections. I systematically test a series of hypotheses on mass support for the PRI derived from my voting model with the use of micro-level evidence.

The Context of the Elections

The 1994 Mexican presidential elections took place after six years of profound economic transformation. The government had removed almost all trade barriers. Mexico had joined the North American Free Trade Agreement, and the country was more fully integrated into international capital markets. Some political commentators and analysts interpreted these elections as a referendum on economic performance. At the time, it seemed that macroeconomic stabilization had been successful, and domestic consumption was booming. The economy, however, was barely growing. Contrary to these views, I find that the electorate reelected the PRI in 1994 despite holding highly negative retrospective assessments of the economy. As they had done in 1988 and 1991, voters exonerated the PRI for mediocre economic performance and chose prospectively, reelecting the incumbent party because they still believed it was more capable of handling the future of the national economy.

The 1994 elections were unique in that they took place during a year of political turmoil, marked by both the Zapatista uprising and the assassination of the PRI's presidential candidate, Luis Donaldo Colosio. Triggered by the first of these violent events, an electoral reform had taken place before the 1994 presidential elections, during the Carlos Salinas term. As will be explored in the next chapter, the reform established the six Citizen Councilmen, who were elected to the board of the IFE, and who were crucial in the organization and credibility of the elections. The reform was successful in that the 1994 electoral process was transparent enough that no major complaints of electoral fraud were lodged.

However, before the 1994 elections, there was a great deal of uncertainty about the workings of the new IFE. As I will demonstrate in the following chapter, most of the opposition electorate, and particularly PRD supporters, perceived that the elections would be fraudulent and that political violence was going to erupt after the elections. A sizable group of voters further doubted that the PRI would allow a winning opposition party to take office. Thus, before the 1994 presidential elections, there was no consensus within the electorate about whether the country had passed the threshold that separates democracy from authoritarianism.

This regime cleavage became less important after the 1994 elections. The PRD first attempted to contest the results, but soon switched to a less confrontational post-electoral strategy, complaining not so much about manipulation of the elections as about the unfair nature of the electoral contest. The PAN and the PRD agreed that the new Citizen Councilmen on the IFE's board provided for the independence of this body and credibly committed the PRI to clean elections. Both parties still complained, however, that the electoral rules were not fair for two main reasons: opposition parties received extremely unequal access to the media, and the PRI received a disproportionate share of campaign resources. The 1996 electoral reform addressed these objections, and after the political parties agreed on the set of fundamental political rules, the regime cleavage between the opposition and the PRI became less salient. Elections increasingly became more conventional, centered on economic evaluations, candidates, and issues.[1]

The 1997 midterm elections took place at a time when the economy was recovering (GNP grew by 7 percent in that year). However, as my empirical analysis will demonstrate, voters assessed the PRI's performance on the basis of its dismal longer-term economic record. Policy issues played a decisive role in these elections, and the opposition was divided into two equally strong blocs. Those defecting to the PRD had policy stances conventionally

[1] For assessments of media effects in the 1997 elections, see Lawson (1999). For assessments of how political awareness, exposure to the media, and campaigns shaped voting decisions, see Moreno (1999a, 2004).

associated with left-wing policies, and those defecting to the PAN were more right-wing than the PRI. The 1997 midterm elections brought about a fundamental change in Mexican politics because the PRI received only 39 percent of the vote, and hence lost its absolute majority in the powerful Chamber of Deputies. The opposition would now actively participate in the drafting of laws and could veto presidential initiatives, including the annual budget.

The aggregate electoral results of 1997 can be summarized as a dramatic decline in the PRI's electoral support, a significant increase in support for the PRD, and a somewhat mediocre performance by the PAN. Indeed, in the local elections taking place in 1995 and 1996, the PAN was a strong beneficiary of voters' massive defections from the PRI. However, in the 1997 midterm elections, the PAN did not increase its absolute number of votes with respect to the previous national elections, although it won two additional governorships, in Nuevo León and Querétaro. The PRD not only won the election for mayor of Mexico City,[2] but also obtained slightly more seats than the PAN in the Chamber of Deputies.

In the 2000 presidential elections, the PRI lost the presidency to the PAN's candidate, Vicente Fox, who had been governor of the state of Guanajuato and had previously worked as a manager for the Coca-Cola Company in Mexico. This time the PRD came in third, far behind the top parties, due mainly to the fact that many of its supporters strategically deserted the PRD to support the opposition candidate most capable of defeating the PRI (see Magaloni and Poiré, 2004b). Issue divisions did not play a significant role in the 2000 presidential elections (see also Magaloni and Poiré, 2004a). At first glance, the 2000 presidential race does not seem to have been significantly shaped by retrospective evaluations. Economic performance in the two years prior to the elections was particularly strong, and the public approval of the president was quite high, as I demonstrated in Chapter 5. The puzzle, then, is how the PRI could lose the election when economic evaluations should have favored it.

My results indicate that the 2000 PRI defeat can be attributed to three main factors. First, Mexican voters had stopped perceiving the PRI as the most competent party to handle the national economy. Second, given voters' memories of past economic crises, Mexicans disregarded the good pre-electoral performance of the economy, instead anticipating an economic crisis after the elections. As a consequence, the PRI could not profit from

[2] Elections in Mexico City took place for the first time in 1997.

high presidential approval and the high growth rates preceding the presidential elections. Third, voter coordination played a significant role in the PRI's defeat. In the 2000 elections, an unprecedented amount of information was available about the relative standing of the parties at the polls, information that was made accessible to the mass public through television. The electorate realized that the PRI could be defeated, and these expectations played a decisive role both in encouraging ruling party voters to strategically defect from the PRI and in enabling strategic voting among opposition supporters.

I will now summarize the set of hypotheses that will be evaluated in the remainder of this chapter as derived from my theoretical model of voting choices in hegemonic-party regimes.

Modeling Voting Choices and Hypotheses

When only one party has governed for decades in an authoritarian regime, voters need to make complex evaluations related to possible futures with and without the hegemonic party (Domínguez and McCann, 1995). Chapter 1 developed three models to explain how voters derive these expectations about the future. The interesting question is why voters arrive at their decisions, not how they behave once they reach the voting booth. Below, I summarize some of the basic arguments and derive the hypotheses that will be assessed using survey data.

Expected Economic Performance

What would happen to the national economy if a party other than the PRI were to win? To answer this question, voters need to calculate the expected economic performance of the parties. Part of the difficulty they face is that only one party, the PRI, has a record in government. The opposition's performance is uncertain (Cinta, 1999; Buendía, 2000). My voting model incorporates uncertainty in the following way: voters infer the parties' expected performance according to a Bayesian model of learning. To evaluate the PRI, they focus on the long-term economic record of the regime, the *prior information*, and update it with new information, namely, the current state of the economy and the PRI's campaign promises. Voters assess the credibility of these promises by observing how much the PRI's actual performance at time $t+1$ deviated from what the party had promised at time t; when the incumbent has deviated from its promises, they are disregarded as unreliable. To evaluate the opposition, voters need to update some "diffuse prior beliefs" with campaign promises, which voters discount due to uncertainty.

One implication of this model is that voters might stick with the "known devil" owing to to uncertainty about the opposition. As argued in Chapters 1 and 5, this mode of prospective voting behavior corresponds to that of a *banker* and tends to be displayed mainly by richer voters, who tend to disregard government transfers and to focus on government performance. Another implication of the model is that voter uncertainty about the opposition may be reduced as these parties win more local races and are thus "tested" by the electorate. A third implication of the model is that voters *learn* from experience to assess the ruling party. As their long-term experiences with the party become more negative, and as voters observe the PRI betraying its campaign promises, they will assign lower prospective expectations to this party. I derive the following hypotheses from my theoretical model.

Hypothesis 1. I expect voters holding higher prior beliefs about the PRI's expected economic performance to have higher expectations about the ruling party's future economic performance than those holding lower prior beliefs. In the Mexican case, prior beliefs are strongly correlated with voters' age: voters born approximately around and after 1960, the so-called crisis generation, have experienced long-term economic stagnation and macroeconomic volatility and thus are expected to give lower prospective marks to the PRI, while voters born before the 1960s also witnessed the years of the so-called Mexican economic miracle and should give higher prospective marks to the PRI.

Hypothesis 2. Those who hold more favorable short-term retrospective assessments and those who approve of the way the president is currently handling the economy are predicted to have a higher probability of expecting the PRI to capably handle future economic performance than those who hold more unfavorable retrospective assessments.

Hypothesis 3. I expect voters to attach low prospective marks to the opposition and to be deterred from supporting these parties owing to uncertainty.

Hypothesis 4. Controlling for regional predispositions to support the different parties, I expect to find more support for the opposition parties in states where the opposition governs at the local level, as this should reduce voter uncertainty about the opposition.

Hypothesis 5. The more the individual expects the PRI to be more competent than the opposition in handling future economic performance, the higher his probability of voting for this party. Conversely, the more he expects the opposition to be more capable than the PRI in shaping future economic performance, the higher his probability of voting for the opposition, all other things held constant.

Expected Government Transfers

Voters also need to assess the impact of the PRI's fate on their personal finances. Expected government transfers must be inferred by solving a simple strategic interaction game. I call this the "punishment regime," in which the ruling party moves second after observing voters' behavior, rewarding loyalty with government transfers and punishing defection with fewer government transfers. One implication of this argument is that fear of losing government transfers can deter voters from defecting, particularly the poorer and least ideologically inclined voters.

Lacking appropriate instruments in opinion surveys for testing the impact of punishment and government transfers on voting choices, I dealt with these issues using aggregate data in Chapter 4. In this chapter, I can test some of the implications of the aggregate patterns.

Hypothesis 6. Mass defections from the PRI are more likely to come from voters who are least dependent on the party's spoils system for their survival. Conversely, those who are more dependent on government patronage and transfers for their survival, are expected to remain more loyal to the PRI. In the Mexican case, peasants are the most vulnerable group and remain dependent on the state transfers and subsidies for survival. I thus expect peasants to vote for the PRI.

Voter Coordination Dilemmas

My theory shows how voter coordination dilemmas help to sustain party hegemony. There are two related coordination dilemmas. First, the punishment regime implies that ruling party voters who would like to defect but fear punishment face a coordination dilemma: if few other voters defect, it is better to support the PRI than to risk punishment in isolation. An implication of this is that *perceptions of invincibility allow the PRI to hold its coalition together*. Ruling party defections occur when voters calculate that other voters will defect in sufficient numbers that they can coordinate to dislodge the

PRI. I call this type of behavior on the part of ruling party voters *strategic defections*. The more voters perceive that the PRI can be defeated, the more they will strategically defect from the party.

The second coordination dilemma exists because of divisions between opposition forces. In order to defeat the PRI, opposition voters need to put aside their ideological differences, strategically supporting the opposition party most likely to defeat the PRI. Ideological divisions can prevent the opposition from coordinating if most opposition voters rank the PRI second. In order for the opposition to be able to coordinate, most opposition voters must possess a preference ranking whereby any outcome is preferable to the PRI – there should be more "tactical" than "ideological" opposition voters. Another requirement for opposition coordination is that the PRI must be vulnerable to defeat. If only the PRI can win, opposition voters possess no incentive to desert their first choice. "Strategic voting," the tendency of voters not to waste their votes on trailing candidates (Duverger, 1963; Riker and Ordeshook, 1968; Riker, 1982), makes rational sense only when voters' second choice has a real chance of winning (Cox, 1997). The third requirement for strategic voting is that information about the parties' relative standing at the polls be common knowledge (Cox, 1997). In the 1994 presidential elections, most observers agreed that the PRD was the trailing candidate. However, the PRD elites claimed to have private polls that gave them the lead (Zinser, 1994). A key difference between the 1994 and 2000 presidential elections was the "emergence and public acceptance of professional public opinion polling and the dissemination of polling information through the mass media" (Domínguez, 2004). In the 2000 presidential elections, there was no doubt that Vicente Fox was the candidate most likely to defeat the PRI, and this played a powerful role in allowing society to coordinate to dislodge it (see also Magaloni and Poiré, 2004b) .

Hypothesis 7. Strategic voting should come from opposition voters (a) who derive a *lower* utility differential from both opposition parties than from their first-ranked party and the PRI, or those whom I have defined as "tactical" rather than "ideological," and (b) who see that their first choice has no chance of winning.

Hypothesis 8. The higher the utility differential a voter derives from both opposition parties and the stronger the ideological polarization of these parties, the less strategic voting there should be.

Hypothesis 9. Given that during the Carlos Salinas presidency there was a strong ideological polarization of opposition party elites, I expect to find little strategic voting on the part of PRD supporters in the 1994 presidential elections.

Hypothesis 10. Perceptions that the PRI can be defeated should increase both strategic defections of ruling party supporters and strategic voting among opposition voters.

I test these hypotheses with individual-level data from the 1994, 1997, and 2000 national elections and do so in three steps. In the first step, I estimate the voters' *comparative prospective assessments* (CPAs), or how they assess the future of the national economy with and without the ruling party. In the second step, I estimate voting choices. In the third step, I assess the extent of both strategic defections and strategic voting. In the course of testing these hypotheses, I employed three national surveys. The 1994 survey was collected by Belden-Rusonello one month before the presidential elections (N = 1,500). The 1997 data was derived from a post-election survey collected by ARCOP one week after the midterm elections (N = 1,200). Finally, the data for the 2000 presidential elections comes from a 2000 Mexico panel study funded in part by the NSF (grant SES-9905703) and collected by *Reforma* newspaper.[3] Although these surveys did not consistently ask the same questions, my goal is to present models that are as similar as possible.

The Economy and the Voters' Comparative Prospective Assessments

Voters in Mexico saw the economy as the most important problem facing the country. In the 1994, 1997, and 2000, 55 percent, 57 percent, and 40 percent of respondents, respectively, saw "the economy" or one economic problem (e.g., unemployment or poverty) as the most important problem facing the nation. Crime and public safety also played an important role, consistently designated as the most important problem by at least 10 percent of the electorate in 1994 and 1997, and by a quarter of the electorate in 2000. Corruption trailed far behind in voters' eyes. However, Mexican elections should not be conceived simply as referendums on the economy. Table 7.1 presents a summary measure of retrospective assessments and voting intentions in the 1994, 1997, and 2000 elections. The summary retrospective

[3] Participants in the Mexico 2000 Panel Study (in alphabetical order) were Miguel Basañez, Roderic Camp, Wayne Cornelius, Jorde Domínguez, Federico Estévez, Joseph Klesner, Chappell Lawson (Principal Investigator), Beatriz Magaloni, James McCann, Alejandro Moreno, Pablo Parás, and Alejandro Poiré. Funding for the study was provided by the National Science Foundation and *Reforma* newspaper.

Table 7.1. *Summary retrospective assessments and the vote (percent)*

National Economy and the Voter's Personal Finances Are	PRI	PAN	PRD	Total
1994				
Much worse	39	20	13	22
Worse	42	20	10	20
Same	49	16	8	26
Better	54	24	7	17
Much better	46	20	5	15
1997				
Much worse	16	26	31	32
Worse	21	22	30	17
Same	36	22	20	28
Better	47	23	10	11
Much better	45	27	13	13
2000				
Much worse	24	32	25	14
Worse	36	34	19	18
Same	35	35	13	42
Better	37	37	10	16
Much better	49	33	9	10

Note: Percentages are weighted for the 1994 survey. The summary retrospective measures add pocketbook and sociotropic evaluations.

measure adds pocketbook and sociotropic evaluations. This creates a measure that ranges from 1, which means that the respondent indicated that both her personal finances *and* the national economy had deteriorated, to a score of 5 for those who assessed improvements in both.

During all three elections, but especially in 1997, more voters felt that the overall economic situation had deteriorated more than improved during the previous three years. The 1994 elections cannot be interpreted as a referendum on the economy: close to 40 percent of those who saw deterioration in *both* their personal finances and the national economy supported the PRI. Although the PRI received more support from those who had positive retrospective assessments, it was also the first choice among those who felt most strongly about the economic decline.

The 1997 elections were different. The PRI received the support of only 16 percent of those holding extremely negative retrospective assessments. Most voters saw deterioration in economic conditions, and they deserted the PRI. At first glance, retrospective assessments also seem to have played a role in 2000: the PRI received less support from those reporting very negative retrospective assessments (24 percent) than from those who had very positive evaluations (49 percent). However, retrospective assessments barely played a role in accounting for Vicente Fox's victory: he in fact received only slightly more support from those who had favorable retrospective evaluations than from those who had very negative assessments.

Another important performance evaluation relates to presidential approval. In both the 1994 and 2000 presidential elections, the PRI had high levels of presidential approval – 63 percent and 59 percent approved of the president in 1994 and 2000, respectively. Presidential approval was much lower in 1997, when only 44 percent of the electorate reported approving of the president.[4] Yet, as I argued in Chapter 5, presidential approval in 2000 was no longer fungible for the PRI: given the post-electoral bust of 1994, this time voters discounted the good economic performance as not credible and became more pessimistic about the future as elections approached. Mexico's aberrant economic cycles had produced a voter both distrustful of governmental promises and accustomed to a boom-and-bust economy. Zedillo's government successfully averted expectations of an end-of-term crisis among investors and analysts, but the Mexican electorate remained quite skeptical. In the 2000 survey, 76 percent of respondents in April/May expected an end-of-term crisis, and the same was true of 76 percent of respondents in June.

Prospective assessments of the parties' capacities to handle the economy, as we will see, are what most powerfully shaped voting decisions. Table 7.2 shows the percentage of voters who identified one of the three major parties (or its candidates in the 2000 survey) as having the best expected performance. With the exception of improving wages in 1997, the PRI is consistently identified as the party most capable of solving the key problems in all three elections. Voters systematically assigned low prospective marks to the opposition parties, possibly because they were too uncertain about them. However, the PRI's prospective marks dramatically fell after the 1994 peso crisis. In 1994, an average of 48 percent cited the PRI as the party most capable of solving key economic problems, and this percentage drops to 22 percent and 25 percent in 1997 and 2000, respectively.

The PAN's prospective marks remained quite constant over the three elections. The PRD's prospective marks increased from 1994 to 1997, and

[4] Approval here comes from adding those who report moderately approving and strongly approving of the president. Percentages for the 1994 survey are weighted.

Table 7.2. *Prospective evaluations of the parties' capacities (percent)*

Party Best Able to	PRI	PAN	PRD	None/Do Not Know
1994				
Fight poverty	46	18	12	20
Improve the national economy	51	18	10	18
Improve personal finances	48	15	10	23
Improve public safety	48	22	9	19
Fight corruption	38	24	12	23
1997				
Fight poverty	22	20	27	18
Generate employment	24	23	27	12
Increase wages	21	24	25	16
Improve public safety	24	22	22	18
Fight corruption	18	19	26	22
2000				
Handle the economy	25	21	6	48
Fight crime	23	19	6	53

Note: Percentages are weighted for the 1994 survey. Percentages for the last column correspond to "do not knows" in the 1994 survey. The question for the 2000 survey is about candidates, not parties, and it comes from the first wave of the panel (W1).

then plunged in 2000, as Mexican voters experienced serious doubts about Cuauhtémoc Cárdenas' capacity to solve key economic problems. The evidence suggests that changes in voters' comparative prospective judgments of the PRI's performance relative to the opposition are accounted for mainly by voters' *decreasing approval* of the PRI, not by increasing approval of the opposition's capability. Mexican voters seem to have arrived at the conclusion that the opposition was better able to handle the future of the national economy not so much because they had overcome their uncertainty about the opposition, but because they had lost faith in the PRI.

To assess voters' expectations about the parties' comparative performance systematically, I construct *comparative prospective assessments* (CPAs). A voter's CPAs for the 1994 and 1997 surveys is a summary measure based on three questions that asked respondents to assess which party was most capable of improving the three economic problems reported in Table 7.2. The 2000 survey did not include similar prospective assessments. Thus, the 2000 data is derived from a question that asked respondents how competent each of the candidates were in handling the economy. Candidate competence data is drawn from the first wave (W1) and voting intentions from the third wave (W3) so as to minimize problems with rationalization. In 1994, 52 percent of respondents thought the PRI was more capable of handling the future of the national economy than either of the opposition parties. CPAs markedly favored the opposition in 1997, when 61 percent of respondents judged that either of the major opposition parties was more competent than the PRI, 12 percent had neutral prospective assessments, and only 27 percent believed that the PRI was more capable. By 2000, more than 50 percent of voters had become neutral about the candidates' comparative capacities to handle the future of the national economy; 28 percent judged that the opposition was more capable; and only 22 percent considered the PRI more capable. Thus, Vicente Fox's victory cannot be interpreted as a sign of voters' optimism about his economic capacity. Rather, his victory must be attributed to the fact that voters had lost confidence in the PRI.

My theory provides hypotheses about why voters reached these conclusions. It argues that voters will employ their prior experiences with the ruling party and their assessments about the current state of the economy, together with the parties' campaign promises, to infer the future economic performance of the PRI relative to the opposition. Thus, a voter's CPAs can be conceived as responding to retrospective assessments, presidential approval, and the voter's prior beliefs plus voter uncertainty about the opposition. Unfortunately, the impact of campaign promises and how voters discount the promises of the opposition due to uncertainty cannot be assessed with the existing data. I will thus estimate the following models to account for the voters' CPAs in each election:

$$\begin{aligned} CPA_i \text{ (PRI-Opposition)} &= \beta_1 + \beta_2 \text{ Prior}_i + \beta_3 \text{ Retrospective}_i \\ &+ \beta_4 \text{ Presidential Approval} + \varepsilon_i \end{aligned} \tag{7.1}$$

I employ a maximum likelihood logit procedure. Respondents who expect the PRI to perform better than the opposition are scored as 1; those who expect the PRI to be worse than the opposition or who are neutral are scored as 0. Regarding voters' priors, I employ an average of the growth rates that each individual has observed since she became politically aware until the preceding elections.[5] Voters born roughly after 1960, the so-called

[5] The measure of actual performance is, of course, a *proxy* for prior beliefs, that is, for how the voter might have experienced and evaluated economic performance during her lifetime. Voters care about a larger set of economic variables, not just about growth rates. And they might attach different weights to these various components of performance. I use growth

crisis generation, have had markedly more negative economic experiences under the PRI's rule.

Results of the logit equation estimations for the voters' CPAs in 1994, 1997, and 2000 are shown in Table 7.3. They lend considerable credence to the manner in which the Bayesian retrospective model derives voters' calculations regarding the parties' expected economic performance. In each case, the coefficients are significant and of the expected sign. Older voters who have had better past economic experiences with the PRI have CPAs more favorable to the PRI. Retrospective assessments and presidential approval also perform as expected: the more favorable the voter's evaluation of the economy and of the president, the more favorable are the incumbent's comparative prospective assessments.

To give a sense of the magnitude of these effects, I simulated the models using Clarify (Tomz et al., 2001) to obtain the mean change in the predicted probability of expecting the PRI to be more competent than the opposition in handling the future of the national economy as the independent variables change from their minimum to their maximum value. The other variables are held at their mean values. Results are shown in Figure 7.1. The effect of presidential approval on voters' CPAs is the strongest. Note that the effects of these variables drop significantly in the 2000 elections, which is an indication that voters' future expectations were no longer significantly shaped by presidential approval and retrospective assessments, as I argued in Chapter 5.

The last model in Table 7.3 for the 2000 election adds voters' expectations of an end-of-term crisis. Expecting an economic crisis reduces voters' confidence in the PRI's capacity to handle the future of the national economy relative to the opposition, and voters' priors are no longer significant. These results are consistent with the findings in Chapter 5 and explain why the PRI could not profit from the high growth rates of the two years prior to the 2000 presidential elections or from Zedillo's approval ratings. To support this last claim, consider the following simulated probabilities coming from Model IV. I examine three types of hypothetical voters: type 1 hold positive retrospective assessments, approve of the president, and do not expect an end-of-term crisis. These voters are predicted to have a 0.55 chance of assessing the PRI as more competent than the opposition. Type 2 voters possess positive retrospective assessments and approve of the

rates because they constitute the one economic indicator for which a longer systematic and reliable time series, which dates back to 1900, can be found.

Table 7.3. *Logit analyses of voters' CPAs: PRI is more competent than the opposition to handle the future of the national economy*

	1994 Model I		1997 Model II		2000 Model III		2000 Model IV	
Independent Variables	Coeff.	Std. Error	Coeff.	Std. Error	Coeff.	Std. Error	Coeff.	Std. Error
Constant term	−2.97***	0.32	1.77**	0.39	−3.75***	0.28	−3.66***	0.44
Prior beliefs	0.11**	0.05	0.21**	0.092	0.09*	0.53	0.12	0.08
Retrospective assessments	0.22***	0.04	0.49***	0.09	0.21***	0.049***	0.28***	0.075
Approval	0.41***	0.05	0.84***	0.08	0.46***	0.053	0.38***	0.07
Crisis expected							−0.18**	0.09
* p < .10	N = 1,378		N = 1,000		N = 2,174		N = 911	
** p < .05	Log ll = −883.16		Log ll = −476.767		Log ll = −1097.15		Log. ll = −466.04	
*** p < .01	Lr Chi2(3) = 119.88		Lr Chi2(3) = 224.74		LR Chi2(3) = 135.83		Chi2(4) = 68.18	
	Prob > chi2 = .0000		Prob > Chi2 = 0.000		Prob > chi2 = .0000		Prob > Chi2 = 0.000	
	65% predicted correctly		85% predicted correctly		78% predicted correctly		77% predicted correctly	

Note: The dependent variable in these models is voters' comparative prospective assessments, or how voters expect the PRI to handle future economic performance relative to the opposition. Regarding voters' priors, I employ an average of the growth rates that each individual has observed since age fifteen. Retrospective assessments are the summary measure presented in Table 7.1. Presidential approval comes from a question that asked respondents to assess the president's performance. End-of-term crisis comes from a question that asked respondents whether they expected an end-of-term crisis after the 2000 elections. All variables in Model III are from the first wave of the 2000 panel. In Model IV, the variable in the last row ("crisis expected") comes from the third wave of the panel, because it was not included in the first. As a consequence, there are fewer observations in the last model.

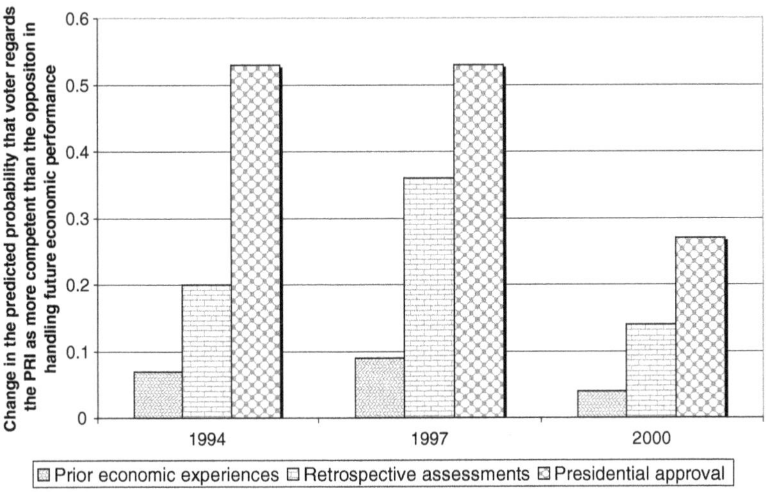

Figure 7.1. Simulating comparative prospective assessments. Predicted probabilities come from simulating Models I to III of Table 7.3 using Clarify (Tomz et al., 2001). 95% confidence intervals are not displayed. The dependent variable in these models is voters' comparative prospective assessments, or how voters expect the PRI to handle future economic performance relative to the opposition. Regarding voters' priors, I employ an average of the growth rates that each individual has observed since age fifteen. Retrospective assessments are the summary measure presented in Table 7.1. Presidential approval comes from a question that asked respondents to assess the president's performance. Simulations are done by moving an independent varible from its minimum to its maximum value, holding the rest at their mean values.

president but expect an end-of-term crisis. Despite having very positive evaluations of the economy and the president, these voters prefer the opposition *because they expect an end-of-term crisis*. These voters are predicted to have a 0.54 chance of assessing the opposition as more competent than the PRI. Type 3 voters disapprove of prior economic performance and of the president, and expect an end-of-term crisis. This last group has a 0.94 chance of expecting the opposition to be more competent in handling the future of the national economy. A voter with average evaluations on the independent variables has a 0.78 chance of favoring the opposition over the PRI, which largely accounts for why the PRI lost the 2000 elections, as I demonstrate below.

Voting Choices in the 1994, 1997, and 2000 Elections

I now turn to testing my hypotheses about voting choices and coordination dilemmas. My goal is to present models that can be compared across the three elections. I am able to present models employing the same economic performance measures (retrospective assessments, prior beliefs, presidential approval, and prospective judgments about the parties' capacities). The voters' retrospective assessments, prior beliefs, and presidential approval are the same variables as in the previous section. A full description of how each of the independent variables was coded is found on my website (www.stanford.edu/~magaloni/).

For the three elections, I also include a dummy for states governed by the opposition. In 1994, opposition parties governed only 10 percent of respondents at the state level; by 1997 and 2000, this percentage had increased to 22 percent and 30 percent, respectively. I seek to assess whether the opposition was able to profit from its local experience, presumably because this helped to reduce voter uncertainty. The models also include a series of regional dummies, to control for preexisting dispositions to support the parties, in an attempt to isolate as much as possible the effect of local opposition governance on the national vote.

The models also include a measure of voter uncertainty. The results should be read with caution because the instruments used to measure voter uncertainty are very different in each election. The models also include four sociodemographic variables: peasant, gender, education, and, for the 1995 and 1997 surveys, state employee. Peasants are presumed to be the most loyal base of the PRI because they are the most dependent upon the PRI's patronage system for their survival.

The models include a series of issues that were unique to each election, or issues that were not included in all three surveys but were relevant. For both presidential elections, there is information about voters' perceptions of the prospects for defeating the PRI. I include two types of policy issues: so-called valence issues – those issues that the voter regarded as the most important problems facing the country – and "policy" issues. I isolate two problems, security and unemployment, to assess differences between support for the PAN and the PRD. Voters who are more concerned about security should vote for the right-wing opposition party, and those who are more concerned about unemployment should vote for the left-wing opposition alternative. The other policy issues vary in each survey. The 1994 survey included a question about NAFTA. The 1997 survey, which was in part designed by the author, included many questions on economic policies, attitudes toward federalism, and some moral issues such as abortion. For the 2000 survey, I include questions about the privatization of the electricity industry and political reform. In each survey, I control for political interest (the extent to which the voter manifested having an interest in politics).

One last comment regarding partisanship: party identification certainly plays an important role in voting decisions. Evaluating the impact of party identification is empirically problematic in the Mexican case, however, because there is a very strong problem of endogeneity, in that voters tend to respond to the conventional question, "Generally speaking, do you consider yourself PANista, PRIísta, or PRDísta?" according to their voting decisions (Magaloni and Poiré, 2004a). One approach to rectifying this problem has been to employ reported past voting intentions as a proxy for party identification (Domínguez and McCann, 1995). This strategy is problematic, however, because of serious levels of misreporting.[6] The 2000 Mexico panel study can mitigate this problem, as one can employ reported party identification in the first wave of the panel to model voting decisions in subsequent rounds (Magaloni and Poiré, 2004a).[7] Since my goal here is to present models that can be compared across the three elections, I exclude party identification from the voting models. I include a dummy for those who report not identifying with any of the three major parties.

Table 7.4 presents the results of these analyses. Overall, the results relevant to my voting model can be summarized as follows:

1. In all three elections and for all parties, prospective economic evaluations played a powerful role, and retrospective assessments were not statistically significant. Voters were future-oriented, supporting the PRI when they perceived this party to be more capable of handling economic performance, and defecting to the opposition otherwise.
2. Presidential approval played a significant role in all of the elections; the greater the approval of the incumbent president, the more voters supported the ruling party.

[6] For example, in the 1994 Belden-Rusonello survey, 67 percent reported having voted for the PRI in 1988, when less than 50 percent probably did; and only 11 percent reported having voted for the PRD in 1988, when probably more than 40 percent did. In the Gallup surveys employed by Domínguez and McCann (1995), the problem of misreporting is of similar magnitude, which implies that the authors' conclusions about the strength and stability of partisan loyalty to the PRI should be tempered.

[7] Another approach would be to instrumentalize party identification, but it is difficult to think of an instrument that can independently cause party identification without simultaneously shaping voting decisions.

Table 7.4. *Multinomial logit analyses of voting choices*

	1994				1997				2000			
	PAN		PRD		PAN		PRD		PAN		PRD	
	Coeff.	SE	Coeff.	SE	Coeff.	SE	Coeff.	SE	Coeff.	SE	Coeff.	SE
South	0.09	0.49	−0.05	0.57	−0.51	0.61	−0.80	0.54	−0.52	0.52	0.51	0.58
North	−0.67	0.35*	−0.77	0.53	0.36	0.43	−0.23	0.48	−0.48	0.52	0.53	0.68
Mexico City	0.41	0.38	0.80	0.58	−0.13	0.63	0.40	0.58	−0.45	0.36	−0.36	0.53
Local Opp.	0.88	0.45**	0.96	0.75	0.64	0.47	−1.03	0.57**	0.09	0.34	0.06	0.51
Education	0.15	0.13	0.26	0.20	0.15	0.13	0.06	0.14	−0.06	0.15	0.37	0.18**
Female	−0.57	0.27**	−0.10	0.38	0.28	0.35	0.01	0.35	−0.34	0.30	−0.80	0.39**
Peasant	−1.08	0.45**	−0.64	0.51	−0.68	0.77	−0.57	0.75	−1.64	0.76**	−0.61	0.78
Bureaucrat	0.83	0.50*	0.26	0.88	−0.13	0.57	0.23	0.55				
Independent	0.15	0.35	−0.44	0.51	−0.26	0.46	0.27	0.42	0.39	0.34	0.98	0.42**
Approval	−0.27	0.13**	−0.43	0.15***	−0.45	0.14***	−0.38	0.15***	−0.35	0.13***	−0.34	0.17**
Retrospective	−0.01	0.11	0.34	0.26	−0.15	0.13	−0.15	0.13	−0.19	0.13	−0.19	0.17
Priors	−0.36	0.15**	−0.07	0.20	−0.05	0.21	−0.01	0.21	−0.18	0.16	0.18	0.20
PRI prospect.	−0.82	0.29***	−1.67	0.36***	−1.08	0.20***	−1.25	0.26***	−0.32	0.12***	−0.60	0.15***
PAN prospect.	1.30	0.25***	−0.89	0.32***	1.13	0.18***	0.07	0.24	0.61	0.12***	−0.05	0.15
PRD prospect.	−0.42	0.37	0.76	0.47*	−0.03	0.18	1.01	0.16***	−0.03	0.12	0.50	0.15***
Uncertainty	0.02	0.30	−0.80	0.38	−0.57	0.22***	−0.46	0.22	0.07	0.19	−0.02	0.21
Interest	0.38	0.22*	0.23	0.32	0.01	0.19	−0.11	0.19	0.20	0.18	0.22	0.22

Security	0.82	0.47*	0.64	0.74	0.54	0.64	0.57	0.61	0.67	0.33**	0.14	0.46
Unemployment	0.03	0.31	0.58	0.44	0.15	0.42	0.22	0.42	−0.13	0.45	0.47	0.53
NAFTA	−0.09	0.14	−0.28	0.21								
Electoral fraud	0.13	0.11	0.26	0.15*								
Can PRI lose?	0.47	0.15***	0.24	0.23								
PAN likely win?	1.04	0.38***	−1.69	0.41***								
Economy private hands					0.15	0.07**	0.07	0.07				
Reduce taxes					0.17	0.08**	0.03	0.08				
Federalism					0.12	0.08*	0.07	0.08				
Pro-life/anti-abortion					−0.23	0.21	−0.33	0.21***				
End of term crisis?									0.40	0.18**	0.63	0.25***
Privatize electricity									0.04	0.04	0.01	0.06
Insufficient pol. reform									0.03	0.04	0.03	0.05
Fox win Labastida?									1.45	0.19***	0.28	0.32
CCS win Labastida?									0.26	0.31	1.33	0.33***
Fox win CCS?									1.18	0.26***	−0.56	0.24**
Constant	−0.28	1.43	1.46	1.72	−3.60	1.45***	−1.06	1.43	0.59	1.14	−0.46	1.39
* p < .10	N = 934				N = 631				N = 582			
** p < .05	Lr Chi2(46) = 1029.06				Lr Chi2(46) = 819.21				Lr Chi2(48) = 611.07			
*** p < .01	Prob > Chi2 = .0000				Prob > Chi2 = .0000				Prob > Chi2 = .0000			
	Pseudo R2 = .62				Pseudo R2 = .59				Pseudo R2 = 0.51			
	Log ll = −318.58				Log ll = −282.65				Log ll = −289.89			
	88% predicted correctly				87% predicted correctly				84% predicted correctly			

3. In both presidential elections, support for the PAN over the PRI is accounted for by a concern for security.
4. In both presidential elections, expectations that the ruling party could be defeated powerfully shaped the decision to support the opposition over the PRI.
5. The 1997 midterm elections were more policy-oriented. An economic cleavage divided the electorate. The PAN received support from those who held more conservative stands on the economy and favored more autonomy for the localities. Those who stood to the left on the economic issues and favored a stronger federal government supported the PRI or the PRD. A second moral cleavage was also present in those elections, with attitudes toward abortion differentiating the more libertarian PRD voters from the more conservative supporters of the PAN and the PRI.
6. In the 1994 elections, expectations that the PAN had a better chance of winning than the PRD discouraged support for the PRD, *in favor of the PRI.* This is evidence, as I will discuss further, both that there was little strategic voting by Cárdenas' supporters in favor of the PAN and of the opposition's coordination dilemmas in the 1994 presidential elections. In the 2000 elections, expectations that Fox could defeat Labastida encouraged strategic voting by PRD supporters in favor of the PAN's candidate, not the PRI's candidate.

Mexican voters have shown a remarkable stability in the logic of their voting decisions since the first presidential elections for which there is survey research. My results here are quite consistent with those in Domínguez and McCann (1995) in two main respects. First, voters are prospective rather than retrospective. Second, what these scholars called "ruling party" factors continued to be the most important factors accounting for voting decisions up until the 2000 elections – in particular, prospects for the future of the national economy with and without the PRI, presidential approval, and prospects for the PRI's defeat. The main difference between the 1997 and 2000 elections relative to the 1988, 1991, and 1994 elections is that Mexican voters stopped seeing the PRI as the party most competent to handle the future of the national economy. The 2000 election was also different in that there was significant opposition coordination, to a large extent because voters' desires for political change became more important than their ideological and partisan divisions. I will now discuss the results of the models in more detail.

The Economy and the Vote

Voters' retrospective assessments had no direct impact on voting choices. Thus, the 1994 PRI reelection cannot be interpreted as a referendum on the economy. Nor were the 1997 and 2000 electoral defeats the product of "conventional" economic or retrospective voting (Key, 1966; Fiorina, 1981). In the three elections, presidential approval and prospective evaluations dominated voting decisions. Disapproval of the president more powerfully shaped support for the PAN than for the PRD in the three elections. In both the 1994 and 2000 presidential elections, voters' prospective evaluations about the parties' competence to handle future economic performance played a much stronger role in accounting for support for the PAN than for the PRD. Thus, part of the reason that the PRD was the third party in both of these elections was that the PRD and Cárdenas failed to convince voters of their ability to solve central economic problems.

The PAN, instead, was perceived as more competent to handle future economic problems, and these perceptions were, to a large extent, generated by its much wider experience in governing at the local level. In the 1994 presidential elections, the PAN profited from its experience in local government; it received more support from voters in states that had governors of this party. In the 1997 midterm elections, the PRD received *fewer* votes from states governed by the PAN. The effect of this variable is substantial: holding the rest of the variables at their mean value, moving a voter from a PRI-held state to a PAN-held state increased the probability of voting for the PAN by 13 percent and decreased the probability of voting for the PRI by 17 percent in 1994. Similarly, in 1997 the change in the predicted probability of voting for the PRD is −0.17 percent, of voting for the PRI is −.02 percent, and of voting PAN is 22 percent if a voter moves from a PRI-held state to an opposition-held state. This variable played no significant role in the 2000 elections.

Punishment and Peasants

Indirect evidence that the "punishment regime," or the regime's threat to withdraw funds from opposition voters, mattered is found in the propensity of peasants to support the PRI disproportionately. This voter group is the most dependent upon government transfers for its survival and, as the model predicts, is the most loyal to the PRI. The effect of this variable was considerable: in the 1994 elections, a peasant had a 0.90 chance of supporting the PRI, a 0.07 chance of supporting the PAN, and a 0.02 chance of supporting the PRD, holding the rest of the variables at their mean value. These probabilities are, respectively, 0.54, 0.24, and 0.21 in 1997; and 0.70, 0.18, and 0.12 in 2000. The propensity of peasants to continue to support the PRI over the years was thus impressive, and I largely attribute this result to the effect of the punishment regime in deterring poor voters from defecting from the PRI. Peasants' loyalty to the PRI might to a large extent also be attributed to the greater effectiveness of the ruling party's clientelistic networks in smaller rural communities, where local party bosses and caciques possess more *local knowledge* about the voters and can more credibly threaten to punish those who manifest sympathies toward the opposition.

Policy Issues

Policy issues played no significant role in the 1994 and 2000 presidential elections, which is consistent with what Domínguez and McCann (1995) found for the 1988 and 1991 elections. The 1997 midterm elections were different. Even after controlling for presidential approval, prospective party evaluations, and the set of sociodemographic variables, policy issues still played a significant role.

Economic issues strongly differentiated support for the PAN over the PRI. The PAN drew support from those conventionally associated with more conservative economic stands. Three issues were important in attracting these voters. First, regarding voters' assessments about the role of the state in the economy, the PAN drew support from those who believed that the economy should be left in private hands. Second, PAN voters were more likely to believe that the government should reduce taxes to promote investment rather than redistribute wealth to alleviate poverty. Third, PAN voters disproportionately favored more autonomy for the localities instead of a stronger federal government. On these economic issues, those who voted for the PRI and the PRD stood to the left of the PAN, and they did not differentiate themselves from each other.

Attitudes toward abortion also played a role in the elections. This moral divide differentiated support for the PRD from support for the PRI, but played no role in a vote for the PAN over the PRI. Thus, on this moral divide, PRD voters stood to the left, more libertarian side of the scale, and PRI and PAN supporters stood to the right, more conservative side of the

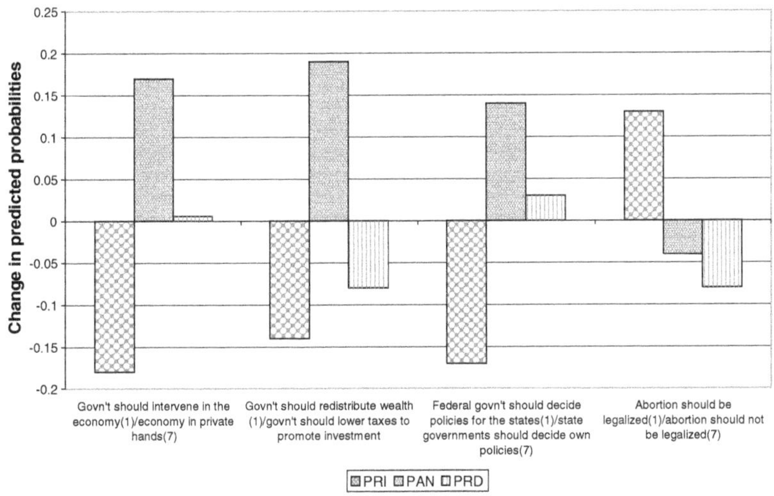

Figure 7.2. Effects of policy issues in the 1997 midterm elections. Change in predicted probabilities of voting for each of the parties comes from changing the issue from the minimum value (1) to its maximum value (7). The predicted probabilities come from simulating the voting models in Table 7.4.

scale. This result are partially at odds with my findings in the previous chapter that demonstrated that voters perceive the PAN as standing to the right of the PRI on value-related issues such as abortion, and that the PRI was perceived as an anticlerical party. The difference between the findings in this and the preceding chapter stems from the fact that here I focus on voters, while the previous chapter focused on voters' perceptions about the parties' stands on the issues. PRI voters seem to be rather conservative on their value-related issue positions and in this sense indistinguishable from PAN supporters. PAN politicians, by contrast, appear to be much more conservative than PRI ones.

The effects of these issues were substantial, as can be seen in Figure 7.2, which presents simulated changes in the probabilities of voting for each of the three parties that result from changing the policy issue position of the voter from its minimum to its maximum value, holding the rest of the independent variables constant. I highlight two conclusions from these simulations. First, policy issues powerfully shaped the decision to support the PAN or the PRI, but barely affected a vote for the PRD. Holding all the variables to their mean values and shifting the voter's opinion from the extreme left to the extreme right on the issue of government involvement in the economy increases the probability of voting for the PAN by 17 percent and decreases the probability of voting for the PRI by 18 percent. The probability of voting for the PRD barely changes. A similar shift to the right on the issue of the redistribution of wealth versus lowering taxes increases the probability of voting for the PAN by 19 percent and reduces the probability of voting for the PRI and the PRD by 14 percent and 8 percent, respectively. The issue of federalism also shows a powerful effect: shifting the voters' opinion from assigning the central government a key role in policy making to devolving to the states the power to decide their own polices increases the chance of voting for the PAN by 14 percent and for the PRD by 3 percent, and decreases the chance of voting for the PRI by 17 percent. Finally, changing the voters' opinion on abortion from most pro-choice to most pro-life increases the chance of voting for the PRI by 13 percent and decreases the chance of voting for the PRD and the PAN by 8 percent and 4 percent, respectively.

To further assess the effects of these issues, consider the predicted probabilities of voting for each of the parties by hypothetical right-wing and left-wing voters who assign the lowest prospective mark on the economy to the PRI and who are indifferent between the two opposition parties in terms of how they assess their competence to handle future economic performance. Thus, the only difference between these hypothetical opposition voters is their policy stands. Those with right-wing and conservative stands on the economic and abortion issues have a probability of 0.61 of defecting to the PAN, and those with left-wing and libertarian policy stands have a 0.45 chance of defecting to the PRD.

Overall, these results indicate that defections to the PAN in 1997 were more issue-oriented than defections to the PRD. The reason is that PRD and PRI supporters held more similar views on all of the issues but abortion. Thus, if a former PRI voter defected to the PRD in 1997, it was mainly because this voter was fed up with the PRI. If a former PRI voter defected to the PAN in 1997, it was because this voter had rightist stands on the issues. This is confirmatory evidence, as I argued in Chapters 1 and 4, that PRD voters were more ideologically akin to the PRI and as a consequence were easier to buy off through patronage than PAN voters. My results also indicate that relative to other elections, those who supported the PAN in the 1997 elections were significantly more homogenous in terms of their policy stands, while the PAN appears more as a catch-all party in the 1994 and 2000 presidential elections (Magaloni and Moreno, 2003).

Voter Coordination and Perceptions that the PRI Could Be Defeated

Perceptions about the PRI's vulnerability encouraged support for the opposition in both the 1994 and 2000 presidential elections.[8] In the 1994 presidential elections, these perceptions strongly shaped support for the PAN over the PRI, but did not affect support for the PRD over the PRI. A similar pattern occurred in the 2000 presidential elections: the more likely a voter was to see that either of the opposition candidates could defeat the PRI, the more likely she was to support the opposition over the PRI.

On both occasions, the PAN benefited most from perceptions of the PRI's vulnerability, because it was seen as the party most likely to defeat the PRI. In the 1994 presidential elections, 66 percent answered that the PAN had a better chance of defeating the PRI than did the PRD or "other" parties. In the 2000 elections, voters also perceived that the PAN was stronger. In the third wave of the panel, the mean vote share calculation was Fox 40 percent, Labastida 40 percent, and Cárdenas 26 percent, a close approximation to the actual results. Furthermore, although more voters thought that Labastida would defeat Fox (48 percent), there was a sizable group (37 percent) that anticipated a Fox victory, and 15 percent believed that there would be a tie between the PAN and the PRI. Cárdenas was perceived as a sure loser by the overwhelming majority of the electorate: 72 percent believed that Labastida would defeat Cárdenas, and 65 percent thought that Fox would defeat Cárdenas.

To what extent did expectations that the PRI could be defeated motivate voter coordination in favor of the strongest opposition party? There are two ways to document voter coordination. The first approach comes from simulating the results of the models according to different voter predispositions to support the parties, and then seeing how these are changed by perceptions of the PRI's vulnerability. The second approach looks at bandwagon effects in the course of the campaign, which requires the use of panel data, available only for the 2000 election. Since my goal is to compare the

[8] Since the 1997 survey was post-electoral, I cannot assess how this issue shaped voting decisions in those elections.

two elections, below I assess how much voter coordination played a role using the first approach.[9]

Simulated Probabilities of Strategic Voting among Opposition Voters

Strategic voting implies abandoning a trailing candidate in favor of one of the front-runners. This form of voting behavior, as explained earlier, depends on relative utility comparisons of the parties and the voter's perception of the parties' probabilities of winning.

Since in both elections the PRD was the trailing party, I evaluate the extent to which PRD supporters deserted their party. PRD supporters are identified as those who assigned the highest prospective marks on the economic competence issues to this party. I take three hypothetical voters, beginning with type I PRD supporters, for whom there is a large utility differential between the PRD and the other two parties, as measured by their comparative prospective marks. Those with a large utility differential give the highest prospective mark to the PRD and the lowest to both the PAN and the PRI. Second, there are type II PRD supporters, for whom there is a mild utility differential between the PRD and the other two parties. Those with a moderate utility differential assign a lower prospective value to the PRD and the lowest prospective marks to both the PAN and the PRI. Thus type I and type II voters are presumed to be indifferent between the PRI and the PAN in terms of the parties' prospective economic performance, but they vary on the intensity of their preference for the PRD. Third, there are average PRD supporters, for whom the parties' prospective marks are given by the average respondent who reported voting for this party. The expectation is that the PRD should have a harder time retaining the support of voters with smaller utility differentials (type II), for whom the difference between their party and one of the front-runners is not too large.

To these three types of voters, I assign the same assessment of the parties' chances of winning: *they perceive the PRD as a sure loser and believe that the PAN can defeat the PRI.* For opposition coordination to take place, it is necessary that PRD supporters abandon their party in favor of the PAN. If, instead, they abandon their party in favor of the PRI, I take this as evidence of coordination failure among the opposition. The simulated probabilities are presented in Table 7.5.

9 Looking at the dynamics across the campaign, Magaloni and Poiré (2004b) assess strategic voting in the 2000 presidential elections.

Table 7.5. *Simulated strategic voting by PRD supporters in the 1994 and 2000 presidential elections (voters in simulation regard the PRD as sure loser)*

1994				2000			
PAN Likely Winner PRI Can Be Defeated				Fox Winner CCS Loses to Both			
Predicted to Vote:	Mean Predicted Probability	[95% Confidence Interval]		Predicted to Vote:	Mean Predicted Probability	[95% Confidence Interval]	
Type I PRD voter (with large utility differential)				*Type I PRD voter (with large utility differential)*			
PRI	.25	[.17,	.33]	PRI	.14	[.04,	.31]
PAN	.10	[.04,	.19]	PAN	**.54**	[.25,	.81]
PRD	**.66**	[.62,	.68]	PRD	.32	[.08,	.65]
Type II PRD voter (with moderate utility differential)				*Type II PRD voter (with moderate utility differential)*			
PRI	**.53**	[.32,	.74]	PRI	.17	[.07,	.33]
PAN	.34	[.16,	.57]	PAN	**.74**	[.55,	.88]
PRD	.13	[.03,	.30]	PRD	.09	[.02,	.24]
Average PRD voter				*Average PRD voter*			
PRI	**.47**	[.31,	.62]	PRI	.11	[.06,	.19]
PAN	.14	[.06,	.27]	PAN	**.85**	[.76,	.92]
PRD	.39	[.25,	.56]	PRD	.04	[.01,	.09]

Note: Simulated probabilities of voting decisions from vote models in Table 7.4 calculated with the use of Clarify (Tomz et al., 2001). PRD supporters are defined as those giving higher prospective marks to the PRD. Those with a large utility differential give the highest prospective mark of 3 to the PRD and the lowest mark of 0 to both the PAN and the PRI. Those with a moderate utility differential assign a lower prospective value of 2, to the PRD and the lowest prospective marks of 0 to both the PAN and the PRI. Both categories of voters are thus presumed to be indifferent between the PRI and the PAN in terms of their prospective marks. Those with average utility differentials assign comparative prospective marks that correspond to those of the average PRD voter. The rest of the independent variables are held at their mean values. All regard the PRD as a sure loser.

There is no evidence of substantial opposition coordination in the 1994 presidential elections. Despite believing the PRD to be a sure loser, the probability of voting for this party is extremely high (66 percent) for those with large utility differentials. As expected, those with low utility differentials show a better chance of deserting the PRD, but 53 percent desert in favor of the PRI and only 34 percent in favor of the PAN. The last row shows that an average PRD supporter who believes his party will be defeated has a higher probability of deserting in favor of the PRI, which underscores the coordination dilemmas faced by the opposition parties in the 1994 presidential elections. Ideological differences, I argue, precluded the opposition from coordinating. Indeed, in the 1994 presidential elections, the average PRD voter slightly preferred the PRI over the PAN, as measured by the prospective marks she assigned to the three parties, which is an indication that more PRD voters were *ideological* rather than *nonideological* or *tactical*.

Voters behaved in a radically different way in the 2000 elections. Even those with large utility differentials show a very low probability (0.34) of remaining loyal to the PRD if they perceive that the PRD is a sure loser and that the PAN can defeat the PRI. To be sure, this apparent higher propensity for voters to abandon the PRD in 2000 might result in part from the different wording of the prospective assessments in these two surveys.[10] What is most significant about the difference between these two elections is that in the 2000 elections, strategic desertions mostly favor the PAN, as these voters show a 0.54 probability of deserting in favor of Fox, as opposed to 0.17 in favor of Labastida; whereas in the 1994 elections, strategic desertions mostly favored the PRI. Opposition coordination in the 2000 elections is even more likely by those with low utility differentials, who show a 0.74 probability of deserting the PRD in favor of Fox. Note that if the average PRD voter believed that Fox could defeat the PRI *and* Cárdenas, he had a 0.85 chance of casting a strategic vote in favor of Fox. Thus, opposition coordination took place in the 2000 presidential elections because this time, the average PRD supporter was *tactical* rather that *ideological* and disliked the PRI more than the PAN.

Another issue that might have complicated opposition coordination in the 1994 presidential elections was that, relative to the 2000 presidential elections, there was less information in the media about the relative standing of the parties at the polls. In the 1994 elections, Cárdenas himself was convinced that he could win, and he claimed to have proprietary polls that gave him the victory (Zinser, 1994). In the 1994 elections, only 18 percent of the PRD supporters believed that the PAN had a better chance of defeating the PRI than the PRD. To assess the extent of strategic voting in 2000,

[10] The 1994 prospective assessments focus on parties and the 2000 prospective assessments on candidates. Another key difference is that in the 2000 survey there are fewer problems with rationalization, since prospective assessments come from the first wave of the panel and voting intentions from the third wave.

Table 7.6. *Change in voter preference by respondent's reported party identification in the first wave of the panel*

	Voted for . . . (percent)			
	PRI	PAN	PRD	
PRI partisan				
February	92	7	1	100
April–May	82	14	4	100
June	75	19	6	100
July (post-electoral)	71	24	4	100
PRD partisan				
February	9	10	81	100
April–May	11	14	75	100
June	10	17	73	100
July (post-electoral)	14	22	64	100
PAN partisan				
February	4	94	2	100
April–May	7	88	5	100
June	10	85	5	100
July (post-electoral)	8	87	5	100
Independent				
February	34	52	14	100
April–May	36	49	15	100
June	30	45	25	100
July (post-electoral)	25	60	15	100

Source: Magaloni and Poiré (2004b).

one crucial question is how many PRDístas believed that Fox could defeat the PRI *and* Cárdenas. Of those who reported being PRDístas at the onset of the campaign, 33 percent believed that Fox would defeat Cárdenas, and 10 percent calculated a tie. Furthermore, only 60 percent of the PRDístas believed that Cárdenas could defeat Labastida.[11] This means that, roughly, Cárdenas risked losing close to 40 percent of his supporters due to strategic desertions. Was this the case? To answer this question, I now make use of the panel data.

To identify PRD supporters, I look at those who reported identifying with this party at the onset of the campaign. Table 7.6 reports how voters

[11] This is an indication that probabilistic assessments are not simple rationalizations of the vote – only 62 percent of those who supported Cárdenas in 2000 believed he could win.

who reported identifying with each of the three major parties changed their voting intentions in the course of the 2000 election campaign. The PRD lost around 40 percent of these voters, 22 percent going to Fox and 14 percent to Labastida.

Strategic Defections from the PRI

The PRI also lost a substantial share of its supporters in the 2000 presidential election. As shown in Table 7.6, 29 percent of those who reported being PRIístas at the onset of the campaign deserted their party, with 24 percent going to Fox and 4 percent to Cárdenas. By contrast, the PAN was highly successful at keeping the support of its core voters. Of those who reported being PANistas at the onset of the campaign, 87 percent reported voting for Vicente Fox. The reasons why PRI supporters abandoned their party are not clear, however. Unless these voters wrongly perceived that Labastida was the trailing candidate, their behavior cannot be attributed to conventional strategic voting.

My hypothesis is that these desertions involve some form of a tipping phenomenon, which was triggered by perceptions that the PRI could be defeated. As with strategic voting, assessing strategic defections first requires identifying those most likely to support the ruling party, and then seeing how their behavior changes in anticipation of what other voters might do. I perform simulations of the models for hypothetical ruling party voters, whom I identify as those assigning to the parties the prospective marks of the *average respondent who reported voting for the PRI*. Naturally, these voters assign higher prospective marks to the PRI than to the opposition. For these voters, I then change their probabilistic assessments in three ways. The first set of voters believes that the PRI cannot be defeated. The second set believes that the PAN can defeat the PRI and that the PRD is the trailing party. The third group assigns average probabilistic assessments. Thus, this last group reveals the intensity of ruling party support by its own voters. If there is some form of tipping phenomenon, desertions should come from those who believe that the PAN can defeat the PRI. Results are presented in Table 7.7.

There is no evidence of tipping in the 1994 presidential elections. The PRI retains the support of its followers *regardless* of probabilistic assessments. Also note that in the 1994 elections the propensity to support the ruling party of someone holding the comparative prospective marks of an average PRI voter is extremely high (0.92). In the 2000 presidential

Table 7.7. *Simulated strategic defections by PRI supporters in the 1994 and 2000 presidential elections*

	1994				2000		
Predicted to Vote	Mean Predicted Probability	[95% Confidence Interval]			Mean Predicted Probability	[95% Confidence Interval]	
	PRI winner				**PRI winner**		
PRI	**.94**	[.90,	.97]	PRI	**.80**	[.73,	.86]
PAN	.01	[.008,	.038]	PAN	.14	[.09,	.21]
PRD	.04	[.015,	.083]	PRD	.10	[.06,	.18]
	PAN likely winner PRI can be defeated				**FOX winner CCS loses to both**		
PRI	**.90**	[.87,	.93]	PRI	.24	[.14,	.38]
PAN	.08	[.05,	.11]	PAN	**.72**	[.56,	.84]
PRD	.009	[.003,	.020]	PRD	.04	[.01,	.10]
	Average probabilistic assessments of PRI voter				**Average probabilistic assessments of PRI voter**		
PRI	**.92**	[.88,	.94]	PRI	**.53**	[.44,	.62]
PAN	.06	[.04,	.08]	PAN	.37	[.29,	.15]
PRD	.02	[.007,	.03]	PRD	.09	[.06,	.16]

Note: Simulated probabilities of voting decisions calculated from vote models in Table 7.4 with the use of Clarify (Tomz et al., 2001). PRI supporters are defined as those who give the parties prospective marks corresponding to the *average respondent who reported voting for the ruling party*. These voters differ in their assessments of which party is most likely to win. The rest of the independent variables are held at their means values.

elections, PRI voters behaved in a dramatically different way for two reasons. First, the propensity to support the ruling party of someone holding the comparative prospective marks of an average PRI voter is much lower (0.53), which reflects the fact that PRI voters now saw only a small utility differential between their party and the opposition.

Second, there appears to be a significant bandwagon effect against the PRI, motivated by the belief that Fox could defeat Labastida. To be sure, some ruling party voters deserted the PRI either because they were more convinced by Vicente Fox or because they were deterred by Francisco Labastida, independent of strategic calculations about their party's chances of losing. But expectations that the PRI could be defeated also played a powerful role in accounting for ruling party desertions. When performing an analysis of ruling party defections making use of the panel data, these conclusions still hold. Assessments about the prospects of defeating the PRI play a strong role in ruling party defections from the first wave of the panel to the third, holding strength of partisanship and candidate prospective evaluations constant. Also, there is no evidence that those who defected from Labastida during the campaign disproportionately voted for the losing candidate, Roberto Madrazo, in the PRI's primary elections (results available upon request). I am thus confident that prospects that the PRI could be defeated played a powerful role in explaining desertions from the PRI by its own supporters.

The crucial question is, how many of the PRI supporters actually held probabilistic assessments that would induce them to desert the PRI? of those who reported being PRIístas at the onset of the campaign, 20 percent believed that Fox would defeat Labastida, and 11 percent calculated a tie. This means that a sizable group of PRIístas had the probabilistic assessments necessary to induce tipping and that strategic defections on the part of ruling party voters in favor of Vicente Fox played a very significant role in the PRI's defeat in the 2000 presidential elections.

Conclusions

In the 1994 presidential elections, voters still believed that the PRI was more capable than the opposition of handling the future of the national economy. Since according to the voters the current state of the economy was mediocre, their positive prospective judgments about the PRI were mostly shaped by their approval of Carlos Salinas. However, presidential approval during that presidential term, as I demonstrated in Chapter 5, was not significantly shaped by objective economic conditions. Richer voters approved of Carlos Salinas in the prospective sense, in part because they believed in his policy initiatives. Poorer voters supported Carlos Salinas in part because of macroeconomic stabilization, and in part because of PRONASOL.

The 1994 post-electoral bust led voters to question the PRI's economic competence *and* to doubt its credibility. By the 1997 midterm elections, voters no longer believed that the PRI was more capable of handling the future of the national economy than the opposition. To arrive to such a conclusion, they observed the party's long-term economic record, together with the current economic situation – mostly focusing on the recent recession and their disapproval of President Zedillo's handling of the economy. Voters' comparative prospective assessments in 2000 were similar to their assessments in 1997 because they no longer favored the PRI. Compared to 1997, voters in 2000 had more positive evaluations of the president and the current state of the economy, which makes sense considering that the economy had fully recovered from the 1994 peso crisis. However, since the overwhelming majority of voters anticipated an end-of-term economic crisis, the PRI no longer received higher prospective marks. The party could not fully profit from the outstanding growth rates of the two years prior to the presidential elections because this time voters anticipated that good things would not last. Thus, the PRI's ultimate demise must be understood in the context of the 1994 peso crisis, which had made voters realize that the economic booms and busts around elections had become a systematic, yet undesired and undesirable, attribute of the party's rule.

Strategic voter coordination played a powerful role in the PRI's defeat. Opposition voters faced a complicated coordination problem to dislodge the ruling party. The coordination dilemma became manifest in the 1994 presidential elections. The average PRD supporter preferred the PRI over the PAN and would not have been willing to put her ideological differences aside to cast a strategic vote in favor of the PAN's candidate. In part, PRD voters disliked the PAN because of its cooperation with the Salinas government in enacting market-oriented reforms. PRD voters also had other reasons to disdain the PAN – the party's leaders, as I explain in the next chapter, had tacitly acquiesced in the 1988 electoral fraud and had behaved as "loyal opposition" during much of the Salinas term. Another issue that complicated coordination in 1994 was the lack of consensus about who the trailing candidate was. PRD leaders claimed to have proprietary polls that gave them the lead. Although many PRD supporters accurately perceived their candidate to be a sure loser, a sizable group believed their party had a better chance of defeating the ruling party that the PAN, and this discouraged voter coordination.

Opposition voters behaved in a dramatically different way in the 2000 presidential elections. This time the average PRD supporter much preferred the PAN over the PRI. Political change and democratization were more salient than the economic policy issues that divided the opposition. Thus, a sizable group of PRD voters were willing to set aside their ideological differences and voted strategically in favor of Vicente Fox. Further, in the 2000 presidential elections, there was plenty of information in the mass media about the relative standing of the parties at the polls. Voters' perceptions of which opposition candidate had a better chance of defeating the PRI were quite accurate. The notion that the PRI could effectively be defeated encouraged both strategic defections by ruling party voters and strategic voting by PRD supporters. All of these voters managed to coordinate successfully and finally to dislodge the long-standing ruling party.

8

Electoral Fraud and the Game of Electoral Transitions

After the 2000 presidential elections, the PRI yielded power peacefully to the PAN's candidate, Vicente Fox. The electoral defeat put an end to one of the most enduring autocracies in the twentieth century. Just twelve years before, the PRI had committed massive fraud against Cuauhtémoc Cárdenas. One key difference between 1988 and 2000 was that Mexico's institutional setting had been transformed in fundamental ways. In 1988, the PRI controlled every single aspect of the organization, monitoring, and certification of the elections, and there were no independent sources of information to verify fraud. In 2000, a truly independent electoral commission, the IFE, was in charge of organizing the elections, from counting the vote to ratifying the results. The 2000 elections were also different because of the massive dissemination of polling information to the mass media. These new institutional and informational settings, I argue, proved critical in motivating the PRI to yield power peacefully in 2000.

This chapter develops a game of "electoral transitions" and employs some of the intuitions derived from it to explain, first, the political rationale, from the PRI's perspective, of granting independence to the IFE in 1994 and, second, some of the key differences between the 1988 and 2000 presidential elections that led the PRI to commit massive fraud in the former and to yield power peacefully in the latter. The model seeks to answer the following fundamental questions: When would a hegemonic party resort to electoral fraud? Under what conditions is a hegemonic party willing to peacefully yield power when it loses elections? What explains why a hegemonic party might choose to tie its hands and not commit fraud, delegating the organization and monitoring of elections to an independent electoral commission? The chapter also brings voters into the transition game by testing, with individual-level data, some of the implications of the game for voters' behavior. To do so, I make use of survey evidence from the Belden-Rusonello survey, collected one month before the 1994 presidential election (N = 1,500).

The chapter unfolds as follows. The first section discusses the game and some of its critical implications. The second discusses the 1988 presidential election in light of the model. The third section presents an analysis, based on the transition game, of the PRI's decision not to commit electoral fraud by delegating power to an independent electoral commission, the IFE, in the 1994 electoral reform. The fourth section brings voters into the game of "electoral transitions," assessing some of the critical assumptions of the game for voters' behavior. The last section discusses some of the key differences between the 1988 and 2000 presidential elections, in light of the transition game.

Electoral Fraud and the Game of "Electoral Transitions"[1]

My game of "electoral transitions" builds upon the strategic approach to transitions to democracy that focuses on elite bargaining and contingent choice during the *process* of transition (O'Donnell and Schmitter, 1986; Przeworski, 1991).[2] Following Karl and Schmitter's (1991) advice, the model seeks to provide a "modest effort to develop a contingently sensitive understanding of a variety of circumstances under which [democratic regimes] may emerge" (270). In terms of the logic of scientific inference (Keohane, King, and Verba, 1994), some of the scholarly research on transitions to democracy tends problematically to sample on the dependent variable, choosing mostly cases of successful transitions (Geddes, 1999). A logically consistent explanation of democratization should account for both successful and unsuccessful cases. The game of "electoral transitions" I develop provides a framework in which peaceful alternation of political power in office, as occurred in Mexico in 2000, is one of the possible

[1] The game draws from Diaz-Cayeros and Magaloni (1995) and from Magaloni (2005).

[2] The strategic approach stresses that democratization is a process, rather than a set of preconditions (see Kitschelt, 1992). Game-theoretic strategic analyses of transitions to democracy are becoming more common. Some relevant contributions are Colomer (1991), Colomer and Pascual (1994), and Weingast (1997). For the most recent works, which explore how the preconditions for democracy shape elite strategies, see Geddes (1999), Fearon (2000), Acemoglu and Robinson (2006), Wantchekon and Neeman (2002), Boix (2003), and Wantchekon (2004).

equilibrium outcomes. But it also provides for the possibility that the incumbent resorts to electoral fraud, as occurred in 1988.

In the transition game, parties are viewed as unitary actors who seek to maximize votes and seats in elective office. The three parties in the model are strategic actors who first define an electoral strategy to maximize votes, and then define a post-electoral strategy for whether they will abide by the election results or contest them through various legal, illegal, violent, or peaceful means. The strategies available differ according to whether the party in question is the ruling party or one of the two challengers in the opposition camp.

The ruling party controls the electoral process, which means that it may carry out electoral fraud using the power of government – or, if need be, use the army – to reverse the results. At this stage of the game, the model does not distinguish among the incumbent party, the army, and the government, because empirically in all of these contexts, the ruling party *is* the government, and the armed forces most often remain under civilian control. However, the model does not presuppose that the support of the armed forces is always guaranteed. The armed forces will cooperate with the ruling party to enforce electoral fraud when only one opposition party challenges the results, engaging in a "failed" rebellion. If the opposition threatens to challenge the results in unison and there is a real risk that social peace will be completely destroyed as a consequence of the parties' post-electoral feuds, the armed forces might choose to back the ruling party to repress the opposition, but they might also decide to back the opposition or to oust the ruling party through a military coup and so impose order themselves.

The challengers, on the other hand, can contest the electoral result through legal processes, massive mobilizations, and, in the most extreme cases, outright rebellion. In that case, a military coup could ensue, with the incumbent typically retaining power; but the situation could get out of hand. With civil strife, even the incumbent could lose.

A "transition to democracy" or democratization outcome occurs when the ruling party refrains from using its power to manipulate the election and both of the challengers accept the result as legal and legitimate – even if they lose. If a challenger wins, democratization has obviously occurred. But defining the model in this way allows for the possibility that democratization can occur even without an alternation in power. This definition of a democratization outcome fulfills Przeworski's requirement that no player

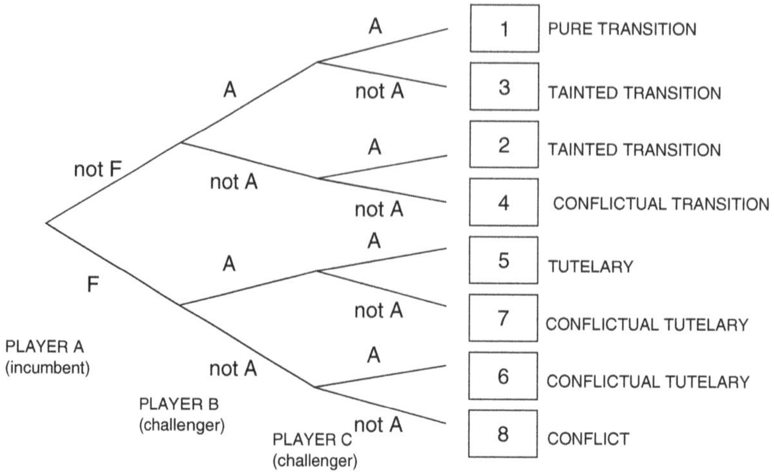

Figure 8.1. The transition game with a divided opposition.

should prevent some political outcome from occurring by exercising ex post (not only ex ante) control over society (1987: 60).

Figure 8.1 presents the extensive form representation of the game. The outcomes are numbered from one to eight. The first four outcomes entail different forms of clean elections, where the ruling party refrains from committing electoral fraud, regardless of whether it wins or loses. If it wins, the election must be clean; but if it loses, the ruling party must also step down from office. Both of these possibilities are regarded as "democratic outcomes," although the real challenge consists in bringing about a transition to democracy when the incumbent loses. The first of these outcomes is a "pure transition to democracy," where alternation in power is not necessary, but the elections must be clean and accepted by everyone. The second and third outcomes are "tainted transitions to democracy" – the ruling party enforces clean elections, one of the opposition parties challenges these results, and the other accepts them. The fourth outcome is "conflictual transition": regardless of the ruling party's impeccably democratic behavior, both opposition parties protest the results of clean elections through massive street demonstrations that may get out of hand.

The last four outcomes all involve the ruling party committing fraud. When there is electoral fraud, but both challengers consent to it, I call it a "pure tutelary autocracy." A "conflictual tutelary autocracy," on the other hand, entails that the incumbent commits fraud, and opposition parties fail to coordinate in challenging the results. Here one of the opposition parties becomes an accomplice of the regime, while the other is left to challenge the results alone. The ruling party will be able to get away with electoral fraud more effectively when the opposition fails to act in unison to challenge the regime.[3] The intuition here is that if at least one of the opposition parties cooperates with the ruling party, social peace is maintained, with the armed forces cooperating in enforcing the fraud. The last outcome involves conflict, where both opposition parties coordinate in contesting the electoral fraud through massive street demonstrations that may get out of hand. Because no opposition party cooperates with the regime, social peace is destroyed, and the armed forces may choose to back the ruling party but may also oust it through a military coup, or may choose to back the opposition in order to dislodge the ruling party by force.

In the game, parties are presumed to aspire to maximize the number of seats and votes at each election. Votes are valuable in and of themselves and because they translate into legislative seats. For all of the players, office is valuable because it confers power and perks, and because it might also be a means to implement policy. The autocrat seeks to maximize votes rather than treating votes as simply being instrumental to winning, for two reasons. First, by winning with huge margins of victory the autocrat is more capable of creating an image of invincibility that will discourage potential challengers – most notably, those coming from within the party – and mass bandwagon effects. Second, the ruling party seeks to control constitutional change and to set the basic rules of the game without the need to forge coalitions with the opposition parties. Constitutional change often requires an oversized legislative coalition, and if a form of proportional representation is employed, more votes will translate into more seats. For opposition parties, votes are valuable because they are the "currency" with which they bargain with the ruling party and with each other, apart from the value they might place on gaining office.

Office is not unique or indivisible; its value depends on the set of electoral rules. I consider two examples of the value of office depending on the electoral rules. A presidential election is by definition winner-take-all: the party that gets the plurality gets the presidential seat, and the losers get nothing. A second electoral rule I consider is "proportional representation," which

[3] This might not be a reasonable structure depending on the levels of electoral support. If one challenger has, say, 60 percent of the votes, it might have enough strength, by itself, to bring the conflict outcome about. Hence this payoff makes sense if all three parties are relatively strong.

simply says that the vote share (including fraudulent votes) is the share of office. Office can be divisible under presidentialism when a presidential election takes place concurrently with a legislative election. In this case, the losers in the presidential race might still get legislative seats, especially if a form of proportional representation is employed for electing the assembly. Institutional details are hence important, because, together with the electoral result, they determine the value of office and how it will be distributed among the parties. Most hegemonic-party regimes are presidential regimes that have vested enormous power on the presidency. One of the central battles of the transition is to convince those ruling parties to cede this enormous power peacefully.

The consequences for the parties of taking different post-electoral actions are the following. Electoral fraud is translated into more votes and seats for the ruling party and fewer votes and seats for the opposition and might make the difference between winning and losing for a party. There is, however, a penalty for the ruling party of governing under fraud in the form of a *legitimacy deficit* that can result in, for example, the loss of foreign aid or in the imposition of international sanctions; it can also result in reprisals from the business community in the form of capital flight.

The game further posits that an *electoral punishment* will follow in the next elections, as a response to the parties' post-electoral strategies. To simplify, I focus on the electoral punishment to the opposition parties. I distinguish two types of opposition voters according to their tolerance for violence. *Moderate opposition voters* are highly averse to post-electoral mobilization and violence. These voters will defect from an opposition party that challenges clean elections in favor of (1) another opposition party that did not challenge the elections, or (2) in favor of the ruling party, whichever is closest in the political spectrum. *Radical opposition voters* are highly committed to democratization, even if this entails post-electoral struggle and violence. These voters will punish an opposition party that acquiesces in electoral fraud by switching their support to the party that challenged the fraud. If both opposition parties acquiesce, these voters are presumed to abstain from voting in the next elections.

These electoral pay-offs presuppose that voters know the actual election results. This assumption is problematic because, when elections take place under authoritarian conditions, the ruling party tends to control the electoral institutions, and there are no independent sources of information to verify the results. When there is no credible information about the actual election results, voters need to find ways to infer whether there was fraud or not. One possibility would be that voters simply mimic elites from their own party – if party elites challenge the results, their supporters believe the elections were fraudulent; if they acquiesce, voters believe the elections were clean.

Opposition party elites, however, possess incentives to mislead their voters. When an opposition party challenges an election, it can be punished by its *moderate* supporters; in that case, it will find it in its interest to have its supporters think there was fraud, even if the elections were clean. But if this party chooses not to contest the results, it will find it in its interest to have its supporters believe the elections were clean, even if there was fraud, because otherwise it could be punished by its *radical* supporters. Thus, opposition voters must find ways to infer what happened in the elections, but if they simply mimic elites of their own party, they could be seriously misled.

Opposition voters, I assume, learn about whether or not there was fraud by listening to what opposition elites of both parties declare. They then filter this information through their own preconceptions about the nature of the political regime. As they are more distrustful of the democratic credentials of the regime, *radical opposition voters* will not believe the elections were clean unless both opposition parties accepted the results. As they are more skeptical of allegations of electoral fraud, *moderate opposition voters* do not believe there was fraud unless both opposition parties challenge the results.

These simple assumptions about how voters construct their beliefs imply that if only one opposition party acquiesces and the other challenges the results, *radical opposition voters* will infer that there was fraud, even if the elections were clean. When only one opposition party claims fraud and the other acquiesces, *moderate opposition voters* will believe the acquiescing party and will punish the opposition party that claimed fraud, even if the elections were actually rigged. The formal solution to the transition game is provided in Magaloni (2005). Here I discuss some of the intuitions derived from the model.

Authoritarian Equilibrium with Electoral Fraud

In the game, the ruling party is able to get away with electoral fraud because opposition parties possess incentives to act as a "loyal opposition" and acquiesce in the electoral fraud. Suppose that the ruling party steals votes from party A. If both opposition parties choose to challenge the electoral fraud, the hegemonic party could more easily be dissuaded to abide by the results of clean elections because it risks conflict. Yet if party A chooses to challenge the electoral fraud, party B will face the following strategic dilemma: acquiesce in the electoral fraud and capture legislative seats and government spoils, or get the expected value of conflict. Further, if party A challenges the electoral fraud, it will lose the support of its *moderate voters* in the next elections – although it will keep the support of its *radical voters*. If party B's electoral base is composed mostly of *moderate* supporters who are averse to violence, and if the official results allow this party to acquire enough legislative seats and possibly policy influence, this party will be better off institutionalizing itself as a "loyal opposition," with the result that the opposition fails to rebel in tandem, which in turn helps the autocrat to get away with various sorts of electoral malpractice.

The game allows for the possibility that the ruling party commits electoral fraud even if it wins. One reason hegemonic party regimes might choose to inflate their vote margins, as argued in Chapter 1, is that they are interested in creating an image of invincibility that serves to discourage potential challengers. Another reason to inflate vote margins is that more votes might also translate into more seats, which the ruling party might need either to retain the supermajority necessary to modify the constitution single-handedly or to keep majority control of the Congress. Fraud can also be carried out in a local and decentralized manner, since there may be some local bosses who, for their own sake or to improve the territorial distribution of votes, want to inflate the electoral result.

Whether the ruling party commits fraud when it is winning depends, on the one hand, on the likelihood that the electoral fraud will produce a major social rebellion, and on the other, on the costs of governing under fraud. If the ruling party anticipates that the opposition will not coordinate to rebel against the fraud (or if the opposition is incapable of rebelling because it is too weak), it will choose to inflate its vote margin as long as the gain – in seats, votes, or both – it obtains from stealing the election outweighs the *legitimacy deficit* for governing under fraud. This explains why such autocratic equilibria, where the ruling party resorts to stealing the elections so as to boost its vote margins, can be long-lasting.

Obviously, the ruling party's temptation to commit fraud is even greater when electoral fraud is needed to win. In this case, the ruling party will be more willing to risk conflict so as to stay in office. The ruling party's calculation depends, first, on its expected pay-off after conflict erupts. The end result of the conflict crucially depends on what the armed forces do. If the ruling party believes it has the unconditional backing of the army, it will probably not hesitate to steal the election. But if the ruling party anticipates major social unrest, it might be better off peacefully stepping down from office before a military coup ousts the incumbent.

Second, the ruling party's decision to risk conflict so as to retain office also depends on the pay-off of losing. The value of losing is shaped in part by the existing electoral institutions for the translation of votes into seats. The ruling party will be more willing to risk conflict to stay in office if electoral rules are winner-take-all, as in presidential elections. Winner-take-all electoral rules and presidential elections increase the ruling party's incentive to risk conflict so as to retain office, making transitions to democracy more violence-prone. However, winner-take-all electoral rules also increase the incentives for opposition parties to challenge the electoral fraud, because the ruling party has less to offer to these parties in exchange for their acquiescence.

By contrast, proportional representation electoral rules decrease the ruling party's incentives to risk conflict, but also increase the incentives for at least one of the opposition parties to acquiesce in the electoral fraud. In these cases, the ruling party can better co-opt one of its opponents into acquiescing by offering legislative seats and possibly some policy influence. Thus, in legislative elections that take place under some form of proportional representation rule, and in presidential elections that take place concurrently with assembly elections, it will be easier for the ruling party to get away with electoral fraud.

One key quandary in the game is that the autocrat is capable of stealing the election because it profits from coordination dilemmas among the opposition camp. If both opposition parties coordinated in challenging the electoral fraud, the ruling party could be deterred more effectively from stealing the elections owing to the threat of conflict. However, given the risks of war, at least one of the opposition parties will cooperate with the regime, especially if it can offer side payments in the form of perks, legislative seats, and policy influence. When only one opposition party challenges the fraud while the other party acquiesces, the ruling party is able to steal the elections at low cost (only a *legitimacy deficit*), without putting its own political survival at stake. The fundamental problem is that opposition forces generally divide too early; long before they are able to defeat authoritarianism, they divide to compete among themselves, seeking to maximize their individual chances under the existing system. The divisiveness of the opposition is in part *endogenous* – shaped by the existing electoral rules, which the ruling party autocrat can unilaterally draft – and in part shaped by preexisting ideological, regional, or ethnic differences (Cox, 1997). Thus, in the transition game, opposition parties possess mixed incentives – namely, to defend their stolen votes while at the same time seeking to maintain their prizes under the current system.

The Role of Public Information about Electoral Outcomes

If there is perfect voter information about the actual elections results, outcomes 2, 3, and 4 are never equilibria, because there is decisive electoral punishment by *moderate* opposition voters against an opposition party that contests the results of clean elections. However, if voters do not know the actual election results, these outcomes can become equilibria of the game. Opposition party elites might choose to contest clean elections for various reasons. One is to destabilize the regime and harm its legitimacy. Another is to maintain the enthusiasm of *radical* voters to continue fighting authoritarianism.

Recall that when voters do not know the actual election results, their reactions to the parties' post-electoral strategies depend, on the one hand, on their preconceptions about the political regime and, on the other, on what the opposition parties do. If both opposition parties challenge the results or if both acquiesce, voters will believe them. But if only one opposition party challenges the results and the other acquiesces, *moderate voters* will believe the acquiescing opposition party and *radical voters* will believe the one that challenged the elections. This means that when there is no public information about the electoral fraud, *moderate voters* will inevitably abandon the opposition party that engages in post-electoral battles in favor of the party that acts as a loyal opposition or in favor of the ruling party, whichever is closest to their views. *Radical voters* will inevitably abandon the opposition party that acquiesces to the official election results in favor of the party that claims fraud and engages in post-electoral battles. If both parties act as a loyal opposition, *radical voters* will abstain.

This means that in the absence of public information about the electoral results, elections will invariably involve allegations of electoral fraud, post-electoral clashes, and even violence as long as the electoral base of at least one of the opposition parties is disproportionately *radical*. Indeed, under this poor information environment, all that it is required for an opposition party to challenge clean elections is that the number of its *radical voters be larger than the number of its moderate supporters.* This provides an explanation of why allegations of electoral fraud need not always be credible.

Another implication of relaxing the assumption of perfect voter information about the actual election results is that the ruling party is not always rewarded for holding clean elections. Suppose that the ruling party knows it can win the elections cleanly and that party B's base is mainly *moderate*, while party C's supporters are mostly *radical*. Looking down the game tree, the ruling party knows that party B will accept the election results, while party C will challenge them. If fraud produces some extra payoff for the ruling party, even if marginal, it will steal votes from the opposition because, regardless of what it does, its legitimacy will be harmed by party C's allegations of electoral fraud. Thus, although allegations of electoral fraud are not always credible, it is also the case that the ruling party's claims of electoral transparency are equally dubious.

A final implication of imperfect voter information about the actual election results is that the coordination dilemma among the opposition camp becomes even more acute. Suppose that the ruling party can successfully buy off party B into acquiescing to fraud. If voters do not know the actual election results, party B will be able to deceive *moderate opposition voters* into believing that the elections were clean, even when there was fraud. The implication of this is striking: the acquiescing opposition party not only receives a payoff in the form of seats, but also receives an electoral payoff for acquiescing in the fraud – namely, the *moderate opposition voters* who desert the more militant opposition party. Obviously, this electoral payoff increases if *moderate opposition voters* all choose to desert to party B and none desert to the incumbent.

Thus, coordination among opponents is more difficult when electoral fraud is not *common knowledge*, because the ruling party will deceive *moderate voters* into believing the elections were clean, even if there was fraud. This result underscores why dictators abhor information dissemination and an independent mass media: public exposure of the rulers' abuses makes coordination against these abuses more likely.

Endogenous Institutional Change and Delegation to an Independent Electoral Commission

Why, then, would an autocratic ruling party accede to the creation of independent electoral institutions that can publicize the actual election results? To provide an answer, my model addresses endogenous institutional change – why an autocrat might sign a "political pact" with the opposition to willingly refrain from committing fraud.

When perfect voter information about the election results exists, opposition parties never challenge the results of clean elections. The same is not true in the game of imperfect voter information. Here, the dilemma for a hegemonic party is that even if it can win elections cleanly, the opposition will *not be willing to endorse the electoral process* as long as its supporters are disproportionately *radical*, and elections will invariably be contested at the risk of producing a violent conflict.

The ruling party's dilemma cannot be solved simply by promising to hold clean elections, because this promise is not credible. In the game of imperfect voter information, the ruling party will commit fraud as long as it produces a marginal payoff that will compensate the *legitimacy deficit*, since regardless of what this party does, at least one of the opposition parties will challenge the results. The only way to commit the opposition to the electoral process is if the ruling party credibly ties its hands ex ante not to commit fraud.

One way of committing the opposition to the elections is to transform the existing institutions. If the ruling party delegates the organization of the elections to an independent electoral commission that is trusted by all major political players, it can then commit the opposition to the elections. The incentives to delegate the organization of the elections to an independent electoral commission arise only when the ruling party can reasonably expect to win clean elections *and* the opposition credibly threatens to challenge the elections and play Conflict, even if there is no fraud, unless the ruling party finds a way to guarantee that the elections will be clean. In addition, the ruling party must not be willing to risk conflict in order to retain its control of the electoral process. If the ruling party cannot win clean elections, then it will always be better off if it retains its ability to commit fraud.

The independent electoral commission removes the ruling party's ability to commit fraud and negotiate the vote behind closed doors. If the ruling party were to lose, it would have to blatantly refuse to step down from office. Because this transgression is public and unambiguous, opposition parties would more easily coordinate to rebel against it. The role of the independent electoral commission is thus twofold. First, it provides clear information about the actual election results, thus facilitating opposition coordination against ruling party transgressions. Second, the independent electoral commission serves to commit an intransigent opposition to the electoral process. Who will follow the opposition into the streets to protest the elections when it is obvious that the ruling party did not control the electoral process and that elections were clean? Of course, this argument works only if the electoral commission is truly credible and independent, so that no single party possesses unilateral control over it and it has enough power to control the elections. In the next section, I apply some of these insights to account for crucial aspects of the process of transition in Mexico.

The 1988 Electoral Fraud and the Opposition's Coordination Dilemma

The post-electoral bargains following the 1988 Mexican presidential elections clearly illustrate the model's understanding of the opposition's coordination dilemma in the transition game. The official results of the 1988 elections gave the victory to the PRI's presidential candidate, Carlos Salinas, with 50.7 percent of the vote, over Cuauhtémoc Cárdenas, of the Frente Democrático Nacional (which eventually became the PRD), with 32.5 percent of the vote.

There is no doubt that the PRI committed fraud. In his recently published memoirs, former president Miguel de la Madrid confesses that the PRI announced its victory prematurely, long before the final vote count was completed, so as to preempt Cuauhtémoc Cárdenas from claiming the elections. De la Madrid also confirms that the PRI and the government were "horrified" after receiving the first electoral returns from Mexico City, other states near the capital, and some of the predominantly urban precincts, which gave a decisive victory to Cárdenas.[4] Results from the rural districts, which arrived much later, gave the victory to the PRI. With the currently available information, it is impossible to know if the PRI would have actually lost the presidency had there been no electoral fraud in 1988.

Within the government, there were two factions. One supported the idea of "cleaning up the elections," examining the electoral information and establishing the real results of the elections. The other faction, which eventually prevailed, was eager to alter the results so as to guarantee the governing party a minimum of 50 percent of the vote and a majority of the single-member districts in the Chamber of Deputies. The 50 percent vote threshold was decisive because with fewer votes, the PRI would not

[4] De la Madrid explicitly says, "I was horrified when I found out about the size of the PRI's debacle in the area" (de la Madrid, 2004: 817).

obtain the cushioned majority it needed in the Electoral College to ratify the presidential election single-handedly (Castañeda, 2000: 86, 232).[5]

On election night, the candidates of the FDN, the PAN, and the PRT (Workers' Revolutionary Party) signed a joint petition, the "Call to Legality," which denounced the fraud. The violations of the electoral laws, they argued, warranted annulling the elections, and they warned the interior minister that "we will not accept the results nor recognize the authorities that come out of fraud" (cited in Bruhn, 1997: 145). Three days latter, Cárdenas proclaimed victory and confirmed his commitment not to recognize the illegitimate authorities selected out of fraud. The PAN soon backed away and decided not to join Cardenistas in calling for annulment of the elections. Instead, the PAN and other minor opposition parties that had cross-endorsed the Cárdenas candidacy chose to ratify the congressional elections. The outcome of the 1988 elections might have been quite different had the opposition parties opted to challenge the PRI in unison. The PRI might have been forced to accede to holding an extraordinary election, or widespread conflict and violence might have resulted.

In light of the model, I highlight the following reasons why the PAN chose not to coordinate with the Cardenistas in challenging the results. First, the PAN concluded that the danger of confronting the government was too great, and it was not willing to risk political violence (Castañeda, 2000: 88). Second, by choosing to acquiesce in the fraud, the PAN opted to defend its own *legislative victories*, seizing the opportunity to acquire policy-making power for the first time since its creation in 1939. Indeed, the distribution of legislative seats, according to the official results, implied that the PRI would keep control of the majority in the Lower Chamber but would no longer control the supermajority needed to modify the constitution single-handedly. PAN support was essential for Carlos Salinas because his economic agenda required modification of the constitution in fundamental ways (e.g., the privatization of the banking system and the restructuring of property rights in the countryside, which were part of the PAN's legislative agenda, required constitutional changes). Thus, siding with the Cardenistas in challenging the results of the elections would have cost the

[5] Although a "governability clause" existed that would grant an automatic majority in the Lower Chamber to the largest party, this entailed distributing seats by a proportional representation formula to the PRI from the multimember races. However, this would have given the PRI only a very narrow majority, 251 of the 500 seats. If it had 50 percent of the vote, the PRI would be assured 261 of the 500 seats, and the ratification of the presidential election could be carried out with fewer problems (Castañeda, 2000: 233).

PAN the opportunity to have policy influence for the first time in its long history of opposing the PRI.

The PAN would use its new power in government strategically. It traded approval of the numerous constitutional reforms proposed by Salinas during his administration for two major electoral reforms that took place in 1990 and 1993. Their major achievement was the establishment of a Federal Electoral Tribunal and the creation of the IFE, which was in charge of organizing and monitoring elections. The 1993 electoral reforms finally eliminated "self-certification" by the Electoral College, granting the IFE authority to certify electoral results. In addition, within the Electoral Tribunal, a second legal entity was created (Sala de Segunda Instancia), whose decisions could not be appealed or reversed by any other authority.[6]

Salinas offered additional payoffs to the PAN for its cooperation with the economic reforms. During his presidency, the PAN obtained official recognition for many of its electoral victories at the local level; it secured three governorships – Chihuahua, Baja California, and Guanajuato – and won many municipal races. The gubernatorial seat in Guanajuato was the result of what came to be known as the *concertacesiones* – post-electoral bargains through which the president transferred the election from the PRI to the PAN, regardless of the actual vote count, when uncertain results emerged from local elections.

PAN supporters did not abandon their party for cooperating with the regime. On the one hand, the extent of the 1988 fraud and the PAN's tacit support for it never became public. Some years after those elections, the PAN would vote in a legislative coalition with the PRI to burn the ballots. The then-leader of the PAN's legislative fraction, Diego Fernández de Cevallos, justified its party's decision to support the PRI's proposal to

[6] The 1990 electoral reform did not modify the so-called governability clause, which gave the largest electoral party (obtaining more than 35 percent percent of the vote) an absolute majority of seats in the Lower Chamber even if that party did not obtain the majority of the vote. In 1993, the electoral rule was transformed. The new electoral rule for the translation of votes into seats in the Chamber of Deputies gave a more-than-proportional share of seats to the largest electoral party as long as it finished above some threshold with respect to the second-largest party. The 1993 reform also changed the electoral rules for the composition of the Senate: three senators were to be elected by plurality, and a fourth was allocated to the second-largest party in the state. The rules for selecting the Senate largely benefited the PAN over the PRD. These rules for the selection of the Senate were to be modified in the 1996 electoral reform, allocating the fourth senator by a form of proportional representation. On this occasion, the rule was meant to benefit the PRD (see Diaz-Cayeros and Magaloni, 2001, for a discussion of the electoral reforms that relate to the translation of votes into seats).

burn the 1998 ballots, which had been stored in the basement of the Mexican Congress, with the following words:

> [A]fter three years those ballots mean and represent nothing; they have been guarded by the government, without a purpose. They might or might not contain the results [of the 1988 elections]. The electoral process of 1988 is now history that nobody can change. Furthermore, National Action [the PAN] has as one of its most distinctive traits that of always looking forward, searching for the unity of all Mexicans. Nobody will benefit from revising papers that tell and mean nothing. The PAN's legislative fraction accepts that those mythical documents be destroyed. (Diario de Debates de la Cámara de Diputados, December 20, 1991: 3276).[7]

With these terrifying words, the leadership of the PAN recognized the party's tacit support for the PRI's electoral manipulations and the 1988 electoral fraud. Had the ballots of the 1988 presidential election been exposed, the 1988 electoral fraud would have become common knowledge, and the PAN would have faced serious difficulties in justifying its cooperation with Salinas's government.

Another reason why PAN did not experience electoral punishment for its alliance with the regime is that its supporters were disproportionately *moderate*, as I will show. Since PAN supporters were more skeptical about allegations of electoral fraud and did not regard the existing institutions as terribly authoritarian, they were willing to support a party that cooperated with the regime.

The PRD, by contrast, was left with the support of mostly *radical voters*, who were extremely distrustful of Salinas's government and the PRI. This party voted against the 1990 and 1993 electoral reforms negotiated between the PRI and the PAN and became increasingly anti-institutional. In most of the local elections that took place after 1988, violent confrontations between PRI local elites and PRD contenders occurred (Eisenstadt, 2004). By the PRD count, during the Salinas presidency close to 500 of its activists were murdered in these electoral confrontations. To be sure, *moderate voters*, distrustful of these allegations of electoral fraud and averse to post-electoral violence, would abandon this party owing to the perception, in part fostered by the regime, that it was violence-prone; but its core *radical voters* would continue to support it.

The effectiveness of the 1990 and 1993 electoral reforms in limiting the PRI's control of the electoral process was limited. On the one hand, neither of these electoral reforms eliminated the key impediment to the

[7] I thank Jeffrey Weldon for helping me find this transcript in the *Diario de Debates*.

establishment of more transparent federal electoral processes. The IFE's board continued to be controlled by the government and the PRI. The board was composed of the Secretario de Gobernación (interior minister), as its president; four congressmen (two belonging to the largest party and two members of the second-largest party); party representatives (whose number varied according to the percentage of votes received by each party); and six Consejeros Magistrados (magistrate councilmen), whose impartiality was severely questioned, as they were elected from a list proposed by the president and ratified by a vote of two-thirds of the Chamber of Deputies.

On the one hand, electoral courts were not very successful in adjudicating electoral disputes. According to Eisenstadt's (2004) careful analysis of post-electoral conflicts in Mexico's local elections during the period, "fewer than a third of the country's first institutional arbiters of electoral fraud successfully adjudicated postelectoral disputes by preventing disagreements from spilling out of the courtrooms and onto the streets" (270). More often, opposition parties, especially the PRD, continued to mobilize in the streets to protest after elections.

The most fundamental institutional reform in the construction of democracy in Mexico was the 1994 granting of true independence to the IFE. Unlike ex post court adjudication of electoral disputes, the IFE offered a way to minimize ex ante violations of the electoral laws by removing the PRI's *institutional capacity* to commit electoral fraud. In light of the "transition game," I now explore why the PRI decided to give up its control of the organization and monitoring of elections, delegating these tasks to an independent electoral body.

The Creation of an Independent IFE

The major achievement of the 1990 and 1993 electoral reforms was the elimination of the "self-certification" of elections by the Electoral College. The IFE was created to organize and monitor the elections, and to certify electoral results. However, the PAN did not have enough leverage to push for the full independence of the IFE's board, which continued to be controlled by the president and hence to act as a puppet of the regime. Through the 1994 electoral reform, the PRI finally prevented itself from committing fraud by granting true independence to the board of the IFE. Six Citizen Councilmen were to be elected to the IFE's board by a two-thirds vote in the Lower Chamber. This time, each of the major parties – the PRI, the PAN, and the PRD – had the right to propose two Councilmen. With this new arrangement, the government lost control of the IFE's board. The 1994 electoral process was transparent enough that the three parties accepted the results with almost no complaints of electoral fraud.

What led the PRI to grant independence to the IFE? The 1994 electoral reform was triggered by the Zapatista guerilla uprising in the southern state of Chiapas. Just after the war erupted, the government invited the PRD and the PAN to negotiate the electoral reform as a way to commit the major players to "peaceful means for attaining power." The government granted independence to the IFE believing that the war in Chiapas could expand – bombings in Mexico City and at various electrical facilities contributed to magnify the impact of the uprising (Castañeda, 1995). Among the first demands of the Zapatistas was clean elections. Salinas felt the need to neutralize the guerrillas with a nationwide political opening, one that particularly included the PRD. The creation of the independent IFE was a way to bring the PRDistas into the electoral contest, to give them a real chance, and above all to commit them to the electoral process so as to avoid violence after the elections.

In light of the model, I argue that the PRI chose to create an independent electoral commission to prevent the 1994 electoral process from bursting into violent conflict. However, it agreed to tie its hands ex ante not to commit fraud only because it knew it would easily win the 1994 elections. The combination of Salinas's economic reforms, his high approval ratings, and the PRI's outstanding performance in the 1991 midterm elections had created such high expectations about the party's lasting strength that politicians thought they would be in office for years to come. At the time, politicians could not anticipate the rapid electoral demise of the PRI that came as a result of the 1994 peso crisis, which struck four months after the presidential elections and took all parties by surprise, including the international financial community.

A possible objection to my argument about the politics of delegation to the IFE is that the PRI might simply have been shortsighted, delegating power in 1994 without anticipating the possible costs of doing so.[8] I offer two points in defense of my argument. First, not even experts and investors, let alone the PRI, predicted the 1994 peso crisis. At the end of the Carlos Salinas presidency, opinions about the future of the Mexican economy were extremely optimistic in the international financial community. It

[8] The game could easily be drawn as a repeated game to account for longer-term considerations.

was believed that Carlos Salinas's reforms had laid a solid groundwork for economic recovery and future prosperity, and the party expected to profit from these reforms in the years to come. Second, the 1994 electoral reform was adopted under a sense of true emergency because at that time Salinas, his advisors, and major elements of the armed forces believed that the war in Chiapas could easily explode.

An alternative theory of delegation would suggest that the PRI granted independence to the IFE's board so as to prevent the next winner from taking advantage of its new role in the opposition. This kind of approach has been persuasively employed to account for why political parties in democratic regimes create institutions such as independent bureaucracies (Geddes, 1994). The PRI, however, did not create an independent IFE to protect itself when it became the opposition. As argued earlier, in 1994 the PRIístas did not think they would lose power in the foreseeable future. Witness the declaration made in 1994 to a group of Japanese investors by Foreign minister José Angel Gurría, that there would be at least "eighteen more years of continuity with the same political party, the PRI, in power." By 1994, the PRI continued to hold around 90 percent of the country's municipalities and had only lost three states to the PAN. The PRI's debacle that began in 1995 was unexpected, a result of the 1994 peso crisis, which erupted almost a year after the independence of the IFE was established.

Voters' Understanding of the Transition Game: Evidence from the 1994 Presidential Elections

The transition game is based on several assumptions about voters' behavior. The game assumes that voters understand the structure of the game, and that they choose to participate or not according to their preexisting beliefs about the political regime. *Moderate opposition voters* tend to punish opposition parties that allege electoral fraud and engage in post-electoral battles, because these voters do not regard the existing electoral system as particularly authoritarian. *Radical opposition voters*, by contrast, are inclined to believe that elections are fraudulent, because they assess the current regime as highly autocratic. Is there evidence that voters understand the implications of this game? Is there evidence of such divisions among the members of the opposition electorate? This section answers these questions through the use of survey research.

To assess voters' understanding of the transition game and its implications for voting behavior, recall the simplified version of the transition game presented in Chapter 1, which assumed that opposition parties coordinate in their actions and that there is information about the actual election results. In this simplified version of the transition game, post-electoral violence occurs only in the lower branch of the game: namely, when the PRI *loses the elections* and chooses to *commit electoral fraud*. Thus, I derive the following five hypotheses with respect to voters' expectations for post-electoral violence.

Hypothesis 1. A voter should expect more violence when she believes that elections will be fraudulent; conversely, if the voter believes that elections will be clean, she should not expect violence.

Hypothesis 2. Those who calculate that the opposition has a good chance of defeating the PRI should expect more violence. Conversely, those who see no chance that the PRI can be defeated should anticipate less violence.

Hypothesis 3. Voters who believe that the PRI will not allow the opposition to take office if it loses the election should expect more violence. Voters who instead believe that the ruling party will yield power to the opposition if it loses should expect less violence.

However, voter's expectations of post-electoral violence might be driven in part by partisan preferences. To put it simply, if violence is the likely result of the PRI's refusal to accept defeat, a voter who is willing to continue to support the ruling party might rationalize his position by concluding that post-electoral violence is not likely. Conversely, voters who expect post-electoral violence presumably prefer one of the opposition parties precisely because they believe the ruling party to be an authoritarian incumbent that can steal elections. As a consequence, I control for partisanship in my modeling of expectations of post-electoral violence.

Hypothesis 4. Those who identify with the PRI will not expect violence; conversely, those who identify with the opposition, and particularly with the PRD, will anticipate more violence.

As stated earlier, during the Salinas presidency the PAN and the PRD followed dramatically different strategies in this game, partly as a result of the differential treatment they received from the PRI. As Eisenstadt (2004), explains, the PAN became less confrontational and chose to resolve most of its post-electoral disputes through the electoral courts. There were two main reasons that the PAN followed this strategy. First, the PAN directly participated with the PRI in the creation of the new electoral courts, and second, the composition of the PAN's electoral base was mostly *moderate*, as I will show. The PRD, by contrast, chose to defend its votes in the streets, in part because this party did not trust the electoral courts – it had not participated in their enactment – and in part because its electoral base was mostly composed of *radical voters*, as I will show.

The average voter may thus have perceived that the PAN was more capable than the PRD of winning elections without bringing about conflict, which, from the perspective of *moderate voters*, must have been more attractive than engaging in continuous post-electoral battles. I thus derive the following hypothesis about how expectations of post-electoral violence shaped support for the PAN and the PRD during this period:

Hypothesis 5. Only the more risk-tolerant *radical voters* are likely to continue to support an opposition party, such as the PRD, that is expected to engage in post-electoral battles. Expectations of post-electoral violence should discourage support for the PRD by *moderate voters*, and should favor the PAN.

I now test these hypotheses using individual-level data from 1994 presidential election survey.

The 1994 survey asked respondents a series of questions that permit me to evaluate how the electorate perceived the transition game. Table 8.1 presents these questions and their relationship to reported voting intentions.

I highlight the following findings: although very few voters expected generalized violence, 52 percent believed that after the elections, violence would erupt "in some parts of the country." Although the majority expected elections to be "clean" or "reasonably clean," there was a sizable minority who expected a "great deal of fraud" (22 percent) or a "huge fraud" (8 percent). The majority of voters (55 percent) saw a real possibility that the PRI could be defeated in the 1994 elections. Before the 1994 presidential election, Mexicans were sharply divided in their assessments of the most crucial test of electoral democracy, namely, whether the PRI would allow an opposition party to take office if it lost. There was almost one individual who believed that the party would not allow the opposition to take office for every Mexican who thought that the PRI would yield power. PRD supporters were highly suspicious of the authoritarian regime. PAN voters, on the other hand, were distributed more evenly across the spectrum.

A *regime cleavage* was salient in the 1994 presidential elections. This term refers to a division among political parties and voters regarding their evaluations of the rules of the electoral game and, ultimately, their assessments of the existing political regime. The cleavage goes from pro-status-quo players, who strongly support the existing rules of the game and the political

Table 8.1. *The transition game as perceived by the electorate and the vote in the 1994 presidential elections (percent)*

	Distribution of Responses	Voted PRI	Voted PAN	Voted PRD
After the election will there be:				
Violence in the whole country	4.9	28.0	19.1	26.9
Violence in many parts of the country	4.8	42.8	25.0	16.9
Violence in only some parts	52.1	47.0	22.0	8.9
No violence	23.8	53.4	17.7	5.4
Election will be:				
Clean	41.8	58.4	16.4	4.9
Reasonably clean	17.4	47.9	22.5	8.2
Some fraud	22.3	34.7	27.3	13.6
A great deal of fraud	8.3	25.5	24.3	23.7
Can an opposition party obtain more votes than the PRI?				
Yes	55	34	27.3	12.9
No	34	64.1	10.6	3.0
Don't know	11	52.2	3.7	8.5
If an opposition party wins:				
It will officially take power.	45.3	51.4	20.8	6.7
Government won't permit it.	41.1	42.1	21.9	13.4
Don't know	13.5	53.7	10.0	5.5

Note: Undecided and "other" are not reported. Percentages are weighted.

regime, to anti-status-quo players, who oppose the political regime and believe that they must confront the system to make their votes count.

To give some sense of how the Mexican electorate was distributed on this cleavage during the 1994 elections, Figure 8.2 presents a summary measure of the electorate's perception of the rules of the electoral game. The summary measure uses three questions: the perceived likelihood of violence, the perceived cleanliness of elections, and the perceived likelihood that an opposition party would be allowed to take office if it won the elections.[9] A

[9] Violence was coded as two if the respondent believed it was not likely; as one if post-electoral violence was expected to take place only in some isolated parts of the country; and as zero if violence in the whole country or in many parts of the country was expected. If the respondent answered "do not know," violence was coded as one. Regarding the cleanness of elections, the same procedure was used, coding two for clean; one for reasonably clean or don't know; and zero if the respondent said that he expected some fraud or a great deal of fraud. However, if the respondent answered "do not know" to both questions, she was eliminated from the analysis. Regarding the expected government behavior if an opposition party won the

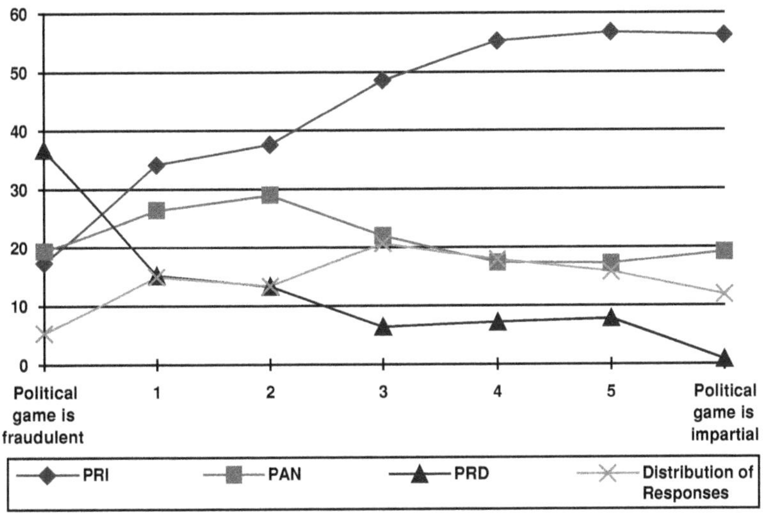

Figure 8.2. Summary measure of the electorate's perceptions of the electoral game and the vote.

seven-point scale was employed, where seven means that the elector believes that the electoral game is impartial, and one means that it is strongly skewed in favor of one player, the PRI. For instance, a score of seven means that the respondent believes post-electoral violence is not likely, that he expects elections to be clean and the PRI to yield power to the opposition if it loses the election.

The majority of the population was concentrated along the middle points of the scale. A voter's standing on this regime cleavage scale is strongly related to partisan preferences. As expected, PRD voters were more *radical*: they tended to perceive the electoral game as clearly antidemocratic – almost 40 percent of those placed at the origin of the scale reported voting for the PRD. These voters believed that there was going to be a great deal of electoral fraud in the 1994 elections, that the PRI would not yield power to an opposition party if it lost the elections, and that post-electoral violence was likely. PAN voters, by contrast, were more *moderate*: they did not perceive the electoral game as being as antidemocratic as PRD voters, nor did they follow PRI voters in their complacent perceptions of the existing rules

election, the response was coded as two if the respondent thought the opposition would be allowed to take office, and as zero if she thought the government would not allow it. In this last case, a "do not know" answer was eliminated from the analysis.

of the game. Hence, on the regime cleavage scale, PRD voters occupied the "anti-status-quo" or *radical* extreme, PRI voters the "pro-status-quo" one, and PAN voters the center or *moderate* position, where the median voter was found.

Some political commentators interpreted the 1994 elections as a conscious decision on the part of voters to support the PRI because they feared that the opposition would not be able to maintain social peace. The guerilla uprising and the Colosio assassination may indeed have created fear about the breakdown of the social order, which the PRI tried to employ to its advantage with slogans such as "vote for PRI, vote for peace." Yet this argument misses the important point that voters in 1994 had as much reason to be suspicious of the PRI's authoritarian control as to be uncertain about the opposition's expected ability to maintain order.

By modeling expectations for post-electoral violence, I test my theory against this view, which I here call the Mexican folk theory – namely, the belief that a vote for the PRI represents fear of political instability caused by the opposition's incapacity to govern. This theory argues that voters fear violence because they think the opposition would not be able to maintain social peace if the PRI were to lose. Instead, my account states that voters' expectations of post-electoral violence result from their assessments of the "transition game," and in particular whether they expect the PRI to commit fraud and refuse to accept an electoral defeat by repressing the opposition.

Modeling Voters' Expectations for Post-Electoral Violence

To model voters' expectations of post-electoral violence, an ordered probit maximum likelihood estimation procedure is appropriate because the dependent variable lies along an ordinal scale. The independent variables are voters' assessments of the transition game presented in Table 8.1. I also control for partisanship. Results are provided in Table 8.2.

All of the variables perform as expected, and all reach reasonable levels of statistical significance. Mexican voters anticipated violence depending on which subbranch of the transition game they thought was being played. Some voters, particularly PRIístas, believed that the PRI could not be defeated and that the election did not put the political order at stake. Other voters, particularly opposition supporters, believed that the opposition could defeat the PRI, but they differed among themselves in their assessments of how this party would react to an opposition victory. Those who believed that the PRI was going to steal the elections and would not

Table 8.2. *The transition game and voters' expectations of post-electoral violence in the 1994 presidential elections (ordered probit estimates)*

Independent Variables	Coeff.	Std. Err.
Fraud	0.17***	0.02
PRD most likely opposition winner	0.49***	0.11
PAN most likely opposition winner	0.43***	0.10
PRI defeated?	0.12***	0.03
Government will not permit opposition to take office	0.11**	0.06
Party ID PRD	0.31**	0.12
Party ID PAN	0.01	0.09
Cut 1	0.25	0.10
Cut 2	0.52	0.10
Cut 3	2.09	0.11
Cut 4	2.78	0.12
N = 1,404		
Log likelihood = 1715.00		
Lr Chi2(7) = 153.75		
Prob > chi2 = .0000		
41% predicted correctly		

*p < .10; **p < .05; ***p < .01

allow the opposition to take office if it won felt that the election would produce violence. Those who believed that the PRI would not steal the elections and would yield power to the opposition if it lost did not expect violence. As expected, the PRDístas expected more post-electoral violence than the PANístas.

To illustrate how expectations of post-electoral violence are powerfully shaped by voters' beliefs about which subbranch of the transition game is being played, I present simulated probabilities for the violence model using Clarify (Tomz et al., 2001). I take three hypothetical voters: the first calculates that the PRI will not be defeated. She thinks that neither the PAN nor the PRD has a chance of defeating the PRI, does not believe there will be fraud, and thinks that the PRI will allow an opposition party to take office if it loses. This type of voter should not expect post-electoral violence.

The second hypothetical voter thinks that the PRI can be defeated, but is uncertain about its reaction. Would elections be clean? Would the PRI allow an opposition party to assume office it lost? To reflect this uncertainty, I assign mean values to these two variables. Finally, the third hypothetical voter also believes that the PRI can be defeated, and is further certain that it will not allow an opposition party to take office and that the election will be fraudulent. These last two voters assign mean values to the PAN's and the PRD's relative chances of defeating the PRI. For all three voters, I hold party identifications at their mean values. Results are presented in Table 8.3.

These results lend considerable credence to my hypotheses with respect to voters' expected levels of post-electoral violence. Mexican voters made clear connections between the ruling party's available strategies in the transition game and post-electoral violence. We can focus on those who expect no post-electoral violence (a value of one for the dependent variable) and on those who expect moderate to high levels of post-electoral violence (values of four and five for the dependent variable). A type I voter shows a 52 percent chance of expecting no violence after the elections. This probability drops to 20 percent for a type II voter and to 9 percent for a type III voter. Thus, as expected, only type I voters cast their votes free from fear, as they think the PRI cannot be defeated and that there will be no electoral fraud. Indeed, the probabilities that type I voters expect high levels of post-electoral violence (values of four and five for the dependent variable) are extremely low (.02 and .005, respectively). By contrast, types II and III cast their votes thinking that if the PRI loses, it will not allow the opposition to take office and will resort to repression and violence in order to maintain power. I have thus demonstrated voters' understanding of the transition game by systematically accounting for their expectations of post-electoral violence. The question I address in the last section of this chapter is why the PRI yielded power peacefully in 2000.

The PRI's Peaceful Defeat in the 2000 Elections

In the 2000 presidential elections, the PRI lost to the PAN's candidate, Vicente Fox, and the ruling party yielded power peacefully. The key difference between the 2000 and 1988 presidential elections was that the institutional and informational settings had been transformed in fundamental ways. In the 2000 elections, the IFE was highly autonomous and professional, and opposition parties could use a vast pool of public funds to disseminate their campaign messages through the mass media.

Although the IFE significantly reduced the PRI's institutional capacity to commit electoral fraud, the party's acceptance of an electoral defeat was not guaranteed. The IFE could prevent the PRI from committing fraud, but

Table 8.3. *Simulated predicted probabilities of levels of post-electoral violence*

Voter Type	Level of Violence	Mean Predicted Probability [95% Confidence Intervals in Brackets]
Type I		
PRI can't lose	1	**0.52** [0.45, 0.61]
No electoral fraud	2	0.11 [0.09, 0.12]
PRI would allow opposition to take office	3	0.34 [0.28, 0.40]
Neither PAN nor PRD have chance of defeating PRI	4	0.02 [0.01, 0.04]
	5	0.005 [0.02, 0.01]
Type II		
PRI can lose	1	.20 [0.17, 0.22]
Electoral fraud mean value	2	.08 [0.07, 0.10]
PRI will allow opposition to take office mean value	3	**.56** [0.52, 0.58]
Chances of defeating the PRI for PAN and PRD at their mean value	4	**.12** [0.10, 0.13]
	5	.05 [0.03, 0.06]
Type III		
Opposition can win	1	0.09 [0.07, 0.11]
Huge fraud	2	0.05 [0.04, 0.06]
PRI will *not* allow opposition to take office	3	**0.55** [0.51, 0.58]
Chances of defeating the PRI for PAN and PRD at their mean value	4	**0.19** [0.16, 0.23]
	5	**0.12** [0.09, 0.16]

Note: Probabilities come from simulating the model in Table 8.2 using Clarify (Tomz, 2001).

had this party refused to yield power peacefully to the winning opposition candidate, Vicente Fox, the IFE could not have forced it to step down. The "transition game" still needed to be played, but in this case, unlike the 1988 presidential election, the PRI's options were more restricted.

In the 2000 presidential election, the PRI could no longer manufacture the results and negotiate the vote distribution with the opposition behind closed doors, as it had done in 1988. The new institutional setting implied that the PRI's options were more limited. Had the PRI attempted to reverse the outcome of the elections, it would have had to openly reject the electoral results presented by the IFE and probably close all democratic institutions, the IFE included. Thus, in the 2000 elections the PRI's only options in the "transition game" were to accept a losing outcome and yield power peacefully, or to reject a losing outcome, defy the IFE, and close all democratic institutions. Why did the PRI choose to accept the losing outcome instead of rejecting it?

The model developed in this chapter argues that a successful alternation of political power in office requires, first, that the opposition can credibly threaten a conflict if the ruling party attempts to steal the elections, and second, that the ruling party sees low prospects of retaining office after such a conflict occurs. I argue that both of these conditions were present in 2000. As occurred in 1988, the left and the right chose not to present a unified opposition front against the PRI.

Despite the fact that the opposition parties did not coordinate in their pre-electoral strategies in either of these elections, the institutional setting of the transition game in 2000 – with clear and unambiguous information about the PRI's defeat and no leeway to negotiate the elections behind closed doors – made post-electoral opposition coordination more credible.

In the 1988 elections, the PRI managed to discourage opposition parties from coordinating in their post-electoral strategies because it was able to offer significant side payments to the PAN to acquiesce in the fraud, including that party's legislative victories and their consequent policy influence. Because the results of elections were unknown to voters, the PAN possessed more leeway to acquiesce without fearing significant electoral punishment from its supporters. The PRI's threat that it would employ force if the opposition contested the results was highly credible in 1988 – as reported by president Miguel de la Madrid in his memoirs, elements of the armed forces had gathered in the basements of several buildings in downtown Mexico City in the event that the opposition decided to take the National Palace by force (de la Madrid, 2004: 819).

In the 2000 elections, the PRI had no such elements at its disposal to discourage the opposition from coordinating against an authoritarian imposition. This time the PRI's electoral defeat was common knowledge, which implied that the PRI could not have misled anyone – segments of the mass public, the mass media, the church, the armed forces, or the business and international communities – into believing that it had won. All the exit polls, which received wide media coverage, had Vicente Fox winning – indeed, by four o'clock in the afternoon, news about Fox's victory was widespread. Moreover, the IFE possessed an impressive central information system that gathered immediate results as the vote counts emerged in each of the precincts, and the mass media was given ample access to this information. By the time the IFE declared that Vicente Fox had won, there could be no doubt of the PRI's defeat. Had the party refused to accept the official results, the authoritarian imposition would have been far too obvious.

In the 2000 elections, the PRI lacked the leeway to offer side payments in the form of legislative seats and policy influence to buy off one of the opposition parties. As noted earlier, reversing the outcome of the 2000 election would have required defying the IFE and closing the existing democratic institutions, Congress included. None of the opposition parties would have accepted this outcome – unless, of course, the PRI offered to make them partners in a new autocratic government. For any opposition party, this would have been impossible to justify to its supporters.

President Zedillo also played a key role. Various sources indicate that by two o'clock in the afternoon on the day of the elections, just after the president's own exit poll had shown Vicente Fox as the clear winner, Zedillo decided to tape an announcement to the public that conceded the election. President Zedillo sent this tape with various members of his presidential guard to the main transmission tower, instructing them to broadcast the message at seven o'clock. President Zedillo also called Francisco Labastida, the PRI's losing candidate, and urged him to concede defeat before the president's announcement was broadcast. With these actions, Zedillo sent a clear message that he would abide by the results and refrain from using the armed forces to defend the PRI. The behavior of Ernesto Zedillo drastically differed from that of Miguel de la Madrid, who was willing to employ the armed forces to repress the opposition after the 1988 electoral fraud.

It is revealing that the PRI's presidential candidate, Francisco Labastida, waited to concede the elections until after Zedillo's message had been transmitted, hours after it was obvious that Vicente Fox had won. Nobody knows what exactly went through the minds of Labastida and his close allies in the PRI during those hours. What is clear is that president Zedillo chose to "burn the bridges" by committing his support to the outcome of the elections before members in the PRI could attempt to reverse them. The signal was clear: the president and the armed forces would defend the constitution and the newly created electoral institutions, not the PRI.

9

Conclusion

This book has focused on the study of the logic of a particular form of autocracy and its demise. The Mexican PRI held multiparty elections with clockwork precision for all elective offices, including the presidency. Yet an authoritarian government hid behind the façade of these elections. As argued by Schedler (2002), "electoral autocracies" such as the PRI constitute one of the most common forms of autocracies in the world today.

Elections under Autocracy

The Mexican PRI was designed with the explicit intent to prevent personal dictatorship. Since its creation in 1929, the PRI used regular elections as a means to share the spoils of office among ruling party politicians and to prevent any single individual from grabbing it all. For that purpose reelection for all elective offices, including the presidency, was ruled out. I hope to have shown that one of the pillars propping up the PRI regime was its massive electoral support. Even when elections were not competitive and the opposition could not dream of winning, the PRI engaged in the mobilization of voters. During the golden years of the PRI, elections were primarily a display of might – billboards, roads, and towns were painted in the party's colors (the same as those of the Mexican flag), and party rallies were packed with voters who were performing their duties, as if somebody was watching them. The PRI employed dense clientelistic networks that allowed it to monitor citizens' partisan loyalties and political predispositions, mobilize voters, and buy off electoral support by distributing benefits ranging from food and credit to land titles, favors, gifts, and cash transfers.

Most electoral autocracies also aspire to huge margins of victory and, like the Mexican PRI, engage in the effective mobilization of voters. Why would these autocracies expend all that effort in mobilizing electoral support when, during most of their histories, the opposition cannot even conceive of victory? Why would an authoritarian regime seek huge margins of victory, rather than settling for a simple win at the polls? I have argued that authoritarian regimes mobilize electoral support to deter potential elite opponents, particularly those coming from within the regime. By mobilizing voters in great numbers, authoritarian regimes signal to elites that the regime is invincible and that potential rivals have little hope of defeating the official party. Autocratic elections play other fundamental roles. They are power-sharing devices employed to distribute office, perks, and spoils among ruling party politicians that make a large number of the elite vest its interest in the survival of the autocratic regime. Autocratic elections also work to divide the opposition. By offering legislative seats and marginal policy influence to its opponents, the autocrat can coopt and divide them. Autocratic parties can better get away with all sorts of electoral malpractice, including electoral fraud, when they confront a divided opposition.

The danger of holding elections, however, is that the autocracy becomes vulnerable to the entry of opponents every time elections are held. During the golden years of the PRI, this party was particularly vulnerable to rivals emerging from within the party. The rule of non-reelection for all elective offices, including the presidency, allowed the party to offer ample opportunities to elites, who remained loyal to the official party hoping to obtain a nomination in the future and thereby to reap the benefits of office. However, regular presidential succession every six years also made the PRI vulnerable to division at the top. As I have argued in this book, elites disappointed by failure to obtain the party's nomination represented the most serious threat to continued party unity. The 1988 split by Cuauhtémoc Cárdenas, who ran against the PRI as a member of an opposition coalition and later formed the PRD, is only the best known. A disappointed prominent ruling party politician who was denied the PRI's presidential nomination faced the following choice: remain within the PRI and hope for a nomination in the future, or exit the party and challenge it through elections. The latter alternative did not look attractive when the overwhelming majority of the electorate was expected to support the ruling party. Thus, the PRI invested in the mobilization of voters in an attempt to signal to elites that millions of individuals supported the ruling party, and that they had a vested interest in its survival. To be sure, the PRI also resorted to ballot stuffing and electoral fraud. However, as I have argued in this book, during the golden years of the PRI fraud was carried out at the margin, to boost the party's vote totals; it was not a substitute for the effective mobilization of voters. Electoral victories obtained simply by stuffing the ballot box would not have convinced potential defectors from the PRI of the regime's invincibility.

A critical implication of my theory of authoritarian elections is that there will be budget cycles *even when elections are not competitive*. I conceive hegemonic-party autocracies as oversized governing coalitions that are glued together by patronage, pork, and spoils. The resources to pay for the hegemonic coalition in Mexico originally came from the landowners, whose power was destroyed or vastly reduced during the revolution. To sustain the hegemonic coalition, the PRI also resorted to the systematic manipulation of the budget and other policy instruments. For a long time, economic growth generated electoral support and provided ample spoils to distribute. As long as the pie kept growing, the PRI could sustain the oversized coalition. Splits within the PRI, as I have demonstrated in this book, occurred when expenditures were systematically lower. The debt crisis of the 1980s transformed the authoritarian equilibrium. The PRI experienced its most severe split in 1987, which resulted in the emergence of a new opposition player, the PRD. In light of the dismal performance of the economy, the Mexican PRI became increasingly more dependent on vote buying and electoral fraud to survive. Voters' disposition to defect the PRI increased, and as a result the ruling party's imperative to manipulate the economy for electoral survival also increased. Budget cycles induced by the PRI and recurrent economic busts ended up undermining the popular support that had sustained this party for so long.

Autocratic Institutions and the Endogeneity of the Constitution

Another reason why the PRI invested in sustaining an oversized governing coalition, rather than a minimally winning one, was that it sought to control institutional change. To control constitutional change, the PRI needed legislative supermajorities. By unilaterally controlling constitutional change, the PRI was able to erect autocratic institutions. The constitution was modified to the PRI's advantage almost 400 times, and many of these changes were substantial, including numerous changes in the electoral institutions and the systematic weakening of the judicial power and the Supreme Court.

Consider the importance of the *endogeneity* of constitutional rules with two examples. To consolidate his power, President Lázaro Cárdenas (1934–40) wanted to begin with the implementation of land reform, to which the 1917 constitution had entitled peasants. The existing Supreme Court, representing the interests of conservative forces and property owners, attempted to block the president's agrarian redistributions. Cárdenas responded by dissolving the Supreme Court and reappointing a new, quite enlarged body with amicable justices; these new justices would serve six-year terms, instead of appointments for life. This reshuffling of the Supreme Court required a constitutional change, which president Cárdenas could accomplish because the PRI had the necessary supermajority in the federal Congress and control of the state's assemblies (Magaloni, 2003). The implementation of land reform would prove crucial for the consolidation of the PRI's hegemony because it gave the party a key instrument to buy off peasants' support.

The PRI also employed its power to change the constitution to erect autocratic electoral institutions and to draft electoral laws to its advantage. First, as a result of some of the elite splits that took place in the 1940s and 1950s, the PRI increased the costs of entry to potential challengers, and it centralized the organization and monitoring of elections in the hands of the federal government and the PRI's central bureaucracy (Molinar, 1991). Second, the PRI drafted electoral rules for the translation of votes into seats in order to reward itself disproportionately, coopt the opposition, and divide its opponents. The PRI accomplished these goals by, among other measures, creating the mixed electoral system for the Chamber of Deputies, originally established in 1978, and by continuously modifying the electoral formulas (Diaz-Cayeros and Magaloni, 2001). The manipulation of constitutional rules to the autocrats' advantage is a very common phenomenon, and this is one key reason why these autocracies aspire to control legislative supermajorities. The democratization agenda in these regimes is thus largely centered on the renegotiation of the basic institutional apparatus – from reducing the powers of the presidency, to redrafting electoral laws and campaign finance legislation, to the establishment of independent electoral comissions.

This book concurs with the common view that these autocratic institutions play a central role in the maintenance of an autocratic regime. However, I hope to have shown that attributing party hegemony solely to autocratic institutions evades a central question: what allows a ruling party to erect and sustain these institutions? The approach taken in this book is that institutions are *endogenous* to the electoral game. A hegemonic party can create and sustain these institutions only because it controls the necessary legislative supermajorities to do so. This implies that there is *no binding set of constitutional rules*. If the ruling party can draft the constitution without the need to forge coalitions with the opposition, the likelihood of erecting authoritarian institutions increases. Yet this logic of institutional design in an autocratic regime is possible only because the ruling party can mobilize enough electoral support to control legislative supermajorities or to have the upper hand in a national referendum.[1] When the ruling party loses its legislative supermajority, the institutional dynamic is transformed in fundamental ways. The opposition becomes an effective veto player in the constitution-making game. After 1988, the PRI lost the legislative supermajority to change the constitution. Every constitutional reform since then, including four major electoral reforms, has been jointly approved by the PRI and at least one of the major opposition parties.

Modernization, Economic Growth, and Authoritarian Demise

The process of democratization of these hegemonic-party autocracies, I hope to have shown, is different from the earlier transitions in Latin America and Europe that inspired much of the existing work on transitions focusing on elite bargaining. The democratization literature stresses that successful democratization is most likely when moderate actors enter into a "political pact " that limits the agenda of policy choice and excludes radical opposition forces and the masses.[2] Transitions from hegemonic-party regimes, however, are fundamentally *electoral transitions* in which mass political parties and voters, not a "select group of actors," play the central role.

My approach provides some predictions that are similar to those of modernization theory with respect to the structural factors that should increase the demand for democracy. In a nutshell, modernization theory predicts that development and urbanization will lead voters to demand more political participation, thus creating the necessary preconditions for democracy to emerge. Yet the causal mechanisms I have offered in this book differ from those provided by modernization theory.

[1] Most constitutions are called "rigid" in that to modify them, a supermajority or a referendum or a combination of the two is required.

[2] The literature stressed different "modes of transition" and argued that if the transition was not pacted, it was most likely to fail (Karl, 1990). As defined by O'Donnell and Schmitter (1986), political pacts take place among a select group of actors who seek to "(1) limit the agenda of policy choice, (2) share proportionally in the distribution of benefits, and (3) restrict the participation of outsiders in decision-making" (p. 41).

Modernization theory sees a sharp division between rural, "pre-modern" societies and urban, "modern" ones; this division is based, above all, on values and attitudes. As Huntington (1968: 32) put it, traditional men and women expect continuity in nature and society, are attached to immediate groups (family, clan, and village), and rely on particularistic values and standards for achievement based on ascription. Modern men and women, in Lerner's (1958) formulation, possess a "mobile personality" that adjusts to change, is attached to broader impersonal groupings (class, party, and nation), and relies on universalistic values and standards of achievement. Conceived as a multifaceted process (urbanization, industrialization, secularization, education, media participation), modernization, in its classic formulation, should lead to a shift in normative commitments that will in turn transform the patterns of political participation. In Deutsch's (1961) formulation, "major clusters of old social, economic and physiological commitments are eroded or broken and people become available for new patterns of socialization and behavior" (494).

It is possible to understand the behavior of traditional and modern societies by using a single set of underlying assumptions, not different ones as required by modernization theory (Bates, 1984a). In my account, voters – rich and poor, urban and rural – all seek to elect governments that can make them prosper. Yet, as I have argued in this book, richer voters can better afford to make "ideological investments" in democratization, supporting opposition parties despite a credible threat by the ruling party to eject them from the party's spoils system. The poor and those living in smaller rural settings, I have argued, are likely to stick with the autocrat because they are more averse to the risk of economic punishment, for two reasons. On the one hand, poorer voters are much more dependent upon the party's spoils system for their survival. On the other, the hegemonic party can better monitor and hence threaten to punish would-be defections by voters living in smaller localities than defections by voters living in bigger, more impersonal urban settings.

The theory provided in this book also differs from modernization theory with respect to some of its *empirical predictions* about democratization. In what Przeworski and colleagues (2000) labeled the endogenous version of modernization theory, development *causes* democracy. In my account, development does not necessarily lead to the establishment of democracy. Modernization is a strong predictor of *voter support for the opposition*, but it does not directly lead to the establishment of democracy. By comparative standards, many of the hegemonic-party regimes survived for many years after their countries reached the income threshold that would be able to sustain democracy (Przeworski et al., 2000). Mexico, as I detailed in Chapter 2, reached this threshold long before the PRI finally lost power, and the same is true for other hegemonic-party autocracies such as those in Malaysia, Taiwan, Singapore, Botswana or Gabon. My approach argues that hegemonic parties are strong when they put in place a series of economic policies that generate prosperity, promote industrialization, and increase wages and employment. Economic growth not only generates electoral support but allows the ruling party to amass enough resources to distribute in the form of patronage, pork, and vote buying that are necessary to glue the hegemonic coalition together.

Further, in modernization theory, all "good things" come together, meaning that economic growth and development are both positively associated with democracy. In my account, economic growth and development have conflicting effects on authoritarian survival. Growth initially helped the PRI to survive, but it also threatened the party in the long run because the richer voters became, the more they were willing to defect from the ruling party and make "ideological investments" in democratization despite the risk of economic punishment. In addition, in my account economic recession weakens an autocratic regime. As the economy deteriorates, voters will be more willing to defect to the opposition unless the ruling party is able to buy them off with more government transfers. Economic recession translates into a decrease in economic resources available for patronage and pork, making the hegemonic party more vulnerable to elite divisions, voter defection, and opposition entry. However, this book has demonstrated that economic recession is not sufficient to account for the breakdown of hegemonic party regimes. Only when economic recession is perceived as systematic will voters defect from the ruling party en masse.

Opposition Coordination and the Formation of Electoral Fronts

My account of democratization is in line with that of Weingast (1997), who stresses that dictators trespass upon citizens' rights by profiting from coordination dilemmas among opponents. The theory provided in this book moves beyond Weingast (1997) by incorporating parties, elections, and voters into the story of strategic interaction. Unlike Weingast, I also provide a theory of endogenous institutional design to explain why an autocrat might willingly sign a political pact with the opposition not to transgress their *electoral rights*.

In Mexico, the opposition never managed to coordinate, making the transition much harder. Ideological differences played a powerful role in accounting for the divisiveness of the opposition. This type of ideological opposition is not very common – most other hegemonic-party regimes possess oppositions divided along ethnic or personality lines, not by ideology. However, I believe that my arguments about how the divisiveness among the opposition allows an autocratic regime to survive apply to these other cases as well. What remains to be explained are the factors that account for opposition coordination against autocratic regimes at the cross-national level.

For example, for a long time the opposition remained divided in Kenya and Senegal, confronting similar dilemmas as those faced by opposition parties in Mexico. However, in both of these countries all-encompassing multiethnic electoral fronts were eventually forged to dislodge their long-standing hegemonic parties. As my transition model makes explicit, when the opposition is unified, the coordination dilemma making transitions so difficult is largely mitigated. If the ruling party chooses to steal the elections, the opposition is likely to stand united to defend its victory, in which case the ruling party must choose between a violent conflict and stepping down peacefully. Although I leave for further research the reasons why the opposition successfully coordinated in Senegal and Kenya and not in Mexico, I now present some preliminary hypotheses.

I believe that opposition coordination in Senegal was facilitated by the following factors. Presidential elections in Senegal take place under a runoff majority system, which allows opposition parties to run as separate players in the first round and coalesce in the second round against the ruling party. Coordination in the second round is further facilitated by the fact that the National Assembly is not elected concurrently with the presidential race; thus, there were no legislative seats in dispute that the PS could selectively use to co-opt its opponents during the presidential race of 2000. Opposition coordination in Senegal was also made easier because the PDS was the only opposition party with national presence and the clear leader of the alliance, and because the opposition was not divided along ethnic lines.

By contrast, presidential elections in Mexico take place under a plurality rule, and the assembly is elected concurrently. The rules for electing the assembly, as I have argued in this book, were designed to co-opt the PRI's opponents and to divide them. In addition, one of the rules that most seriously discouraged the formation of opposition electoral fronts in Mexico was the prohibition of cross-endorsement of presidential candidates, established in the electoral reform of 1993. Opposition parties interested in endorsing a common presidential candidate had to craft alliances for all 628 legislative races for federal deputy and senator taking place concurrently. Finally, the current electoral code awards each alliance the amount of public funding that its largest constituent party would have received, rather than the sum of the financing that each party in the alliance would have received had it fielded a separate candidate. Despite these rules, the PAN and the PRD formed electoral fronts to compete in the 2000 presidential elections, making alliances with other, much smaller coalition partners that were closer on the ideological spectrum. This suggests that, in addition to ideology, the electoral strength of the players might also play a role in the logic of coalition making. In line with Cox (1997), when there is one dominant opposition player, opposition coordination might be easier than when both opposition parties are closer in strength.

In Kenya, the opposition was much more fractionalized than in Senegal, mostly along ethnic lines. However, in the 2002 presidential elections, all the opposition parties united behind the Rainbow Coalition. Opposition coordination is harder to account for in Kenya than in Senegal. One possibility is that there was an important learning process on the part of opposition leaders. Twice before, KANU had been able to win with 36 and 40 percent of the vote, making it evident that the opposition had no chance unless it stood united. In Mexico, by contrast, the PRI had always been able to win the presidential elections with an absolute majority of the vote, if not by huge margins, and this worked to discourage opposition party elites from coordinating. If only the ruling party can win, why bother to sacrifice ideology and internal party dynamics in order to create an opposition coalition? If this hypothesis is correct, I would expect significant opposition fractionalization to prevail in hegemonic-party autocracies that win with large margins.

Another factor that might help to explain why opposition coordination occurred in Kenya in 2002 and not before is the 1997 constitutional reform, which finally permitted the formation of coalition governments among different parties. The constitution used to require the president to form a government from among members of his own party only, even if the party had no parliamentary majority. This clause directly discouraged the formation of electoral coalitions among opposition parties by preventing them from forming a coalition government in case one of the opposition candidates won the presidency (Foeken and Dietz, 2000). A third possible reason why opposition coordination occurred in Kenya in 2002 and not before, as Kasara (2005) explains, is that with the impending constitutional reform politicians expected a significant reduction in presidential power after the elections, making pre-electoral power sharing agreements more credible.

Electoral Malpractice and the Game of Fraud

My game-theoretic account of "electoral transitions" provides three main lessons that can be extended to other electoral autocracies to explain why authoritarian equilibria in countries where there is significant electoral corruption can be long-lasting. First, the autocrat can selectively buy off its opponents by offering legislative seats, perks, and policy influence. By dividing and co-opting the opposition, the autocrat can more easily get away with electoral malpractice.

Second, electoral incentives are not well aligned to fight authoritarianism: because *moderate opposition voters* are averse to post-electoral violence, opposition parties confront the paradoxical result that allegations of electoral fraud can turn against them. To deter the ruling party from committing fraud, the opposition must be composed of a large enough number of *radical voters* willing to support opposition parties that engage in violent struggles to make their votes count. If the opposition's electoral base is mostly *moderate*, the ruling party will find it easier to co-opt one of its opponents into acquiescing in the electoral fraud.

Third, my approach underscores the idea that limited information about the extent of the electoral fraud makes opposition coordination against autocratic transgressions much harder. Fearon (2000) argues that the convention of holding elections as such is valuable primarily as a device for coordinating rebellion against would-be dictators. "In a democratic equilibrium, if the ruling party cancels or blatantly rigs the elections, out-of-power factions infer that the terms of the bargain are about to be unilaterally changed to their advantage. Because the signal is public, like a traffic light, they gain assurance that other out-of-power individuals or factions will also protest" (12). Fearon's vision assumes that it is unambiguous when the ruling party rigs elections.[3] It also assumes that all voters will mobilize against the fraud. However, in autocratic regimes, the extent of electoral fraud is often not common knowledge because autocrats normally control every aspect of the organization and monitoring of elections *and* the mass media.

[3] Fearon (2000) is aware of this problem when he talks abut "partially rigged elections."

Only when voters know that elections are rigged can party elites count on the support of their *moderate electorate*, not only their *radical voters*, to engage in post-electoral battles, making opposition coordination against transgressions more likely. Furthermore, I have also argued that not all voters will be willing to mobilize against the electoral fraud. Electoral authoritarian regimes can be long-lasting to a large extent because *moderate* voters are willing to tolerate the corrupt incumbents rather than risking political turmoil and violence.

For years, the opposition in Mexico complained about electoral fraud. Since the PRI controlled every aspect of the organization of the elections and there were few independent sources of information that could verify the fraud, the mass public remained uncertain about the veracity of these accusations. Voters reacted to these accusations according to their own preconceptions about the political regime. Some regarded the PRI as excessively authoritarian and readily believed these accusations, even if the elections were clean. Others were highly suspicious of allegations of electoral fraud, even if elections were rigged. Under this poor informational environment regarding the extent of the electoral fraud, whichever opposition party chose to engage in post-electoral battles risked losing electoral support among its *moderate* followers. These *moderate opposition voters* valued political stability and tended to stay away from parties that engaged in post-electoral protests. Other opposition voters were *radical* or truly anti-system. They were more committed to bringing democratic change, even at the risk of violence, and would punish a political party that acquiesced in fraud. The PRD was trapped in this dilemma throughout the Salinas presidency. It engaged in continuous post-electoral battles, which ended up discouraging *moderate voters* from supporting this party.

I have argued in this book that the PRI was able to co-opt the PAN into acquiescing in the infamous 1988 electoral fraud by offering legislative seats and policy influence. The official results of the 1988 presidential elections implied that the PRI had lost the supermajority necessary to modify the constitution, and that the PAN had acquired veto power in the constitution-making game. The PAN opted not to contest the official results, in part because it calculated that the risks of confronting the government were too high, and in part because it wanted to keep its newly acquired policy-making power. The PAN's strategy to play the "loyal opposition" during those critical years paid dividends – this party was able to push for electoral reform and also to access office at the local level by counting with the president's alliance against recalcitrant state PRI politicians.

Although there was no doubt that Cuauhtémoc Cárdenas had been the victim of electoral fraud in the 1988 elections, nobody can know with certainty whether the fraud was decisive for the PRI to win the presidency, or whether fraud had rather been employed to manufacture a 50 percent vote threshold and a more comfortable majority in the legislature for the PRI. The PRI and the PAN employed this uncertainty to their advantage. On the one hand, this uncertainty would help to discourage ordinary citizens, the business community, the church, and many civic associations from mobilizing more forcefully against the fraud. On the other hand, this ambiguity about the extent of the 1988 electoral fraud reduced the electoral punishment the PAN received for playing the "loyal opposition" during the Salinas presidency. PAN's *moderate supporters* remained loyal to the party under the impression that Cárdenas had falsely accused the government of preventing him from assuming the presidency through massive fraud. In 1991, elites from the PAN made sure that voters remained ignorant about the extent of the electoral fraud by voting in a legislative coalition with the PRI to burn the ballots from those elections.

Thus, my transition model and discussion of the Mexican case illustrate why autocrats find it relatively easy to steal elections and get away with this behavior. Electoral incentives are misaligned to fight electoral fraud. The average voter is likely to be averse to violence, which is often necessary to force the autocrat to count votes fairly. In the absence of credible information about the the autocrats' transgressions, opposition parties that play the "loyal opposition" and acquiesce in the electoral fraud will tend to be rewarded by the *moderate* electorate; opposition parties that are willing to challenge the autocrat's transgressions will face the paradoxical result that allegations of electoral fraud will trun against them, leaving them with only the support of *radical voters*. Legislative seats, perks, and policy influence are additional benefits the autocrat can offer in order to co-opt its more moderate opponents into acquiescence. To fight against electoral fraud, the major forces in the opposition camp must all be willing to give up their institutional payoffs, credibly threatening major social unrest if the autocrat steals the elections.

The Creation of an Independent Electoral Commission and the Transition

A key reason why autocrats abhor an independent news media is that information dissemination makes coordination against transgressions more likely. Why, then, would an autocratic ruling party accede to the creation of independent electoral institutions that can publicize the actual election results? To provide an answer to this question, this book provided a theory of endogenous institutional change – why an autocrat might willingly sign a "political pact" with the opposition to refrain from committing fraud. The threat of violence, I have argued, created the incentives for the PRI to credibly pledge itself not to commit electoral fraud by delegating true independence to the IFE, putting it in charge of organizing and monitoring the elections.

Just after the Zapatista uprising erupted, the government invited the PRD and the PAN to negotiate the electoral reform as a way to commit the major players to "peaceful means for attaining power." The PRI thus attempted to neutralize the guerrillas with a nationwide political opening. The creation of the independent IFE prior to the 1994 presidential elections was a way to commit the PRDistas to the electoral process so as to avoid a major violent confrontation after the elections. Who was going to follow Cuauhtémoc Cárdenas into the streets to contest the elections if it was clear that the PRI did not control the electoral process? However, as I have argued in this book, the PRI pledged ex ante not to commit fraud only because it knew it would easily win the 1994 elections. At the time, politicians could not have anticipated the rapid electoral demise of the PRI as a result of the 1994 peso crisis, which was almost totally unpredicted. Granting independence to the IFE was an irreversible measure because it required a constitutional reform, and the PRI no longer controlled the required legislative supermajority.

The subsequent 1996 electoral reform was also important because it contributed to leveling the playing field by increasing campaign financing and media access for the opposition parties. The 1996 reform also incorporated the Federal Electoral Tribunal within the judicial branch and gave the Supreme Court the power to review the constitutionality of electoral laws. This last reform finally generated the incentives for the PRD to break ties with the Zapatistas and other radical social movements.[4] The PRD also won Mexico City in 1997 and acquired significant policy influence in the Chamber of Deputies after the 1997 midterm elections, when the PRI for the first time lost majority control of the assembly. In becoming a party-in-government, the PRD acceded to the existing institutions and moderated its opposition to the regime.

[4] I thank Guillermo Trejo for clarifying this for me.

As my discussion of the Mexican case suggests, an independent electoral commission can play a powerful role in democratizing an authoritarian electoral regime. This type of institution can provide clear information about the actual election results to facilitate opposition coordination against potential ruling party transgressions. An independent electoral commission also serves to commit an intransigent opposition to the electoral process and discourages post-electoral violence. To work as a guarantor of electoral transparency, the electoral commission must be truly independent of the government; both the ruling party and the opposition must have equal representation on its board, and it must be given enough power to control the electoral process. However, this set of institutions comes about only when a political bargain is struck between the ruling party and the opposition, when the former comes to realize that unbiased elections constitute the best means to pursue its goals. As the Mexican case illustrates, two conditions must hold for a pact creating an independent electoral commission to be signed: the ruling party must believe it can go on winning elections cleanly, and the opposition must be able to credibly threaten a post-electoral insurrection, regardless of whether there is fraud or not, unless the ruling party finds a way to guarantee the transparency of the elections ex ante.

In the creation of an independent electoral commission, a semblance of the rule of law in the electoral realm emerged in Mexico. My results are consistent with those of Maravall and Przeworski (2003), who offer the following, highly persuasive view of how that rule of law emerges: "Rule of law emerges when, following Machiavelli's advice, self-interested rulers willingly restrain themselves and make their behavior predictable in order to obtain a sustained, voluntary cooperation of well-organized groups commanding valuable resources" (3).

The Resiliency of Electoral Autocracies

I want to close these concluding remarks by reflecting on the relative durability of hegemonic-party autocracies in light of the Mexican case. Geddes (1999) has compellingly demonstrated that single-party regimes are significantly more resilient than military regimes and personal dictators. She attributes the resiliency of these regimes to their relative immunity to elite splitting. Gandhi and Przeworski (2001) also demonstrate that autocratic regimes that have legislatures and hold elections are more resilient. They argue that autocrats create these institutions in order to co-opt the opposition by giving them a place in the legislature and limited control over policy.

Huntington (1968) also noted the relative stability of party autocracies and attributed their durability to their superior "institutionalization."

My study of the Mexican PRI suggests that each of these approaches has a great deal of merit, yet they are incomplete. An electoral autocracy employs the institution of elections as a way of regularizing payments to its supporters and implementing punishment to its enemies, among both the elite and the masses. In doing so, it gives citizens and ruling party politicians a vested interest in the survival of the regime. The pillar of this type of autocracy is its monopoly of electoral support, cemented through a combination of economic performance, government transfers, ideological appeals, and voters' fears about the breakdown of political order if they defect to the opposition. Monopoly of electoral support serves to deter intra-elite divisions. Supermajorities also allow an autocratic ruling party to unilaterally control constitutional change and to create institutions designed to, among other things, divide and co-opt opponents. As electoral support withers, an electoral autocracy becomes more vulnerable to elite divisions and opposition rivals; it also comes to rely more on fraud and coercion to survive in office. Voters under autocracy cannot simply "throw the rascals out" of office because their choices are constrained by a series of strategic dilemmas that compel them to support the autocrat, even if reluctantly.

References

Abramson, Paul R., John H. Aldrich, Phil Paolino, and David W. Rohde. 1992. "'Sophisticated' Voting in the 1988 Presidential Primaries." *American Political Science Review* 82: 55–69.

Acemoglu, Daron K., and James Robinson. 2006. *Economic Origins of Dictatorship and Democracy*. Cambridge: Cambridge University Press.

Achen, Chris. 1989. "Prospective Voting and the Theory of Party Identification." Unpublished manuscript.

Achen, Christopher H. 1992. "Breaking the Iron Triangle: Social Psychology, Demographic Variables and Linear Regression in Voting Research." *Political Behavior* 14(3): 195–211.

Achen, Christopher H. 1996. "The Timing of Political Liberalization: Taiwan as the Canonical Case." Paper presented at the annual meeting of the American Political Science Association.

Alesina, Alberto. 1987. "Macroeconomic Policy in a Two-party System as a Repeated Game." *Quarterly Journal of Economics* 102: 651–78.

Alesina, Alberto. 1988. "Credibility and Convergence in a Two-party System with Rational Voters." *American Economic Review* 78: 796–805.

Alesina, Alberto, Gerald D. Cohen, and Nouriel Roubini. 1993. "Macroeconomic Policy and Elections in OECD Democracies" *Economics and Politics* 4: 1–30.

Alesina, Alberto, and Howard Rosenthal. 1995. *Partisan Politics, Divided Government and the Economy*. Cambridge: Cambridge University Press.

Alesina, Alberto, and Nouriel Roubini. 1997. *Political Cycles and the Macroeconomy*. Cambridge, Massachusetts: MIT Press.

Alvarez, Michael R. 1997. *Information and Elections*. Ann Arbor: University of Michigan Press.

Alvarez, Michael R., and Jonathan Nagler. 2000. "A New Approach for Modelling Strategic Voting in Multiparty Elections." *British Journal of Political Science* 30(1): 57–75.

Ames, Barry. 1970. "Bases of Support for Mexico's Dominant Party." *American Political Science Review*. 64(1): 153–167.

Ames, Barry. 1987. *Political Survival*. Berkeley and Los Angeles: University of Califorina Press.

Arendt, Hannah. 1968. *The Origins of Totalitarianism*. New York: Harvest Books.

Arriola, Leonardo. 2004. "Managing Political Risks: Coups and Clients in African States, 1971–2001." Unpublished manuscript, Stanford University.

Bailey, John. 1994. "Centralism and Political Change in Mexico: The Case of National Solidarity." In Wayne Cornelius, Ann Craig, and Jonathan Fox (eds.), *Transforming State-Society Relations in Mexico: The National Solidarity Strategy*. La Jolla, California: Center for U.S.–Mexican Studies, UCSD.

Banks, Arthur. 1976. *Cross-national Time Series, 1815–1973*. Ann Arbor, Michigan: Inter-University consortium for Political and Social Research. CD-ROM.

Barro, Robert. 1997. *Determinants of Economic Growth*. Cambridge, Massachusetts: MIT Press.

Basánez, Miguel. 1994. "Encuestas y Resultados de la Eleccion de 1994." *Este Pais* 43: 13–21.

Bates, Robert. 1984a. "Some Conventional Orthodoxies in the Study of Agrarian Change." *World Politics* 36(2): 234–54.

Bates, Robert. 1984b. *Markets and States in Tropical Africa*. Berkeley: University of California Press.

Bates, Robert. 1989. *Beyond the Miracle of the Market*. New York: Cambridge University Press.

Bates, Robert. 2001. *Prosperity and Violence*. New York: Norton.

Bates, Robert, Avner Greif, Margaret Levy, Jean-Laurent Rosenthal, and Barry Weingast. 1998. *Analytic Narratives*. Princeton, New Jersey: Princeton University Press.

Baumhogger, Goswin. 1999. "Zimbabwe." In Dieter Nohlen et al., *Elections in Africa: A Data Handbook*. Oxford: Oxford University Press.

Beck, Thorsten, George R. Clarke, Alberto Groff, Philip Keefer, and Patrick Walsh. 2001. "New Tools in Comparative Political Economy: The Database of Political Institutions." *World Bank Economic Review* 15(1): 165–76.

Bensusán, Graciela. 2004. "A New Scenario for Mexican Trade Unions: Changes in the Structure of Political and Economic Opportunities." In Kevin J. Middlebrook (ed.), *Dilemmas of Political Change in Mexico*. London: Institute of Latin American Studies, University of London / Center for U.S.–Mexico Studies, UCSD.

Boix, Carles. 2003. *Democracy and Redistribution*. Cambridge: Cambridge University Press.

Boix, Carles, and Susan Stokes. 2003. "Endogenous Democratization." *World Politics* 55 (July): 517–78.

Box, G., and G. Tiao. 1992. *Bayesian Inference in Statistical Analysis*. New York: John Wiley and Sons.

Brandenburg, Frank. 1955. "Mexico: An Experiment in One-Party Democracy." Ph.D. dissertation, University of Pennsylvania.

Brandenburg, Frank. 1964. *The Making of Modern Mexico*. Englewood Cliffs, New Jersey: Prentice-Hall.

References

Bratton, Michael, and Nicholas van de Walle. 1997. *Democratic Experiments in Africa: Regime Transitions in Comparative Perspective*. New York: Cambridge University Press.

Bruhn, Kathleen. 1996. "Social Spending and Political Support: The 'Lessons' of the National Solidarity Program in Mexico." *Comparative Politics* 26(January): 151–77.

Bruhn, Kathleen. 1997. *Taking on Goliath*. University Park: Pennsylvania State University Press.

Buendía, Jorge. 1996. "Economic Reform, Public Opinion and Presidential Approval in Mexico 1988–1993." *Comparative Political Studies* 29(October): 566–92.

Buendía, Jorge. 2001. "Economic Reforms and Political Support in Mexico." In Susan Stokes (ed.), *Public Support for Market Reforms in New Democracies*. Cambridge: Cambridge University Press.

Bueno de Mesquita, Bruce, et al. 2003. *The Logic of Political Survival*. Cambridge, Massachusetts: MIT Press.

Camp, Roderic. 1992. *Generals in the Palacio: The Military in Modern Mexico*. New York: Oxford University Press.

Camp, Roderic. 1995. *Political Recruitment across Two Centuries: Mexico 1884–1991*. Austin: University of Texas Press.

Camp, Roderic. 1999. *Politics in Mexico: The Decline of Authoritarianism*. Oxford: Oxford University Press.

Campbell, Angus, Philip E. Converse, Warren E. Miller, and Donald E. Stokes. 1960. *The American Voter*. New York: Wiley.

Campuzano, Irma. 1995. *Baja California en los Tiempos del PAN*. México: La Jornada Ediciones.

Castañeda, Jorge. 1995. *The Mexican Shock*. New York: The New Press.

Castañeda, Jorge. 2000. *Perpetuating Power: How Mexican Presidents Were Chosen*. New York: The New Press.

Casar, María Amparo. 2002. "Executive-Legislative Relations: The Case of Mexico (1946–1997)." In Benito Nacif and Scott Morgenstern (eds.), *Legislative Politics in Latin America*. New York: Cambridge University Press.

Chand, Vikram. 2001. *Mexico's Political Awakening*. South Bend, Indiana: University of Notre Dame Press.

Chandra, Kanchan. 2004. *Why Ethnic Parties Succeed: Patronage and Ethnic Head Counts in India*. Cambridge: Cambridge University Press.

Chehabi, H. E., and Juan J. Linz, eds. 1998. *Sultanistic Regimes*. Baltimore: Johns Hopkins University Press.

Chull Shin, Doh. 1994. "On the Third Wave of Democratization. A Synthesis and Evaluation of Recent Theory and Research." *World Politics* 47 (October): 135–70.

Cinta, Alberto. 1999. "Uncertainty and Electoral Behavior in Mexico in the 1997 Congressional Elections." In Jorge I. Domínguez and Alejandro Poiré (eds.), *Toward Mexico's Democratization: Parties, Campaigns, Elections and Public Opinion*. New York: Routledge.

Collier, David, and Ruth B. Collier. 1991. *Shaping the Political Arena*. Princeton, New Jersey: Princeton University Press.
Collier, Ruth B. 1992. *The Contradictory Alliance: State-Labor Relations and Regime Change in Mexico* (Research Series No. 83). Berkeley: Institute of International Studies, University of California.
Colomer, Josep. 1991. "Transitions by Agreement: Modeling the Spanish Way." *American Political Science Review* 85(4): 1283–1302.
Colomer, Josep, and Margot Pascual. 1994. "The Polish Games of Transition." *Communist and Post-Communist Studies* 27(3): 275–94.
Cornelius, Wayne A. 1975. *Politics and the Migrant Poor in Mexico City*. Stanford, California: Stanford University Press.
Cornelius, Wayne. 2004. "Mobilized Voting in the 2000 Elections: The Changing Efficacy of Vote Buying and Coercion in Mexican Electoral Politics." In Jorge Domínguez and Chappell Lawson, eds. *Mexico's Pivotal Democratic Election: Campaign Effects and the Presidential Race of 2000*. Stanford, California: Stanford University Press.
Cornelius, Wayne, Ann Craig, and Jonathan Fox, eds. 1994. *Transforming State-Society Relations in Mexico: The National Solidarity Strategy*. La Jolla, California: Center for U.S.–Mexican Studies, UCSD.
Cornelius, Wayne, Judith Gentleman, and Peter Smith, eds. 1989. *Mexico's Alternative Political Futures*. La Jolla, California: Center for U.S.–Mexico Studies, UCSD.
Cox, W. Gary. 1991. "SNTV and d'Hont are 'Equivalent'." *Electoral Studies* 10: 118–32.
Cox, W. Gary. 1994. "Strategic Voting Equilibria under the Single Nontransferable Vote." *American Political Science Review* 88: 608–21.
Cox, Gary. 1997. *Making Votes Count: Strategic Coordination in the World's Electoral Systems*. Cambridge: Cambridge University Press.
Cox, W. Gary, and Mathew D. McCubbins. 1986. "Electoral Politics as a Redistributive Game." *Journal of Politics* 48(May): 370–89.
Cox, W. Gary, and Michael Thies. 2000. "How Much Does Money Matter? 'Buying Votes' in Japan, 1967–1990." *Comparative Political Studies* 33(1): 37–57.
Cowen, Michael, and Liisa Laakso. 2002. *Multi-Party Politics in Africa*. New York: Palgrave.
Craig, Ann, and Wayne Cornelius. 1995. "Houses Divided. Parties and Political Reform in Mexico." In Scott Mainwaring and Timothy R. Scully (eds.), *Building Democratic Institutions: Party Systems in Latin America*. Stanford, California: Stanford University Press.
Crespo, José Antonio. 1992. "Crisis Economica = Crisis de Legitimidad." In Carlos Bazdresch (ed.), *Mexico: Auge, Crisis y Ajuste*. Vol. 1. México: Fondo de Cultura Económica.
Crespo, José Antonio. 2004. "Party Competition in Mexico: Evolution and Prospects." In Kevin Middlebrook (ed.), *Dilemmas of Political Change in Mexico*. London: Institute of Latin American Studies, University of London/Center for U.S.–Mexico Studies, UCSD.

References

Cukierman, Alex, and Allan Meltzer. 1986. "A Positive Theory of Discretionary Policy, the Cost of Democratic Government, and the Benefits of a Constitution." *Economic Inquiry* 24: 367–88.

Dahl, Robert. 1971. *Polyarchy*. New Haven, Connecticut: Yale University Press.

Dahl, Robert, ed. 1973. *Regimes and Oppositions*. New Haven, Connecticut: Yale University Press.

Dahlberg, Matz, and Eva Johansson. 2002. "On the Vote-Purchasing Behavior of Incumbent Governments." *American Political Science Review* 96(1): 27–40.

Davids, A. Otto, Melvin J. Hinich, and Peter C. Ordeshook. 1970. "An Expository Development of a Mathematical Model of Electoral Process." *American Political Science Review* 64: 426–48.

De la Madrid H., Miguel. 2004. *Cambio de Rumbo*. México: Fondo de Cultura Económica.

Deutsch, Karl W. 1961. "Social Mobilization and Political Development." *American Political Science Review* 55(3): 493–514.

Di Palma, Giuseppe. 1990. *To Craft Democracies*. Berkeley: University of California Press.

Diamond, Larry. 2002. "Elections without Democracy: Thinking about Hybrid Regimes." *Journal of Democracy* 13.2(April): 21–35.

Diamond, Larry, et al., eds. 1989. *Democracy in Developing Countries: Asia*. Boulder, Colorado: Lynne Rienner.

Diaz-Cayeros, Alberto. 1997. "Political Responses to Regional Inequality: Taxation and Distribution in Mexico." Ph.D. dissertation, Duke University.

Diaz-Cayeros, Alberto. 2004. "Decentralization, Democratization and Federalism in Mexico." In Kevin Middlebrook (ed.), *Dilemmas of Political Change in Mexico*. London: Institute of Latin American Studies, University of London / Center for U.S.–Mexico Studies, UCSD.

Diaz-Cayeros, Alberto, Federico Estévez, and Beatriz Magaloni. 2002. "The Erosion of One-Party Rule: Clientelism, Portfolio Diversification and Electoral Strategy." Paper presented at the annual meeting of the American Political Science Association, Boston, August 29–September 1.

Diaz-Cayeros, Alberto, and Beatriz Magaloni. 1995. "Transition Games: Initiating and Sustaining Democracy." Paper presented at the annual meeting of the American Political Science Association, September.

Díaz-Cayeros, Alberto, and Beatriz Magaloni. 2001. "Party Dominance and the Logic of Electoral Design in Mexico's Transition to Democracy." *Journal of Theoretical Politics* 13(3): 271–93.

Diaz-Cayeros, Alberto, Beatriz Magaloni, and Barry Weingast. 2004. "Democratization and the Economy in Mexico: Equilibrium (PRI) Hegemony and Its Demise." Unpublished manuscript, Stanford University.

Dixit, Avinash, and John Londregan. 1996. "The Determinants of Success of Special Interests in Redistributive Politics." *Journal of Politics*. 58(November): 1132–55.

Domínguez, Jorge. 1999. "The Transformation of Mexico's Electoral and Party Systems 1988–97." In Jorge Domínguez and Alejandro Poiré (eds.), *Toward Mexico's*

Democratization: Parties, Campaigns, Elections and Public Opinion. New York: Routledge.

Domínguez, Jorge. 2004. "Why and How Did Mexico's 2000 Presidential Election Campaign Matter." In Jorge Domínguez and Chappell Lawson (eds.), *Mexico's Pivotal Democratic Election: Campaign Effects and the Presidential Race of 2000*. Stanford, California: Stanford University Press.

Domínguez, Jorge, and Chappell Lawson, eds. 2004. *Mexico's Pivotal Democratic Election: Campaign Effects and the Presidential Race of 2000*. Stanford, California: Stanford University Press.

Domínguez, Jorge I., and James A. McCann. 1995. "Shaping Mexico's Electoral Arena: Construction of Partisan Cleavages in the 1988 and 1991 National Elections." *American Political Science Review* 89: 34–48.

Domínguez, Jorge, and James McCann. 1996. *Democratizing Mexico: Public Opinion and Electoral Choices*. Baltimore: Johns Hopkins University Press.

Domínguez, Jorge, and Alejandro Poiré, eds. 1999. *Toward Mexico's Democratization: Parties, Campaigns, Elections and Public Opinion*. New York: Routledge.

Dow, Jay K., and James W. Endersby. 2004. "Multinomial Probit and Multinomial Logit: A Comparison of Choice Models for Voting Research." *Electoral Studies* 23(1): 107–122.

Downs, Anthony. 1957. *An Economic Theory of Democracy*. New York: Harper and Row.

Dresser, Denise. 1991. *Neopopulist Solutions to Neoliberal Problems: Mexico's National Solidarity Program*. La Jolla, California: Center for U.S.–Mexican Studies, UCSD.

Dresser, Denise. 1994. "Bringing the Poor Back In: National Solidarity as a Strategy of Regime Legitimation." In Wayne Cornelius, Ann Craig, and Jonathan Fox (eds.), *Transforming State-Society Relations in Mexico: The National Solidarity Strategy*. La Jolla, California: Center for U.S.–Mexican Studies, UCSD.

Duverger, Maurice. 1963. *Political Parties*. New York: Wiley

Duverger, Maurice. 1986. "Duverger's Law: Forty Years Later." In Bernard Grofman and Arend Lijphart (eds.), *Electoral Laws and Their Political Consequences*. New York: Agathon Press.

Edwards, Sebastian, and Rudiger Dornbusch, eds. 1991. *The Macroeconomics of Populism in Latin America*. Cambridge, Massachusetts: MIT Press.

Eisenstadt, S. N., and Rene Lemarchand. 1981. *Political Clientelism, Patronage and Development*. London: SAGE Publications.

Eisenstadt, Todd. 2004. *Courting Democracy in Mexico*. Cambridge: Cambridge University Press.

Enelow, M. James, and Melvin J. Hinich. 1984. *The Spatial Theory of Voting*. New York: Cambridge University Press.

Erikson, Robert S. 1989. "Economic Conditions and Presidential Vote." *American Political Science Review* 83: 567–73.

Estévez, Federico, and Magaloni, Beatriz. 2000. "Partidos Legislativos y sus Electorados en la Batalla Presupuestal de 1997." ITAM Working Papers in Politics.

Fearon, James. 2000. "Why Use Elections to Allocate Power?" Unpublished manuscript, Stanford University.

References

Ferejohn, John A. 1986 "Incumbent Performance and Electoral Control." *Public Choice* 50: 5–25.

Fiorina, Morris P. 1981. *Retrospective Voting in American National Elections*. New Haven, Connecticut: Yale University Press.

Foeken, Richard, and Tom Dietz. 2000. "Of Ethnicity, Manipulation and Observation: The 1992 and 1997 Elections in Kenya." In Jon Abbinik and Gerti Hesseling (eds.), *Election Observation and Democratization in Africa*. New York: St. Martin's Press.

Fox, Jonathan. 1994. "The Difficult Transition from Clientelism to Citizenship: Lessons from Mexico." *World Politics* 46(2): 151–84.

Gandhi, Jennifer, and Adam Przeworski. 2001. "Dictatorial Institutions and the Survival of Dictators." Paper presented at the annual meeting of the American Political Science Association, August 30–September 2.

Geddes, Barbara. 1994. *Politician's Dilemma: Building State Capacity in Latin America*. Berkeley: University of California Press.

Geddes, Barbara. 1999. "Authoritarian Breakdown: Empirical Test of a Game Theoretic Argument." Paper presented at the annual meeting of the American Political Science Association, Atlanta, Georgia, September.

Geddes, Barbara. 2003. *Paradigms and Sand Castles: Research Design in Comparative Politics*. Ann Arbor: University of Michigan Press.

Gellner, Ernest, and Waterbury, John. 1977. *Patrons and Clients*. London: Duckworth.

Gershberg, Alec Ian. 1994. "Distributing Resources in the Education Sector." In Wayne Cornelius, Ann Craig, and Jonathan Fox (eds.), *Transforming State-Society Relations in Mexico: The National Solidarity Strategy*. La Jolla, California: Center for U.S.–Mexican Studies, UCSD.

Glickman, Harvey, ed. 1995. *Ethnic Conflict and Democratization in Africa*. Atlanta, Georgia: African Studies Association Press.

Golden, Miriam. 2004. "International Economic Sources of Regime Change: How European Economic Integration Undermined Italy's Postwar Party System." *Comparative Political Studies* 37(December): 1238–74.

Golden, Miriam, and Eric Chang. 2001. "Competitive Corruption: Factional Conflict and Political Malfeasance in Postwar Italian Christian Democracy." *World Politics* 53(4): 588–622.

Gómez, Edmund T., and K. S. Jomo. 1997. *Malaysia's Political Economy: Politics, Patronage and Profits*. Cambridge: Cambridge University Press.

Gómez López, Marcela, and Sandra Pineda Antúnez. 1999. *El Reparto Municipal del Pronasol: Criterios de Asignación en Aguascalientes y Michoacán*. B.A. thesis, ITAM, Mexico.

Gómez Tagle, Silvia. 1997. *La Transición Inconclusa: Treinta Años de Elecciones en México*. México: El Colegio de México.

González, María de Los Angeles. 2002. "Do Changes in Democracy Affect the Political Budget Cycle? Evidence from Mexico." *Review of Development Economics* 6(2): 204–24.

González Casanova, Pablo. 1965. *La Democracia en México*. México City: ERA.

Haggard, Stephan, and Robert Kaufman, eds. 1992. *The Politics of Economic Adjustment*. Princeton, New Jersey: Princeton University Press.
Haggard, Stephan, and Robert Kaufman. 1995. *The Political Economy of Democratic Transitions*. Princeton, New Jersey: Princeton University Press.
Haggard, Stephan, and Kaufman, Robert. 1999. "The Political Economy of Democratic Transitions." In Lisa Anderson (ed.), *Transitions to Democracy*. New York: Columbia University Press.
Haggard, Stephan, and Steven Webb. 1994. *Voting for Reform*. Washington, D.C.: World Bank.
Hansen, Roger D. 1974. *The Politics of Mexican Development*. Baltimore and London: Johns Hopkins University Press.
Havel, Vaclav. 1992. *Open Letters*. New York: Vintage.
Heath, Jonathan. 1999. *Mexico and the Sexenio Curse: Presidential Successions and Economic Crises in Modern Mexico*. Washington, D.C.: Center for Strategic and International Studies.
Hibbs, Douglas A. 1987. *The American Political Economy*. Cambridge, Massachusetts: Harvard University Press.
Hilley, John. 2001. *Malaysia: Mahathirism, Hegemony and the New Opposition*. London: Zed Books.
Hinich, Melvin, and Michael Munger. 1994. *Ideology and the Theory of Political Choice*. Ann Arbor: University of Michigan Press.
Hirschman, Albert. 1981. "Exit, Voice and the State." In his *Essays in Trespassing*. Cambridge: Cambridge University Press.
Hiskey, Jonathan. 1999. "Does Democracy Matter? Electoral Competition and Local Development in Mexico." Ph.D. dissertation, University of Pittsburgh.
Hiskey, Jonathan. 2003. "Demand Based Development and Local Electoral Environments." *Comparative Politics* 36(1): 41–60.
Honaker, James, et al. 2001. "AMELIA: A Program for Missing Data (Windows Version)." Cambridge, Massachusetts: Harvard University Press.
Huntington, Samuel P. 1968. *Political Order in Changing Societies*. New Haven, Connecticut: Yale University Press.
Huntington, Samuel P. 1970. "Social and Institutional Dynamics of One-Party Systems." In Samuel P. Huntington and Clement H. Moore (eds.), *Authoritarian Politics in Modern Society*. New York: Basic Books.
Ingham, Kenneth. 1990. *Politics in Modern Africa: The Uneven Tribal Dimension*. New York and London: Routledge.
Joseph, Richard. 1999. "Democratization in Africa after 1989: Comparative and Theoretical Perspectives." In Lisa Anderson (ed.), *Transitions to Democracy*. New York: Columbia University Press.
Karl, Terry L. 1990. "Dilemmas of Democratization in Latin America." *Comparative Politics* 23(1): 1–23.
Karl, Terry L. 1997. *The Paradox of Plenty: Oil Booms and Petro-States*. Berkeley: University of California Press.
Karl, Terry L., and Philippe Schmitter. 1991. "Modes of Transition in Latin America, Southern and Eastern Europe." *International Social Science Journal* 128(May): 269–84.

Kasara, Kimuli. 2005. "A Prize Too Large to Share: Opposition Coalitions and the Kenyan Presidency, 1991–2002." Unpublished manuscript, Stanford University.
Kaufman, Robert. 1977a. "Corporatism, Clientelism, and Partisan Conflict: A Study of Seven Countries." In James M. Malloy (ed.), *Authoritarianism and Corporatism in Latin America*. Pittsburgh: University of Pittsburgh Press.
Kaufman, Robert. 1977b. "Mexico and Latin American Authoritarianism." In Jose Luis Reyna and Richard S. Weinert (eds.), *Authoritarianism in Mexico*. Philadelphia: Institute for the Study of Human Issues.
Kaufman, Robert, Carlos Bazdresh, and Blanca Heredis. 1994. "Mexico: Radical Reform in a Dominant Party System." In Stephen Haggard and Steven B. Webb (eds.), *Voting for Reform*. New York: Oxford University Press.
Kaufman, Robert R., and Guillermo Trejo. 1996. "Regionalismo, Transformación del régimen y Pronasol: La Política del Programa Nacional de Solidaridad en Cuatro Estados Mexicanos." *Política y Gobierno* 3(2): 245–80.
Kaufman, Robert R., and Guillermo Trejo. 1997. "Regionalism, Regime Transformation, and PRONASOL: The Politics of the National Solidarity Programme in Four Mexican States." *Journal of Latin American Studies* 29: 717–45.
Kaufman, Robert, and Leo Zuckerman. 1998. "Attitudes toward Economic Reform in Mexico: The Role of Political Orientations." *American Political Science Review* 92(2): 359–75.
Keech, William. R. 1995. *Economic Politics*. Cambridge: Cambridge University Press.
Keefer, Phil. 2003. "Clientelism, Development and Democracy." Unpublished manuscript, World Bank.
Keohane, Robert, Gary King, and Almond Verba. 1994. *Designing Social Inquiry: Scientific Inference in Qualitative Research*. Princeton, New Jersey: Princeton University Press
Key. V. O., Jr. 1955. "A Theory of Critical Elections." *Journal of Politics* 17(February): 3–18.
Key. V. O., Jr. 1966. *The Responsible Electorate: Rationality in Presidential Voting 1936–1060*. Cambridge, Massachusetts: Harvard University Press.
Kiewiet, Roderick D. 1983. *Macroeconomics and Micropolitics*. Chicago: University of Chicago Press.
King, Gary, et al. 2001. "Analyzing Incomplete Political Science Data: An Alternative Algorithm for Multiple Imputation." *American Political Science Review* 95(1): 49–69.
Kitschelt, Herbert. 1992. "Review: Comparative Historical Research and Rational Choice Theory: The Case of Transitions to Democracy." *Theory and Society*. 22(3): 413–27.
Kitschelt, Herbert. 2000. "Linkages between Citizens and Politicians in Democratic Politics." *Comparative Political Studies* 33(6/7): 845–79.
Klesner, Joseph. 1988. "Electoral Reform in an Authoritarian Regime: The Case of Mexico." Ph.D. dissertation, MIT.
Klesner, Joseph. 1993. "Modernization, Economic Crisis and Electoral Alignment in Mexico." *Mexican Studies/Estudios Mexicanos* 9(2): 187–223.
Klesner, Joseph. 1994. "Realignment or Dealignment? Consequences of Economic Crisis and Restructuring for the Mexican Party System." In Maria Lorena Cook,

Kevin J. Middlebrook, and Juan Molinar, (eds.), *Politics of Economic Restructuring State-Society Relations and Regime Change in Mexico*. La Jolla: center for U.S.–Mexican Studies, University of California at San Diego.
Klesner, Joseph, and Chappell Lawson. 2004. "Political Reform, Electoral Participation, and the Campaign of 2000." In Jorge I. Domíguez and Chappell Lawson (eds.), *Mexico's Pivotal Democratic Elections*. Stanford, California: Stanford University Press.
Kuran, Timur. 1991. "Now Out of Never: The Element of Surprise in East European Revolutions of 1989." *World Politics* 44: 7–48.
Laver, Michael, and Norman Schofield. 1991. *Multiparty Government: The Politics of Coalition in Europe*. Oxford: Oxford University Press.
Lawson, Chappell. 1999. "Why Cárdenas Won: The 1997 Election in Mexico City." In Jorge I. Domínguez and Alejandro Poiré (eds.), *Toward Mexico's Democratization: Parties, Campaigns, Elections and Public Opinion*. New York: Routledge.
Lawson, Chappell. 2002. *Building the Fourth Estate: Democratization and the Rise of a Free Press in Mexico*. Berkeley: University of California Press.
Lawson, Chappell. 2004a. "Television Coverage, Vote Choice, and the 2000 Campaign." In Jorge Domínguez and Chappell Lawson (eds.), *Mexico's Pivotal Democratic Election: Campaign Effects and the Presidential Race of 2000*. Stanford, California: Stanford University Press.
Lawson, Chappell. 2004b. "Building the Fourth Estate: Media Opening and Democratization in Mexico." In Kevin Middlebrook (ed.), *Dilemmas of Political Change in Mexico*. London: Institute of Latin American Studies, University of London/Center for U.S.–Mexico Studies, UCSD.
Lemarchand, Rene. 1972. "Political Clientelism and Ethnicity in Tropical Africa: Competing Solidarities in Nation Building." *American Political Science Review* 66(1): 68–90.
Lemarchand, Rene, and Keith Legg. 1972. "Political Clientelism and Development: A Preliminary Analysis." *Comparative Politics* 4(2): 149–78.
Lerner, Daniel. 1958. *The Passing of Traditional Society*. Glencoe, Illinois: Free Press.
Levitzky, Steven, and Lucan A. Way. 2002. "The Rise of Competitive Authoritarianism." *Journal of Democracy* 13(2): 51–65.
Lewis-Beck, Michael. 1988. *Economics and Elections*. Ann Arbor: University of Michigan Press.
Lichbach, Mark. 1998. *The Rebel's Dilemma*. Ann Arbor: University of Michigan Press.
Lijphart, Arend. 1984. *Democracies: Patterns of Majoritarian and Consensus Government in Twenty-One Countries*. New Haven, Connecticut: Yale University Press.
Lin, Jih-weh. 2003. "Transition through Transaction: Taiwan's Constitutional Reforms in the Lee Teng-hui Era." In Wei-chin Lee and T. Y Wang (eds.), *Sayonara to the Lee Teng-hui Era*. Lanham: University of Maryland Press.
Lindbeck, Assar. 1976. "Stabilization Policies in Open Economics with Endogenous Politicians." *American Economic Review Papers and Proceedings*, 1–19.
Lindbeck, Assar, and Jörgen Weibull. 1987. "Balanced-Budget Redistribution as the Outcome of Political Competition." *Public Choice* 52(2): 273–97.

References

Linz, Juan J. 2000. *Totalitarian and Authoritarian Regimes*. Boulder, Colorado: Lynne Rienner.

Lipset, Seymour Martin. 1957. *Political Man: The Social Basis of Politics*. Baltimore: Johns Hopkins University Press.

Lipset, Seymour Martin. 1959. "Some Social Requisites of Democracy: Economic Development and Political Legitimacy." *American Political Science Review* 53(1): 69–105.

Loaeza, Soledad. 1989. *El Llamado a las Urnas*. Mexico City: Cal y Arena.

Loaeza, Soledad. 1999. *El Partido Acción Nacional, la larga marcha, 1939–1994: Oposición Leal y Partido de Protesta*. México: Fondo de Cultura Económica.

Loaeza, Soledad. 2003. "The National Action Party (PAN): From the Fringes of the Political System to the Heart of Change." In Scott Mainwaring and Timothy Scully (eds.), *Christian Democracy in Latin America*. Stanford, California: Stanford University Press.

Lohmann, Sussane. 1994. "The Dynamics of Informational Cascades: The Monday Demonstrations in Leipzig, East Germany, 1989–91." *World Politics*. 47(1): 42–101.

Lujambio, Alonso. 2000. *El Poder Compartido*. México: Oceano.

Lujambio, Alonso. 2001. "Democratization through Federalism? The National Action Party Strategy, 1939–1995." In Kevin J. Middlebrook (ed.), *Party Politics and the Struggle for Democracy in Mexico: National and State Level Analyses of the Partido Accion Nacional*. La Jolla, California: Center for U.S.–Mexican Studies, UCSD.

Lustig, Nora. 1992. *Mexico: The Remaking of an Economy*. Washington, D.C.: Brookings Institution.

Lust-Okar, Ellen. 2005. *Structuring Conflict in the Arab World*. Cambridge: Cambridge University Press.

MacKuen, Michael B., Robert S. Erikson, and James A. Stimson. 1992. "Peasants and Bankers: The American Electorate and the US Economy." *American Political Science Review* 86: 597–611.

Magaloni, Beatriz. 1994. "Elección Racional y Voto Estratégico: Algunas Aplicaciones al caso Mexicano." *Política y Gobierno* 1(2): 309–44.

Magaloni, Beatriz. 1996. "Dominio de Partido y Dilemas Duvergerianos en las Elecciones Presidenciales de 1994." *Política y Gobierno* 3: 281–326.

Magaloni, Beatriz. 1997. "The Dynamics of Dominant Party Decline: The Mexican Transition to Multipartyism." Ph.D. dissertation, Duke University.

Magaloni, Beatriz. 1999. "Is the PRI Fading? Economic Performance, Electoral Accountability and Voting Behavior in the 1994 and 1997 Elections." In Jorge I. Domínguez and Alejandro Poiré (eds.), *Toward Mexico's Democratization: Parties, Campaigns, Elections and Public Opinion*. New York: Routledge.

Magaloni, Beatriz. 2003. "Authoritarianism, Democracy and the Supreme Court: Horizontal Exchange and the Rule of Law in Mexico." In Scott Mainwaring and Christopher Welna (eds.), *Democratic Accountability in Latin America*. Oxford: Oxford University Press.

Magaloni, Beatriz. 2004. "Contested Elections, Electoral Fraud and the Transition Game." Unpublished manuscript, Stanford University.

Magaloni, Beatriz. 2005. "The Demise of Mexico's One-Party Dominant Regime: Elite Choices and the Masses in the Establishment of Democracy." In Haggopian Frances and Scott Mainwaring (eds.), *The Third Wave of Democratization in Latin America*. Cambridge: Cambridge University Press.

Magaloni, Beatriz, Alberto Diaz-Cayeros, and Federico Estévez. (forthcoming) "Private versus Public Goods as Electoral Investments: A Portfolio Diversification Model with Evidence from Mexico." In Herbert Kitschelt and Steven Wilkinson (eds.), *Patrons, Clients and Policies: Patterns of Democratic Accountability and Competition*. London: Cambridge University Press.

Magaloni, Beatriz, Alberto Diaz-Cayeros, and Federico Estévez. 2000. "Federalism, Redistributive Politics and Poverty Relief Spending: The Programa Nacional de Solidaridad in Mexico (1989–1994)." Paper delivered at the annual meeting of the American Political Science Association, Washington, D.C.

Magaloni, Beatriz, and Alejandro Moreno. 2003. "Catching All Souls: The Partido Acción Nacional and the Politics of Religion in Mexico." In Scott Mainwaring and Timothy Scully (eds.), *Christian Democracy in Latin America*. Stanford, California: Stanford University Press.

Magaloni, Beatriz, and Alejandro Poiré. 2004a. "The Issues, the Vote and the Mandate for Change." In Jorge Dominguez and Chappell Lawson (eds.), *Mexico's Pivotal Democratic Election: Campaign Effects and the Presidential Race of 2000* Stanford, California: Stanford University Press.

Magaloni, Beatriz, and Alejandro Poiré. 2004b. "Strategic Coordination in the 2000 Mexican Presidential Race." In Jorge Dominguez and Chappell Lawson (eds.), *Mexico's Pivotal Democratic Election: Campaign Effects and the Presidential Race of 2000*. Stanford, California: Stanford University Press.

Mainwaring, Scott, and Aníbal Perez Liñán. 2005. "Latin American Democratization since 1978." In Frances Haggopian and Scott Mainwaring (eds.), *The Third Wave of Democratization in Latin America*, Cambridge: Cambridge University Press.

Mainwaring, Scott, and Matthew Shugart, eds. 1997. *Presidentialism and Democracy in Latin America*. Cambridge: Cambridge University Press.

Malloy, James A., ed. 1977. *Authoritarianism and Corporatism in Latin America*. Pittsburgh: University of Pittsburgh Press.

Marawall, Ignacio, and Adam Przeworski. 2003. "Introduction." In Ignacio Marawall and Adam Przeworski (eds.), *Democracy and the Rule of Law*. Cambridge: Cambridge University Press.

Marshall, Monty, and Keith Jaggers. 2003. "Political Regime Characteristics and Transitions, 1800–2003." <www.cidcm.umd.edu/inscr/polity>

Medina, Luis. 1978. *Evolución Electoral en el México Contemporáneo*. México: Gaceta Informativa de la Comisión Federal Electoral.

Middlebrook, Kevin. 1986. "Political Liberalization in an Authoritarian Regime: The Case of Mexico." In Guillermo O'Donnell, Philippe Schmitter, and Lawrence Whitehead (eds.), *Latin America, Pt.2, Transitions from Authoritarian Rule: Prospects for Democracy*. Baltimore: Johns Hopkins University Press.

Middlebrook, Kevin. 1995. *The Paradox of Revolution: Labor, the State and Authoritarianism in Mexico*. Baltimore: Johns Hopkins University Press.

Middlebrook, Kevin. 2004. "Mexico's Democratic Transitions: Dynamics and Prospects." In Kevin J. Middlebrook (ed.), *Party Politics and the Struggle for Democracy in Mexico: National and State Level Analyses of the Partido Acción Nacional*. La Jolla, California: Center for U.S.–Mexican Studies, UCSD.

Molinar Horcasitas, Juan. 1987. "Regreso a Chihuahua." *Nexos* 111(March): 21–32.

Molinar Horcasitas, Juan. 1991. *El Tiempo de la Legitimidad. Elecciones, Autoritarismo y Democracia en México*. México: Cal y Arena.

Molinar Horcasitas, Juan. 1996. "Changing the Balance of Power in a Hegemonic Party System: The Case of Mexico." In Arendt Lijphart and Carlos Waisman (eds.), *Institutional Design in New Democracies: Eastern Europe and Latin America*. Boulder, Colorado: Westview Press.

Molinar Horcasitas, Juan, and Jeffrey Weldon. 1990. "Elecciones de 1988 en Mexico: Crisis del Autoritarismo." *Revista Mexicana de Sociología* 52(4): 229–62.

Molinar Horcasitas, Juan, and Jeffrey Weldon. 1994. "Electoral Determinants and Consequences of National Solidarity." In Wayne Cornelius, Ann Craig, and Jonathan Fox (eds.), *Transforming State-Society Relations in Mexico: The National Solidarity Strategy*. La Jolla, California: Center for U.S.–Mexican Studies, UCSD.

Moore, Clement H. 1970. "The Single Party as a Source of Legitimacy." In Samuel Huntington and Clement H. Moore (eds.), *Authoritarian Politics in Modern Society*. New York: Basic Books.

Moreno, Alejandro. 1998. "Party Competition and the Issue of Democracy: Ideological Space in Mexican Elections." In Mónica Serrano (ed.), *Governing Mexico: Political Parties and Elections*. London: University of London Press.

Moreno, Alejandro. 1999a. "Campaign Awareness and Voting in the 1997 Mexican Congressional Elections." In Jorge Domínguez and Alejandro Poiré (eds.), *Toward Mexico's Democratization: Parties, Campaigns, Elections and Public Opinion*. New York: Routledge.

Moreno, Alejandro. 1999b. *Political Cleavages: Issues, Parties, and the Consolidation of Democracy*. Boulder, Colorado: Perseus.

Moreno, Alejandro. 2003. *El Votante Mexicano*. México: Fondo de Cultura Económica.

Moreno, Alejandro. 2004. "The Effects of Negative Campaigns on Mexican Voters." In Jorge Domínguez and Chappell Lawson (eds.), *Mexico's Pivotal Democratic Election: Campaign Effects and the Presidential Race of 2000*. Stanford, California: Stanford University Press.

Morgenstern, Scott, and Elizabeth Zechmeister. 2001. "Better the Devil You Kow than the Saint You Don't? Risk Propensity and Vote Choice in Mexico." *Journal of Politics* 63(1): 93–119.

Neocosmos, Michael. 2003. "The Politics of National Elections in Botswana, Lesotho and Swaziland." In Michael Cowen and Lisa Laakso (eds.), *Multiparty Elections in Africa*. New York: Palgrave.

Nie, Norman H., Sidney Verba, and John Petrocik. 1979. *The Changing American Voter*, enl. ed. Cambridge, Massachusetts: Harvard University Press.

Niemi, Richard G., and Herbert F. Weisberg. 1993. *Classics in Voting Behavior*. Washington, D.C.: Congressional Quarterly.

Nordhaus, William. 1975. "The Political Buisnesss Cycle." *Review of Economic Studies* 42: 169–90.
O'Donnell, Guillermo. 1973. *Modernization and Bureaucratic Authoritarianism: Studies in South American Politics*. Berkeley: University of Califorinia, Institute of International Studies.
O'Donnell, Guillermo, and Philippe C. Schmitter. 1986. *Transitions from Authoritarian Rule: Tentative Conclusions about Uncertain Democracies*. Baltimore: Johns Hopkins University Press.
Olson, Mancur. 2000. *Power and Prosperity: Outgrowing Communist and Capitalist Dictatorships*. New York: Basic Books.
Ordeshook, Peter C., and Olga Shvetsova. 1994. "Ethnic Heterogeneity, District Magnitude, and the Number of Parties." *American Journal of Political Science* 38: 100–23.
Ozbudun, Ergun. 1989. "Turkey: Crisis, Interruptions, and Reequilibration." In Larry Diamond et al. (eds.), *Democracy in Developing Countries: Asia*. Boulder: Lynne Rienner.
Pacheco Méndez, Guadalupe. 1995. "Los Resultados Electorales de 1994." In Pablo Pascual Moncayo (ed.), *Las Elecciones de 1994*. México: Cal y Arena.
Palfrey, Thomas. 1989. "A Mathematical Proof of Duverger's Law." In Peter C. Ordeshook (ed.), *Models of Strategic Choice in Politics*. Ann Arbor: University of Michigan Press.
Pempel, T. J., ed. 1990. *Uncommon Democracies: The One-Party Dominant Regimes*. Ithaca, New York: Cornell University Press.
Persson, Torsten, and Guido Tabellini. 1990. *Macroeconomic Policy, Credibility and Politics*. Chur, Switzerland and New York: Harwood Academic Publishers.
Pessino, Carola. 1991. "From Aggregate Shocks to Labor Market Adjustments: Shifting of Wage Profiles under Hyperinflation in Argentina." Unpublished manuscript.
Pinkney, Robert. 1997. *Democracy and Dictatorship in Ghana and Tanzania*. Ipswich: MacMillan Press.
Poiré, Alejandro. 1999. "Retrospective Voting, Partisanship and Loyalty in Presidential Elections: 1994." In Jorge I. Domínguez and Alejandro Poiré (eds.), *Toward Mexico's Democratization: Parties, Campaigns, Elections and Public Opinion*. New York: Routledge.
Posner, Daniel. 2005. *Institutions and Ethnic Politics in Africa*. Cambridge: Cambridge University Press.
Powell, G. B., and G. D. Whitten. 1993. "A Cross-National Analysis of Economic Voting: Taking Account of Political Context." *American Journal of Political Science* 37(2): 391–414.
Przeworski, Adam. 1987. "Democracy as a Contingent Outcome of Conflicts." In Jon Elster and Rune Slagstad (eds.), *Constitutionalism and Democracy*. Cambridge: Cambridge University Press.
Przeworski, Adam. 1991. *Democracy and the Market*. Cambridge: Cambridge University Press.
Przeworksi, Adam et al. 2000. *Democracy and Development: Political Institutions and Well-Being in the World, 1950–1990*. Cambridge: Cambridge University Press.

References

Rae, Douglas. 1971. *The Political Consequences of Electoral Laws*, rev. ed. New Haven, Connecticut: Yale University Press.

Reed, Steven R. 1990. "Structure and Behaviour: Extending Duverger's Law to the Japanese Case." *British Journal of Political Science* 20(3): 335–56.

Remmer, Karen. 1993. "The Political Impact of Economic Crisis in Latin America in the 1980s." *American Political Science Review* 85(3): 777–800.

Riker, William H. 1962. *The Theory of Political Coalitions*. New Haven, Connecticut: Yale University Press.

Riker, William H. 1976. "The Number of Political Parties: A Reexamination of Duverger's Law." *Comparative Politics* 9: 93–106.

Riker, William H. 1982. "The Two Party System and Duverger's Law: An Essay on the History of Political Science." *American Political Science Review* 76: 753–66.

Riker, William H., and Peter C. Ordeshook. 1968. "A Theory of the Calculus of Voting." *American Political Science Review* 62: 25–43.

Robinson, James A., and Thierry Verdier. 2002. "The Political Economy of Clientelism." Unpublished manuscript, University of California, Berkeley.

Rodríguez, Victoria E. 1995. "Municipal Autonomy and the Politics of Intergovernmental Finance: Is It Different for the Opposition?" In Victoria E. Rodríguez and Peter M. Ward (eds.), *Opposition Government in Mexico*. Albuquerque: University of New Mexico Press.

Rodríguez, Victoria E., and Peter M. Ward. 1995. *Opposition Government in Mexico*. Albuquerque: University of New Mexico Press.

Rodríguez, Victoria E., and Peter M. Ward. 1998. *Political Change in Baja California: Democracy in the Making?* La Jolla, California: Center for U.S.–Mexican Studies, UCSD.

Roggoff, Kenneth. 1990. "Equilibrium Political Budget Cycles." *American Economic Review* 80: 21–36.

Roggoff, Kenneth, and Anne Sibert. 1988. "Elections and Macroeconomic Policy Cycles." *Review of Economic Studies* 55: 1–16.

Rojas, Carlos. 1994. *El Programa Nacional de Solidaridad*. México: Fondo de Cultura Económica.

Romero, Vidal. 2005. "Misaligned Interests and Commitment Problems: A Study of Presidents and Their Parties with Application to the Mexican Presidency and Privatization in Latin America." Ph.D. dissertation, Stanford University.

Ross, Michael. 2001. "Does Oil Hinder Democracy?" *World Politics* 53(April): 325–61.

Rudebeck, Lars. 2003. "Multi-Party Elections in Guinea-Bissau." In Michael Cowen and Lisa Laakso (eds.), *Multiparty Elections in Africa*. New York: Palgrave.

Rustow, Dankwart A. 1970. "Transitions to Democracy: Towards a Dynamic Model." *Comparative Politics* 2: 337–63.

Sartori, Giovanni. 1976. *Parties and Party Systems: A Framework for Analysis*. Cambridge: Cambridge University Press.

Schady, Norbert R. 2000. "The Political Economy of Expenditures by the Peruvian Social Fund (FONCODES), 1991–95." *American Political Science Review* 94(2): 289–304.

Schedler, Andreas. 2000. "Mexico's Victory: The Democratic Revelation." *Journal of Democracy* 11(3): 5–19.

Schedler, Andreas. 2002. "Elections without Democracy: The Menu of Manipulation." *Journal of Democracy* 13(2): 36–50.

Schelling, Thomas. 1980. *The Strategy of Conflict*. Cambridge, Massachusetts: Harvard University Press.

Schmidt, S. W. et al. 1977. *Friends, Followers and Factions: A Reader in Political Clientelism*. Berkeley: University of California Press.

Schmitter, Philippe. 1974. "Still the Century of Corporatism?" *Review of Politics* 36: 85–131.

Scott, James. 1972. "Patron-Client Politics and Political Change in Southeast Asia." *American Political Science Review* 66(1): 91–113.

Scott, Robert E. 1959. *Mexican Government in Transition*. Urbana: University of Illinois Press.

Secretaría de Desarrollo Social (México). 1994. *Hechos en Solidaridad*. CD-ROM.

Serrano, Mónica. 1995. "The Armed Branches of the State: Civil–Military Relations in Mexico." *Journal of Latin American Studies* 27(2): 423–48.

Share, Donald, and Mainwaring, Scott. 1986. "Transitions through Transaction: Democratization in Brazil and Spain." In Wayne Selcher (ed.), *Political Liberalization in Brazil: Dilemmas and Future Prospects*. Boulder, Colorado: Westview Press.

Sheiner, Ethan. 2006. *Democracy without Competition in Japan*. Cambridge: Cambridge University Press.

Smith, Peter H. 1979. *Labyrinths of Power: Political Recruitment in Twentieth-Century Mexico*. Princeton, New Jersey: Princeton University Press.

Stepan, Alfred. 1971. *The Military in Politics: Changing Patterns in Brazil*. Princeton, New Jersey: Princeton University Press.

Stokes, Susan. 1996. "Public Opinion and Market Reforms: The Limits of Economic Voting." *Comparative Political Studies* 29: 499–519.

Stokes, Susan. 2001. *Mandates and Democracy: Neoliberalism by Surprise in Latin America*. Cambridge: Cambridge University Press.

Stokes, Susan. 2001. *Public Support for Market Reforms in New Democracies*. Cambridge: Cambridge University Press.

Stokes, Susan. 2005. "Perverse Accountability: A Formal Model of Machine Politics with Evidence form Argentina." *American Political Science Review* 99(3): 315–25.

Stokes, Susan, Valeria Brusco, and Marcelo Nazareno. 2003. "Selective Incentives and Electoral Mobilization: Evidence from Argentina." Unpublished manuscript, University of Chicago.

Taagepera, Rein, and Mathew S. Shugart. 1989. *Seats and Votes*. New Haven, Connecticut: Yale University Press.

Tilly, Charles. 2004. *Contention and Democracy in Europe, 1650–2000*. Cambridge: Cambridge University Press.

Tomz, Michael, et. al. 2003. *CLARIFY: Software for Presenting and Interpreting Statistical Results*, version 2.0. Cambridge, Massachusetts: Harvard University Press. <http://gking.harvard.edu.>

Tsebelis, George. 2002. *Veto Players: How Political Institutions Work*. Princeton, New Jersey: Princeton University Press.

Tufte, Edward R. 1978. *Political Control of the Economy*. Princeton, New Jersey: Princeton University Press.
Van de Walle, Nicolas. 2001. *African Economies and the Politics of Permanent Crisis, 1979–1999*. Cambridge: Cambridge University Press.
Van de Walle, Nicolas. 2001. "Presidentialism and Clientelism in Africa's Emerging Party Systems." Unpublished manuscript.
Van de Walle, Nicholas. (forthcoming) "The Evolution of Political Clientelism in Africa." In Herbert Kitschelt and Steven Wilkinson (eds.), *Patrons, Clients and Policies: Patterns of Democratic Accountability and Competition*. Cambridge: Cambridge University Press.
Villarreal, Andrés. 1999. "Public Opinion of the Economy and the President among Mexico City Residents: The Salinas Sexenio." *Latin American Research Review* 34(2): 132–51.
Wantchekon, Leonard. 1999. "On the Nature of First Democratic Elections." *Journal of Conflict Resolution* 43(2): 245–58.
Wantchekon, Leonard. 2004. "The Paradox of 'Warlord' Democracy: A Theoretical Investigation." *American Political Science Review* 98(1): 17–33.
Wantchekon, Leonard, and Zvika Neeman. 2002. "A Theory of Post-Civil War Democratization." *Journal of Theoretical Politics* 14(October): 439–64.
Weingast, Barry. 1997. "The Political Foundations of Democracy and the Rule of Law." *American Political Science Review* 91(2): 245–63.
Weldon, Jeffrey. 1997. "The Political Sources of Presidencialismo in Mexico." In Scott Mainwaring and Mathew Soberg Shugart (eds.), *Presidentialism and Democracy in Latin America*. Cambridge: Cambridge University Press.
Weyland, Kurt. 2002. *The Politics of Market Reform in Fragile Democracies*. Princeton, New Jersey: Princeton University Press.
Wintrobe, Ronald. 1998. *The Political Economy of Dictatorship*. Cambridge: Cambridge University Press.
Wood, Elisabeth Jean. 2000. *Forging Democracy from Below*. Cambridge: Cambridge University Press.
Zechmeister, Elizabeth. 2002. "What's Left and Who's Right in Mexican Politics?" Paper presented at the annual meeting of the Midwest Political Science Association, Chicago, Illinois, April 25–28.
Zinser, Aguilar. 1994. *Vamos a ganar*. México: Cal y Arena.

Index

Other Books in the Series *(continued from page iii)*

Valerie Bunce, *Leaving Socialism and Leaving the State: The End of Yugoslavia, the Soviet Union, and Czechoslovakia*
Daniele Caramani, *The Nationalization of Politics: The Formation of National Electorates and Party Systems in Europe*
Kanchan Chandra, *Why Ethnic Parties Succeed: Patronage and Ethnic Headcounts in India*
Ruth Berins Collier, *Paths toward Democracy: The Working Class and Elites in Western Europe and South America*
Donatella della Porta, *Social Movements, Political Violence, and the State*
Alberto Diaz-Cayeros, *Federalism, Fiscal Authority, and Centralization in Latin America*
Gerald Easter, *Reconstructing the State: Personal Networks and Elite Identity*
M. Steven Fish, *Democracy Derailed in Russia: The Failure of Open Politics*
Robert F. Franzese, *Macroeconomic Policies of Developed Democracies*
Roberto Franzosi, *The Puzzle of Strikes: Class and State Strategies in Postwar Italy*
Geoffrey Garrett, *Partisan Politics in the Global Economy*
Miriam Golden, *Heroic Defeats: The Politics of Job Loss*
Jeff Goodwin, *No Other Way Out: States and Revolutionary Movements*
Merilee Serrill Grindle, *Changing the State*
Anna Gryzymala-Busse, *Redeeming the Communist Past: The Regeneration of Communist Parties in East Central Europe*
Frances Hagopian, *Traditional Politics and Regime Change in Brazil*
Gretchen Helmke, *Courts Under Constraints: Judges, Generals, and Presidents in Argentina*
Yoshiko Herrera, *Imagined Economies: The Sources of Russian Regionalism*
J. Rogers Hollingsworth and Robert Boyer, eds., *Contemporary Capitalism: The Embeddedness of Institutions*
John D. Huber and Charles R. Shipan, *Deliberate Discretion? The Institutional Foundations of Bureaucratic Autonomy*
Ellen Immergut, *Health Politics: Interests and Institutions in Western Europe*
Torben Iversen, *Capitalism, Democracy, and Welfare*
Torben Iversen, *Contested Economic Institutions*
Torben Iversen, Jonas Pontussen, and David Soskice, eds., *Union, Employers, and Central Banks: Macroeconomic Coordination and Institutional Change in Social Market Economies*
Thomas Janoski and Alexander M. Hicks, eds., *The Comparative Political Economy of the Welfare State*
Joseph Jupille, *Procedural Politics: Issues, Influence, and Institutional Choice in the European Union*
Stathis Kalyvas, *The Logic of Violence in Civil War*

David C. Kang, *Crony Capitalism: Corruption and Capitalism in South Korea and Philippines*
Junko Kato, *Regressive Taxation and the Welfare State*
Robert O. Keohane and Helen B. Milner, eds., *Internationalization and Domestic Politics*
Herbert Kitschelt, *The Transformation of European Social Democracy*
Herbert Kitschelt, Peter Lange, Gary Marks, and John D. Stephens, eds., *Continuity and Change in Contemporary Capitalism*
Herbert Kitschelt, Zdenka Mansfeldova, Radek Markowski, and Gabor Toka, *Post-Communist Party Systems*
David Knoke, Franz Urban Pappi, Jeffrey Broadbent, and Yutaka Tsujinaka, eds., *Comparing Policy Networks*
Allan Kornberg and Harold D. Clarke, *Citizens and Community: Political Support in a Representative Democracy*
Amie Kreppel, *The European Parliament and the Supranational Party System*
David D. Laitin, *Language Repertoires and State Construction in Africa*
Fabrice E. Lehoucq and Ivan Molina, *Stuffing the Ballot Box: Fraud, Electoral Reform, and Democratization in Costa Rica*
Mark Irving Lichbach and Alan S. Zuckerman, eds., *Comparative Politics: Rationality, Culture, and Structure*
Evan Lieberman, *Race and Regionalism in the Politics of Taxation in Brazil and South Africa*
Julia Lynch, *Age in the Welfare State: The Origins of Social Spending on Pensioners, Workers, and Children*
Pauline Jones Luong, *Institutional Change and Political Continuity in Post-Soviet Central Asia*
Doug McAdam, John McCarthy, and Mayer Zald, eds., *Comparative Perspectives on Social Movements*
James Mahoney and Dietrich Rueschemeyer, eds., *Historical Analysis and the Social Sciences*
Scott Mainwaring and Matthew Soberg Shugart, eds., *Presidentialism and Democracy in Latin America*
Isabela Mares, *The Politics of Social Risk: Business and Welfare State Development*
Isabela Mares, *Taxation, Wage Bargaining, and Unemployment*
Anthony W. Marx, *Making Race, Making Nations: A Comparison of South Africa, the United States, and Brazil*
Joel S. Migdal, *State in Society: Studying How States and Societies Constitute One Another*
Joel S. Migdal, Atul Kohli, and Vivienne Shue, eds., *State Power and Social Forces: Domination and Transformation in the Third World*

Scott Morgenstern and Benito Nacif, eds., *Legislative Politics in Latin America*
Layna Mosley, *Global Capital and National Governments*
Wolfgang C. Müller and Kaare Strøm, *Policy, Office, or Votes?*
Maria Victoria Murillo, *Labor, Unions, Partisan Coalitions, and Market Reforms in Latin America*
Ton Notermans, *Money, Markets, and the State: Social Democratic Economic Policies Since 1918*
Roger D. Petersen, *Understanding Ethnic Violence: Fear, Hatred, and Resentment in Twentieth-Century Eastern Europe*
Simona Piattoni, ed., *Clientelism, Interests, and Democratic Representation*
Paul Pierson, *Dismantling the Welfare State? Reagan, Thatcher, and the Politics of Retrenchment*
Marino Regini, *Uncertain Boundaries: The Social and Political Construction of European Economies*
Lyle Scruggs, *Sustaining Abundance: Environmental Performance in Industrial Democracies*
Jefferey M. Sellers, *Governing from Below Urban Regions and the Global Economy*
Yossi Shain and Juan Linz, eds., *Interim Government and Democratic Transitions*
Beverly Silver, *Forces of Labor: Workers' Movements and Globalization since 1870*
Theda Skocpol, *Social Revolutions in the Modern World*
Regina Smyth, *Candidate Strategies and Electoral Competition in the Russian Federation: Democracy Without Foundation*
Richard Snyder, *Politics after Neoliberalism: Reregulation in Mexico*
David Stark and László Bruszt, *Postsocialist Pathways: Transforming Politics and Property in East Central Europe*
Sven Steinmo, Kathleen Thelen, and Frank Longstreth, eds., *Structuring Politics: Historical Institutionalism in Comparative Analysis*
Susan C. Stokes, *Mandates and Democracy: Neoliberalism by Surprise in Latin America*
Susan C. Stokes, ed., *Public Support for Market Reforms in New Democracies*
Duane Swank, *Global Capital, Political Institutions, and Policy Change in Developed Welfare States*
Sidney Tarrow, *Power in Movement: Social Movements and Contentious Politics*
Kathleen Thelen, *How Institutions Evolve: The Political Economy of Skills in Germany, Britain, the United States, and Japan*
Charles Tilly, *Trust and Rule*

Joshua Tucker, *Regional Economic Voting: Russia, Poland, Hungary, Slovakia, and the Czech Republic, 1990–1999*
Ashutosh Varshney, *Democracy, Development, and the Countryside*
Stephen I. Wilkinson, *Votes and Violence: Electoral Competition and Ethnic Riots in India*
Jason Wittenberg, *Crucibles of Political Loyalty: Church Institutions and Electoral Continuity in Hungary*
Elisabeth J. Wood, *Forging Democracy from Below: Insurgent Transitions in South Africa and El Salvador*
Elisabeth J. Wood, *Insurgent Collective Action and Civil War in El Salvador*